Rousing minds to life

Rousing minds to life

Teaching, learning, and schooling in social context

ROLAND G. THARP
University of Hawaii

RONALD GALLIMORE
University of California, Los Angeles

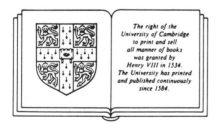

The right of the
University of Cambridge
to print and sell
all manner of books
was granted by
Henry VIII in 1534.
The University has printed
and published continuously
since 1584.

CAMBRIDGE UNIVERSITY PRESS

Cambridge
New York   Port Chester
Melbourne   Sydney

Published by the Press Syndicate of the University of Cambridge
The Pitt Building, Trumpington Street, Cambridge CB2 1RP
40 West 20th Street, New York, NY 10011, USA
10 Stamford Road, Oakleigh, Melbourne 3166, Australia

First published 1988
Reprinted 1990
First paperback edition 1991

Printed in the United States of America

Library of Congress Cataloging-in-Publication Data

Tharp, Roland G., 1930–
Rousing minds to life : teaching, learning, and schooling in social context /
Roland G. Tharp, Ronald Gallimore.
p. cm.
Bibliography: p.
Includes index.
ISBN 0-521-36234-2
1. Teaching.   I. Gallimore, Ronald.   II. Title
LB1025.2.T446   1988
371.1′02-dc19   88-20224
                  CIP

British Library Cataloging-in-Publication Data

Tharp, Roland G.
Rousing minds to life : teaching, learning, and schooling in social context.
1. Schools.   Teaching
I. Title   II. Gallimore, Roland
371.1′02

ISBN 0-521-36234-2 hardback
ISBN 0-521-40603-X paperback

For
Donald, Thomas, Michael, and Julie Tharp
Christine and Andrea Gallimore

Contents

vii

Acknowledgments

The work reported in this book was made possible by our opportunities to associate with many people of unusual vision, intelligence, and learning. Our respective universities supported these efforts in many ways, through many agencies and agents. We express our appreciation to our primary academic affiliations: the Department of Psychology, University of Hawaii, and the Sociobehavioral Research Group (Mental Retardation Research Center), University of California, Los Angeles. Many colleagues there have provided support through administrative, consultative, and technical assistance. Additional support for work reported here has been provided by the Bernice Pauahi Bishop Museum, the Social Science Research Institute at the University of Hawaii, the Hawaii Progressive Neighborhoods Act (299), the Queen Liliuokalani Trust, the Samuel N. and Mary Castle Foundation, the Freer Eleemosynary Trust, the Juliette M. Atherton Trust, the McInerny Foundation, the National Institute of Mental Health, the National Science Foundation, the Carnegie Corporation, the Ford Foundation, and the National Institute of Health and Human Development, to each of which we extend our thanks. We are also grateful for support from the Linguistic Minority Research Project of the University of California and from the Department of Psychiatry and Biobehavioral Sciences and Graduate School of Education at UCLA.

The Kamehameha Elementary Education Program (KEEP), which serves as a principal example in this volume, has been operated since 1970 by The Kamehameha Schools/Bernice Pauahi Bishop Estate, Honolulu, Hawaii, and it is this institution that provided the bulk of the financial, political, and human resources for the work. The KEEP program was developed from 1970 through 1983 by the contributions of many people, but particularly (in alphabetical order) Mele Ah Ho, Claire Asam, Kathryn Hu-pei Au, Karen Bogert, Rodrick Calkins, Doris Crowell, Stephanie Dalton, Sally Dowhower, Sherlyn Chun Franklin, Ramona Hao, Cathie Jordan, Thomas W. Klein, Karen O'Neal, Kim C. M. Sloat, Kenneth Smith (of the University of Arizona), Gisela Speidel, Sarah Sueoka, and Lynn Baird Vogt.

xi

During the creative years of this program, a set of trustees of the Bishop Estate exhibited extraordinary vision and patience. It is almost unique to find a commitment to research and development, in education or social science, solid enough and patient enough to allow the trials, the errors, and the corrections that allowed this model program to grow and to flourish for over a decade. Those trustees were Myron Thompson, Matsui Takabuki, Hung Wo Ching, Richard Lyman, and Frank Midkiff. Their executive officers, Jack Darvill and Thomas Hamilton, contributed guidance and support both to us and to the trustees.

Consultations to the KEEP project, and comments on earlier publications, were provided by David Berliner, Donald Campbell, Fred Erickson, Wayne Fox, Donna Gelfand, Donald Guthrie, Donald A. Hansen, Marjorie Martus, Karl Minke, Robert Newbrough, Clifford O'Donnell, David Pearson, Douglass Price-Williams, Barbara Rogoff, Jim Turner, and James V. Wertsch. Carol Feldman encouraged us to consider Vygotsky's ideas early in the research, a suggestion for which we are very grateful. External evaluation of the KEEP program has been accomplished by teams that have included George Guthrie and Ronald Johnson (1975); Robert Calfee, Courtney Cazden, Richard Duran, Margaret "Peg" Griffin, Marjorie Martus, and H. D. Willis (1981); Richard Anderson, Courtney Cazden, Thomas Cook, Michael Doss, Irene Gaskins, and Dorothy Strickland (1986).

In the preparation of this volume, helpful suggestions were made by Vera John-Steiner, Luis Moll, Claude Goldenberg, Sandra Kaufman, Thomas Weisner, Phyllis Schneider, John Hyland, Stephanie Dalton, Grace Omura, Deborah Stipek, Barry McLaughlin, Merle Wittrock, Barbara Keogh, Robert Rueda, Richard Duran, Henry Trueba, Concha Delgado-Gaitan, Donald A. Hansen, Lynn Johnson, Jaana Juvonen, Barbara Hawkins, Robert Springer, and Richard Shavelson.

Extensive technical assistance was provided by Mark Troy, Caleb Burns, Linda Kobayashi, Sandra Kaufman, Candace Fox-Henning, Lupe Montano, Janell Demyan, Darlene Plunkett, Joyce Metzger, Helen Chang, Mary Note, and Sylvia Clay. Transcribers for some lessons quoted were Donna Tanimura, Teresa Yates, John Lee, Steve Monroe, and Afton Sells.

Manuscript preparation was completed by Joyce Metzger with characteristic skill, patience, and wit. She was assisted by Alyssa McKinney, Janell Demyan, Grace Davis, Cynthia Ratekin, and Andrea Gallimore.

Surviving errors are ours alone.

Roland G. Tharp   Ronald Gallimore
Honolulu   Santa Monica

Introduction

The problem of teaching: its contemporary context in historical perspective

Once again, America has become concerned with its schools. It is only the most recent of the irregular series of national spasms that, from time to time, grip the nation. No less than nine recent national commissions and reports have offered a painful picture of American education (Griesemer & Butler, 1983). The torrent of comment, proposal, dispute, and accusation generated by these reports has become a contemporary version of the "great school debate" (Gross & Gross, 1985).

The last previous round of concern was generated some 30 years ago by the highly publicized Soviet Sputnik success and its rousing of the American competitive spirit (Sarason, 1983). The continuity of issues is revealed in the echoes of the Sputnik crisis that can be heard in the current debate, as in *A Nation at Risk* (National Commission on Excellence in Education, 1983).

In *A Nation at Risk,* and other reports of the same ilk, two themes are common. The first is the theme of standards. In one form or another, all conclude that students must be held to a higher standard, including more homework, better comportment, longer school hours, higher expectations, and a solid academic curriculum.

The second theme is the quality of teaching, which the reports hold to be generally poor. A recognition that teaching must be improved has been, sooner or later, the conclusion of all educational reformers, including the most recent wave (Sarason, 1971, 1983; Warren, 1985).

That this great debate, after some casting about, has found its focus on teachers and teacher education is entirely predictable: This has been the course of earlier debates and "reforms" (Warren, 1985). However, "If the pattern holds, general interest in the ways teachers prepare for their professional roles will be temporary." In the meantime, while the "hyperbole borders on silliness . . . it gives historians something to chew on" (Warren, 1985, p. 5).

1

To improve teaching, the reports argue, we must provide higher initial salaries and differentiated pay based on merit, thereby bringing more capable individuals into the teaching profession. We must increase the ratio of content courses to method courses for teachers in training and demand that they meet a higher academic standard (Stedman & Smith, 1983). Many would-be reformers are optimistic that these and other reorganizations of policy and power will lead to fundamental changes in schools, in the conduct of teaching, and in the way that individual students experience education – an optimism that can only be based in the mistaken belief that these ideas are new and untried (Sarason, Davidson, & Blatt, 1986). Sarason sometimes despairs that though there may be a voice, there are no ears in the wilderness:

> [Current reformers] fail to realize that everything being said and proposed was said, proposed, and acted upon earlier as a reaction to the narcissistic wound experienced by our society when the Soviet Union orbited the first sputnik in 1957. (Sarason, 1983, p. 4)

> If the book has been widely read [referring to Sarason, 1971], if there has been general agreement that the issues I raised are valid and crucial, there is no evidence whatsoever that those responsible for these commission reports considered any of them. On the contrary, these reports are based on a conception of change by legislative and administrative fiat. . . . [What] they recommend for improving the preparation of teachers has been recommended countless times in the past without discernable effect, e.g., better grounding in specific subject matter and the arts and sciences generally, better supervision, more in service and continuing education opportunities, stricter and more objective standards for judging teacher performance and competency, and greater and material recognition of superior teachers. . . . [These] recommendations . . . do not speak to the question of how to prepare teachers better for the realities of the classroom, the school, and the school system. . . . *It has long been obvious that learning their appropriate implementation in a classroom has not been valued.* (Sarason et al., 1986, pp. vii–ix; emphasis added)

Now history girds itself for another repetition. Again, current reform proposals do not directly address the practice of the profession of teaching. What *is* acceptable teaching practice? This is always left to someone else to define. How is acceptable teaching practice to be instantiated? This is always assumed to be a mere technical matter, secondary to the resolution of policy and power wars.

There is cause enough for pessimism about the outcome of the 1980s reform movement, in its neglect of the history of teaching practices, and in its neglect of the history of "reform." Even if more intelligent, motivated, and educated teachers are recruited and retained, there is no reason to think that teaching itself will be improved *pari passu*. In the torrent of reform proposals, too few define how teachers should conduct themselves in the classroom, or the means through which they will learn higher standards of teaching. We did not heed him in 1971, so let us listen again to Sarason describing the fate of the New Math innovation:

... the intended consequences – the basic goals and outcomes – always intended a change in the relationships among those who are in or related to the school setting. But these intended consequences are rarely stated clearly, if at all, and as a result, a means to a goal becomes the goal itself, or it becomes the misleading criterion for judging change. Thus, we have the new math, but we do not have those changes in how teachers and children relate to each other that are necessary if both are to enjoy, persist in, and productively utilize intellectual and interpersonal experience – and if these are not among the intended consequences, then we must conclude that the curriculum reformers have been quite successful in achieving their goal of substituting one set of books for another. (Sarason, 1971, p. 48)

Despite good intentions, hard work, and success in the policy wars, little was gained – unless one was satisfied to see teachers using unfamiliar textbooks to instruct material they did not understand very well, using the same teaching practices that the reformers had proposed to improve.

The New Math reform is not an isolated case. Other massive efforts at reform of teaching have often produced only superficial change. "Often ... changes are largely symbolic ... without changing the quality of teacher or student performance [Berman & McLaughlin, 1978]. Thus schools can at once be innovative and unchanging" (Rosenholtz, 1986, p. 514).

How can that be? Because the preoccupation of the reformers with policy and power redistribution involves matters remote from the practices of teaching and schooling, or the daily experiences of teachers before or after they enter the profession. Ignoring such details and their effective implementation puts even the soundest of reforms at risk.

In the current wave of reform, there are glimmers of attention being paid to the details of training and development of excellent teachers (e.g., Darling-Hammond, 1986; Rosenholtz, 1986). But for the most part, current enthusiasts are as disinterested as their predecessors in the details of teaching and schooling practices, and how they will be changed (cf. Gross & Gross, 1985; Sarason et al., 1986).

What is it about teachers and teaching that reformers have tried to change without success? What is it that the latest effort must also address? What is the problem on which reform must focus if history is not to be repeated? In American classrooms, now and since the 19th century, teachers generally act as if students are supposed to learn on their own. Teachers are not taught to teach, and most often they do not teach. The problem does not lie in individual incompetence or the incompetence of individual institutions. It does not lie in the incompetence or cupidity of teachers or teacher-educators or of educational researchers or theorists. All participants in the educational enterprise have suffered from the same lack of knowledge. Schools have been administered in ways that make teaching unlikely if not impossible. All participants in the educational enterprise have shared an inadequate vision of schooling.

Contemporary critics attribute this miserable condition to one or another recent variation of educational policy, and they tend to argue as though the problem's origin is recent. In fact, contemporary descriptions of impoverished teaching (Goodlad, 1984; Gross & Gross, 1985) differ little from the instructional practices described by Stevens in 1912 and by Rice in 1893 – observations made before the era of colleges of education and the rise of philosophies that some critics blame for contemporary school problems (Oldenquist, 1983). In their review, Hoetker and Ahlbrand (1969) found a "remarkable stability" in the patterns of instruction observed over the past century, patterns that have been condemned as "nonteaching" by successive waves of reform, yet that survive virtually unchanged (p. 163).

Given this history, there is little hope that most of the frequently debated policy proposals will have the impact the reformers seek. We are confronted with this troubling conclusion: It is essential to recruit and retain more able teachers through adequate pay and better working conditions. They must have a liberal education and a substantive knowledge of their subject matter. School curricula must be broad and deep. The school facilities, equipment, and materials must be appropriate. The schools and their surrounding communities must be safe from drugs and violence. But these necessary changes are not sufficient to ensure that teaching will occur. They will not alter the implicit attitude that students are to learn on their own. That attitude is inculcated in teachers throughout their own educational histories, beginning with elementary school and continuing throughout college-level courses.

Professors of arts and sciences faculties may often treat their colleagues and students from schools of education as unworthy of place. Yet three-quarters of U.S. teacher preparation is in the arts and sciences faculties (Kerr, 1983). If teacher education is poor, a good share of the problem is with the curriculum of arts and sciences. Arts and sciences faculties seldom recognize, and even less often acknowledge, the role they play in teacher education. Few critics on university faculties offer much beyond contempt for "methods" courses, and few solutions beyond disempowering the already flaccid methods-oriented teacher-training programs. Although we hold no brief for methods-course orientations, we could all be well reminded that little will be advanced in pedagogy by tossing intended teachers back to the models of the thoughtless "teaching" of the average arts and sciences classroom in which students are expected to learn on their own.

The attitude that individuals must learn from their textbooks on their own, without teaching, will not be altered easily. In the words of Secretary of Education William Bennett, we must have

a new and rigorous science of pedagogy – not the quasi-academic material now found in "methods" courses, but a discipline that will really teach potential teachers the intellectual roots of their work. A new pedagogy would deal at a profound level with the "knots" that complicate children's understanding, not with the drawing-up of lesson plans. (Bennett, 1986, p. 50)

In the pages to follow, we offer a science and discipline to address the problem. It is a unified theory and practice of teaching, literacy, schooling, and education, distinguished by its roots in developmental, behavioral, and anthropological sciences.

The problem of schooling: its contemporary context in historical perspective

If teachers suffer from lack of preservice opportunity for learning how to teach, they find things no better once the doors of their first classrooms close behind them. As now organized, schools do not provide for professional development or for the introduction of innovations in teaching practices. This is clearly demonstrated in studies of teachers of varying lengths of service showing that

most experienced teachers who work in isolation from peers continue to do the same thing they did when they first entered teaching 10, 15, or 20 years ago and now find their jobs monotonous and unchallenging. . . . Beginners develop initial skills by trial-and-error learning and begin to deplete their fund of ideas after about the fifth year of teaching [McLaughlin & Marsh, 1978; Rosenholtz, 1985; Summers & Wolfe, 1977]. (Rosenholtz, 1986, p. 524)

Teachers do continue to learn after many years in the profession, but the sources of new learning are extremely limited. More important, the major source of new learning for teachers is the school itself: Rosenholtz (1985) compared relative newcomers who had taught between 1 and 5 years and veteran teachers who had taught 10 to 15 years. She reported that organizational conditions in their schools explained 60% of how much learning beginners reported, but a staggering 72% of how much learning veterans reported (Rosenholtz, 1986, p. 524).

Given these circumstances, the most widely discussed and proposed reforms – higher standards for entry into the field, better salaries, merit pay, and career-ladder plans – will not be enough. As crucial as these reforms are, they will prove disappointing in their impact because they will not change teaching practices, unless at the same time we change the settings in which teachers work – unless we change school culture and redefine schooling. Indeed, efforts that focus exclusively on individuals may simply reinforce the features of contemporary school culture that now hamper development of teachers and teaching. For example, reforms that seek improvements through salary differentials may, in some forms, suppress conditions that would foster better teaching: "Because teachers' skill development depends heavily on collaborative support and exchange, *competitive rewards will thwart efforts to improve*" (Rosenholtz, 1986, p. 518; emphasis added).

Teaching will not be reformed until schools are reformed. Schools will not be reformed until it is understood that schools must be a context for teaching, and that context must itself be a teaching context. To demand that teachers truly teach in existing schools is like demanding that a surgeon achieve asepsis under water in a stagnant pond.

What is needed is a new theory of schooling that will guide organizational and operational decisions toward the correct priorities – achieving an institution that teaches. As we need a new science and discipline of pedagogy, so we must have a new discipline and science of schooling, one that unites analysis of the social circumstances in which educators work to the details of the teaching interactions that schools are intended to create and sustain. Such a unified theory is needed if we are to overcome the barriers to change about which Sarason has written so persuasively and so long.

In the pages that follow, we shall attempt to offer such a science and discipline – one that unifies our understanding of teaching and schooling in terms of both theory and practice.

The basis for a theory of teaching and schooling

Although social and behavioral research has never had much effect on the practice of teaching and schooling, a potential basis to guide change is now discernible. It is an emergent contextualist and interactionist view of human development that draws from the achievements of 20th-century English-speaking social science and from what we refer to as "neo-Vygotskianism" (e.g., Bruner, 1962, 1966, 1984; Fischer & Bullock, 1984; Greenfield, 1984; Minick, 1987; Moll & Diaz, 1985; Ochs, 1982; Rogoff, 1982; Rogoff & Lave, 1984; Tharp, Gallimore, & Calkins, 1984; Vygotsky, 1978; Wertsch, 1985a, 1985b; Wood, 1980). This view has profound implications for teaching, schooling, and education. A key feature of this emergent view of human development is that higher-order functions develop out of social interaction. Vygotsky argued that a child's development cannot be understood by a study of the individual. We must also examine the external social world in which that individual life has developed. Cognitive and communicative skill appears "twice, or in two planes. First it appears on the social plane, and then on the psychological plane. First it appears between people as an interpsychological category, and then within the child as an intrapsychological category" (Vygotsky, 1978, p. 163). Through participation in activities that require cognitive and communicative functions, children are drawn into the use of these functions in ways that nurture and "scaffold" them.

In formal and informal instruction, information regarding cultural tools and practices (such as use of calculators, mathematics and writing systems, event scripts, and mnemonic strategies) is transmitted from experienced members to inexperienced members [Vygotsky, 1962, 1978]. Vygotsky proposed that the higher mental functions appear first on the social level, between people, and later on the individual level, inside the child. . . . This growth occurs in the "zone of proximal development," that phase in the development of a cognitive skill where a child has only partially mastered the skill but can successfully employ it and internalize it with the assistance and supervision of an adult. The adult structures and models the appropriate solution to the problem, engaging the child in this solution, as the adult monitors the child's current level of skill and supports or "scaffolds" the child's extension of current skills and knowledge to a higher level of competence [Wertsch, 1979; Wood, 1980]. Social interaction with people who are more expert in the use of material and conceptual tools of the society is thus an important "cultural amplifier" to extend children's cognitive processes. (Rogoff & Gardener, 1984, p. 97)

An example: A 6-year-old child has lost a toy and asks her father for help. The father asks where she last saw the toy; the child says, "I can't remember." He asks a series of questions: "Did you have it in your room? Outside? Next door?" To each question, the child answers no. When he says, "In the car?" she says "I think so" and goes to retrieve the toy.

In this mundane interaction are the roots of higher mental functions. When the father organizes the strategic aspects of this simple recall task by a series of questions, it becomes clear that the child has the relevant information stored in memory. Without the father's assistance, she is able to recall only (as is typical for her age) isolated bits of information; she is unable to choose a strategy to organize the information toward a particular goal-oriented purpose. But with his assistance, her performance reveals a level of development to come. To ask oneself questions as a strategy for organizing recall of information is a well-researched example of a metamemorial "tool" (Brown, 1978; Brown & Campione, 1986); it is an "internally mediated cognitive tool" characteristic of literate societies (Brown, 1978). It is part of a sociocultural heritage transmitted to children through "teaching," in that zone of performance that "reveals a level of development to come."

The collaboration of the father and daughter reveals the social interactional origins of higher mental functioning, the idea that gave name to the well-known collection of Vygotsky's writings: *Mind in Society* (Vygotsky, 1978). Through this small domestic collaboration, the father is rousing to life significant cognitive functions. Such teaching – understood as assisted performance of apprentices in joint activity with experts – becomes the vehicle through which the interactions of society are internalized and become mind. Such a definition of teaching can guide training and practice and yet remain firmly rooted in theory.

This contextualist/cognitive view of human development provides a basis for understanding and correcting teaching and schooling. As yet, neither Vygotsky nor his followers have attended adequately to the processes by which assistance is achieved. Adequate understanding of the processes of assisted performance requires that the achievements of Western behavioral science of this century, achievements that have detailed the processes of learning in social interactions, be brought into conjunction with the new cognitive/contextualist understanding now being developed. It is our purpose to unite behavioral science with neo-Vygotskianism and thereby illuminate the full issue of teaching, schooling, and literacy development. To the extent that we are successful, there will be available for discussion a unified, integrated theory of education that is based on a culture-sensitive theory of human learning and development.

Plan of the book

In developing this argument, we treat the current state of teaching and schooling in Chapter 1. In Chapter 2 we present the interactionist theory of development that has emerged from Vygotsky's ideas and discuss examples from the natural teaching and learning that characterize everyday life in most cultures. After establishing those general patterns by which cognitive development is fostered, we articulate in Chapter 3 the theory of teaching. That theory also requires an understanding of the means by which assistance can be provided. A review of those means, as discovered by the Western behavioral science of this century, will be articulated with examples drawn from transcripts of a single reading lesson.

In Chapter 4, we return to the contextual level to consider the organization of schools and to develop a general theory of schooling in which all members of the organization are seen as learners and teachers.

In Chapter 5, we present the third leg of our theoretical structure – a theory of what is developed through interaction in social context, a theory of literacy, understood as the patterns of language and cognitive development that can develop through teaching and schooling.

In Part II of this book, the idea of the school as an institution for assisting performance is presented in practical terms, replete with examples. In 1969, we were given the opportunity to design and build a school. For the next 10 years we had authority to select the student population, hire teachers, design curricula, conduct research, learn from mistakes, and test alternatives. That small demonstration school grew into the Kamehameha Elementary Education Program (KEEP), a system of related educational development activities that spanned three states, 3,000 students, many cultures, many languages, and many more corrections and alternatives. Chapter 6 gives an overview of that program, which serves in this book as the major "good example" for teaching, classroom and school organization, teacher training, and research and development.

In Chapters 7 and 8, we discuss the principal activity settings of schooling and examine the teaching, learning, and patterns of assisted performance that emerge in each setting.

We then turn to an examination of systems for assisting teacher performance, through training, consultation, and support. Chapter 9 details the interpersonal plane of the activity settings that assist teacher performance. Chapter 10 presents a detailed case study of a single teacher, who, by having her own performance assisted, becomes competent in assisting the performance of students. Chapter 11 follows the processes of internalization, as teacher competency moves from the stage of assisted performance into the stages of self-assistance and automaticity.

Finally, Chapter 12 discusses the broader social context in which schooling is nested and returns to the question of how – and indeed whether or not – teaching, schooling, and literacy can be reformed. Throughout the volume, we examine the contextual conditions for our "good example" – KEEP – that have allowed such thoroughgoing innovation; in the final chapter we examine the conditions that led to its decline. From both its rise and fall there are lessons to be learned for educational reform.

Part I

Teaching, schooling, and literacy: a unified theory of education

1 The redefinition of teaching and schooling

Go back in memory. To the school of your childhood. Go further, if you can – travel back in time, to the North American classrooms of your great great grandmothers. Go back a century. The trick would be to keep your eyes closed. Of course there are fewer jeans, and the skirts are different. Textbooks are less brightly colored. But blindfolded, you might not notice the time warp. Listening to the teachers, you would hear speech almost indistinguishable from the way teachers are talking to your son and daughter today.

Before the Civil War

Young teachers are very apt to confound rapid questioning and answers with sure and effective teaching.

> (Morrison, 1860, p. 303; quoted in Hoetker & Ahlbrand, 1969, p. 153)

At the turn of the century

Sara Burstall, an Englishwoman, visited American schools in 1908 and was struck by the ubiquity of the "time-honoured" question–answer recitation.... In the European schools the teacher was at the center of the learning process; he lectured, questioned the pupils, and "buil[t] up new knowledge in class." In contrast, in the American classroom, "clearly ... the master is the textbook." The teacher does not really teach but "acts rather as chairman of a meeting, the object of which is to ascertain whether [or not the students] have studied for themselves in a textbook.

> (Burstall, 1909, pp. 156–158; quoted in Hoetker & Ahlbrand, 1969, p. 150)

Today

In three major studies, the National Science Foundation found that most science education follows the traditional practice: "At all grade levels the predominant method of teaching was recitation (discussion) with the teacher in control, supplementing the lesson with new information (lecturing). The key to the information and basis for reading assignments was the textbook" [Smith, 1980, p. 166]. If science is presented like this, is it any wonder that children's natural curiosity about their physical world turns into boredom by the time they leave grade school – and into dangerous ignorance later on?

> (Bennett, 1986, p. 26)

13

The redefinition of teaching

The recitation script

"Recitation." It is everywhere in North American schools. "Recitation." It is the most frequently reported form of interactive teaching (Hoetker & Ahlbrand, 1969). "Recitation" has been described in the educational literature for over 90 years. It constitutes a major portion of all interactive teaching (Duffy, 1981; Durkin, 1978–1979; Hoetker & Ahlbrand, 1969).

What is this ubiquitous "recitation"? It consists of a series of unrelated teacher questions that require convergent factual answers and student display of (presumably) known information. Recitation questioning seeks predictable, correct answers. It includes up to 20% yes/no questions. Only rarely in recitation are teacher questions responsive to student productions. Only rarely are they used to assist students to develop more complete or elaborated ideas (Hoetker & Ahlbrand, 1969).

Other studies of interactive teaching are no more encouraging: Teachers are mainly guided by preselected activities and commonsense ideas about child development and educational practice (Anderson, Hiebert, Scott, & Wilkinson, 1985; Duffy, 1981; Durkin, 1978–1979; Goodlad, 1984; Hoetker & Ahlbrand, 1969; Joyce & Clift, 1984; Shavelson & Stern, 1981). Teachers seldom report being reflective during interactions with students; they do not refer to educational theories, and they engage in little pedagogical maneuvering. This unresponsive, "automatic" teaching seems devoted to creating and maintaining activity and assessing pupil progress.

This dismal portrait describes not only the schools of time past, or some few unlucky or deprived communities of the present. Goodlad (1984) conducted a broadly based survey of 38 American schools in 13 communities and seven regions of the United States. Hundreds of students and teachers were interviewed and observed in small and large schools, in low- and middle-socioeconomic communities, in both rural and metropolitan areas with diverse cultural and ethnic populations. Goodlad's researchers found a striking similarity in the kinds of teaching across these seemingly diverse situations. For the most part, teachers controlled what transpired, and the focus was on the total group of students, rather than small groups or individuals. Teachers emphasized rote learning and immediate responses, a pattern rather like television game shows. On the average, only 7 of 150 min of the school day involved a teacher responding to a student's work. Most of the time, teachers lectured and explained. Almost never were there opportunities for give-and-take between a challenging teacher and learning students. The student role was passive, and few teachers made any effort to adapt instruction to individual differences.

Quizzing students is a favorite activity. Sarason (1983) summarized previous studies of classrooms and reported that teachers frequently did question students in these large groups – from 45 to 150 times per half hour. Unfortunately, they quizzed students in such a way that students responded with few questions of their own. The more questions asked by the teacher that are answerable by simple recall, the fewer questions children asked. When teachers asked personally relevant questions, children's questions increased; unfortunately, 67% to 95% of teachers' questions required straight recall for the answers. The most damning statistic, however, is this: Children asked fewer than two questions per half hour! These rates were not different for students according to IQ or social class (Sarason, 1983, p. 97).

The recitation–questioning pattern is supported by the educational apparatus at every level, including standard curriculum materials. We quote again from Secretary Bennett's *First Lessons*:

Classroom materials provided to teachers may frustrate their attempts. . . . Teacher manuals have docility embedded in the teachers' directions and questioning techniques. . . . Answers are right, wrong, but mostly short, thus smothering the student's efforts to be an effective and intuitive thinker. (Bennett, 1986, p. 47)

Even naive beliefs about schooling presume that active teaching is the business of classroom instruction. The laity envision expert teachers assisting apprentices to learn new knowledge and skills. Little reported in these studies supports such a view.

Recent progress in the reform of teaching

In recent years, the "effective teacher" movement (based on process–product research) has succeeded in identifying existing classroom practices associated with greater student learning. On the whole, this movement is a salutary development, even though it suffers from being atheoretical (Good & Weinstein, 1986), which has constrained the movement to studies of existing practices, rather than experimenting with fresh forms. Duffy and his associates (Duffy, 1981; Duffy, Lanier, & Roehler, 1980) summarized the work on teacher effectiveness and drew two conclusions: (a) The most effective teachers of basic skills generate the greatest opportunity to learn. (b) Such teachers are technical managers of instructional materials and activities, rather than theory-driven and reflective decision makers. Even in these "more effective" classrooms,

there is little evidence of instruction of any kind. Teachers spend most of their time assigning activities, monitoring to be sure the pupils are on task, directing recitation sessions to assess how well children are doing and providing corrective feedback in response to pupil errors. Seldom does one observe . . . teaching in which a teacher presents a skill, a strategy or a process to pupils, shows them how to do it, provides assistance as they make initial attempts to perform the task and assures that they can be successful. (Duffy et al., 1980, pp. 4–5)

Few writers, and certainly not ourselves, would dispute the value of highly organized, technical, and direct forms of didactic instruction. Such classrooms are far more effective than those that rely on unstructured, informal teaching, where students have broad latitude to select what they will do (Brophy & Good, 1986; Rosenshine & Stevens, 1986). Among such practices associated with higher achievement are daily and weekly review, checking homework, correction of errors, and independent practice (seatwork). "Time on task" or "engaged time" is another important factor: In the "technical" classroom, where "automatic teaching" is the norm, pupils are engaged on task for longer amounts of time and thus have more opportunity to learn (Duffy, 1981). Not only is this intuitively sound, but educational research has repeatedly shown that time on task is a positive factor for student performance (Rosenshine, 1979).

One can also make a case for a selective value of recitation and didactic instruction from the cross-cultural literature (Hirsch, 1987, pp. 30–31). Memorization is widely and effectively used to teach sacred texts and rituals; other "chunks" of cultural knowledge may also be best taught in this way. For example, it is essential that students have "automatic" control of the alphabet and sound–symbol relationships, build "automatic" sight vocabulary, know essential facts of history (including dates), and internalize abstract categories. For these abstract, symbolic, decontextualized forms of learning, various forms of didactic teaching may be the most effective, but they are not sufficient. They are particularly inadequate if students are to acquire some mastery and understanding of the knowledge and literature of the world's civilizations – that mastery that distinguishes the literate mind (Adler, 1983; Hirsch, 1987).

In its worst forms, "automatic" didactic teaching is little more than the recitation script of earlier eras (Hoetker & Ahlbrand, 1969; Rice, 1893; Stevens, 1912). It emphasizes rote learning and student passivity (Goodlad, 1984), facts and low-level cognitive functions (Durkin, 1978–1979); it prevents implementation of many curricula (Sarason, 1971). It can contribute to poor morale because it diminishes the teacher role in order to make programs "teacher-proof." It works best with highly structured materials such as worksheets and "manufactured" reading materials. Duffy (1981) remarked that however adaptive this "automatic" teaching may be, in many classroom contexts it reflects inadequate training, the limits of current pedagogical theory, and an overreliance on commercial materials to the exclusion of real literature, art, and science. It does little to promote intellectual development, cultural literacy, and thoughtful citizenship of the kinds that *A Nation at Risk* identified as crucial.

We must develop ways of balancing "automatic," didactic teaching with teaching that assists learning. But does an alternative exist? Yes. Is "automatic and didactic teaching" the best we can do? No.

Teaching as assistance

Another kind of teaching

The literature of U.S. educational research is filled with efforts to define and study interactive teaching that goes beyond recitation and "automatic" didactic teaching. Such teaching has been described in many ways: guided practice, quality teaching, reciprocal teaching, active, hypothetical, artistic, natural, proleptic, responsive, Socratic, maieutic teaching, instructional assistance and more (Adler, 1983; 1988; Berliner, 1986; Bloom, 1976; Brookover et al., 1978; Brown & Campione, 1986; Brown & Palinscar, 1987; Bruner, 1966, 1973b; Cazden, 1981; Duffy & Roehler, 1980; Fisher et al., 1978; Gage, 1978; Gallimore, Dalton, & Tharp, 1986; Good & Grouws, 1979; Greenfield, 1984; Korth & Cornbleth, 1980; Medley, 1977; Palinscar, 1986; Palinscar & Brown, 1984; Rosenshine, 1979; Rosenshine & Stevens, 1986; Shavelson & Stern, 1981; Shulman, 1986; Wertsch & Stone, 1979; Wittrock, 1974, 1978). In this literature, recurrent themes and positions can be discerned. Also, in contemporary theory and research on behavior, cognition, and human development, there is theory ready at hand to explain and unify these many efforts to construct better teaching. Our task is to review this theory and research and, through it, to propose a reliable general teaching method. Through this theory and method, we then derive a general theory of schooling, a general theory of literacy, and consequently a general theory of education.

Of what does this "other" kind of teaching consist? For one thing, it clearly involves subject-matter competence. To do more than manage activities and allow students to learn on their own, teachers must command the knowledge and skills they seek to impart (Hyland, 1984; Hyland, Gallimore, & Schneider, in press; Shulman, 1986). The point of teaching is to impart knowledge and the capacity to process that knowledge. In this respect, we come down fully on the content side of the debate over content versus process. Teachers and students alike must know the subject matter; they must learn and have the facility to access the accumulated knowledge and important facts of our civilization and the world's cultures. But knowing the subject matter is not sufficient for teachers.

Pedagogical expertise is also required (Berliner, 1986), of which there are many kinds. Among those to be commended are use of instructional objectives, positive and efficient classroom and behavior management, provision of effective and varied activities, properly conducted recitation and drill, orderly monitoring and assessment of progress, checking for comprehension, and any number of other expert practices (Brophy & Good, 1986; Rosenshine & Stevens, 1986). The fully professional teacher will command all of these useful and desirable practices and learn to apply them to those aspects of the curricula for which they are most efficient. Judicious use of recitation and other forms of automatic, technical, and didactic teaching surely is part of the effective teacher's armamentarium.

But at best, recitation and technical, didactic, and automatic teaching are not sufficient. Other kinds of teaching are also necessary, and more important.

This point was made by Adler (1983, 1988), who discussed three kinds of teaching in ascending order of importance: didactic, coaching, and Socratic. Three kinds of learning are produced, respectively: (1) acquisition of knowledge (not information, which is the memory of facts without any understanding of them), (2) intellectual skills, which are possessed as habits, and (3) understanding, which can be developed only through Socratic questioning in discussion (Adler, 1988).

This third method, this Socratic teaching, has bemused Western teachers for more than two millennia. Like Adler, Beck (1985), a recent analyst of the teaching of Plato and Socrates, insists that they recognized different levels of teaching. One method is "nothing but recall ... but there is room for something quite different from the clever leading of remembrance ... [that something different is] to be taught, to have the service of an intellectual midwife-dialectician" (Beck, 1985, p. 120).

This kind of teaching cannot be reserved for graduate seminars. Adler (1988) insists that high schools cannot do their job unless Socratically conducted discussion plays a major role in our schools from the early grades on.

Recitation, coaching, and Socratic questioning/discussion together compose effective teaching, and they must all be present in judicious measure throughout the educational experience. A unified practice of teaching must incorporate them all. The task of this book is to produce a unified theory of teaching that conceptualizes and articulates these forms of teaching within a general theory of education.

Our effort is by no means the first. Numerous theories of teaching have been proposed in recent decades, many of which are embedded in broad "models" of educational performance that cover not only teaching but also learning, instruction, motivation, curriculum, and other processes (Bloom, 1976; Bruner, 1966, 1973b; see Haertel, Walberg, & Weinstein, 1983, and Walberg, 1986, for reviews). These efforts, combined with the steady accretion of understanding in the psychological, developmental, and social sciences, have made possible the unified theory of teaching and education that we propose.

Indeed, developments in the human sciences during the last half century have now reached a critical mass: It is now possible to articulate a new theory of teaching, an overarching, unified conception that puts into perspective and mutual association all those forms of assistance that result in increased cognitive and performance capacities in learners. Evidence discovered in behavioral science in the English-speaking world during this century has prepared the ground. Linchpin concepts that allow a systematic theory of teaching have been provided recently by translations of the work of L. S. Vygotsky and by those neo-Vygotskian researchers in various nations who are now attempting to elaborate, correct, and develop this body of work.

Rousing minds to life

Vygotsky argued that a child's development cannot be understood by a study of the individual; one must also examine the external social world in which that individual life has developed. In schools, we can understand the child's developing mind by studying the social interactions of teaching and learning.

An example: This excerpt is from a transcription of a reading-comprehension lesson. The teacher and children are reading and discussing a story, *Freddie Finds a Frog.* Freddie has proudly shown his new frog to Mr. Mays. Mr. Mays says that he just might take Freddie's new frog fishing. None of the children understands the double meaning of Mr. Mays's remark, and they are missing both the grisly joke and Freddie's revulsion. In this brief example, the teacher can be seen assisting the children – by a series of four questions – to assemble their knowledge, from the text and from their own experience, into a coherent understanding of Mr. Mays's joke.

Teacher: What did Mr. Mays say he would do with the frog?
Lon: He would take . . .

Mele: ... water, 'um fishing
Teacher: Do frogs like to go fishing?
Group: Noooo. [When the teacher repeats the question, one child says "yes," and
        several say "no"]
Teacher: Why don't they like to go fishing?
        [The children give several opinions] Frogs don't like water, don't like flies,
        don't like fish.
Bill: They use for da bait.
Teacher: If you use it for bait, what do you have to do to the frog?
        [The children give several opinions, including one exclamation of disgust]
Alice: Put it on a hook.

The teacher assists by providing the structure, and the children participate by providing the information. This is true teaching. Such teacher
behavior can never be entirely automatic. In its absence, this group of
children would never have been able to understand the story, no matter
how well they were able to read its individual words and phrases. But
with the teacher's assistance, they understood and were able to proceed.

In the example, we can see the social origins of an eventual mental tool,
or cognitive strategy. When faced with the puzzle of Mr. Mays's remark,
the children were baffled. The group solved the meaning by the strategy
of querying each possible explanation, until the one best meaning – frog
as bait – satisfied the logic of the story. The children had the bits of information necessary to solve the puzzle, and the teacher assisted them by
providing the structure and the questions that provoked the retrieval of
that information. By adolescence, most children will have internalized
that strategy. They will query themselves as to possible meanings of puz-
zling events, until the one best explanation emerges. However, until
internalization occurs, *performance must be assisted.*

Assisted performance identifies a fundamental process of development
and learning. The instructional activity of teaching-and-learning "*is good
only when it proceeds ahead of development. It then awakens and rouses
to life those functions which are in a stage of maturing*" (Vygotsky, 1956,
p. 278; italics in original; quoted in Rogoff & Wertsch, 1984, p. 3). In
natural teaching as it occurs in the socialization of young children into
their families and communities, interactions that assist higher-order
mental functions are commonplace (Bruner, 1983; Ochs, 1982; Wertsch,
1979, 1985b; Wood, 1980). In every culture, natural teaching transmits
skills of immense variety and power – a "curriculum" of far greater complexity than anything attempted in schools. Such interactions awaken
and arouse mind, communication, and expression and assist the instantiation of culture and society (Vygotsky, 1978; Wertsch, 1985b).

Yet, as we have seen in the foregoing review of teaching research, the
forms of assisted performance that are commonplace in everyday life are

seldom used by teachers in classrooms. Instead, since the last century, "teaching" in North American classrooms has consisted only of providing tasks and assessing individual development. This must be changed: Students cannot be left to learn on their own; teachers cannot be content to provide opportunities to learn and then assess outcomes; recitation must be deemphasized; responsive, assisting interactions must become commonplace in the classroom. Minds must be roused to life.

Teaching must be redefined as assisted performance. Teaching consists in assisting performance. Teaching is occurring when performance is achieved with assistance.

How can this be brought about? Education cannot improve until the processes and responsibilities of teaching are taken seriously at every link in the chain of education. The theory of teaching and schooling can and must be applied equally to every level of interaction in schools.

Thus far we have emphasized that the interactions between teacher and child must be improved. This level of analysis requires the most detailed and dedicated examination. However, all such interactions take place in the context of the social organization of the schools. Without an effective theory and practice of that social organization, no effective interactional reform can occur. The interactionist and contextualist levels of analysis must be conducted in full coordination. We need a theory not only of teaching but also of schooling.

The redefinition of schooling: toward a change in the culture of the school

Behind the classroom door: isolation, boredom, stagnation

Will the reform movement of the 1980s, set in motion by *A Nation at Risk,* be different? It is too soon to judge, but we can predict that reform will depend on the degree to which we heed certain elements in current calls for change – change in the school culture so that it will more reliably support teaching development and excellence. The Carnegie Foundation Forum on Education and the Economy (1986) wants reforms that will include making teaching more a profession than a trade. The "Goodlad consortium" is modeling new partnerships between schools and universities in an effort to revivify both. The California Commission on the Teaching Profession supported Rosenholtz's syntheses of research that identified a vital problem: "If we seek to promote the quality of teaching, reforms ... should also provide [teachers] some means to improve" (Rosenholtz, 1986, p. 518).

In the introduction, we quoted Rosenholtz on the isolation, monotony, and boredom of experienced teachers and the degree of their dependence on the school itself to provide continuing learning: Organizational conditions explained 60% of how much learning beginners reported, but a staggering 72% of how much learning veteran teachers reported (Rosenholtz, 1986, p. 524).

In 1972, Sarason made this same point as well as anyone has before or since, and the situation has changed not one whit:

> Nobody would disagree with the statement that schools are primarily for the education of children. People may disagree about what education is but they would all agree that the primary purpose of schools is to do something for and with children. . . . I have spent thousands of hours in schools and one of the first things I sensed was that the longer the person had been a teacher the less excited, or alive, or stimulated he seemed to be about his role. . . . Being a teacher was on the boring side. Generally speaking, these teachers were not as helpful to children as they might have been or as frequently as the teachers themselves would have liked to have been. . . . *Schools are not created to foster the intellectual and professional growth of teachers. The assumption that teachers can create and maintain those conditions which make school learning and school living stimulating for children, without those same conditions existing for teachers, has no warrant in the history of man.* That the different efforts to improve the education of children have been remarkably short of their mark is in part a consequence of the implicit value that schools are primarily for children, a value which gives rise to ways of thinking, to a view of technology, to ways of training, and to modes of organization which make for one grand error of misplaced emphasis. (Sarason, 1972, pp. 123–124; italics added)

How are we to achieve in schools the conditions that will make them places for teachers as well as students? The solution will involve others besides teachers.

Teaching, the bureaucratic organization, and the redefinition of schooling

Little actual teaching occurs in schools, and this is also characteristic of transactions within the entire educational apparatus. Teachers do not teach children, but then professors of education do not teach principals, principals do not teach grade-level chairpeople, and curriculum specialists do not teach teachers. Educational administrators teach no one, and neither do educational researchers. The educational establishment is organized as a series of unconnected independent positions whose occupants believe that somewhere below them, surely someone is teaching someone. Certainly the occupant of each position attempts to create educational opportunities for those down the chain – good textbooks, good workshops, even good performance objectives – but no one attends to assisting the performance of those objectives.

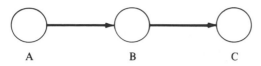

Figure 1.1. The bureaucratic supervisory chain.

Why? Schools are organized bureaucratically into chains of authority through which supervisory responsibility is exercised (Figure 1.1). Schools are by no means unique in this respect; even in organizations of the newer structural forms, such as the matrix and "Z" systems, each member of the organization looks to someone else, located "above" in the hierarchy, for "supervision." This "overseeing" usually means *direction and evaluation.* But in schools, this bureaucratic organizational structure has had most deleterious effects on the competence of the schools to teach.

Let us return to an earlier time and go down the hallways of a New York school of a century past. Apparently the bureaucratic, supervising culture in the American school has been as unchanging as its recitation script:

Principals and heads of departments do not teach classes. They are supposed to spend their whole time in supervision. There is one supervisor who does not teach for every eleven classes. In my judgment the number of non-teaching supervisors is unnecessarily large. The excessive development of supervision has resulted in several clearly defined evils in our schools. (Thomas, 1985; quoted in Sarason et al., 1986)

These evils in the schools of the late 19th century included a reduction in the status of teaching and an increase in the status of supervision, a harmful interference in the classroom by central authority, an unnecessary increase in evaluation of pupils, and a waste of money. Bureaucratic organization of schools, needless to say, decreases the amount of teaching that is done.

Nor is the situation different today:

Teachers are bureaucratically accountable for doing certain specific and standardized things that are hierarchically imposed, while they are supposed to be professionally accountable for doing uniquely appropriate things for individual clients. Though these things could conceivably be orthogonal, in practice they generally are not. If detailed prescriptions for practice could, indeed, improve the quality of teaching, they might substitute for meaningful evaluation of teachers. When they make it more difficult for good teachers to teach well, they defeat both the goals of quality assurance and of accountability. (Darling-Hammond, 1986, p. 537)

Given these organizational strictures that hinder good performance, teachers are now subjected to political and reformist demands for "accountability." Accountability is certainly a reasonable demand on any profession, but it is not reasonable when the demands are for performance that is entirely unassisted, indeed is obstructed. Accountability, when accompanied by assisted performance, is an ultimate goal. Teachers should be held accountable and recognized for their performances throughout their careers. Consider two views of how that might be done. In one view, the definitions of teaching and teachers are straightforward and readily mastered: Teaching can be reduced to a few days of standard in-service training that teachers can implement on their own. Such teaching can be assessed with an observation form, and teachers can be assessed with a test. The results of teaching can be checked by standardized achievement tests. In this view, teachers are moved primarily by their expectation of a pension, by fear that their incompetence will be detected, or by respect for authority. This is a caricature of talk one hears about teachers; it is more accurate as a description of behavior toward teachers.

In another view, teaching is a complex, humane activity at which a teacher can grow steadily more proficient over the years by means of disciplined curiosity, continuous training, and skillful assistance. Teachers can be supported and evaluated by persons – including principals – who join with them in mastering and advancing the craft. In this view, one influences teachers primarily by organizing the support and recognition that will permit them to realize the higher motives of service that bring them to teaching (Bird & Little, 1986, p. 507).

Sarason and associates (1986) have observed that none of the reformists, commissions, or policymakers have ever dealt directly or meaningfully with these leadership and administrative features of the school culture – this in spite of the fact that the school culture systematically assumes incompetence on the part of the teacher and, through paternalistic authoritarianism, ultimately makes not only teachers but also schools themselves incompetent for teaching (Sizer, 1984). It is the ossified administrative/organizational structures of the schools themselves that perpetuate the infantilization and unprofessionalism of the American teacher, because the schools will not allow teachers to become professional. This state of affairs is now marching blindly and triumphantly into its third century.

Redefining "supervision" does not mean ignoring teachers. Educators will not be made more professional and more competent by further isolating them in their classrooms. The human resource of the supervisor could become the agent for professional growth, were "supervision" defined as more than "directing and evaluating." There are other ways to oversee; this larger view can be used to assess the context in which the individual works and to provide opportunities for professional growth. *Supervision should be defined – particularly in an institution devoted to teaching – as assisting performance in precisely the terms we used to define teaching.*

New teachers left to cope on their own can be compared with those who are assisted to perform through mentorship and other collaborative enterprises. We then see the enormous benefits of such a redefinition of supervision:

Mentoring may assist new teachers, the group that defects most frequently [Schlechty & Vance, 1983]. Many beginning teachers who receive no guidance from experienced, successful teachers undergo severe "reality shock" as idealism gives way to an understanding that one must manage students' sometimes unruly behavior before one can teach. For beginning teachers who are isolated from colleagues, reality shock prompts negative attitudes. The view that each student has different needs gives way, usually within the first year, to a custodial view in which new teachers stress order, distrust students, and are punitive toward them [Ashton, Webb, & Doda, 1983; Bishop, 1977].

New teachers in collaborative settings, however, appear to maintain the view that tending to the individual needs of students is essential [Ashton et al., 1983; Bishop, 1977]. The emphasis on skill development and on ways to resolve teaching problems helps beginners avoid a custodial attitude, which in turn lessens reality shock. (Rosenholtz, 1986, p. 524)

Such conditions in schools also have a desirable effect on veteran teachers, from whom assistance is available through opportunities for collaboration:

In collaborative settings, teachers acquire and develop better skills through their collective analysis, evaluation, and experimentation with new teaching strategies [Armor et al., 1976; Little, 1982; Rosenholtz, Bassler, & Hoover-Dempsey, 1985a; Rutter, Maughan, Mortimore, & Ouston, 1979; Venezky & Winfield, 1979]. Unlike more typical school settings where teachers believe that they alone are responsible for running their classrooms and that to seek advice somehow implies a lack of teaching competence, in collaborative settings, teachers believe that help from others is both necessary and legitimate, and there are far more requests for and offers of assistance among colleagues and supervisors [Glidewell, Tucker, Todt, & Cox, 1983]. Ideas that are generated in collaborative settings give rise to greater classroom experimentation, greater teaching success, and ultimately to larger psychic benefits. (Rosenholtz, 1986, p. 518)

In Chapters 4 and 5, and again in Chapters 8 through 12, we explore the structures, roles, responsibilities, and consequences of a new culture of the school – one in which each member of the supervisory chain assumes the responsibility of *assisting, not controlling,* the performance of the next.

Before leaving this topic, however, it should be noted that the practice of supervision in schools is largely this: to assess, to direct, and otherwise to ignore. *The administrative/bureaucratic practice of assessing and directing is organically related to the classroom practice of assessing and directing the recitation script.* At neither level is there sufficient assistance, responsiveness, joint productive activity, or the building of common meanings and values. Teachers have virtually no interaction with their supervisors; when they do, they are expected to "recite," be assessed, and receive directions. Earlier in this chapter, we wondered at the vitality of the recitation script, which, like some ineradicable classroom mold, has lived long and done nothing. We should wonder no longer: In schools, it is everywhere – in the classroom, in the boardroom, and in the principal's office.

In any school organization, one of the duties of each individual should be to assist the performance of the person in the next subordinate position: The superintendent assists the principal, the principal assists the teacher, the teacher assists the pupil. Of course, assisting performance is only one of the responsibilities; each must also see to fair compensation, arrange vacations, respond humanely to family emergencies, and the like. Having granted this, let us also recognize the central responsibility of the teaching organization: assisting the performance of each member. This assistance, with its accompanying cognitive and behavioral development, is the justifying goal of the school, and all other duties should be in its service.

We have had the opportunity to experiment with the culture of the school, to produce an alternative form, and to observe several other instances in which glimmers of a new kind of school life could be discerned. In Chapter 5, we illustrate these points with a full case study. In Chapter 12, we examine the conditions that made such a school culture possible, and we describe those conditions that led to its decline. In the next four chapters, we elaborate an integrated theory of teaching, of schooling, and of literacy.

2 A theory of teaching as assisted performance

The development of cognition in society

It is ironic that the school – which alone among formal institutions has teaching as its primary goal – is notable for a lack of teaching, whereas all societies, including the most primitive, succeed in teaching the vast majority of their young members all those basic cognitive, social, and attitudinal structures that constitute cultural socialization. This teaching occurs largely without formalization, and largely without awareness.

This embarrassing comparison is often dismissed as a function of the schools' "more complex curriculum" of literacy and technology. Schools do indeed have particular constraints and unique technical demands, which we shall discuss in detail; nevertheless, schools have much to learn by examining the informal pedagogy of everyday life. The *principles* of good teaching are not different for school than for home and community. When true teaching is found in schools, it observes the same principles that good teaching exhibits in informal settings.

Long before they enter school, children are learning higher-order cognitive and linguistic skills. Their teaching takes place in the everyday interactions of domestic life. Within these goal-directed activities, opportunities are available for more capable members of the household to assist and regulate child performances. Through these mundane interactions, children learn the accumulated wisdom and the cognitive and communicative tools of their culture. They begin to develop functional cognitive systems; they begin to generalize their new skills to new problems and to novel aspects of familiar situations; they learn how to communicate and think.

In this informal socialization, neither communication nor cognition is the subject of direct instruction. Children's participation is sustained by the adults assuming as many of the strategic functions as are necessary to carry on (Wertsch, 1979, 1985b). Children often are unaware of the goal of the activity in which they are participating, but at the earliest levels

27

this is not necessary to learning. The caretakers' guidance permits children to engage in levels of activity that could not be managed alone. The pleasures of the social interaction seem sufficient to lure a child into the language and cognition of the more competent caregiver (Bernstein, 1981).

The process begins early, much earlier than was once thought, and takes place mainly without the conscious awareness of the participants (Ochs, 1982). Without awareness, a caregiver may engage in a collaborative enterprise with the most profound implications for the development of a participating child. Revealed in the interpersonal exchanges are the precursors of cognitive and communicative functions that will someday be self-regulated by the child. In the Introduction, we gave an example of children who could retrieve from memory the individual bits of information necessary to solve a problem, but were unable to assemble them by using the simple strategy of self-interrogation (see Brown, 1978, for additional discussion). The more competent individual assisted the learners by asking a series of questions. The problem was solved by each participant making a vital contribution – the child contributing the information, and the assistor providing a strategy for solving the problem. Eventually these same questions will be self-generated by the developing children, and the entire strategy self-regulated from beginning to end.

Such scenes are repeated many times during ontogenesis, and it is through such mundane interactions that children learn the cognitive and communicative tools and skills of their culture. This insight from Vygotsky has the most profound implications for how we think about development and teaching:

From the very first days of the child's development his activities acquire a meaning of their own in a system of social behavior and, being directed towards a definite purpose, are refracted through the prism of the child's environment. The path from object to child and from child to object passes through another person. This complex human structure is the product of a developmental process deeply rooted in the links between individual and social history. (Vygotsky, 1978, p. 30)

Thus, to explain the psychological, we must look not only at the individual but also at the external world in which that individual life has developed. We must examine human existence in its social and historical aspects, not only at its current surface. These social and historical aspects are represented to the child by people who assist and explain, those who participate with the child in shared functioning:

Any function in the child's cultural development appears twice, or in two planes. First it appears on the social plane, and then on the psychological plane. First it appears between people as an interpsychological category, and then within the child as an intrapsychological category. This is equally true with regard to voluntary attention, logical memory, the formation of concepts, and the development of volition. (Vygotsky, 1978, p. 163)

The process by which the social becomes the psychological is called *internalization*: "The process of Internalization is not the *transferral* of an external activity to a preexisting, internal 'plane of consciousness': It is the process in which this plane is *formed*" (Leont'ev, 1981, p. 57). The individual's "plane of consciousness" (i.e., higher cognitive processes) is formed in structures that are transmitted to the individual by others in speech, social interaction, and the processes of cooperative activity. Thus, individual consciousness arises from the actions and speech of others.

However, children reorganize and reconstruct these experiences. The mental plane is not isomorphic with the external plane of action and speech. As the external plane is internalized, transformations in structure and function occur. In this regard, Vygotsky's thought is closer to that of Piaget than to others. For example, Vygotsky expressly denies Watson's assumption that the internal speech of thinking is identical with external speech save for the vocalization. A child does learn to speak by hearing others speak – indeed, learns to think through hearing others speak – but as private speech sinks "underground" into thought, it is abbreviated and finally automatized into a form that bears little surface resemblance to speech itself. This transformation of form is a part of the developmental process.

The child is not merely a passive recipient of adult guidance and assistance (Baumrind, 1971; Bell, 1979; Bruner, 1973a; Rogoff, in press); in instructional programs, the active involvement of the child is crucial (Bruner, 1966). To acknowledge the inventive role of the child in transforming what is internalized, some developmentalists have begun to use the term *guided reinvention* – a term that connotes both social learning and cognitive reconstructivist arguments. Fischer and Bullock (1984) credit Vygotsky for having best anticipated the guided reinvention perspective, which expressly excludes the extreme positions found in some versions of modern social learning and cognitive-stage theories. Guided reinvention

acknowledges the social learning theorists' insistence that social guidance is ubiquitous. It also acknowledges, however, the Piagetian insight that to understand is to reconstruct. Thus, guided reinvention elaborates the theme that normal cognitive development must be understood as a collaborative process involving the child and the environment. (Fischer & Bullock, 1984, pp. 112–113)

In summary, the cognitive and social development of the child (to the extent that the biological substrate is present) proceeds as an unfolding of potential through the reciprocal influences of child and social environment. Through guided reinvention, higher mental functions that are part of the social and cultural heritage of the child will move from the social plane to the psychological plane, from the intermental to the intramental, from the socially regulated to the self-regulated. The child, through the regulating actions and speech of others, is brought to engage in independent action and speech. In the resulting interaction, the child performs, through assistance and cooperative activity, at developmental levels quite beyond the individual level of achievement. In the beginning of the transformation to the intramental plane, the child need not understand the activity as the adult understands it, need not be aware of its reasons or of its articulation with other activities. For skills and functions to develop into internalized, self-regulated capacity, all that is needed is performance, through assisting interaction. Through this process, the child acquires the "plane of consciousness" of the natal society and is socialized, acculturated, made human.

The zone of proximal development

Assisted performance defines what a child can do with help, with the support of the environment, of others, and of the self. For Vygotsky, the contrast between assisted performance and unassisted performance identified the fundamental nexus of development and learning that he called the zone of proximal development (ZPD).

It is conventional and correct to assess a child's developmental level by the child's ability to solve problems unassisted – this is the familiar protocol of standardized assessment, such as the Stanford-Binet. The child's *learning,* however, exceeds the reach of the developmental level and is to be found by assessing those additional problems that the child can solve with social assistance.

The distance between the child's individual capacity and the capacity to perform with assistance is the ZPD, which is

the distance between the actual developmental level as determined by individual problem solving and the level of potential development as determined through problem solving under adult guidance or in collaboration with more capable peers. The zone of proximal development defines those functions that have not yet matured but are in the process of maturation, functions that will mature tomorrow but are currently in an embryonic state. These functions could be termed the "buds" or "flowers" of development rather than the "fruits" of development. (Vygotsky, 1978, p. 86; italics in original)

In contemporary neo-Vygotskian discussions, the concept of the ZPD has been extended to a more general statement, in which the "problem solving" of the preceding quotation is understood to mean performance in other domains of competence (Cazden, 1981; Rogoff & Wertsch, 1984). There is no single zone for each individual. For any domain of skill, a ZPD can be created. There are cultural zones as well as individual zones, because there are cultural variations in the competencies that a child must acquire through social interaction in a particular society (Rogoff, 1982). Boys in Micronesia, where sailing a canoe is a fundamental skill, will have a ZPD for the skills of navigation, created in interaction with the sailing masters. A girl in the Navajo weaving community will have experiences in a zone not quite like any ever encountered by the daughters of Philadelphia. Whatever the activity, in the ZPD we find that assistance is provided by the teacher, the adult, the expert, the more capable peer. Through this assistance,

learning awakens a variety of internal developmental processes that are able to operate only when the child is interacting with people in his environment and in cooperation with his peers. Once these processes are internalized, they become part of the child's independent developmental achievement. (Vygotsky, 1978, p. 90)

Distinguishing the *proximal zone* from the *developmental level* by contrasting assisted versus unassisted performance has profound implications for educational practice. It is in the proximal zone that teaching may be defined in terms of child development. In Vygotskian terms, teaching is good only when it *"awakens and rouses to life those functions which are in a stage of maturing, which lie in the zone of proximal development* (Vygotsky, 1956, p. 278; quoted in Wertsch & Stone, 1985; italics in original).

We can therefore derive this general definition of teaching: *Teaching consists in assisting performance through the ZPD. Teaching can be said to occur when assistance is offered at points in the ZPD at which performance requires assistance.*

By whom performance is assisted is less important than that performance is achieved, and thereby development and learning proceed. To the extent that peers can assist performance, learning will occur through that assistance. In terms of pedagogy, assistance should be offered in those interactional contexts most likely to generate joint performance.

Vygotsky's work principally discusses children, but identical processes can be seen operating in the learning adult. Recognition of this fact allows the creation of effective programs for teacher training and offers guidance for organizational management of systems of assistance. Developmental processes, arising from assisted performance in the ZPD, can be observed not only in the ontogenesis of the individual but also in the microgenesis of discrete skills as they develop throughout the life course. The role of assisted performance for adults in the educational enterprise is discussed in detail in Chapters 4, 5, and 9–12. In the remainder of this chapter, however, the discussion will draw on examples from adult–child interactions in the ZPD.

Paths through the zone

The transition from assisted performance to unassisted performance is not abrupt. We can again use the example of an interaction between a father and a daughter who cannot find her shoes; the father asks several questions ("Did you take them into the kitchen? Did you have them while playing in your room?"). The child has some of the information stored in memory ("not in the kitchen; I think in my room"); the father has an interrogation strategy for organizing retrieval of isolated bits of information in order to narrow the possibilities to a reasonable search strategy. The child does not know how to organize an effective recall strategy; the father knows the strategy, but he does not have the information needed to locate the shoes. Through collaboration, they produce a satisfactory solution. When the child is older, perhaps the father will have to say less ("Well, think of where you last saw the shoes"), leaving the more specific interrogation to the now self-assisting strategies of the child. This example of memory function provides an account of the origins of what are typically called metacognitive processes (Brown, 1978; Wertsch, 1978).

The developmental stages of higher cognitive, communicative, and social functioning always involve new systemic relationships among more basic functions. Vygotsky's discussions of higher-order mental processes all emphasize the shifting nature of such relationships during the course of development (Vygotsky, 1987). Attentional processes may be used as an example. In the first days of school, children can solve even simple problems only if attentional processes are brought into a new relationship with perception and memory. The attention capacity of the child entering kindergarten may be in the ZPD, so that a 5-year-old is capable of attending to teacher instruction and direction, but only if a rich diet of teacher praise is available. The teacher praise assists the child's attending by both cueing and reinforcing it. With time, the amount of praise required may be expected to decline (Tharp & Gallimore, 1976b). As the capacity for attending advances through the ZPD, assistance often is provided by peers, who may remind a daydreamer that attention to the teacher is wise. For most pupils, after the third grade, assistance by either teachers or peers is rarely needed; attention processes can be invoked when the situation is judged appropriate; they have become self-regulated.

The development of any performance capacity in the individual also represents a changing relationship between self-regulation and social regulation. We present progress through the ZPD in a model of four stages. The model focuses particularly on the relationship between self-control and social control.

The four stages of the ZPD

Stage I: Where performance is assisted by more capable others

Before children can function as independent agents, they must rely on adults or more capable peers for outside regulation of task performance. The amount and kind of outside regulation a child requires depend on the child's age and the nature of the task: that is, the breadth and progression through the ZPD for the activity at hand.

Wertsch (1978, 1979, 1981, 1985b) has pointed out that during the earliest periods in the ZPD, the child may have a very limited understanding of the situation, the task, or the goal to be achieved; at this level, the parent, teacher, or more capable peer offers directions or modeling, and the child's response is acquiescent or imitative. Only gradually does the child come to understand the way in which the parts of an activity relate to one another or to understand the meaning of the performance. Ordinarily, this understanding develops through conversation during the task performance. When some conception of the overall performance has been acquired through language or other semiotic processes, the child can be assisted by other means – questions, feedback, and further cognitive structuring. Consider a child perplexed by the myriad pieces of a puzzle. Thus, the adult might say, "Which part of the puzzle will you start to do?" The child may respond by putting in all the wheels, and thus see a truck take shape. Such assistance of performance has been described as *scaffolding,* a metaphor first used by Wood, Bruner, and Ross (1976) to describe the ideal role of the teacher. Greenfield (1984) noted that the characteristics of the carpenter's scaffold indeed provide an apt analogy for the teaching adult's selective assistance to a child. She added that scaffolding is similar to the concept of "behavior shaping," except in one important way. Shaping simplifies a task by breaking it down into a series of steps toward the goal. Scaffolding, however, does not involve simplifying the task; it holds the task difficulty constant, while simplifying the child's role by means of graduated assistance from the adult/expert (Greenfield, 1984).

Scaffolding is a concept that has been of unusual importance to the study of child development. However appealing this metaphor may be, the field has advanced to the point that a more differentiated concept can be developed. For example, scaffolding suggests that the principal variations in adult actions are matters of quantity – how high the scaffold stands, how many levels it supports, how long it is kept in place. But many of the acts of the adult in assisting the child are qualitatively different from one another. "Sometimes, the adult directs attention. At other times, the adult holds important information in memory. At still other times, the adult offers simple encouragement" (Griffin & Cole, 1984, p. 47).

The various means of assisting performance are indeed qualitatively different. By discussing these different means of assisting performance, we have the opportunity to connect neo-Vygotskian ideas with a broader literature of American and British psychology, a task taken up in Chapters 3 and 4.

For the present, we can discuss the issue in terms of the various kinds of assistance that are regular features of Stage I. Rogoff (1986) discusses some of these issues in terms of *structuring situations*. Even before interacting with the child, a parent or teacher assists by an age grading of manipulanda: The choice of puzzles, the selection of kindergarten tasks, and the selection of appropriate tools and materials for an apprentice are all important features of assisting performance.

In addition to grading manipulanda, the assistor provides a "grading" of tasks, by structuring tasks into sub-goals and sub-sub-goals. The Saxe, Gearhart, and Guberman (1984) work on assisting children to learn to count is an example of structuring a teaching situation by careful task analysis and sub-goal selection, until the entire script is assembled back from its parts.

During Stage I, a child (or an adult learner) may not conceptualize the goal of the activity in the way that the adult assistor does (Figure 2.1). A child's initial goal might be to sustain a pleasant interaction or to have access to some attractive puzzle items, or there might be some other motive that adults cannot apprehend. As interaction proceeds, different goals and sub-goals emerge and change as the participants work together. The adult may shift to a subordinate or superordinate goal in response to ongoing assessment of the child's performance. The child's goals will also shift in response to adult help and their growing intersubjectivity. In a careful analysis of such interactions, Saxe and associates concluded that because the goal structure is located

neither in the head of the mother nor in that of the child, this goal structure is negotiated in the interaction itself. Thus, the emergent goal structure simultaneously involves the child's understandings and the historical achievements of culture as communicated by the mother. . . . As children generate coherent means to achieve these socially negotiated goals, they create for themselves a system of rep-

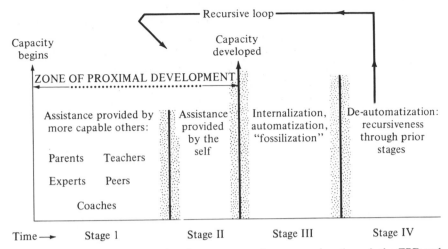

Figure 2.1. Genesis of performance capacity: progression through the ZPD and beyond.

resentation that reflects achievements that have been generated in our culture's social history. (Saxe et al., 1984, p. 29)

The shifting of goals by the adult to achieve intersubjectivity is the fundamental reason that a profound knowledge of subject matter is required of teachers who seek to assist performance. Without such knowledge, teachers cannot be ready to promptly assist performance, because they cannot quickly reformulate the goals of the interaction; they cannot map the child's conception of the task goal onto the superordinate knowledge structures of the academic discipline that is being transmitted. This fundamental aspect of interaction in the ZPD will emerge repeatedly in our analysis of teaching and the development of teaching.

During Stage I, we see a steadily declining plane of adult responsibility for task performance and a reciprocal increase in the learner's proportion of responsibility. This is Bruner's fundamental "handover principle" – the child who was a spectator is now a participant (Bruner, 1983, p. 60). The developmental task of Stage I is to transit from other-regulation to self-regulation. The transit begins while performance is still being carried out on the interpsychological plane of functioning, because the child can begin to use language exchanges with the adult to engender assistance. For example, in the analysis of joint puzzle-solving, the child can begin to ask the adult for strategic direction (e.g., "Which part do I do next?") (Wertsch, 1979, p. 19).

Indeed, by asking questions and adopting other sub-routines of the adult's assistance, children gradually take over the actual structuring of the task and thereby acquire not only the performance but also the process of transfer of the performance (Rogoff, 1986). The adult's task is to accurately tailor assistance to the child by being responsive to the child's current effort and understanding of the task goal. By asking "Which part do I do next?" the child begins to influence the level of help provided. *This assists the adult to assist.* Children, and other learners, are never passive recipients of adult or teacher input. As infants, they attracted adult attention through cries, smiles, and other responses. "Rocking and walking are not only effective ways of calming babies but also provide them with adult legs to move on and with access to new scenes of regard that yield information about the environment" (Rogoff, Malkin, & Gilbride, 1984, p. 32).

"Legs" of a different kind are needed to solve puzzles, learn to read, and acquire all the other skills that have their origins in social interaction. But at each stage, the developing child contributes to the success of an activity. Asking for strategic direction is, in this sense, no different than the infant's cry that makes locomotion possible. In both cases, the child's partial performance provokes adult assistance, thus permitting an achievement not possible without the collaborating other.

The task of Stage I is accomplished when the responsibility for tailoring the assistance, tailoring the transfer, and performing the task itself has been effectively handed over to the learner.

Of course, this achievement is gradual, with progress occurring in fits and starts. The line between any two stages in the diagram of the ZPD is represented as a zone itself.

Stage II: Where performance is assisted by the self

If we look carefully at the child's statements during this transition, we see that the child

has taken over the rules and responsibilities of both participants in the language-game. These responsibilities were formerly divided between the adult and child, but they have now been taken over completely by the child. The definitions of situation and the patterns of activity which formerly allowed the child to participate in the problem-solving effort on the interpsychological plane now allow him/her to carry out the task on the intrapsychological plane. (Wertsch, 1979, p. 18)

Thus, in Stage II, the child carries out a task without assistance from others. *However, this does not mean that the performance is fully developed or automatized.*

This point can be seen most clearly at the level of individual, ontogenetic development. In neo-Vygotskian theory, whether we consider the genesis of a particular performance capacity (microgenesis) or the development of an individual (ontogenesis), the same four stages describe the preponderance of self-control/social-control relationships. During Stage II, the relationships among language, thought, and action in general undergo profound rearrangements – ontogenetically, in the years from infancy through middle childhood. By the age of 2 years or so, child behavior can be inhibited by adult speech ("Don't kick!"). In the next stage of development, this same *self*-instruction ("Don't kick!") also inhibits the kicking impulse. Control is passed from the adult to the child speaker, but the control function remains with the overt verbalization. The transfer from external to internal control is accomplished by transfer of the manipulation of the sign (e.g., language) from others to the self.

The phenomenon of self-directed speech reflects a development of the most profound significance. According to Vygotsky, and his follower Luria, once children begin to direct or guide behavior with their own speech, an important stage has been reached in the transition of a skill through the ZPD. It constitutes the next stage in the passing of control or assistance from the adult to the child, from the expert to the apprentice. What was guided by the other is now beginning to be guided and directed by the self.

There is now substantial experimental and observational evidence (Gallimore et al., 1986; Tharp, Gallimore, & Calkins, 1984; Watson & Tharp, 1988) that a major function of self-directed speech is "self-guidance, that its developmental origins have to do with early social experiences, and that it increases under task circumstances involving obstacles and difficulties" (Berk & Garvin, 1984, p. 24; Berk, 1986). Developmental analysis places self-assistance as a stage in the ZPD.

Self-control may be seen as a recurrent and efficacious method that bridges between help by others and fully automated, fully developed capacities. Meichenbaum (1977) sought to teach self-instruction to children with deficient self-control. "Impulsive" children were taught to instruct themselves with cognitive strategies (e.g., "Go slow and be careful") before and during a variety of performance tasks; they demonstrated improved performance in such tasks as paper-and-pencil mazes. For children older than 6 years, semantic meaning efficiently mediates performance (Gal'perin, 1969). Children also employ self-directed vocalization to assist performance under conditions of stress or task difficulty (Berk, 1986; Berk & Garvin, 1984; Kohlberg, Yaeger, & Hjertholm, 1968; Roberts, 1979; Roberts & Mullis, 1980; Roberts & Tharp, 1980).

Thus, for children, a major function of self-directed speech is self-guidance. This remains true throughout lifelong learning. At the microgenetic level, when we consider the acquisition of some particular performance capacity, adults during Stage II consistently talk to themselves, and indeed assist themselves in all ways possible. Later in this volume, we present many examples of both students and teachers using self-assistance as they progress through the ZPD (see Chapters 10 and 11 for accounts of the teacher's use of self-assistance). The self-conscious, systematic use of self-directed assistance strategies is one of the most vigorous movements in applied psychology (Watson & Tharp, 1988).

Self-speech is more than instrumental in skill acquisition; it is itself an aspect of cognitive development of the most profound sort (Diaz, 1986); it forms the basis for writing and thus is transformed into the highest forms of communication available to the literate life (Elsasser & John-Steiner, 1977).

Stage III: Where performance is developed, automatized, and "fossilized"

Once all evidence of self-regulation has vanished, the child has emerged from the ZPD into the *developmental stage* for that task. The task execution is smooth and integrated. It has been internalized and "automatized." Assistance, from the adult or the self, is no longer needed. Indeed, "assistance" would now be disruptive. It is in this condition that instructions from others are disruptive and irritating; it is at this stage that self-consciousness itself is detrimental to the smooth integration of all task components. This is a stage beyond self-control and beyond social control. Performance here is no longer developing; it is already developed. Vygotsky described it as the "fruits" of development, but he also described it as "fossilized," emphasizing its fixity and distance from the social and mental forces of change.

Stage IV: Where de-automatization of performance leads to recursion back through the ZPD

The lifelong learning by any individual is made up of these same regulated, ZPD sequences – from other-assistance to self-assistance – recurring over and over again for the development of new capacities. For every individual, at any point in time, there will be a mix of other-regulation, self-regulation, and automatized processes. The child who can now do many of the steps in finding a lost object might still be in the ZPD for the activities of reading, or any of the many skills and processes remaining to be developed in the immature organism.

Furthermore, once children master cognitive strategies, they are not obligated to rely only on internal mediation. They can also ask for help when stuck, for example, in the search for lost items of attire. During periods of difficulty, children may seek out controlling vocalizations by more competent others (Gal'perin, 1969). Again, we see the intimate and shifting relationship between control by self and control by others.

Even for adults, the effort to recall a forgotten bit of information can be aided by the helpful assistance of another, so that the total of self-regulated and other-regulated components of the performance once again resembles the mother-and-child example of shared functioning. Even the competent adult can profit from regulation for enhancement and maintenance of performance.

Indeed, enhancement, improvement, and maintenance of performance provide a recurrent cycle of self-assistance to other-assistance. A most important consideration is that *de-automatization and recursion* occur so regularly that they constitute a Stage IV of the normal developmental process. What one formerly could do, one can no longer do. This de-automatization may be due to slight environmental changes or individual stress, not to mention major upheavals or physical trauma. The analogy between microgenesis and ontogenesis is again clear; at the end of life, capacities fall into general decline. After de-automatization, for whatever reason, if capacity is to be restored, then the developmental process must become recursive.

The first line of retreat is to the immediately prior self-regulating phase. We have already discussed how children doing more difficult problems talk to themselves about it more, and quite competent adults can recall talking themselves through some knotty intellectual problem, or through the traffic patterns of a strange city. Making self-speech external is a form of recursion often effective in restoring competence. A further retreat, to remembering the voice of a teacher, may be required. "Hearing the voice of the teacher" has been shown to be one of the middle stages in the development of complex skills (Gallimore et al., 1986; see a full discussion in Chapter 11). Intentionally recurring to that point in the zone – consciously reconjuring the voice of a tutor – is an effective self-control technique.

But in some cases no form of self-regulation may be adequate to restore capacity, and a further recursion – the restitution of other-regulation – is often required. The readiness of a teacher to repeat some earlier lesson is one mark of excellent teaching. The profession of assisting adults (psychotherapy) is now a major Western institution. In all these instances, the goal is to re-proceed through assisted performance to self-regulation and to exit the ZPD again into a new automatization.

Responsive assistance

In the transition from other-assistance to self-assistance (and automatization) there are variations in the means and patterns of adult assistance to the child. At the earlier phases, assistance may be frequent and elaborate. Later, it occurs less often and is truncated. Adult assistance is contingent on and responsive to the child's level of performance. In the earliest stages, when the child does not comprehend the purpose of an activity or see the connection between component steps, adult help tends to be relatively narrow in focus: "Pick up the blue one, and put it next to the yellow one."

As the child's comprehension and skill increase, adults begin to abbreviate their help (Rogoff & Gardener, 1984; Wertsch & Schneider, 1979). The adult may say something like "OK, what else could you try?" Such a truncated bit of help may prompt the child to take another look at the model of the puzzle, or scan the finished part, or poke through the pile of pieces for a different one. In narrative retelling, the adult may ask if the child remembers any more of the story, whereas earlier queries were about more specific details ("What did the other brother do?") (McNamee, 1979).

If the truncated guidance fails, the adult may add additional hints, testing to find that minimum level of help the child needs to proceed. This continual adjustment of the level and amount of help is *responsive to the child's level of performance and perceived need.* Assisting adults appear to keep in mind the overall goal of the activity, to stay related to what the child is trying to do. New information or suggestions are made relevant to furthering the child's current goal, and at the same time furthering the overall goal.

The tuning of adult assistance appears to begin quite early. For example, Cross (1977) studied 16 children ranging in age from 19 to 32 months. Although the average difference among their mean lengths of utterance (MLU) was only two words, correlations between mothers' speech adjustments and child speech levels ranged from .65 to .85. More significantly, the best predictor of mother adjustments to child utterances was the mean of the 50 longest utterances (out of 500), *not* the MLU for the entire 500. The mothers' MLUs were, on average, about three morphemes longer than their children's and less than half a morpheme longer than the children's longest utterances. The mothers probably were tracking their children's best performance, which probably was at or near the capacity level for the age of the children. This suggests that mothers' contingent speech adjustments are well "tuned" to the leading edge of child communicative competence – to the ZPD of social communication.

For older children, responsive adult assistance can become quite varied within a single episode of collaborative activity – and the reciprocity of adult–child interactions quite complex. Attempts by assisting adults to assess a child's readiness for greater responsibility often are subtle and embedded in the ongoing interaction, appearing as negotiations of the division of labor. For example, in Rogoff's study (1986), at the beginning of sessions, mothers often provided redundant information to ensure correct performance; this decreased over the session, as in the study of Wertsch and Schneider (1979). Mothers and children used hesitation, glances, and postural changes, as well as errors by the children, to adjust relative responsibilities for problem-solving. For example, one mother encouraged her child to determine where the next item went. When the child hesitated, the mother turned slightly toward the correct location. When the child still hesitated, the mother glanced at the correct location and moved the item slightly toward its intended location. Finally, she superficially rearranged other items in the correct group, and with this hint the child finally made the correct placement. Thus, the mother encouraged greater responsibility by the child and masked her assistance as random activity rather than correction of error, adjusting her support to the child's level of understanding.

However, patient, contingent, responsive, and accurately tuned adult assistance does not always occur. A major variable here is the nature of the task or performance. If efficient production is needed, the adult will likely be more directive and less tolerant of such costly child errors as failing to correctly care for animals on which the family's survival is partly dependent (Wertsch, Minick, & Arns, 1984). In joint productive activities of some importance, a child's participation may be relatively passive – observing the adult/expert carry out the task, and joining in to help at those points where the child's skill matches the task demands. This is the classic pattern of informal teaching that has been described in the anthropological literature for 50 years (Fortes, 1938).

But when the development of independent child skill is defined as a goal, the pattern of assistance provided by the adult is more responsive, contingent, and patient. The adult graduates the assistance, responsive to the child's performance level: The more the child can do, the less the adult does (Wertsch et al., 1984).

This illuminates an important pedagogical principle. "Assistance" offered at too high a level will disrupt child performance and is not effective teaching. Once independent skill has been achieved, "assistance" becomes "interference." For this reason, our definition of teaching emphasizes that *teaching can be said to occur when assistance is offered at points in the ZPD at which performance requires assistance.* Careful assessment of the child's abilities, relative to the ZPD and the developmental level, is a constant requirement for the teacher. This becomes imperative when we remember that the processes of development are recursive.

Assisted performance: child, parent, and teacher

As common as assisted performance is in the interactions of parents and children, it is uncommon in those of teachers and students. Study after study has documented the absence in classrooms of this fundamental tool for the teaching of children: assistance provided by more capable others that is responsive to goal-directed activities (see Chapter 1).

The absence of assisted performance in schools is all the more remarkable because most teachers are members of the literate middle class, where researchers have most often found such interactions. Why is it that this adult–child pattern – no doubt a product of historical, evolutionary processes – is so seldom observed in the very setting where it would seem most appropriate? Such interactions can be found in every society, in the introduction of children to any task. But this basic method of human socialization has not generally diffused into schools. Why?

There are two basic reasons. First, to provide assistance in the ZPD, the assistor must be in close touch with the learner's relationship to the task. Sensitive and accurate assistance that challenges but does not dismay the learner cannot be achieved in the absence of information. Opportunities for this knowledge, conditions in which the teacher can be sufficiently aware of the child's actual, in-flight performing, simply are not available in classrooms organized, equipped, and staffed in the typical American pattern. There are too many children for each teacher. And even if there is time to assess each child's ZPD for each task, more time is needed – time for interaction, for conversation, for joint activity between teachers and children. Occasionally, now and through history, these opportunities have existed: the classical Greek academies, Oxford and Cambridge, the individual tutorial, the private American school with classes of seven or less. But all involve a pupil–teacher ratio that exceeds the politicians' judgment of the taxpayers' purse. Public education is not likely to reorganize into classrooms of seven pupils each.

This does not make the case hopeless. Emerging instructional practices do offer some hope of increased opportunities for assisted performance: the increased use of small groups, maintenance of a positive classroom atmosphere that will increase independent task involvement of students, new materials and technology with which students can interact independent of the teacher. In Chapters 6–8 we report a system of classroom organization that does allow for a sharply increased rate of assisted performance by teachers and peers.

There is a second reason that assisted performance has not diffused into the schools. Even when instructional practices allow for increased use of assisted performance, it will not necessarily appear as a regular feature of a teacher's activity. It may not be practiced even by those teachers who are from homes and communities where, outside of school, such interactions are commonplace. It will not necessarily be forthcoming from teachers who themselves provide assisted performance for their own children. Even with the benefits of modern instructional practice, there is still too large a gap between the conditions of home and school. Most parents do not need to be trained to assist performance; most teachers do.

By "training," we mean that teachers cannot rely on lay skills that are sufficient for parental socialization of offspring. Lay or parental skills provide a foundation, but they are not enough. Teachers need a more elaborate set of skills in assistance, and they need to be more conscious of their application.

Teachers need to learn good pedagogical practices: the expert pedagogy of which Berliner (1986) and others have written (e.g., various chapters in Wittrock, 1986). They must learn the professional skills of assisting performance and learn to apply them at a level far beyond that required in private life. Also, they must master the subject matter they are to teach, an accomplishment too rare in teacher-training programs (Hyland, 1984; Shulman, 1986); the level of knowledge that makes for an informed citizen will not be sufficient for the teacher who must pass this knowledge on to others.

For pedagogical skills to be acquired, there must be training and development experiences that few teachers encounter – opportunity to observe effective examples and effective practitioners of assisted performance, and opportunities to practice nascent skills, to receive video and audio feedback, and to have the gentle, competent "coaching" of a skilled consultant. Teachers themselves must have their performance assisted if they are to acquire the ability to assist the performance of their students.

A development in social science offers hope that such a professionalization of teaching can occur. Decades of psychological research have identified the technical means by which assistance to performance is achieved. We move now to a discussion of those means of assistance.

3   The means of assisting performance

In Western psychology in this century, intense attention has been paid to the means of assisting performance: *modeling, contingency managing, feeding back, instructing, questioning,* and *cognitive structuring.* The studies of these various means of assistance have "belonged" to different theories, to different disciplines, and even to different nations. By considering them together, we can link large areas of knowledge into an articulated structure – a theory of teaching – and by linking the achievements of Western psychology to the neo-Vygotskian theory of development, the explanatory power of each is increased substantially.

In discussing the social origins of cognition, Vygotsky insisted on the primacy of linguistic means in the development of higher mental processes. The signs and symbols of speech are primary "tools" of humankind. Only when linguistic tools are integrated with the tools of physical action can the potential for full human cognitive development be reached. Indeed, he wrote that semiotics – the study of signs – is the only adequate method for investigating human consciousness. Writers in this tradition have continued to presume the primacy of interpersonal speech for the development of intrapsychological functioning, and language is featured almost exclusively in their detailed accounts of the internalization process.

This emphasis is in part due to the easily observable role of speech in the processes of internalization. Language appears to be like Mercury, the messenger who carries content from the interpsychological plane to the intrapsychological plane, a messenger with unique gifts for translation from one plane to another. What is spoken *to* a child is later said *by* the child to the self, and later is abbreviated and transformed into the silent speech of the child's thought. Indeed, in mature adults, much systematic thinking continues to occur in the patterns of conversation. Problemsolving thought has the characteristics of dialogue and can be analyzed as though it were a two-person (or multiperson) discourse. This conversational thought may take the form of query and answer ("Let me see

44

now, is it this? Is it that? No. Yes."). It may also take the form of a dialectic ("It must be this! No, it is probably the opposite. Most likely, something between."). Adults' (and even adolescents') typical form of thinking-discourse is rooted in the forms of the conversations in the homes and schools of their childhood.

Even with this close linking of speech and thought, a full account of development must also include an understanding of nonlinguistic means of assisting performance. We agree that, as Vygotsky argued, much thinking, certainly in schooled societies, originates and is perpetuated in speech. This does not mean, however, that all means of assisting performance are linguistic. Thinking is representational, but it employs the full range of icons available from all the sense modalities.

One of our goals is the integration of neo-Vygotskianism with those considerations central to behaviorist and cognitive studies of learning and self-control. Modeling, contingency management, and feedback – these are also major mechanisms for assisting learners through ZPDs. As we shall see, these same mechanisms are used by learners during emergent self-control. In the same way that speech carries signs into the "underground" of thought, these other means of assistance are also carried by representations and icons into the emerging plane of consciousness.

In industrialized, urban society, linguistic means of assistance do appear to be dominant. The predominance of social science evidence comes from this society, and we run the risk of distorting our understanding of human processes by considering only a narrow range of cultural interactions. Our own technological culture may seem to require verbal explanation before children can understand adult activities, but this is a requirement of a particular society, not a requirement of cognitive development (Nerlove & Snipper, 1981; Rogoff, 1982; Scribner & Cole, 1981).

In nontechnological societies, adult behaviors are learned and understood with only occasional verbal explanation. Such societies rely heavily on "observational" learning; this is practical where adult behaviors and role performances are available for prolonged and careful scrutiny by children – in cultures that are "within the direct reach of the sensory organs" of the child (Fortes, 1938; Pettit, 1946). This means that children are incorporated into the activity settings of the society. The process has been put succinctly by Margaret Tafoya, doyenne of American Indian potters, herself both daughter and mother in a family of distinguished artists in clay:

My girls, I didn't teach them . . . they watched and learned by trying. I was taught to stay with the traditional clay designs, because that was the way it was handed down to my mother and me. I am thankful for my mother teaching me to make the large pieces (which require special skill and understanding). I watched her and tried to do like she did. And, I did. (Tafoya, 1983)

John-Steiner & Oesterreich discuss this Pueblo Indian culture and provide a link from typical interpersonal events to intrapsychological processes:

Children listening to the many legends of their people learn to represent these visually . . . because they are not allowed to ask questions or verbally reflect on what they hear. They are to say only *aeh hae* to acknowledge auditory attention. As a result, while the verbal representations of some of these legends are fairly simple nursery tales, the inner representations of the same legends, for older children and adults, are replete with highly abstract visual and symbolic articulations of cultural values. (John-Steiner & Oesterreich, 1975, p. 192)

That which is modeled is internalized and represented by the learner as an image, a paradigm-icon, for self-guidance. The image of the expert's hands on the loom is transformed into an intrapsychological standard for comparison and feedback as the learning weaver watches her own fingers fly. (For a detailed discussion of these issues, see Jordan, Tharp, & Vogt, 1985; Tharp, 1985, 1987; White, Tharp, Jordan, & Vogt, 1987.)

Of course, modeling and feedback as means of assistance are not limited to nontechnological societies. Everyday life is replete with examples, such as athletic coaching (Tharp & Gallimore, 1976a). To include a broader consideration of means of assistance in a theory of teaching does not demote semiotics. The study of signs is congruent with cognitive science's emphasis on cognitive representations. We do, however, propose to expand the discussion, to broaden the range of modalities of those representations that are internalized from interpersonal processes into cognitive processes. Western behaviorism and cognitive science, in fact, are as likely to emphasize visual means as linguistic means; this is equally true of some prominent neo-Vygotskian theorists (John-Steiner, 1985).

Therefore, the means of regulation are not restricted to language. In the full list must also be represented those nonlinguistic and paralinguistic means that have been identified over several decades of research in behaviorist and cognitive psychology.

A note on the examples

In preceding chapters, examples were chosen primarily from interactions in early childhood. The means of assistance are observable in all teaching contexts – and, indeed, in most joint-activity settings where the participants have different skills and levels of skill. Examples could be drawn from teacher preservice training, from principal–teacher interactions, from peer interactions in the classroom or playground. In the second half of this book, the means of assistance are illustrated in teaching/learning interactions at every level of the school organization. However, in this chapter, the examples are drawn from a single third-grade reading lesson in order to emphasize certain points: (a) means of assistance are encountered regularly in competent, responsive teaching; (b) no matter how abstract our theory of teaching, the principles find expression in ordinary interactions in the elementary school classroom; (c) the means of assistance are necessarily intertwined, occurring in combination and sometimes simultaneously; and (d) they can be observed in continuous operation – in fact, a good lesson *consists* in providing assistance in performance.

The reading lesson consisted of two sessions and took place in a community school on a Navajo reservation in northern Arizona. Videotapes of the lesson were collected and made available to us by Cathie Jordan, Roland Tharp, Lynn Vogt, and the teacher, Afton Sells, as part of a joint KEEP/Rough Rock Project. The four children were in the medium-level-ability group of their classroom. They all spoke Navajo as their first language, and the development of bilingualism was one of the goals of the school's curriculum. In this lesson transcript, they can sometimes be seen struggling for growth in English, and the Navajo teacher can be observed assisting them in language development. The primary purpose of the lesson was to teach reading comprehension. At the time of this lesson, the teacher had received 6 weeks of training in responsive, assisting teaching (for a full discussion of this project, see Jordan et al., 1985; Tharp, 1985; Vogt, Jordan, & Tharp, 1987).

We now turn to a detailed examination of the six means of assistance included in our theory of teaching: *modeling, contingency management, feeding back, instructing, questioning,* and *cognitive structuring.* These will be discussed in turn.

Modeling

Modeling is the process of offering behavior for imitation. Imitation of others is a fundamental tendency that begins a great distance below *Homo sapiens* in the phylogenetic scale. Imitation is probably the principal mechanism by which new behaviors are initiated, at least until language maturity is reached. Language development itself is pulled along through imitation. One could make the case that a problem of maturity is to resist imitating others, so strong is the native proclivity.

Not all imitated models are intentionally offered, of course. The socialization of children and other new members into cultures is largely accomplished by their imitation of mature members' culturally organized but unreflective acts. Most traditional and pretechnological cultures teach their offspring largely through modeling, rather than through a verbal emphasis (Scribner & Cole, 1973). These acts of modeling take place during activities created by the family's ecocultural niche – working the fields, caring for domestic animals, collecting and preparing food, caring for children, weaving, and other such tasks. Children take part in these activities through a process of guided participation (Rogoff, 1986), in which opportunities to learn through modeling are seamlessly woven into the fabric of everyday life. What is modeled are the skills of subsistence and family maintenance.

This foundational means of performance assistance – modeling – has been exhaustively studied in this century (Bandura, 1977). Many parameters of the modeling-imitating process are now known: Whether or not imitation of models will occur is affected by the comparative ages and sexes of modeler and imitator, the presence of reinforcement for the behavior, whether the model is live or depicted, relationship factors among the actors, and many other variables, all of which are complexly interactive. We know, too, that imitation itself, as a generalized repertoire, can be strengthened or weakened by reinforcement and punishment (Staats, 1968).

The processes that underlie the modeling-imitation connection are far more complicated than simple mimicry. They involve central processing of the modeled behavior, prior to performance. Modeled activities can be transformed into images and verbal symbols that guide subsequent performances. Indeed, research has shown that active coding of modeled activities into descriptions or labels or vivid imagery increases learning and retention of complex skills. Through watching others, then, a person can form an idea of the components of a complex behavior and can begin to visualize how the pieces could be assembled and sequenced in various other settings. All of this can be achieved through central processing, without having performed the action:

The basic modeling process is the same regardless of whether behavior is conveyed through words, pictures, or live actions. Different forms of modeling, however, are not always equally effective. It is often difficult to convey through words the same amount of information continued in pictorial or live demonstrations. In addition, some forms of modeling may be more powerful than others in commanding attention. Children – or adults, for that matter – rarely have to be compelled to watch television, whereas oral or written reports of the same activities would not hold their attention for long. Furthermore, the symbolic modes rely more heavily upon cognitive prerequisites for their effects. Observers whose conceptual and verbal skills are underdeveloped are likely to benefit more from behavioral demonstrations than from verbal modeling. (Bandura, 1977, p. 40)

Modeling is a powerful means of assisting performance, one that continues its effectiveness into adult years and into the highest reaches of behavioral complexity. In the educational setting, peer models are highly important sources of assisted performance, for children and adult alike. In our own work, modeling by trainers for teachers (Sloat, Tharp, & Gallimore, 1977) has an important place, a means of assisting performance that we can commend to colleges of education for increased emphasis. In Chapter 9, we review studies of modeling as a teacher-training tool.

In our experience, modeling as a means of assisting performance of students is underemployed in public schools. This point has been made forcefully by Joyce and Clift (1984) and other writers cited in Chapters 1 and 9. Often teachers demand that students perform skills without having observed an expert performance of those skills within a relevant task context. Instructors of activities that are more obviously psychomotor – from coaches to musicians (Tharp & Gallimore, 1976a) – understand that modeling is indispensable to assisting performance. Certainly, the demonstration of motor acts is intuitively sound. But verbal-cognitive activity is also composed of acts, and is in fact often imitated.

Modeling has been shown to be a highly effective means of establishing abstract or rule-governed behavior. On the basis of observationally derived rules, people learn, among other things, judgmental orientations, linguistic styles, conceptual schemes, information-processing strategies, cognitive operations, and standards of conduct. Evidence that generalizable rules of thought and conduct can be induced through abstract modeling reveals the broad scope of observational learning. (Bandura, 1977, p. 42)

The use of modeling to assist psychomotor performance is such a well-known technique that we need give no detailed examples here. Teachers of skills from tennis to tractor driving to potting use demonstrations as a primary mode of teaching. Assisting *cognitive* performance through modeling is less well understood, and for that reason an example can be illuminating.

In the lesson that follows, the teacher models a cognitive strategy that is central in teaching reading comprehension: searching the text's words and pictures for evidence that bears on a particular question. In the early stages of reading comprehension, children do not clearly differentiate among sources of their beliefs. They construct understandings of a story from their assumptions and personal experiences, as well as from the content of the text itself. What they say in response to a text is often a gloss of these sources, the independent contributions of which they cannot identify. In the following sequence, the teacher models exactly the strategy she wants the children to employ when things are not clear: *Refer back to the evidence in the text.* The text for the lesson is a book about John Glenn, astronaut (Education Research Council of America, 1974).

At this point in the story, Glenn has returned from his orbiting and is being honored in Washington. The teacher has been reviewing the section they read the day before. She has been asking about the specific honors Glenn received. She wants the children to recall that Glenn got a medal, but the children think he got a hat.

Teacher: [Distributes the textbooks, then flips through the pages of her own copy] Okay . . . let's see now if you're right.
Jimmie: We passed that. We passed that.
Teacher: [Continues to look for the right page.] You passed this one?
Jimmie: Passed that.
Cindy: Passed that.
Emma: [Leaning across the table to look at the teacher's book] Passed that. We . . .

In this sequence, the teacher *models* the physical act of searching the text for the page that contains the evidence that will determine whether Glenn was awarded a medal or a hat. The children begin to assist her and to engage in the search themselves.

Teacher: Oh, here's the army cap, and it says . . .
Children: [Chorusing] U.S.A.!
Jimmie: President. It says . . .
Teacher: John F. Kennedy, president, U.S.A. Was it given to him? Or . . .
Cindy: John Glenn.
Teacher: . . . was it given to the president?

Now the teacher has begun to model the examination of the evidence. She looks at the picture; then the children look at it with her. They talk about the marking on the hat, and they see that the president is holding it.

Emma: Given to the . . .
Jimmie: President.
Emma: John Glenn.
Cindy: President. Given to the . . .
Jimmie: Given to John Glenn.
Emma: To the president.

Now the teacher will model drawing a conclusion from the evidence. She agrees with Emma that it appears to have been given to the president because he's holding it in the picture.

Teacher: [Examining the picture] It looks like it because he's on the platform with it in here.
Cindy: [Leans over to look at the picture with the teacher] Maybe . . . umm . . . the president gave it to him and now he just holding it like that.

Cindy has learned from the teacher's model. She, too, is examining the book and proposing an explanation that will not contradict the evidence.

She suggests that the president did in fact give the hat to Glenn, but now the president is "just holding it like that." Emma, though, is not persuaded.

Emma: [Points to the picture] Hey, right there. President.
Jimmie: [Touches the picture] Kennedy president.
Teacher: Yeah. [Pointing to the picture] President Kennedy is here. John F. Kennedy.
Emma: President Kennedy with John Glenn.
Teacher: Okay. Now we want to talk about how they let the world know about John Glenn.

This is an example of effective teaching by focusing on a particular cognitive strategy as the goal of instruction and providing a model to assist the children to perform the strategy. She does not side with either Emma or Cindy; both have examined the evidence and proposed solutions that are congruent with the limited evidence available in the picture. They have both, with her modeling assistance, performed the cognitive operation.

Notice, too, that the modeling is not isolated, labeled, and taken out of context. The teacher is, consciously or not, offering a model by doing what adults do when they do not remember what a book said. The children see her merely participating with them in an investigation. This interpersonal process, however, is the basis for the eventual internalization of the strategy of adducing evidence.

Contingency management

Contingency management is the means of assisting performance by which rewards and punishments are arranged to follow on behavior, depending on whether or not the behavior is desired. It is composed of a set of techniques so well known by now that few readers will want another explication. Review can be had on a research level from Bandura (1969), or on the level of practice from Tharp and Wetzel (1969). Briefly, all manner of rewards have been used in contingency management – the social reinforcements of praise and encouragement, material reinforcements of consumables or privileges, tokens and symbolic rewards. Ordinarily, punishments are radically minimized and restricted to the loss of some positive opportunity ("time-out" or removal from a social situation) or to brief, firm reprimands.

Jimmie: [Disappears under the table.]
Teacher: [Taps Jimmie's back with her hand as she says] Jimmie, Jimmie, sit up. Okay? You're disturbing the Center when you do that. Just sit and watch if you aren't going to talk with us.

In effective teaching, contingency management is focused overwhelmingly on positive behavior and positive rewards.

Later in the session, the teacher shows the children flash cards, each containing a new vocabulary word drawn from the John Glenn book. The children's task is to state the antonym of the word. During the first part of this session, when the stimulus word is "work," the children offer a variety of words as antonyms.

Teacher: Work. Yes, What's the opposite of work?
Emma: Lazy.
Teacher: Well that would describe a person who doesn't want to work, but . . . the opposite of work . . .
Emma: Opposite of work.
Teacher: Instead of work, you would probably . . .
Emma: Clean.
Cindy: Play.
Nick: Tickle. Tickle.
Teacher: Maybe play . . .
Nick: Tickle!
Teacher: Play.

The teacher appears to have judged that the suggestions have gone on long enough. It is time that they learn the antonym. She suggests, "Maybe play. . . . " Nick, however, continues to act as though it is appropriate to suggest others. Then the teacher simply announces the correct word. She says it unambiguously: "Play."

Emma: Clean.
Nick: Tickle.
Teacher: No, work would mean the same thing as cleaning, right?
Nick: Job?
Teacher: Opposite. Doing the opposite.
Nick: It's job. [Nick leaves the table]

Now the teacher has lost some control over the process. Not only did Emma suggest a new and incorrect word ("clean"), but Nick continues to insist that "tickle" is the opposite of "work," until another nominee occurs to him. He proposes "job" and walks away from the group. The teacher needs to assist the children in performing the skill of quickly and precisely announcing an antonym. She assists by the means of contingency management.

Teacher: [Returns the "work" card to the deck, and turns over another]
Children: [Chorus] Cool!
Teacher: Okay, what's the opposite of cool?
Cindy: Hot.
Jimmie: Warm.

Teacher: [Looking at Jimmie and smiling] Good job . . . Next one . . . [She turns
     over the next card]
Children: [Reading the card as a chorus] Inside!
Teacher: Opposite!
Children: [Chorus] Outside!

The contingent praise of Jimmie for the correct answer appears not only
to have reinforced Jimmie's appropriate behavior but also to have provided a modeled reinforcement for the entire group, which then returned
to the correct pattern of interaction with the teacher in the task of briskly
naming antonyms.

When correctly used, as praise was used in this example, classrooms
that employ contingency management as a means of assistance are productive and pleasant in emotional tone. The professional teacher will be
aware of these principles of human behavior and use them to foster a
positive atmosphere and productive outcomes.

Like any of the means of assisting performance, contingency management can be misused. A wave of popularity of contingency management
in the preceding decade led to many incompetent applications that in fact
did not manage contingencies at all, but did rouse passionate opposition
to the concept. Some opposition was also in response to the mechanistic,
reductive theory of conditioning by which contingency management was
often and inappropriately justified. This is unfortunate, because contingency management is not operant conditioning. Homme (1966) began
making this point 20 years ago; Tharp and Wetzel (1969) insisted on it,
and by now it is generally understood. The effects of contingencies on
behavior are strong; they do not need to be explained by operant conditioning and indeed are as well explained by philosophical utilitarianism,
cognitive science, game theory, and a host of competing theories.

Although contingency management is a powerful means of assisting
performance, it cannot be used to originate new behaviors. This is an
important point, one that distinguishes contingency management from
other means of assisting performance. New behaviors are not originated
by managing contingencies; developmental advances are originated by
other means of assistance – modeling, instructing, cognitive structuring,
and questioning. In the preceding example, the praise itself did not teach
Jimmie or the others the antonyms. It did, however, restore the cooperative engagement of the children in the task, from which position they
could attend and learn.

The rewards, praises, and encouragements that follow a behavior are
like props or buttresses that strengthen each point of advance through the
ZPD, preventing loss of ground. This bulwarking of gains already made
is a signal contribution to performance assistance. In the absence of but-

tressed and secured steps, movement will be more fitful and unsystematic. With reinforced progress, we can observe the steps of development and learning that are potentially orderly and forward-thrusting. Only when gains are made good by systematic reinforcement are we allowed to observe the processes of movement through the zone. In this way, the development of a reliable system of contingency management is a necessary condition for understanding the true functions of the other means of assistance.

Contingency management, then, is something less than its doctrinaire proponents would have us believe, and it is far more than the dehumanized manipulation its detractors consider it. It is folly either to depend on it exclusively or to disregard it. It is one of the means available to assist performance through the ZPD.

Feeding-back

Feeding-back information on performance is a powerful means of assistance. On the experiential level, it often seems a sufficient means. Mere feedback frequently is enough to guide a student to substantial improvement in performance on the next try. In self-regulation, providing for feedback is the most common and single most effective means of self-assistance – this has been demonstrated for virtually all problematic behaviors in which self-regulation has been studied (Watson & Tharp, 1988). Providing feedback for the self is such an ingrained part of normal life that it goes unnoticed, but one can imagine the collapse of performance on the tennis court, for example, if one were unable to track the flight of a ball after it was struck. This tracking information is used to regulate the next shot; without feedback, no correction – or even maintenance – is possible.

In educational programs, feedback regarding performance is vital to every participant, although the form it takes in current practice often is inconsistent or too remote to be useful. Feeding-back performance information to students can be done in many forms: criterion-referenced test data, achievement test data, instantaneous teacher responses to children's conversation, and grade worksheets, among others. In our own program, to be discussed in the second half of this book, feedback to teachers is provided by coded, live observations of their work, by interaction with consultants, and by videotapes that teachers can examine privately. For program operators, feedback in the form of evaluation data of several types serves to regulate program development.

Feedback is a concept derived from cybernetics, and it must be understood in the context of other concepts in that system. Feedback in any system does not refer to information traveling along an unconnected line. It implies the existence of a closed loop; that is, for information to be considered feedback, it must be fed to a system that has a standard, as well as a mechanism for comparing a performance to the standard. Simply providing performance information is insufficient; there will be no performance assistance unless the information provided is compared to some standard. In the self-regulation literature, therefore, much is made of the necessity for setting standards (as goals and sub-goals) and for setting up specific procedures for regular comparison of feedback information to that standard (Carver & Scheier, 1981; Tharp, Gallimore, & Calkins, 1984; Watson & Tharp, 1985). Specific standards for performance need to be established for students and for teachers, and indeed for educational institutions.

The use of tests, scores, grades, and the like is the common means of feeding-back in education. It is also possible to observe feeding-back in interactive teaching. During responsive teaching, many opinions from children are solicited and accepted. When the discussions have to do with matters of fact, however, it is important that they get feedback about accuracy. The setting of standards for accuracy is an important part of this process.

The following excerpt from the continuing example of the John Glenn lesson illustrates simple feedback provided in responsive teaching. The teacher provides three acts of assistance by feeding-back: First, she affirms that Cindy is pronouncing a word correctly; second, she feeds back the information that Jimmie is answering the wrong question; third, she tells Jimmie that his answer is incorrect. The latter two assist Jimmie to continue searching, to bring his answer into line with the standard, which is to answer accurately in terms of the text information.

Teacher: Okay, go ahead and finish the rest of the story and see what happens.
Children: [Mumbling aloud as they read, only half-silently]
Cindy: Or . . . bit?
Teacher: Yeah, orbit.
Emma & Jimmie: [Turn pages and look at each other]
Jimmie: First! I finished first.
Emma: Me.
Jimmie: I finished first.
Teacher: [Reaching over to hold Jimmie's shoulder] Could you answer a question about that? Who are the two men that went to the moon?
Emma: Ummmmm . . .
Jimmie: John Glenn and . . .
Teacher: To the moon?
Jimmie: Yes.
Teacher: Read again. Who went to the moon?
Emma & Jimmie: [Open their books again and read]

Emma: [Turns her book around and shoves it in front of Teacher; points at a
        word]
Teacher: Astronaut.
Emma: Astronaut. [Points again]
Teacher: [Again providing a correct pronunciation] Armstrong.
Cindy: The first man on the moon was . . .
Jimmie: Armstrong!
Teacher: Aldrin. Aldrin.

The teacher gives unambiguous feedback. The correct answer is "Aldrin."
The children, especially Jimmie, were not meeting the performance standard, which was to answer correctly in terms of the text information.

How are performance standards established? Modeling provides standards; teachers in our demonstration school have often remarked that
simply observing their trainer's high competence has provided a standard
for their own aspirations. Students can observe peers who are rewarded
for prompt completion of work, and thereby have a standard set by example. Standards can be set by simple instructions. Indeed, all the means of
assisting performance can be used to regulate standard-setting. In the
foregoing example, the standards for performance are exemplified by the
teacher instructing the children to repeat the process until accuracy is
achieved. This is an example of the interdependence of the means of
assisting performance, a topic that will become clearer as we consider the
remaining means of assistance.

Instructing

The next three means of assistance are specifically linguistic: instructing, questioning, and cognitive structuring. Among these three, there
are important differences in the assisting acts themselves and in the
responses that they elicit. Instructing calls for specific action. Questioning
calls specifically for a linguistic response. Cognitive structuring does not
call for a specific response; rather, it provides a structure for organizing
elements in relation to one another.

Instructing is surely the most ubiquitous of all the means of assisting
in ordinary life. People are forever telling one another, and particularly
children, to do this or do that. Compliance with these instructions is
somewhat less frequent, because effective instructions must be embedded
in a context of other effective means, notably contingency management,
feeding-back, and cognitive structuring.

In typical educational settings, instructions are used primarily in two
contexts: on matters of deportment and in assigning tasks. Instructing to
assist the performance of the next specific act needed to move through
the ZPD is much more rare. Instruction, like other forms of assistance,

can be expected to occur only when teachers assume responsibility for assisting performance, rather than expecting students to learn on their own.

In the foregoing lesson example, there are two specific instances of instructing. In the first, the teacher sets the assignment:

Teacher: Okay, go ahead and finish the rest of the story and see what happens.

In the second, she instructs the children to re-read in order to find the answer to the question. She could simply have given them the answer, but instead she assists them to perform the strategic acts that are the meta-goals of the day's instruction:

Teacher: Read again. Who went to the moon?

A few moments later, the children are proposing (incorrectly) that a picture in the book is of Glenn's family and friends. They are using their own experience – in their part of the reservation, when many Navajo people are gathered together, it must be family. But that is not what the text says. She instructs them in using the problem-solving strategy: Read the book for the information.

Teacher: [Pointing to the picture in Jimmie's book, and then in Cindy's book, and over to Emma's book] Where does it say that? Read. Read in here.

The children, with some struggle, discover that the picture is of the United States Congress.

If instructions become too authoritarian, they can provoke opposition. A harangue of instructions can get anyone's back up, and the harangue is avoided by even some stern coaches of athletics (Tharp & Gallimore, 1976a). The measured use of instructing, however, does not create opposition. Even more important, a good mix of the three types of verbal assistance – instructing, questioning, and cognitive structuring – produces a lively and cooperative teacher–learner interaction.

It is important that instructing be acquitted of any bad name, because the instructing voice of the teacher becomes the self-instructing voice of the learner in the transition from apprentice to self-regulated performer. The noninstructing teacher may be denying the learner the most valuable residue of the teaching interaction: that heard, regulating voice, a gradually internalized voice, that then becomes the pupil's self-regulating "still, small" instructor.

Questioning

It was Plato who first argued that questioning is the *sine qua non* of teaching, because all ideas are discovered by the dialectical method of questioning and answering. Since those first Socratic seminars, questioning has been the most characteristic means of assistance in formal learning, school and academic learning. Of course, questioning is used in all assisting interactions, but neither in the same bulk nor with the same social dynamic as in the formal instructional setting. School is a place where teachers ask questions. Regrettably, questions in classrooms are most often embedded in the recitation script and are concerned with assessment – tests, seatwork, and homework. Few questions are used in responsive, in-flight discussion.

It is not clear to most teachers that questioning can be a powerful means of assistance. Questions work on a level that lies below the surface. For example, it may be useful to distinguish between the ways that questions assist and the ways that instructions assist. Some linguists have emphasized the similarities between questions and instructions. For example, Ervin-Tripp (1976, 1977) considers both instructions and questions as subclasses of *directives*. For example, we may say to a child, "What flowers did you see yesterday?" Or we may say, "Tell me what flowers you saw yesterday." These are functionally equivalent in assisting the child by requiring recall and categorization. At one level of analysis, the question contains implicit instruction: "(Tell me) or (think of) what flowers you saw." According to Ervin-Tripp, whether or not this regulation is phrased explicitly is a matter of courtesy, or role regulation, not of the process per se.

Let us examine this position by taking a hypothetical example. A sergeant is unlikely to say, "Will you march?" He is much more likely to instruct, "March!" Obedience is both presumed and reinforced in the instruction, whereas to phrase the communication as a question lacks those presumptions of role. Even though marching results from both, it is easy to see that a question on the parade ground is socially and contextually inappropriate.

We agree that a part of the difference between questions and instructions has to do with managing acquiescence. But acquiescence is managed by more than niceties of syntax; reinforcement, modeling, and belief structures are all of more consequence. But matters of courtesy and compliance aside, there are important distinctions between questions and instructions in the interpersonal processes of teaching. If the speaker wants action, but phrases the directive as a question, this is likely to produce "misfires" (Ervin-Tripp, 1976, 1977). "Will you march?" and "March!" are not the same, in that the interrogative form, in linguistic logic, *requests a reply in language*. If the troops are asked "Will you march?" they might shout "Yes!" but stand still. The instructional form, "March!" requests a reply in action. Wertsch (1979) has also given examples of this kind of misfiring.

In linguistic logic, all questions require a linguistic reply; logically and socially, a question is a request to speak. Questions and instructions are not interchangeable. When instructions are translated into questions, there is a risk of changing the social and cognitive interaction, whereas questions can be translated into instructions by the trivial manipulation of adding the implicit "tell me."

Therefore, we can see the distinct and valuable means of assisting performance that questioning provides uniquely. In education, questioning is a central device, because questions call up the use of language and in this way assist thinking.

This is not to say that questioning is the only means of assisting cognitive performances. Instructing can also put cognition through its paces: "Think of all the flowers you saw yesterday. Think of all the flowers listed in the passage you just read. Compare the two lists. Establish a new list of those flowers appearing in both. Commit this list to memory." Notice, however, that in this sequence of instructions, no assistance of the required *subprocesses* of cognition is possible, because they are invisible and inaudible. The question form, calling for audible reply, is superior in that the subprocesses become audible and then subject to other means of assisting performance. During early instruction this is particularly vital. Because the development of linguistic fluency is a central goal in itself, and because it is coterminal with many aspects of verbal intelligence, a failure to assist performances of young children through questioning is regrettable indeed.

Questioning, then, calls for an active linguistic and cognitive response; it provokes creations by the pupil. Socrates either can ask "What is the good?" or can give a lecture on the subject. But if Socrates questions, he gains two great teaching advantages. The first is in the mental and verbal activation of the pupils, which provides them with practice and exercise. Second, during this exercise of the pupils' speech and thought, Socrates will be able to assist and regulate the students' assembling of evidence and their use of logic. If he only lectures, he will never see the images of his pupils' minds, projected on the screen of their language.

Now let us distinguish two kinds of questions: those that *assess* and those that *assist*. Durkin (1978–1979), Hoetker and Ahlbrand (1969), and Duffy and Roehler (1981), among others, have noted the predominance of the assessment type in typical classrooms; assessment questions compose the major interaction of the recitation script. The *assessment question* inquires to discover the level of the pupil's ability to perform without assistance.

All assessment questions are not bad; when they are in the service of tailoring instruction to the ZPD, they are an aspect of competent instruction. In the following excerpt, our astronaut lesson is continued into the next day. The teacher asks a series of assessment questions that allows her to gauge the point at which today's instruction should commence.

Teacher: Emma, what was the last thing we talked about yesterday?
Emma: Uh, the . . . John Glenn.
Teacher: Okay, what about John Glenn?
Emma: There was a parade.
Teacher: Like a parade. What was the parade about?
Emma: John Glenn!
Teacher: Why? Why were they having a parade about him?
Emma: Because he . . . umm . . . he . . . went back down.
Teacher: He went back down from where?
Emma: Uh . . . his parachute.
Teacher: He went down in the parachute from what?
Nick: Astronaut!
Emma: Uhhhh . . . the spaceship.
Teacher: He's an astronaut, right; and he came down from the spaceship.
Cindy: From the capsule!

These assessment questions establish the level of the children's memory of yesterday's lesson. With this information in hand, the teacher is able to make a judgment about the "instructional level" appropriate to the next stage of the lesson; she can now move into their ZPDs.

The skillful teacher may interpolate such inquiries whenever information about the pupils' knowledge or progress is needed to direct the course of assistance. Properly used, even recitation questions play a vital role. This is such a basic tactic for teaching that it appears superfluous to discuss it here, except that many teachers do not distinguish the two types. Unfortunately, this lack of discernment usually results in the teacher assuming that a request for information constitutes *teaching*. It does not. Though necessary to teaching, assessment is not itself a means for directly assisting performance.

The *assistance question,* on the other hand, inquires in order to produce a mental operation that the pupil cannot or will not produce alone. The assistance provided by the question is the prompting of that mental operation. In the following example, the teacher occasionally interpolates assessment questions, but the transcript demonstrates an excellent sustained use of questioning as a means of assistance.

The teacher's immediate purpose is to help the children make a connection between two pieces of text information. The textbook states that "the world waits for news of John Glenn." In a later paragraph, it mentions that news of Glenn's return was broadcast on television. The teacher's larger goal is to assist the children to see that the world's hunger for news of this dramatic event was satisfied in many ways. Her line of questioning follows them through meandering paths, but allows the children to emerge with a high-level, and quite lovely, insight.

Teacher: Okay, and everybody waited [for news]. Emma said even all of *us* waited to hear from him. How did they let the world know? How did they let everybody know . . .
Cindy: Maybe they call . . . ed . . .
Teacher: Maybe they called out. Who would call out?
Emma: The boss.
Nick: [Inaudible]
Emma: The . . . the . . . the . . . principal! [Emma is no doubt thinking of the school's loudspeaker system, which frequently interrupts classes with the principal's loud blasts of "news"]
Teacher: Somebody like the principal?
Emma: Yes!
Teacher: The president.
Cindy: The boss.
Jimmy: Nick!
Teacher: A boss. His boss.
Cindy: The president, he calls in and they call all the people.
Emma: The president . . .
Cindy: It was on the radio.
Emma: The president invite the . . . his . . . [Striking the table as she tries to find the right word]
Teacher: His?
Emma: His family.
Teacher: Family. Okay. They could invite . . . invite people over. They could call. They could phone. What else could they do?
Cindy: They put on the radio.
Teacher: They could put it on the radio. So there's . . .
Emma: Newspaper.
Teacher: Newspaper is another way. What else? [To Jimmie and Nick] Okay, we need [your] help. These two girls are . . .
Emma: Just tell them.
Cindy: Just call them.
Jimmy: Or talk on TV.
Teacher: TV. They could use TV. We named five different things.

To this point, the teacher has used several variations on one basic question: What are the ways that the world was informed about Glenn's return? After a brief digression, she returns to the line of thought, but this time she assists the children to "brainstorm" other ways that news could be spread to the people.

Teacher: What else could you use, Jimmie? How about those things you use in a parade, those things that . . . make things sound louder?
Nick: Flute. [Nick's English vocabulary is very small. "Flute" may be the only name of an instrument he knows.]
Cindy: Flu . . . ute?

Emma: Oh, horns!

Jimmie: Horns!

Teacher: It's the shape of a horn. What do you call those?

Emma: Like Don [the gym teacher] has.

Teacher: Yeah, Don has one of those. He holds it up to his mouth and says something and you can hear it louder.

Jimmie: Speak . . . *ers!*

Teacher: Yeah, it has a speaker in it.

Nick: [Inaudible, in Navajo]

Jimmie: Talk English.

Emma: Talking to them, you could . . .

Cindy: You could have a meeting.

Teacher: Like we have a Chapter House meeting? [The Chapter House is the community center of each Navajo area]

Emma: Uh huh.

Teacher: Then could everybody know?

This question assists the children to realize that the Chapter House kind of meeting could reach only a few people.

Cindy: TV could tell them.

Teacher: Yeah, we mentioned TV, that you could tell everybody if you put something on TV. . . . Who are all these people in the picture [in the textbook]?

Have the children realized the magnitude of the audience? By another question, the teacher assists them further in conceptualizing the problem. She asks them, "Who are all these people?" about a picture representing a multitude, all waiting for news.

Cindy: His family, his friends, his . . .

Teacher: These people?

Jimmie: No!

Emma: The whole world of people.

Teacher: What does it say in the book about one way we didn't mention? This first sentence here.

Children: [Reading aloud] "Many news stories are written about John Glenn."

Emma: This book. [She partially closes her text and taps it]

Teacher: Right. This book. She's right. [The teacher taps Jimmie's book]

Emma: In our book.

Teacher: We can read about him because they've written it down for us. And that's how they let *us* know. Right?

Cindy: Yes.

Jimmie: [Opens his book and points to it] In here. Now *I* know.

Through this series of questions, the teacher assists the children from a point of puzzlement and naiveté to a level of comprehension that is highly sophisticated. Now they understand their own textbook's role in spreading the news of John Glenn's accomplishment, and they recognize themselves as part of the "whole world of people."

Cognitive structuring

Cognitive structuring assists by providing explanatory and belief structures that organize and justify. They function differently than questioning, which provokes creations by the pupil. Socrates either can ask "What is the good?" or can give a lecture on the subject. The advantages of the lecture are obvious; the wise teacher can economically and influentially provide structures of understanding not yet – and perhaps never – available to the pupil.

Cognitive structuring, of all the means of assistance, is the most comprehensive and most intuitively obvious; it has the widest ramifications and is the least likely to decompose. It is, in all likelihood, the most frequently practiced. It is without doubt the most difficult to put into practice. Paradoxically, psychology has studied it the most and understands it the least.

As a preliminary definition, "cognitive structuring" refers to the provision of a structure for thinking and acting. It may be a structure for beliefs, for mental operations, or for understanding. It is an organizing structure that evaluates, groups, and sequences perception, memory, and action. In science, it is theory; in religion, it is theology; in games, it is rules. In everyday life, cognitive structures are like all of these, more or less formalized, more or less conscious.

All action and mentation are organized into sets, within which evaluation, grouping, and sequencing occur, and by which we regulate our own lives and the lives of others. These sets may be small or large, closed or fuzzy. The set for "cosmology" will include, for some, a vague knowledge of the sun, moon, and planets by which the moon's shape and the lengths of the days are understood and predictable; for some others, that set will include knowledge of the farthest galaxies and the complexities of theoretical physics. The set for "cooking" may include, for some, complex interactions involving pot sizes, foodstuffs, and heat; for others, that set may include only egg boiling and bacon frying. These sets are ordinarily autonomous, though they are subject to interrelationships, by means of combining, or through creating sets of sets, structures of structures.

Some cognitive structures are universal, in the sense that Piaget meant. The redundancy of the physical world, which consists of permanent, three-dimensional objects that have weight and substance, that respond to gravity, and that stand in topological relationships to one another, represents environmental factors that provide experiences necessary for building an adequate and probably universal conception of the world. Thus, one can acquire the principle of conservation regardless of medium (Feldman, 1980); if one lives in a village of potters, then clay can serve as a medium (Price-Williams, Gordon, & Ramirez, 1969). There are also pan-human factors that contribute to the development of universal cognitive structures, including internal states, as well as conditions created by social interaction – confrontation with different social perspectives, regularities in bodily processes, sleep patterns, and physical, perceptual, and neurological consistencies in responses.

Other cognitive structures are neither universal nor spontaneously achieved by a majority of a culture's population. They are not necessarily mastered at the highest or even the initial levels by all children in all cultures; they are achievements that depend on ecocultural opportunities – "the cognitive consequences of cultural opportunity" (Nerlove & Snipper, 1981).

In most cultures, literacy, numeracy, and understanding of kinship and religion are achieved at some level by virtually all individuals. The domains of opportunity will vary from culture to culture, so that the cognitive structures achieved by the majority will differ accordingly. Only a minority of highly trained individuals in most cultures absorb the structures of medicine, aviation, chess, or carpentry. However, what constitutes a specialized discipline will vary from culture to culture depending on what is required for everyday subsistence and adaptation.

Discipline-based structures cut across cultural domains, so that science-based medical knowledge in the United States is more similar to that in India than are religious domains in the two societies. Thus, the discovery of the structure of deoxyribonucleic acid (DNA) has the potential to change a large part of the world forever. In less dramatic ways, each time a child acquires a new cognitive structure – by whatever means of assistance – that child's world is also changed forever.

Cognitive structures – at whatever level of attainment – may be conscious or not. That is, some structures can be verbalized by some individuals, but not necessarily. They may be automatic, in the sense of operating without attention. This automaticity may occur as part of what Vygotsky (1978) called "fossilization" – their passing out of the ZPD, so that they are fixed. Neither self-directed speech nor the speech of others is needed for these fixed structures, and indeed they would be disrupted by assistance, and perhaps even destroyed. These structures, though we describe them as cognitive, are not entirely so; they may be partly motoric, and different structures certainly produce different actions.

From the point of view of the teacher, various kinds of cognitive structures can be provided. They can be grand: worldviews, philosophies, ethical systems, scientific theories, and religious theologies. Or they can be as modest as giving a name to a thing.

The words attached to things, according to Vygotsky (1987), are the basic units of analysis for all psychological functioning, because "word meaning" is both the basic unit of thought and the basic unit of social interaction. "Word," here, means discourse, not only "vocabulary item," and we can easily see how much performance can be assisted by providing the social meaning, the tool for thinking that these verbal cognitive structures provide.

The domain of cognitive structuring has been mapped in various ways (Duffy, Roehler, Meloth, & Vavrus, 1986; Paris, Lipson, & Wixson, 1983). We commend these sources to readers for detailed treatments, explanations, and examples of ways in which students are assisted by providing cognitive structure.

Most writers make a distinction between cognitive structures of two types: (I) structures of explanation and (II) structures for cognitive activity. Type I may be an explanation that molecular activity increases with temperature, as gases expand in a third-grade experiment. Or the teacher may say that the story for today is about how a girl feels toward her cat. In such cases, structure serves to organize perception in new ways: Ice and steam fall into the new science structure. In reading the new story, readers can group their own feelings of affection with the theme of the girl's protecting her pet. Evaluation, grouping, and sequencing of both old and new information are performances assisted by these newly developed cognitive structures.

Type II, structures for cognitive activity, operate similarly, but the stuff of the structure is mentation. Children may be given structures for memorization, or for recall, or for rules for accumulating evidence, as in the following example: "So, whenever you are reading any place and you come to a word that is new to you and you are not sure what the word is, you first look for clues, then put the clues together with what you already know about the word and you decide on a meaning, and finally you check to see if that meaning fits in with the rest of the sentence" (Duffy et al., 1986, p. 211).

The procedures for cognitive structuring are simple. The teacher assists the pupil to organize the raw stuff of experience – both that which is at hand and that deriving from like instances. The assistance of cognitive structuring often can be achieved merely by making a general statement. Cognitive structures *organize* content and/or functions and (as a corollary) *refer to like instances*. These are the features that distinguish cognitive structuring from simple instructing.

Cognitive structuring can be distinguished from the other forms of linguistic assistance by the following hypothetical examples, which all deal with the same issue:

> *Instructing:* "Think about the main theme of this story."
> *Questioning:* "What do you think the main idea of this story is or will be?"

Cognitive structuring (Type I): "All of this story's parts are connected to its main idea: the girl's feelings toward her cat. The word we use for her feelings is *loving.* She is loving toward her cat."
Cognitive structuring (Type II): "Stories have main ideas. The pieces of any story are related to this main idea."

The instruction calls for a specific action, the question calls for a verbal response, but the cognitive structures provide an organization without calling for a particular action. These three means are not on a scale of abstraction: Some instructions can call for much more complex operations than some lower-level cognitive structures can provide. Neither do they relate to any developmental scale: Each of the means of assistance has its place, for advanced and beginning pupils, and indeed for adults in the ZPD. In assisting actual performances, the good teacher alternates the means; their combination is part of the activity of teaching.

As yet there is little evidence on whether Type I or Type II structures are superior, or when, or why (Tharp & Gallimore, 1985). We do not yet know under what circumstances cognitive structuring is to be preferred over questioning, or vice versa. The *potential* power of cognitive structuring is not in doubt. As in instances of religious conversion, the acceptance of a cognitive structure can have the most revolutionary effects on human behavior and experience. How and why this occurs remain largely mysteries, although our understanding of these remarkable processes is increasing (Brown, Bransford, Ferrara, & Campione, 1983; Brown & Campione, 1986).

On the other hand, there is reason for optimism: Of all the means of assisting performance, cognitive structuring is currently under the most intense study. This is occurring in various fields, disciplines, and theories. As a background for considering cognitive structuring within a theory of assisted performance, the cross-cultural study of healing practices is vital. Frank (1961), for example, establishes as a universal requirement for "psychotherapy" the provision of an accepted explanatory system. The similar work of Ellis (1986) has recently been revivified by cognitive neo-behaviorism. Our Type II cognitive structuring – generally referred to as "metacognition" – can be followed in the work of Brown (1978), Flavell and Wellman (1977), and Tharp and Gallimore (1985). Cognitive-strategy training in the therapeutic context has been reviewed by Meichenbaum and Asarnow (1979), and in the educational setting by Keogh and Hall (1984).

We know that cognitive structuring is an intimate part of the development of cognition. Recall the discussion of "guided reinvention"; Fischer & Bullock (1984) point out that "to understand is to reconstruct." As we have repeatedly emphasized, normal cognitive development is a collaborative process involving the child and the environment. *But the learner will invent cognitive structures during learning,* continually providing the self with explanations and schema. It is often necessary for the teacher to assist by providing these structures, both to accelerate learning and to correct any idiosyncratic or unreliable structures.

In assisting performance, cognitive structuring need not be simply "announced" by the teacher. The interpersonal process of guided reinvention is one in which the teacher assists the children to develop cognitive structures through mutual participation.

In the following example, the teacher assists the children to develop the concept of "hero." In the first section, the teacher assists primarily by means of questioning and feedback. When she judges that they have reached the point in the ZPD where it is appropriate, she announces the definition of "hero" that the group has developed. The discussion begins with John Glenn, but the cognitive structure of "hero" develops through, and comes to include, some surprising companions.

Teacher: Okay. What about "the American hero"? Who's the hero?
Jimmie: John Glenn.
Teacher: Why? What do they think?
Jimmie: Cause he went to the . . . moon.
Teacher: He went to the moon?
Jimmie: Yeah.
Teacher: Does it say he went to the moon in the story?
Jimmie: No.
Teacher: What did he do that made him a hero?
Emma: Wow.
Jimmie: Went around the earth three times.
Teacher: Okay. You're right, he was the first person to go into space and travel around the earth three times.
Teacher: Who lets him know that he's a hero now?
Emma: Ummm, the men and the women.
Jimmie: President Kennedy.
Teacher: The men and women, the president . . .
Emma & Cindy: Kennedy!
Emma: Everyone calls him an American hero.
Teacher: Everyone. Everyone would mean who?
Emma: Everybody, us too.
Teacher: Do you think he's a hero?
Jimmie: Yes!
Emma: No!
Jimmie: Cause the astronaut . . . [Inaudible]
Emma: He goes up, up. . . . He's a hero.
Nick: [Inaudible]
Teacher: Jimmie, what would you call a hero? Who would you call a hero?
Cindy: John Glenn.
Jimmie: Superman!

Teacher: What did he have to do to make him a hero?
Nick: Apache Chief.
Teacher: Okay, what would Apache Chief have to do to be a hero?
Jimmie: He-Man!
Emma: John Glenn! John Glenn!
Teacher: Or He-Man.

The teacher feels that these nominees are useful: Superman, He-Man, Apache Chief, and John Glenn are all acceptable as members of the class "heroes," and these like instances will help the group to work out the concept. Unfortunately, the children begin to drift off on a tangent of associations, from He-Man to cartoons in general.

Emma: A rocket, blah blah.
Jimmie: Cartoons! Cartoons!
Emma: Bugs Bunny! [Emma and Nick laugh]

The teacher ignores Bugs Bunny and assists the children back on the track by a pointed question.

Teacher: What could Superman do that would make him a hero?
Jimmie: Bullets! [In Navajo: He dodges the bullets!]
Teacher: Oh, he doesn't dodge any bullets.
Nick: Helps people.
Teacher: Who helps people?
Nick: Superman.
Jimmie: He-Man.
Teacher: Superman?
Nick: And He-Man.
Teacher: What about the chief you were talking about?
Nick: [Explains in Navajo that he saw "Apache Chief" on television]
Teacher: What does he do?
Jimmie: [Explains in Navajo by citing an incident]
Nick: He helps people.
Teacher: Yeah.
Nick: [Says softly in Navajo that Superman helps people too]

In the next sentence, the teacher finally uses the specific means of cognitive structuring – she announces the defining characteristics of the concept of hero:

Teacher: I think that it's good because . . . if somebody helps people, then I would
         think he's a hero.
Nick: A hero.

Cognitive structuring, however, invokes not only the case at hand but also like instances. Therefore, the teacher allows the children to drift away from the John Glenn story. This section now concludes with a discussion of a cartoon in which Superman helped people escape from giants. By involving Superman – a character far more familiar to the children than John Glenn – the teacher reinforces the concept of hero and allows the group to "create" the concept for themselves. In the following final exchange, the discussion returns for a moment to a hero who has even more special meaning to these Indian children, and more poignant meaning for their teacher.

Jimmie: Apache Chief!
Teacher: Yes. He used to help people.

The teacher has assisted the children to develop the cognitive structure of hero in several ways: by exploring their opinions; by eliciting common characteristics of the members of the class of heroes; by ignoring and excluding from the class an inappropriate suggestion (Bugs Bunny); by eliciting the defining criterion for hero; and by discussing not only John Glenn but also similar individuals.

Notice particularly that she developed this cognitive structure by many means of assistance, particularly through questioning and contingency managing (through praise and the reinforcement of repetition). She did formally state the defining criterion for the hero. But this example illustrates well that often the structure can be first elicited from the learners themselves. To do so, however, requires assistance. It requires teaching.

Interdependence of the means of assistance

Our purpose here is to develop a theory of teaching. To do so, we have drawn from research and concepts in the theories of learning, of cognition, of linguistics, and of development. Thus, our category system of the means of assistance is subject to the criticism of being an eclectic *pastiche,* which, from the point of view of other theories, it surely is. Our means of assistance are derived from behaviorism and information theory and linguistic analysis and cognitive neobehaviorism; all of these theories are capable of discussing all the means in their own terms. The razing of rival camps by explanatory raids provides much of the motivation and delight of science. For example, feedback effects can be "explained" in terms of reinforcement, and it has been argued that the "effective" component of reinforcement lies only in its feedback function. In the same way, it is possible to describe other means as "nothing but" one's own favorite.

Despite these varying theoretical views, the different means of assistance remain distinguished one from the other by the different dynamic effects that each creates when applied. For a teacher to praise or otherwise reward a child produces a different reverberation than for her to compare his performance to a standard. The acts, for teacher and child, are distinctly different; any explanatory system that reduces them to equivalence is operating on a level that, however intellectually amusing, is unhelpful to teaching.

Our selection of means, then, does not argue that they are independent, nor does it deny their potential intertranslatability. They have been described in their own theoretical terms, in order to carry the best available account of the dynamics of the social interactions to which they refer.

The means of assistance are drawn from Western social science, and they make possible a science of teaching. But the means of assistance are not narrowly prescriptive. They are infinitely variable in their selection and patterning by individual teachers. This is because the responsiveness to the ZPD requires individualization according to the exigencies of the moment and movement through the ZPD. The developmental level of the learner and the complexities of activities all require close accommodation. There is ample room for the personalities and proclivities of individual teachers. There is also an art of teaching. Teaching itself is the art of using the science.

4 The social organization of assisted performance

Concentrating on the role of a single adult in direct interaction with children, as in the preceding two chapters, is useful for fine-grained analysis of the processes of assistance, but it does not fully represent the social realities of human life. It is a rare circumstance when only one person influences a learner. In the community and in schools, all teaching – including the teacher/child dyad – is embedded in complex organizations. This point is fundamental in neo-Vygotskian theory:

> If Vygotsky's insights concerning the role of social interaction in psychological development are to be effectively incorporated . . . the links between dyadic or small group interactions and the broader socio-cultural system must be recognized and explored . . . actions are at one and the same time components of the life of the individual and the social system [and] will be defined and structured in certain respects by the broader social and cultural system. (Minick, 1985, p. 257)

Therefore, we cannot concentrate solely on psychological aspects of adult–child interaction. We must also consider the social context of the interaction (Rogoff, 1982); for specific examples, see Donaldson (1978).

Taking context seriously means treating the ZPD as more than a psychological phenomenon. For a ZPD to be created, there must be a joint activity that creates a context for teacher and student interaction. Once the zone is open, the "expert" can use any of the means of performance assistance described in Chapter 3. But our analysis cannot end there, because the qualities of the assistance rendered in the zone are determined by the nature of the joint activity.

This is a generalization of the most profound significance for schooling and teaching. A theory of education not only must deal with the psychological aspects of teacher–student interaction but also must simultaneously address the social context of that interaction. Without analyses of the context of teaching and schooling, we can never hope to achieve that ideal of teaching we seek: assisted performance in children's ZPDs. That

71

ideal can be achieved only when the context provides for joint activity by expert and apprentice, parent and child, teacher and student.

This chapter presents two concepts for understanding the social context of assisted performance. Use of these two concepts will allow educators to design effective social settings and effective schools. The two concepts are *activity settings* and *triadic analysis*. Following the pattern of previous chapters, we shall first examine the concept of activity settings in the teaching and learning activities of early socialization and community life. We shall then be in a position to understand what schools must do in order to be as effective as the larger society. The chapter will conclude with a discussion of *assisting triads* and the principles that can guide the creation of successful school activity settings.

Activity settings

The concept of activity settings: introduction

Contexts in which collaborative interaction, intersubjectivity, and assisted performance occur – in which *teaching* occurs – are referred to as *activity settings*. What are these activity settings, and how can they be considered, evaluated, and designed? Although activity settings can be subject to abstract theoretical analysis, such as that to come in this chapter and that of Wertsch (1985b, pp. 210–216), they are as homely and familiar as old shoes and the front porch. They are the social furniture of our family, community, and work lives. They are the events and people of our work and relations to one another. They are the who, what, when, where, and why, the small recurrent dramas of everyday life, played on the stages of home, school, community, and workplace – the father and daughter collaborating to find lost shoes, the preschooler recounting a folk tale with sensitive questioning by an adult, the child who plays a board game through the help of a patient brother, the Navajo girl who assists her mother's weaving and who eventually becomes a master weaver herself. We can plot our lives as traces of the things we do, in dissolving and recombining social groups and energy knots. Those are activity settings.

The name "activity settings" incorporates cognitive and motoric action itself (activity), as well as the external, environmental, and objective features of the occasion (settings). For example, learning centers in classrooms that allow peer assistance can be activity settings that have specific purposes, occasions, and participants. Independent self-study groups for teachers are activity settings, with goals, values, collaborative activity, and a spatial locus. As the following discussion will attempt to show, it is crucial that we understand activity settings as including cognitive components as well as external, social components. We must understand especially the meaning attached to the activity by participants, which in turn determines important matters such as strategies applied or the manner in which participants interact. Rogoff (1982) described this as the "integration of cognition and context."

Activity settings arise from the pressures and resources of the larger social system of which the participants are a part – the habitats or ecocultural niches of human groups (Weisner, 1984; Weisner & Gallimore, 1985). This means that collaborative interaction, intersubjectivity, and assisted performance do not occur at random. In fact, their occurrences are determined absolutely by restriction to the context of *goal-directed action*. Goal-directed action does not occur at random; it occurs only in the times and places that specify settings in a given ecocultural niche. Many goals show the invisible hand of ecocultural factors (Weisner, 1984), though these factors may not be understood or acknowledged by participants.

Activity settings do not include persons at random; the personnel who can achieve the goal of an action are determined by the goal and the setting. Assisted performance is not guaranteed by random assemblies of persons in given places; it is only the goal-driven activity that makes the maximum contribution of each individual desirable to the entire group, thus motivating assistance by the less competent for the good of all. The operations performed in the service of the goal are not random; they are distributed according to the personnel mix and are given shape by the goal itself.

Activities in given settings do not occur at random with respect to time; an activity can be performed only when the time is congruent with the character of the operations and the nature of the personnel. The meanings of activities, and thus the motivations for them, are to a degree given by the goal, but not entirely; in the emergent intersubjectivity of group performance in its time and place, meaning continues to develop, to emerge, to explain, and to perpetuate.

In short, the activity setting cannot be unpackaged without wrenching out its explanatory roots. "Activity settings" – the name itself simultaneously incorporates cognitive and motoric actions and the external environmental and objective features of the occasion. Maintaining a unit of analysis that incorporates simultaneously all these features – features that social science has always separated – requires some discipline of thought.

The activity setting as a unit of analysis: who, what, when, where, and why

To describe an event, one must specify the who, what, when, where, and why. These famous five W's can assist us here as an outline for considering the interlocked dimensions of activity settings.

The "who" of activity settings. The persons present in activity settings are not there by accident. The personnel are there as a function of the opportunities and constraints of the ecocultural niche in which a given social group lives and to which it adapts (Weisner, 1984; Whiting & Whiting, 1975; Whiting, 1980). These opportunities and constraints can include ways to earn a living, family size and rules regarding co-residence, the division of labor by age or sex or other criteria, participation in religious groups, and participation in the social and political affairs of community life, as well as many others. For instance, where and when parents go to work are well-known examples of ecocultural effects on childcare. In rural settings in Kenya, mothers work in the fields for many days of the year, leaving their children in the family compound; this means that many younger children are cared for and taught by older siblings, slightly older relatives, and aged members of the family who can no longer do the hard work of subsistence agriculture. When these same mothers and children visit Nairobi, where the fathers work in the wage economy to supplement the family income, the daily routine differs drastically from that typical at the rural homesteads. In the city, the mothers are not employed, and the older children, being unemployable, are left on the rural homestead, where their work is needed. Thus, the mothers are alone with the children for many hours each day, often without the older children's help as sibling caretakers (Weisner, 1976, 1979, 1984).

These differences in urban and rural ecocultural niches produce different combinations of family members present, with different scripts and roles to play. These varying activity settings are associated with significant differences in behavior. In the rural setting, more of the burden of childcare falls on siblings, there is more prosocial behavior displayed within sibcare, and the overall mother interaction with children is less. In the urban setting, mothers make more direct requests for children to comply and are much more directive, and the siblings display more aggression (Weisner, 1979). Differences in performances on memory and cognitive tasks are also associated with participation in different activity settings (Weisner, 1976), consistent with the principle that there are "cognitive consequences of cultural opportunity" (Nerlove & Snipper, 1981).

The "what" of activity settings. The "what" of the activity setting involves two dimensions: a description of the things that are done, and a description of how they are done, that is, the operations themselves and the scripts by which the operations are orchestrated.

Operations may include such things as the handling of religious paraphernalia in church, the hammering and sawing at a construction site, or the distribution of textbooks and the reading of passages in a reading lesson. They also include the eventually internalized "mental" operations that appear on the interpersonal plane, as when a father provides a "metacognitive" strategy of questioning that assists the child to retrieve from memory the bits of information needed to locate missing shoes.

Scripts describe the stable patterns of these behaviors in the particular contexts of the activity settings (Abelson, 1981, p. 719). A script can be distinguished from a habit because "a script is a knowledge structure, not just a response program, and thus there is access to it symbolically as well as through direct experience" (Abelson, 1981, p. 722). Many interaction scripts arise in the context of culturally generated activities. They are grounded in the ecocultural niche of each family; it is the niche that makes certain activities more salient and important; it is the activities that influence the choice of scripts. Scripts need not be consciously known to be used routinely in the course of everyday life; in fact, many of the most pervasive scripts in childcare and socialization are so embedded in the culture that they are taken for granted (Weisner, 1984).

In California, for example, middle-class families who own pets are using the activity of caring for the animals to foster empathy and responsibility among children. Some risk to the animal may be involved as the parent assists the child by means of questioning: "What time is it? Why is Spot standing at his bowl and whimpering?" Such assisting questions may prompt the child to responsible action, without the parent ever having to make explicit what is required. Errors, in such contexts, can be tolerated, because a delay will do no lasting harm to a well-fed household pet. In this interaction, as in the puzzle tasks, the literate households put into practice a script that is widely valued, in the society at large, as a means of assisting the development of adaptive skills and behaviors.

Contrast that pet feeding with the interactions in a household in Guatemala, where the feeding of animals is also a daily routine. The *operations* of the tasks, and their cognitive demands, may be virtually identical in Guatemala and southern California: choosing the proper foodstuffs, measuring out correct amounts, distributing the food among the animals to be fed, timing the distribution according to a schedule, and so forth. But in the Guatemalan case, the well-being of the family may be partially dependent on the survival of the animal. In this circumstance, errors can be tolerated much less well. Allowing children to make mistakes so that they will ultimately be able to act independently may not be worth the risk to the health of the animals in question. The consequence of such subsistence-driven activities will be a script in which children are co-participants who gradually assume responsibilities as they display their advancing skills (Nerlove & Snipper, 1981; Weisner, 1984; Weisner & Gallimore, 1977, 1985; Weisner, Gallimore, & Jordan, 1986; Wertsch et al., 1984).

The "when" of activity settings. Activity settings, in ordinary community, family, and work life, are patterned in time: Board meetings are scheduled at particular intervals; tournaments at the chess club occur only on first Saturdays; the float-building committee works only during December; father and son go fishing together at dawn on Sundays. Even though obvious, it is worth attending to the variety of schedules: They may be virtually permanent, as in the Sunday worship services of the community church; or once may suffice, as when the congregation raises a new roof over the sanctuary.

In everyday life, activity settings, because they are driven by productive activity, occur as often and for as long as the product requires. Rehearsals of the play end when the play is on the boards; when the stage is struck, the cast stops meeting, even though they may all regret the loss of the society. To continue meeting in the absence of the work would produce an empty form, and an activity setting will quickly dribble out when the product that drives it has been completed.

To adumbrate the issues of designing activity settings for schools, two points are vital here: Activity settings cannot exist without time, and authorities who would organize them had better make time for them. The second point is that an activity setting should occur when, and only when, there is a product to drive it. When the product is produced or the goal achieved, the scheduled activity should be ended.

The "where" of activity settings. As it is with "when," so it is with "where." Activity settings must have a place to exist. In ordinary life, that place is where the production can best occur – it is where the tools, the materials, or the uses of the product dictate. A rancher will not socialize his daughter into animal husbandry by discussions held in the living room; she will learn in the pens and stalls, as they work together there.

For more cerebral products, the place is less restricted, perhaps, but it is clearly important. Schools are notable in that their activity settings are perhaps more ill-placed than those of any other major institution. This is often discussed as the "decontextualization" of the schools: Instruction "takes place" far removed from the intended tools, the intended materials, or the intended eventual use of the product. There is much truth in the adage that schools teach no thing, but teach only how to talk about things – a state of affairs in part attributable to the inadequacies of the places where instruction occurs.

Designers of schools' activity settings must take the "where" into account also; not only the classrooms but also the activity settings for the adult members of the school community must be in places appropriate to the tools and products.

The "why" of activity settings. The activity setting is a unit of analysis that consists of individual(s) engaged in goal-directed behavior within a framework of implicit cultural assumptions and expectations, within which actions and operations are carried out (Cole, 1985; Leont'ev, 1981; Wertsch, 1981, 1985b; Wertsch et al., 1984).

Therefore, the "why" of the task can have substantial impact on the scripts that influence how the actors behave. Tasks may seem equivalent at the level of external activity, but we cannot safely conclude generality across settings at the level of "why" (at the level of motive) unless we can be certain of the meaning an individual attributes to a task. How people perform, then, provides a potentially deceptive basis on which to make inferences about cognitive activity, or any other process. To be the same, tasks must be equivalent not only at the level of "what" but also at the level of "why." Thus, to the other four descriptive dimensions of an activity setting we must add the "why."

Why an activity setting exists and functions may be described in terms of two facets: the *motivation* and the *meaning*.

The goal of an activity setting usually provides its motivational impetus. If the goal is canoe building, the canoe itself – which may be important for the subsistence of the family and group – carries within it the motivation for the activity, at least for the more powerful authorities who sanction it and who make available the needed resources. This is not necessarily the motive for participation by every member of the activity setting: Some may join in because their friends are participating; less powerful members, such as children, may participate only under threat by their parents, or because they like the society of the uncles who are carving.

A parallel classroom example might be a reading-lesson activity setting: Its goal is to teach reading, and that energizes the teachers for the performance of the operations. However, for many beginning readers – and for many unenthusiastic students – this goal, as articulated by the powerful members who control the activity, provides no motive. Therefore, the more powerful members must provide supplementary motivation for students until they incorporate the values and meanings (and thus the motives) of the controlling members. (That is why assistance by contingency management is useful in working through the ZPD until the motives of the larger institution have been internalized by the child.)

We shall return to this point in later chapters, because it is of fundamental importance in the design of effective settings. For our purposes here, we note that motivations are not always identical for all members of the activity setting, but activity settings tend to create motivational homogeneity for members through the processes of emergent intermental subjectivity.

The second facet of the "why" of an activity setting is its meaning. The understanding, explanation, and meaning of the activity provide part of the reason that activity settings exist and continue. Eventually, to fully participate in scholarly activities, the child must come to share many of the motives of the social system of the school and the larger sociocultural system that organizes the school (Leont'ev, 1981; Minick, 1985). Cole (1985) suggested that this portion of activity theory overlaps with what cognitive psychologists mean by schemata. That is, the concept of activity includes the task, but it also includes the organizational structures in the minds of individuals and the cultural meaning of the interaction. However, the organizations of motives within an individual and within the society need not be isomorphic. Portions of an activity may be more motivating for one individual than for another, and neither may rank the motive as highly as do other members of the society or even other members of the same activity setting (Leont'ev, 1981; Minick, 1985).

Researchers interested in cross-cultural or cross-group comparisons often use a task that the investigator mistakenly thinks is perceived the same by persons from different groups. For instance, suppose that in two different cultures, child and mother are asked to solve a simple jigsaw puzzle. In terms of the "what," the activity settings are similar: The child is to solve the puzzle by placing the pieces correctly, and the mother is requested to help in any way she chooses. The puzzle is the same for all groups tested; the instructions are the same. Very often the attention of the researcher turns exclusively to how mothers and children from different groups interact around this seemingly common task.

Beneath that undifferentiated surface, however, lie most profound differences having to do with why the activity is done. Literate, middle-class mothers are far more likely to interpret the puzzle task as a teaching opportunity; they commonly adopt a strategy in which they allow their children to do as much of the task as possible. They see their role as that of a "teacher" who sits back from the task and uses talk to guide the child through it. In other cultures, mothers behave quite differently (Hess & Shipman, 1965; Jordan, 1977, 1981a, 1985; Wertsch et al., 1984).

For example, Jordan (1977) reported that Hawaiian mothers provide little verbal assistance, in contrast to literate Anglo mothers' heavy reliance on regulatory directives and questions. Although reliance on nonverbal assistance has been interpreted as a deficient form of socialization (Hess & Shipman, 1965), a closer look at the Hawaiian mothers' behavior suggests another view. Hawaiian mothers appear to regard the puzzle task as a joint, cooperative activity in which the goal is to solve the problem as quickly and efficiently as possible; apparently, they do not regard the puzzle as an opportunity to teach strategies that the child may use independently, in subsequent situations, on other similar tasks. They sometimes watch their children in silence, pointing to pieces or spots in the puzzle. Smoothly and seamlessly they shift roles, with the child becoming the silent observer and occasional regulator of the mother's efforts to solve the puzzle.

Thus, the "who," the "when," the "where," and the *operations* portion of the "what" may be the same for Anglo and Hawaiian dyads, but they differ substantially regarding the "why," and this creates major differences in the scripts by which the two groups operate. For Anglos, the motive is to foster independent, self-regulated activity; for the Hawaiians, the motive is to get the job done. As a result of the "why," the "what" of the interaction varies substantially.

Again we must note that the meanings of activities need not be the same for all participants. With an example of a reading lesson, Au and Jordan (1981), following Wallace (1961), have described the meaning of the lesson in the mind of the teacher as substantially different from that of beginning readers, who understand the activity as story-talking. Over time, children will understand events in ways more congruent with those of their teachers, because the tendency of activity settings, and their accompanying semiotically mediated interactions, is to develop a mutual meaning structure, an evolving, developing, and converging common understanding.

In the remainder of this chapter we shall consider schools and analyze them in terms of the components of activity settings.

Activity settings and the schools

Applied to schools, the concept of activity setting immediately identifies some of the reasons why true teaching so seldom occurs in U.S. schools. Assistance in the ZPD requires the assistor to be in close touch with the learner's relationship to the task, in the context of joint productive activity. Opportunities for this knowledge, conditions in which the teacher can be sufficiently aware of the child's actual, in-flight performing, are too seldom available in classrooms organized, equipped, and staffed in the typical American pattern, because there are too many children for each teacher, as well as too little time for interaction, conversation, and joint activity among teacher and children. These same points can be made for each position in the school organization.

There are insufficient opportunities, personnel, time, and commitment for principals to interact with teachers, for superintendents to interact with principals, for district-level experts to interact with grade levels, for program designers to interact with program operators. Activity settings in which assistance can occur must be created and supported at all levels of the school organization. Therefore, if we wish to design a school organization in which assisted performance occurs at all levels, *the task is to create activity settings.*

The task of designing systems for assistance is that of designing activity settings. The criterion for activity settings is that they should allow a maximum of assistance by the members in the performance of the tasks at hand. They must be designed to allow teachers to assist children through the ZPD toward the goal of developing higher-order mental processes. These settings engage children in goal-oriented activities in which the teacher can participate as an assistor and/or co-participant as the need arises. The purpose of these settings is principally to assist the child through the stages from other-regulation to self-regulation and thence to internalization and full development. Other activity settings allow assistance from child to child.

Further up the chain of assistance, other activity settings allow consultants, trainers, principals, or specialists to assist the performance of teachers. Some activity settings can allow occasions for self-assistance, or teacher–teacher assistance. Others can provide for assistance to specialists from program developers.

Schools are activity settings that can be analyzed in terms of the basic components outlined earlier. But the qualities of educational activity settings differ sharply from those in other contexts. For example, Wertsch (1985b, pp. 210ff.) points out that school settings tolerate mistakes more often than do labor settings, because of the teacher "script" that pupils can and do learn from their mistakes; in labor settings, mistakes interfere with productivity.

We can add more drastic differences. In schools, there is too seldom *joint productive activity.* That is, teachers, principals, curriculum specialists, and other authorities merely direct their subordinates to accomplish a task, but do not participate in the productivity. This violates one basic condition for the good functioning of activity settings: their "jointness." Not to participate removes the supervisor from the possibility of assisting performance, of affecting the cognitive structures of the learners, and of being affected by the contributions of the learners in the emerging group intersubjectivity.

In schools' activity settings there is too seldom a product at all. This removes another basic condition needed for good functioning of any human group. As our earlier discussion demonstrated in a number of contexts, the activity of a group, the helpfulness of members to one another, and the motivation to participate in the activity are all indispensable conditions that are, in ordinary life, *driven by the product itself.* In classrooms, even when there *is* a product, it is likely to be numbing worksheets that pour out of duplicating machines to the point of suffocation. Worksheets for the map-interpretation unit can bore an entire class into desuetude, whereas the joint production, by teacher and class, of a map of the schoolyard could energize, drive assisted performance, create cognitive structures with the reliability of real life, and prepare students to acquire a knowledge of geography.

Activity settings for adult members of the school community are themselves neither joint nor driven by valued products. When principals create teacher committees, they are likely to produce some report or bureaucratic requirement that has no value whatsoever to the participants. Indeed, the products of bureaucratically organized school activity settings are products that merely enable other bureaucrats to assess their supervisees. This is organically related to the directing-and-assessing functions of supervision, just as the paucity of classroom products is organically related to the recitation script. If everyone in the school authority line is merely reciting and assessing, it is no wonder that joint productive activity, including supervisor and supervisee, teacher and learner, so seldom occurs. Supervisors who concentrate on their direct supervisees, and concentrate on controlling and assessing them, will find little common ground, create little common activity, and have little influence.

To be sure, most organizations respond in some way to the task of incorporating and orienting new members. Regulation of new members begins immediately, through such systems as orientation and training programs. The acquisition, enhancement, and maintenance of specific individual competencies are the conditions for the survival of the institutions: Mail must be delivered, products manufactured and distributed. Many successful organizations also have settings for enhancement and maintenance of appropriate institutional behaviors: thus workshops, consultants, or retreats. These few and limited settings are organized to "teach" and so are viewed by managers as different in purpose from other systems for ensuring good performance, such as inspections, merit reviews, or performance incentives.

All these systems – from orientation programs to salesmen's incentives – involve means of assistance: modeling, contingencies, feedback, instructions, questions, cognitive structuring. Institutions may apply them self-consciously as teaching devices during "training," but the contingencies and feedback of inspections, the performance reviews and incentive programs, are viewed by management and worker alike as motivational and regulatory. Nevertheless, these interpersonal transactions affect performance, and *pari passu,* create patterns of meanings, values, and cognitive structures, thereby perpetuating the culture of the institution.

However, most institutions accept a very limited responsibility for "teaching" per se. Performances of members may be assessed and differentially rewarded, but the provision of assistance is limited. When performance weakens, and the usual dosage of instructions and incentives does not cure, employees or recruits can be dismissed. Perhaps because such institutions have a limited commitment to teaching, they rarely conceive their relationships to personnel as "teaching through assisting performance."

Schools are, in various ways, both like and unlike such institutions. Schools also accept highly limited responsibility for assisting the performances of their personnel; however, schools have a specific responsibility for teaching. Teaching is the sole formal purpose for the existence of schools, and therefore schools bear a unique relationship to the acts of teaching. Toward some members of their communities – the pupils themselves – public schools have a teaching responsibility as broad as does society itself, and only in extreme situations are pupils permanently dismissed from the institution.

Therefore, schools should be in a position to understand a corollary of our theory of teaching: *A primary operational principle for schools should be to assist the performance of all their members,* from kindergartners to superintendent. Sadly, it is not so.

Organizing schools for teaching: a triadic model of assisted performance

In Chapter 1, we discussed the administrative system common to most organizations, including schools, in which individual A directs and assesses B, who directs and assesses C, and so on. We suggested there that this recitation-like, infantilizing structure prevented the professionaliza-

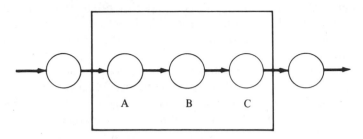

Figure 4.1. The triad in a chain of assistance.

tion of teaching and indeed was organically related to the paucity of teaching interactions in American classrooms. Here we shall detail an alternative organizational structure based on a theory of schooling as assisted performance and the concepts we have already introduced, including activity settings.

The chain of responsibility for assisting

In this kind of organization, the functions are not primarily directing and assessing; in this "new culture of the school" the first responsibility of A is to assist B, the first responsibility of B is to assist C (Figure 4.1). This triad of A–B–C is embedded in a much longer chain of responsibility that may extend to many levels. Typically, the higher authority generates more regulatory lines than the lesser. In a school, for example, the superintendent might generate as many regulatory lines as there are principals, who then regulate grade-level chairs, who regulate classroom teachers, who regulate the pupils.

For our purposes, it is not necessary to treat each possible position and combination of positions in order to understand the basic organization of a teaching school. The crucial elements can be illuminated by considering any three successive positions. Just as the dyad was appropriate for the fine-grained analysis of the assisting process, the triadic analysis is the smallest unit appropriate to a study of the social organization of assistance. A triadic template can be fitted to any three consecutive positions, and this minimal triadic model is sufficient to illuminate the structural issues of the organization for teaching. In particular, we may now ask what it is that A is to assist B to do.

In a school, the final common pathway of all efforts is the performance of the classroom teacher, and the final goal is the development of the students' potential. Presumably, therefore, the ultimate concern of the superintendent is the pupils, but the superintendent is separated from them by many levels; the superintendent's direct interaction is restricted to the principals, or to positions even further separated from the classroom.

The insight provided by the triadic analysis is this: Each position in the organization is restricted in its range of contacts. Most contact is with the next individual in the chain of supervision. In general, then, we can suggest that good work in each position consists in assisting the next position to assist the third, and so forth down the chain for the ultimate benefit of the student. The good work of the superintendent lies in assisting the principal to assist the grade-level chairs; their good work consists in assisting teachers to develop the children by assisting them through their ZPDs.

Now answer the general theoretical question: What is it that A is to assist B to do? A's supervisory responsibility is to B. B's good performance consists in assisting C. Therefore, the first responsibility of A is to assist B to assist C. A is to assist the behavior of B so that B correctly assists C.

This triadic analysis offers a radical option to supervision through bureaucracy. No school supervisor should merely direct and evaluate a supervisee; every supervisor should assist the supervisee to assist. In the triadic school culture, every supervisor's target of concern is two positions away, because each individual in the culture is assisting others.

Others as (nonformal) sources of assistance

The development of any member of an institution is only partially through these formal lines of responsibility. Teachers often have more influence on one another than does their principal. Peers influence one another at every level – from superintendent to pupil. Individuals altogether outside the institution often provide interactions with profound developmental consequences, even for professional skills. The institution is bombarded with other influences that change and teach members at every point in the formal regulatory chain.

This distinction between formal and "other" sources of assistance has to do with differentiating between the exercise of authority and the exercise of teaching. Effective teaching does not require authority. The assistance of performance can sometimes be provided more effectively in its absence. Even authorities can assist performance only through the exercise of modeling, contingency managing, feeding-back, instructing, questioning, and cognitive structuring. Authority can certainly affect other conditions on which learning depends: the mobilization of attention, the

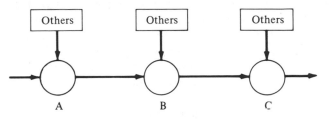

Figure 4.2. The influence of others in the triad.

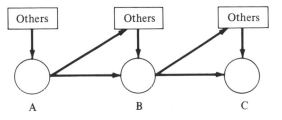

Figure 4.3. Supervisory and informal lines of assistance.

setting of standards, the making available of rewards to use in managing contingencies, and especially the use of authority to create the activity settings in which assistance can really occur. Rather than teaching being dependent on authority, it is more nearly the opposite; indeed, teaching is the process on which authority depends to achieve its aims (Figure 4.2).

One of the major forms of nonsupervisory assistance is that of *peers.* Vygotsky emphasized this issue in stating that a child's ZPD is extended through problem-solving under adult guidance or in collaboration with more capable peers. In the classroom, the formal assistance provided by teacher to child occurs in a context of contemporaneous child-to-child guidance. Ordinarily, the child-to-child line is not planned, supervised, or regulated formally by the school. At the level of teachers, their mutual influence and assistance to one another ordinarily are left unconsidered by the principal. These and other nonformal (and often unrecognized) influences impact on every unit, sometimes in ways congruent with the formal assistance, sometimes in opposition to it.

However, "informal" influences can be structured so as to maximize the coherence of the overall system of assistance provided by the school (Figure 4.3).

The person in position A may arrange opportunities to bring particular others into contact with B, even though A does not, cannot, or may not wish to regulate the specific content of such influence on B. The effective administration of an institution requires many such arrangements. Indeed, A's ultimate impact on C often relies not only on A's good assistance to B but also on A's accurate knowledge of B's social network. That knowledge can allow A to creatively alter the network by establishing activity settings that will make others' influences on B congruent with A's goal for C.

Several examples of such arrangements are discussed in this volume. In Chapters 6 and 8, we discuss a system for arranging student worktables to maximize peer assistance for children so that they will always contain children of varying levels of competence for the task at hand. The rules of the worktables allow for peer helping. The teacher does not regulate the peer assistance, but merely allows it to occur. In terms of the theoretical diagrams, the consultant (A) assists the teacher (B) to arrange a classroom structure for peers (others) that will maximize their opportunity to assist the work of the student (C). One task of the consultant in this chain of assistance is to assist the teacher to maintain this structure for the peers.

In Chapter 9, we discuss in detail a strategy of systematically organizing faculty peers to assist teachers. In the case study of Chapter 10, the consultant (A) creates an activity setting in which the teacher (B) observes a more competent peer and discusses teaching issues with her. The consultant assists the peer to provide relevant modeling and discussions, so that the direct supervisory line of assistance from A to B is congruent with that between the other teacher and B. Both sources of assistance to B are in the service of improving her assistance to the student (C).

It is well to recall here that all of the acts of teaching, by whomever employed, are those six means of assistance already discussed. The task of any institution is to orchestrate the *means* and *sources* of assistance into harmony with its goals. This orchestration is a dynamic process, because the ZPD of each individual (and of each particular skill) is always moving and changing.

As previously discussed, the latter phases of the ZPD are self-assisted, and proper development requires the lessening of interpersonal influence as self-regulation begins. Although the means of assistance remain the same (modeling, instructing, etc.), whether employed by others or by the self, the sources of assistance shift. A full analysis of these sources requires consideration of the self as source.

The self as a source of assistance

Humans as it were preserve the "function of social interaction" even in their own individual behavior; they apply a social means of action to themselves.

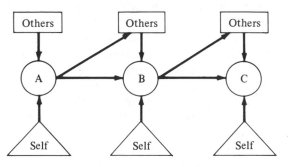

Figure 4.4. The sources of assistance: formal, others, and self.

In this case their individual functioning in essence represents a unique form of internal collaboration with oneself. (Vygotsky, 1960, pp. 450–451, quoted in Wertsch & Stone, 1985, p. 173)

All the means of assistance are used in this self-collaboration. The self as a general source of influence and regulation was discussed in the theory of behavior change of Tharp (1975, 1984) and has been extensively studied in Western psychology since the 1970s (Berk, 1986; Berk & Garvin, 1984; Tharp, Gallimore, & Calkins, 1984; Watson & Tharp, 1988).

Thus, the self is one of the three sources of assistance (formal supervisory, nonformal others, and self). The self as source does not differ from the other sources in regard to means, nor is it different in potential. The self-source *is* different, however, in regard to the time when it is operative. Its use accompanies internalization in the middle ranges of the ZPD.

Of course, self-instruction, self-questioning, self-praise, and self-punishment may be present even during the earlier stages of skill acquisition. Eventually, self-assistance and assistance from the teacher will be brought into harmony, but before teacher and learner have achieved an intersubjectivity of common values and understandings, the learner may be operating on old scripts, attempting residual and possibly competing skills. Thus, particularly in early stages of learning, self-talk and self-regulation may not be congruent with the teacher's goals; they may even be opposed. Whatever is going on in self-assistance must be considered and included in the orchestration of means and goals (Figure 4.4).

In Vygotsky's discussions, "self-speech" is both the manifestation and the mechanism of internalization. His practical work explores the social level as the independent variable, as it were, and the self-assisting level as the consequence or dependent variable. However, we know now that the acts of self-assistance themselves can be taught and learned (Tharp, Gallimore & Calkins, 1984; Watson & Tharp, 1988). The teaching of self-assisting skills has become a good in itself, because the skills can then be used not only "in collaboration with the self," but also in collaboration with the teacher.

In the course of this volume, several examples of the self as source of assistance will be discussed. In Chapters 10 and 11, teachers' developing use of self-assistance will be detailed, with examples of self-modeling, self-reinforcement, self-instructing, and the like (Gallimore, et al., 1986).

Self-assistance occurs in the final stage of the ZPD, and so it signals that full, automatic competence is approaching. Therefore, it is one goal of the teacher that the learner reach the stage at which self-assistance occurs. But this does not mean that the institution ever escapes from the responsibility of having assistance ready. The requirement would be permanent even were new members not brought in, because enhancement and maintenance of competence must be ensured. The automatization of a performance is not a permanent acquisition; de-automatization and recursiveness through the ZPD require that assistance be ready as needed. This is a permanent and preeminent responsibility for teaching institutions.

Restraint in assisting performance

Continually offering assistance is not a requirement for good performance. Performances that are fully developed – automatized – will be disrupted by "assistance" that becomes interference. The supervisor who begins giving instructions to someone performing automatically will only disrupt good performance. In the developmental course, even self-assistance drops out; the "collaborating" self can disrupt smooth execution (Calkins & Tharp, 1984; Tharp, Gallimore, & Calkins, 1984; Watson & Tharp, 1988). Self-directed speech, and even self-conscious attention, will hamper fully developed, automatized execution.

Good teaching involves restraint in collaboration and assistance. Making judgments about when assistance is appropriate, and when restraint is wise, requires careful assessment that can come about only through the processes of intersubjectivity.

The reciprocities of assistance in the interpersonal plane

We do not suggest that influence, assistance, and teaching flow in one direction only – from the supervisor, teacher, or person of more skill to the "learner." This is almost never so. Employees also assist supervisors, pupils teach teachers, teachers assist principals (Figure 4.5). In any interaction, influences are reciprocal, and indeed produce reverberations, so that A's influence on B is itself affected by B's influence on A.

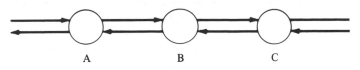

A   B   C

Figure 4.5. Reciprocal assistance.

The contribution of the "learner" to task performance, to problem-solving, and to the continued development of the "teacher" is a well-known possibility (Baumrind, 1971; Bell, 1979; Rogoff, in press). It is discernible even in infancy (Rogoff, Mistry, Radziszewska, & Germond, in press). Certainly young children contribute to the social processes that create their own planes of consciousness:

> The effectiveness of adults in structuring situations for children's learning is matched by children's eagerness and involvement in managing their own learning experiences. Children put themselves in a position to observe what is going on; they involve themselves in the ongoing activity; they influence the activities in which they participate; and they demand some involvement with the adults who serve as their guides for socialization into the culture that they are learning. Together, children and adults choose learning situations and calibrate the child's level of participation so that the child is comfortably challenged. (Rogoff, 1986, p. 38)

If these contributions are present in infancy and early childhood, they are more intensified in the school years and provide a foundational condition for adult activity settings. Obviously, *assistance* most often flows from the more competent to the less competent participant – from teacher to learner, from trainer to trainee – but *influence,* a more general concept, is inevitably reciprocal and shared. The interpersonal plane, created in joint activity, is a joint product.

A central feature of the interpersonal plane is its intersubjectivity. In joint activity, the signs and symbols developed through language, the development of common understanding of the purposes and meanings of the activity, the joint engagement in cognitive strategies and problem-solving, are all aspects of interaction that influence each participant. Although the more able member of a joint activity exercises more influence, through providing more assistance, it is one task of the teacher to understand the subjectivity of the learner and (for the task at hand) to share it so as to influence it. As new members coalesce in a new activity, a new intersubjectivity is created, and for all members it is internalized into a new cognitive development.

For example, trainers of teachers know that children influence teachers, sometimes in ways counter to a given goal of teacher training. A field supervisor may change the composition of pupils in the class of a teacher in training so that the pupils themselves can assist the teacher to perform the target skill.

For most activity settings in the natural environment, the participants are not divided sharply into expert and trainees. Rather, in any group, the various members will have different competencies, and one will offer the assistance of modeling and guidance to others in one's own areas of greatest development. Schools could well be guided by such considerations; for example, mobilizing this potential through self-assisting groups of teachers is a powerful way of organizing assisted performance.

If we emphasize the actions and responsibilities of A, supervising B for the benefit of C, it is not because we are deluded about the nature of the supervisory chain of command. Very often, A is not as expert as is B in the matter at hand. But one need not be more expert in order to assist. In designing activity settings for assistance, A should use supervisory authority to arrange activity settings in which joint productive activity will produce the assistance that will increase B's competence. All those who participate with B (including A, if she is present) will be influenced, will be assisted, will develop a new intersubjectivity, and will advance in the development of capacities to assist.

Authority, in the supervisory line, should not mean only directing and evaluating. Authority will not *ipso facto* produce assistance. Authority, however, often is indispensable in the creation of new activity settings and in providing the time, place, and resources necessary for their operation.

The design of assisting systems

It is a rare institution that maintains a flawless overall orchestration of means and sources of assistance. The most effective systems are dynamic and thus unstable, shifting and thus imperfectly synchronized. The most responsive and flexible systems are those that involve a large number of members, up and down the authority chain, in system design.

Designing and orchestrating systems for teaching are not necessarily reserved for policymakers and authorities. Any person who asks "How can I help B to assist C?" is in the A position of the triadic model and wants to orchestrate the triad's teaching performance.

What are the principles that can guide effective system design? Obviously, a good roster of the sources of assistance is the first requirement; one must not only have knowledge of the formal regulatory line but also understand the informal influences, as well as the content of self-regulation as it affects the competence being developed. Beyond that, the task is to marshal the sources that will assist the performances of B and C and to eliminate the sources that would hinder or obstruct their performances.

Without a full triadic analysis, persons in the position of A (and B) often suppose that they are the sole sources of regulation and that nothing real is happening unless they are the actors. The entire theory of teaching argues against that supposition. An understanding of teaching as assisted performance makes it clear that the source of the assistance is irrelevant to acquisition. Because assisted performance itself is the condition under which learning occurs, the task of the designer is simply to ensure that effective assistance occurs. That one principle will suffice; the quality of teaching systems will then be limited only by inventiveness and the practical limitations of the institution.

Good design and management of assisted performance can be seen as the creation of appropriate activity settings.

Summary

An analysis of the social structure in which teaching occurs reveals these central issues: First, the phenomena of teaching and learning cannot be understood outside the complex social context. Second, a teaching organization has the responsibility to provide an orchestrated assisting environment for all its members. Third, any assistor is ordinarily separated from the ultimate target of the teaching by one or more intermediaries; the triadic model reveals that A's assistance of B has as its purpose B's developing ability to assist C. Fourth, these considerations, combined with the concept of ZPD, emphasize that the ultimate goal of the regulating apparatus is to increase self-regulation by each member. A fully developed skill, one that is automatized, does not guarantee permanent or perfected competence. Enhancement of competences is a higher-order goal, and recursiveness through the ZPD requires assisting performance as the permanent and preeminent responsibility for teaching institutions.

It is here that the triadic model can inform and direct the creation of school organizations that will foster joint productive activity and thus produce a climate of assisted performance. When the first responsibility of A is to assist B to assist C, then the supervisor (A) always has common ground with B, because they are both concerned with B's good assistance to C. A's concentration on B helping C will provide A, in perpetuity, with a realization of joint goals with B, foci for work with B, and products valuable to them both. When a curriculum specialist asks himself "What can I do to assist this teacher to become a better assistor of his students?" there will be no end of answers. This is certain to be one answer: Construct an activity setting by finding a time and a place to work together on a product that we shall both value and through which we can come to a common and advancing understanding.

The principles by which school activity settings can be designed and implemented can be summarized as follows:

1. Whether or not the supervisor is more competent than the supervisees for the task at hand, the ideal is for the supervisor to participate at all times in at least one activity setting with the supervisees.

2. The authority of the supervisor should be exercised primarily to organize activity settings and to make resources of time, place, persons, and tools available to them. Within the activity setting, the authority of the supervisor should be shared with the members of the setting, whose influences should be proportionate and specific to their competences. The authority of the supervisor should be asserted within the activity setting only insofar as it is necessary to see to the continuation of the setting. Authority should not override the emerging intersubjectivity and freedom in problem-solving of the activity's members.

3. Each activity setting should have a product as its goal, a product that will be motivating for the participants, whether or not the ultimate goal of the supervisor is shared by the supervisees.

4. Each activity setting should have as its focus the ability of the supervisor to assist the supervisee; that is, A and B should focus on B's assisting of C. Obviously, the pupils have no supervisees; however, even pupils can be assisted to assist one another in settings of cooperative learning, *and students should be assisted to assist themselves.*

5. Activity settings should be either "permanent" or "temporary" as dictated by the goal and product.

6. Every member of the school community should be engaged in the joint productive activity of activity settings whose purpose is an ever-increasing competence to assist performance.

7. The task of every supervisor, from the board of education to the classroom teacher, is to design activity settings. This principle will create products, assist performance, foster intersubjectivities, promote the cognitive growth of each individual, refocus accountabilities, and turn schools into a culture of learning.

5 Language, literacy, and thought

After the theory of teaching, and after the theory of schooling, we are now prepared to consider the third leg of a theoretical tripod: What shall the schools teach? The question is addressed to a higher level than one of content; the answer should be provided at a level inclusive of content. The answer is that schools should teach students to be literate in the most general sense of the word – capable of reading, writing, speaking, computing, reasoning, and manipulating visual as well as verbal symbols and concepts. Together, the three theoretical legs of teaching, schooling, and general literacy support a theory of education.

For coherent education to exist, all three legs must be supportive. We have already argued that teaching cannot be expected to occur unless schooling itself is organized in ways that support teaching. Likewise, literacy will not be achieved unless teaching is present. Literacy itself, as the basic goal and value of education, requires that schools teach; teaching, as the indispensable process by which literacy is achieved, requires that schools be organized as teaching institutions; schooling, if reorganized to allow teaching, will create a literate citizenry. This concept of the three legs of a tripod emphasizes the interconnectedness of these considerations: If one collapses, all fall down.

Language and meaning

There is a level at which theory can guide education, no matter whether the schools choose to teach differential equations, the poet's "pretty kings of France," or the state constitution of Nebraska. *Concepts* are the goal; meaningful *discourse* is the medium in which society creates minds, and by which minds create society. For literacy, meaningful discourse is both destination and vehicle.

For each of the legs of this theory of education, there is a crucial concept, and in each instance that concept is simultaneously social and psychological, interactional and contextual, intramental and intermental.

93

For the theory of teaching, the ZPD is the cornerstone, and it describes both social interaction and cognitive development. For the theory of schooling, the activity setting is the crucial concept, and it describes both social action and individual mentation. For a theory of knowledge and its expression in discourse, the key concept is "word meaning."

Vygotsky found word meaning to be the basic unit for the analysis of consciousness, because word meaning is both an intramental and intermental phenomenon. Word meaning is an obviously cognitive concept, because it is the stuff of verbal thinking. It is also a sociocultural concept, because word meaning also resides in the community of language users. Through the use of language in activity settings, the dialectic between the intramental and the intermental planes produces constant, evolutionary development in word meaning.

Vygotsky uses "word" (the Russian *slovo*) in two senses: in the simple, lexical form, as symbol for a concept, and in the "biblical" form – the Word, as it is used in Genesis and the Gospel of St. John. In the latter sense, "word" might better be represented today as "discourse." But the translation as "word" has now been honored by decades of use; besides, the simpler use of "word meaning," as in "vocabulary item," should not be overlooked by theoreticians or educators, particulary for young children.

Word meaning, then, as both vocabulary and discourse competences, develops in the context of social use in joint activity. The intersubjectivities of activity settings are created through the use of words, of discourse; these signs and symbols take on new and shared meanings as they are hallowed by use during joint productive activity. The social meanings of words are internalized by individuals through self-directed speech, taken underground, and stripped down to the lightning of thought. When we turn our attention to word meaning and a theory of knowledge development and expression, we are merely attending to another facet of the ZPD and the activity setting. But this facet is a vital one; word meanings are the threads by which society weaves itself into one cloth.

The major task of schools is to promote the development of discourse competences, word meanings, and conceptual structures in a variety of content areas. To examine how this may best be done, we again turn to an examination of how language is taught and learned in the natural environments of home, community, and culture. As in our other two theoretical legs, we shall see that natural methods – in this case of language acquisition – have much to teach the school.

Developing language and concepts in natural settings

Children acquire their first language instruction through interaction with more competent speakers (Bruner, 1983; John-Steiner & Tatter, 1983;

Moerk, 1983; Snow & Ferguson, 1977; Speidel, 1987b; Vygotsky, 1962). Ochs and Schieffelin reviewed the current state of knowledge and concluded the following:

Briefly, these studies indicated not only that adults use well-formed speech with high frequency but that they modify their speech to children in systematic ways as well. These systematic modifications, categorized as a particular speech register called baby-talk register [Ferguson, 1977], include the increased (relative to other registers) use of high pitch, exaggerated and slowed intonation, a baby-talk lexicon [Garnica, 1977; Sachs, 1977; Snow, 1972; 1977b], diminutives, reduplicated words, simple sentences [Newport, 1976], shorter sentences, interrogatives [Corsaro, 1979], vocatives, talk about the "here-and-now," play and politeness routines – peek-a-boo, hi–good-bye, say "thank you" [Andersen, 1977; Gleason & Weintraub, 1978], cooperative expression of propositions, repetition, and expansion of one's own and the child's utterances. (Ochs & Schieffelin, 1984, p. 279)

In these exchanges, which begin early in life, neither children nor caregivers regard their interactions as a language-learning process (Ochs, 1982). However, caregivers do adjust their language closely to that of their children (Bruner, 1983; Cross, 1977; Moerk, 1983). For example,

caregivers *simplify* their speech in addressing young children (e.g., slowing down, exaggerating intonation, simplifying sentence structure and length of utterance). . . . Other studies . . . report that caregivers appear to adjust their speech to a child's cognitive and linguistic capacity [Cross, 1977]. And as children become more competent, caregivers use fewer features of the baby-talk register. (Ochs & Schieffelin, 1984, pp. 279–280; italics in original)

Caregivers act toward children's (and even tiny infants') imperfect efforts as though the children are intending to communicate.

For example, the caregiver attends to what the child is doing, where the child is looking, and the child's behavior to determine the child's communicative intentions (Foster, 1981; Golinkoff, 1983; Keenan & Schieffelin, 1976) . . . caregivers often request clarification by repeating or paraphrasing the child's utterance with a questioning intonation. . . . These studies indicate that caregivers make extensive accommodations to the child, assuming the perspective of the child in the course of engaging him or her in conversational dialogue. Concurrent research on interaction between caregivers and prelinguistic infants supports this conclusion. (Ochs & Schieffelin, 1984, pp. 280–281)

In natural speech communities, adults usually do not teach language intentionally. Instead, they are concerned with understanding the child and tailoring responses to the child's level so that a dialogue can be maintained. From the child's point of view, language occurs when and where there is something to communicate; "teaching" takes place in goal-directed activity. Language learning is not the goal: The child learns language as a means to an end.

Language, in the natural, everyday context is learned partly through topic-centered pragmatic conversation (Bruner, 1983; Dore, 1979; Halliday, 1975; Krashen, 1981). Through interaction, the child's expressive ability is stretched. Dialogue provides meaning and significance to incomplete and truncated utterances of the child. These utterances are structured and expanded by the adult as a basis for sustaining dialogue, with the adult assuming as much responsibility as is necessary to carry on the talk. This process permits the child to be "lured" into language by using language (Bernstein, 1981).

In pragmatic communication, adults tend to correct a child's speech only if there is some purpose, as when the communication clearly fails. For example, if the child asks for "the ball" (wanting the red one) and is handed the blue ball, this nonverbal response can provide feedback to the child and an important "learning trial" (Conant, Budoff, & Hecht, 1983; Conant, Budoff, Hecht, & Morse, 1984). Learning through such natural consequences typically occurs without the child or the adult necessarily being aware that teaching and learning of language are in progress.

However, an emphasis on teaching language as a set of forms and rules does sometimes occur (Schacter, 1979); Schieffelin (1985) reported in detail on the Kaluli, of New Guinea, who believe that young children must be taught to speak, and they do so by modeling long and complex conversational routines. Several methods used by mothers of South Baltimore have recently been described by Miller (1982), who labels as "direct instruction" such interactions as rhyming, singing, and directing the children to say "please" and "thank you," recite the alphabet, name the colors, converse with dolls, and call out the names of objects and persons.

Here is an example of this natural language instruction (Miller, 1982, pp. 105–106) that is about as "direct" as we are likely to find; the exchange is between toddler Amy and her mother.

> [Amy feeds chip to doll]
> [Amy looks at mother]
> [Amy moves toward coffee table and back to doll]
> *Mother:* What are you doin'? Give the baby some? Give the baby some?
> [Amy feeds doll again]
> *Mother:* Tell her say "bite."
> [Amy still feeding doll]
> *Amy:* baby bite.
> *Mother:* Yeah. Say "take a bite."
> [Amy moves about]
> [Amy feeds doll again]
> *Amy:* Mommy.
> *Mother:* What?
> [Amy still feeding doll]
> *Amy:* No bite.

Mother: Say "chew it up." Tell the baby. Say "chew it up."
    [Amy begins to move away]
Amy: Bite.
Mother: Yeah. Say "chew it up."
    [Amy peers into cup]
Amy: Chew up.

Miller emphasizes, however, the way in which doll play functions less as a formal language lesson than as a way of transmitting a social role to one's daughters: the caregiving scenario involving mothers and babies. Miller also emphasizes that such "direct instruction" occurs within the context of verbal interactions, so that the children are also learning how to converse.

If we think of "language" as a system of elements, rules, and linguistic forms with certain properties, young children have a limited awareness of it (Clark, 1978; Hakes, 1982; van Kleeck, 1982). No doubt this is a reason that caregivers attend so little to "language" as a topic of instruction. Indeed, some years must pass in the lives of children before they can explicitly reflect on language. According to Vygotsky (1987), this capacity actually develops through schooling or by learning alternative language systems, as will be discussed later. Because schooling is by no means universal, the ability (or inclination) to reflect on language may not be present in many of the world's adults, who nevertheless successfully pass on language capacities to their children, and have done so for millennia. As in the area of metacognition, so in metalinguistic development: "knowing how" precedes "knowing the rules" (Tharp & Gallimore, 1985). Drawing attention to violations of rules presumably will have little meaning if children are not aware of linguistic forms and functions. So rather than talking about language, a caregiver talks about topics that are the child's focus of attention at the moment. Grammatical errors of young children are ignored (Miller, 1982); instead, the "truth" value of the child's utterance is the focus of the caregiver response. Adults modify their speech according to the child's utterance, by simplifying, repeating, and paraphrasing. In effect, adults guess what the children are trying to say and respond in terms of those guesses; they collaborate with children to help them communicate. In this way, adults use the context and their own contributions to create communicative settings in which children can be successful. As the child's capacity to communicate expands, adults modify accordingly, giving over to children as much responsibility as they can manage to handle.

This natural teaching of language to children is a major example of the principles we elaborated in Chapters 2 and 3 for effective operation in the ZPD. As we describe in Chapter 7, when language development is the goal of interaction, the means of assistance most common are questioning, feeding-back, and modeling. We can see this in operation in the following example, taken from a long and instructive example by Peters (1987). For a period of some weeks, "Dad" has been teaching "Seth," his 2-year-old son, a story about a crocodile and a monkey. (Speech transcriptions from Peters, 1987, pp. 4–5; commentary added.)

Means of assistance: questioning, feedback, modeling

[23.2]
Dad: An' he told the monkey . . . [Questioning by cloze technique] Wha' did he tell her? [Questioning directly]
Seth: #ho' = zowly. [Answers correctly and enthusiastically]
Dad: The whole story. [Models enunciation]
[28.1]
Dad: The #monkey said . . . [Questions by cloze technique]
Seth: Ohhh no! [Produces wrong line]
Dad: The monkey said, "That's okay." [Feeding-back and modeling by providing correct line]
Seth: That's okay! [Produces correct line]

As in schools, natural caregivers *do* teach children the names of things. They establish word meanings in conversation. It is particularly evident in such "compromise" words as "chicken" in the excerpt to follow (Miller, 1982, p. 85):

[Beth and her mother are looking at a book. Beth points to a picture]
Beth: Duck.
Mother: What is that? That's a hen.
Beth: Duck.
Mother: Just call it a chicken. That's too hard for you.
Beth: Chicken.
Mother: Yeah.
[Beth points to another picture]
Beth: That a cat.
Mother: Oh, where?
[Beth still pointing]
Beth: Cat there.
[Mother points to picture of cat]
Mother: No, that's a baby pig. There's the cat.

Mother and child are creating an intersubjectivity through the vehicle of these word meanings and by building a catalog of the names of things. This intersubjectivity, mediated by the signs and symbols of language and common visual experiences, also teaches much more than just "language":

Regardless of the particular goal of an interaction – to assert a claim, to name a picture, to recite a rhyme – the child is actively engaged in mastering the local resources of communication and the mother is actively engaged in lending her assistance. This is one way by which young children become acculturated: they develop the feelings, motivations, and intentions that enable them to speak and act like members of the community. (Miller, 1982, p. 128)

In spite of the ubiquity in natal settings of conversation as the vehicle of language instruction, quite a different pattern of language teaching is used in schools.

The absence of language development in the schools

With the pattern of instruction of the recitation script, learners have few natural language learning opportunities during their school lives. Five-year-old children in Bristol, England, talk significantly less in the classroom than at home, address fewer utterances to adults, are spoken to individually less than at home, engage in shorter sequences of conversation, and speak with less syntactic complexity. The teachers tend to "ignore children, talk over them, and generally dominate the proceedings" (Wells, 1986; Wood, McMahon, & Cranstoun, 1980).

This inferiority of school discourse is characteristic of recitation-script classrooms wherever they are found, and it is particularly handicapping to minority-dialect speakers whose home activity settings do not include discourse in the language of schooling. Hyland (1984) conducted a long-term ethnographic study of eighth-grade social studies classes in a large urban school district in which 90% of the students were Hispanic. After hundreds of hours of observation, he saw almost no opportunities for students to engage in connected discourse with an adult during school hours. The typical social studies period consisted of the teacher talking or the students working silently on teacher assignments. When talking occurred, it was mostly about school and classroom routines, almost never about academic matters. When the teacher did lead class discussions, they were in the form of the ubiquitous recitation script, and poor versions of it at that.

Given opportunities to engage in connected discourse, students from these same classrooms displayed an eagerness to carry on conversations and discussions about current events and text assignments (Schneider, Hyland, & Gallimore, 1985). They also imitated the preceding utterances of the teacher and peers. This clearly suggests that these students – many of whom speak English as a second language – can and will use such opportunities for extended meaningful discourse as opportunities for language development. By "meaningful discourse" we mean conversations focused on history, science, English, and mathematics. The introduction of instructional conversations does not require a massive overhaul in curricula. It does, however, require a massive change in what is defined in American public schools as teaching.

Children of poverty, and many ethnic and cultural minorities who do
not perform well in classrooms, *do* need language-development conversations in the schools. Rather than provide such programs, however,
teachers usually blame families and the culture for failure to provide adequate language development at home, and they castigate such families for
their lack of interactions that would prepare verbal-conceptual thinking.
The irony would be laughable, were it not tragic: The schools themselves
have adopted the interactional patterns so often attributed to disadvantaged homes.

The failure of many disadvantaged children in school is often explained by referring to their unfamiliarity with the middle-class ethos of school. But many schools
operate in a way that is similar to the disadvantaged home in terms of using language and developing thinking skills. . . . Teachers need a new understanding of
the part they can play in children's education. They need insight into the role that
language plays in learning and [into] the way in which children learn to use language through interaction with adults. . . . Teachers need to recognize that many
children will not have experiences through which their thinking might be
extended unless these are provided in school and to recognize the critical importance of the experiences they themselves provide through their own talk with children. (Tough, 1982, pp. 14–15)

Conversational instruction versus direct instruction of language in school programs

Many schools that do offer some language instruction in English use programs for teaching language that rely on a nonconversational style of
instruction quite unlike anything observed in natal settings. These programs of *direct language instruction* focus on the medium of communication, not the messages a speaker wishes to communicate (Dodson,
1984). Such approaches emphasize either (a) learning grammatical rules
and vocabulary lists or (b) pattern drills; the student usually is not free to
express ideas and thoughts, because the lesson usually focuses on learning
features of the language, not on discussion of an interesting topic (Speidel, 1987b). Many linguists and language researchers reject this direct
instruction approach (Krashen, 1981; Terrell, 1982).

This rejection was supported by research conducted by the KEEP
group on our own population of students, whose first language code is a
Hawaiian English, a de-Creolized dialect of English (known popularly as
"pidgin"). In a series of studies, we were able to determine that the
approach of direct language instruction, either in controlled experiments
or under classroom conditions, produced no generalized effects on standard English production (Gallimore & Tharp, 1976, 1981: Speidel, 1987a;
Speidel & Tharp, 1980).

It is entirely possible, however, for schools to conduct language-development activities entirely in a conversational context. A comparison of conversation-focused instruction with direct instruction (or medium-oriented instruction) was undertaken by Speidel (1987a). A group of KEEP kindergartners was instructed with a conversation-interaction analogue developed by the Far West Regional Laboratory (Ward & Kelley, 1971). Both in absolute terms and in comparison with a direct-instruction group (selections from a Peabody program emphasizing pattern drill, repetition, and nursery rhymes), the conversation group made large and significant gains on verbal-expressive subtest skills (Speidel, 1987a). Although neither treatment significantly increased standard English grammatical speech, the conversational approach was clearly superior in fostering a variety of expressive language skills.

The emergence of literacy

Just as language learning begins long before the child utters the first word, literacy development begins long before formal reading instruction (Teale & Sulzby, 1986). Literacy development is part of a continuum that has its roots in the mother–infant conversations so well described by the child-language researchers cited earlier (Bruner, 1983; Moerk, 1983; Ochs & Schieffelin, 1984; Snow & Ferguson, 1977; Vygotsky, 1962). "The notion of reading preceding writing, or vice versa, is a misconception. Listening, speaking, reading and writing abilities (as aspects of language – both oral and written) develop concurrently and interrelatedly, rather than sequentially" (Teale & Sulzby, 1986). The recognition of this concurrency and relatedness has prompted researchers to adopt Clay's concept of emergent literacy (1966).

Literacy emerges in the sense that a child gradually develops as a reader/writer in everyday activity settings. These settings are varied in terms of activities, participants, purposes, and styles of interaction, including the nature and extent of child involvement. Literacy events take place in settings that include domestic chores (the writing and reading of shopping lists, paying bills, making schedules), entertainment (reading TV guides, rules for games), school-related tasks (homework, playing school with siblings), work tasks (carryovers from parents' jobs), religious activities (Sunday-school materials, bible reading), communication (letters, notes, holiday cards), and storybook time. Such literacy events are experienced by children, almost always, as social and collaborative enterprises, with goals embedded in everyday activity settings – only rarely in family contexts is the teaching of reading itself a purpose of everyday literacy events, even after formal schooling commences.

Some of these literacy experiences seem to be most strongly related to early reading and writing development. Mason has summarized them:

At home children have their own alphabet books, they are read to frequently and hear story records, they use the library.... They are encouraged to print their names, write headings on their pictures, and read labels and simple stories ... and they enjoy demonstrating their ability to read to each other, and to adults. (Mason, 1977, p.30)

Not all children are engaged in emergent literacy experiences to the same degree. Variations in literacy opportunities for children have been most often studied in terms of family cultural and socioeconomic status. On the basis of grouped data, low-income and minority families are less likely to read to their children than are middle-class families (Feitelson & Goldstein, 1986; Teale, 1986; Wells, 1985) and indeed are far less likely to create activity settings that engage their young children in other literary events. Yet individual families in all these groups do engage in some literacy-promoting activities (Teale, 1986). Moreover, there is evidence that those working-class families who do engage in storyreading at home have children with higher levels of school achievement (Durkin, 1966; Mason & Allen, 1986; White, 1982).

Being poor does not itself create reading problems; rather, the kinds of literacy activity settings that are generated in the home are affected by the ecocultural niche. Thus, a major source of variation in home literacy events is "the interface between various social institutions (school, workplace, government, or church, for example) and the home ... certain literary activities conducted in the home arise as virtually unavoidable consequences of participating in a literate society" (Teale, 1986, p. 194).

For example, church-generated literacy events are a significant feature in some children's early experience and could well play a role in emergent literacy (Heath, 1983; Teale, 1986; Weisner et al., 1986). Workplace-generated literacy has also been examined, with mixed results. Hoffman (1982) found substantial impact of workplace activity on home literacy activities. Teale (1986), on the other hand, observed few home literacy events associated with workplace activities among low-income whites, blacks, and Hispanics.

This is consistent with Delgado-Gaitan's study (1987) of Mexican families in a California city; she reported frequent observations of blue-collar Spanish-speaking parents who urged their children to read, who discussed teacher reports with their children, who read to their children, who engaged in language-developing conversations over family photo albums, and who assisted their children with homework. However, she observed that those parents "have limited interaction with written text as a result of their limited need for literacy in their work-place and social set-tings. . . . The most frequent literacy activity that takes place in the home centers around the children's school work" (Delgado-Gaitan, 1987, p. 23).

Indeed, some Hispanic families of at-risk children become quite involved in their children's schoolwork. Goldenberg's ethnographic study (1987) indicated that some Hispanic parents took active steps to promote early reading skills that they perceived to be called for by school requirements; a few purchased books and games, and some even insti-tuted regular study periods. Those who did not take more active roles in their children's academic achievements either were unaware that their children's reading achievements were less than satisfactory or were not informed as to what they could do to help their children at home. All were capable of helping their children learn to read to some degree and expressed a willingness to do so.

However, in one significant respect there was a pattern among the fam-ilies Goldenberg observed that foreshadows a crucial discontinuity await-ing low-income Hispanic children as they enter and proceed through school. The parents did not or could not recognize the significance of cer-tain kinds of early literacy behaviors displayed by their children. If a child attempted to read (without knowing how), parents reported that they interpreted this as "pretend" play and considered it merely amusing, not something to be encouraged or nurtured. Early attempts at writing were considered "pure scribbling" (Goldenberg, in press-a). Parents did not recognize the developmental significance of such behavior as being an early precursor of literacy development, an omission of significance, according to Teale (1978).

When asked to select two factors they considered most important for children's early reading achievement, only 2 of 27 kindergarten parents (7%) named "books in the home." Nearly 60% had four or fewer chil-dren's books in the home; another 28% had between 5 and 10 books. Over three-fourths of the children had not been to the library during kin-dergarten (outside of school); only one had been more than twice.

These parents did not undervalue education, nor were they reluctant to actively help their children do well in school. They selected "parents' help and support" most often (59%) as a crucial factor in children's early reading achievement (Goldenberg, in press-a, in press-b). Furthermore, they took such actions as they understood to be helpful; their attendance at parent–teacher conferences ran as high as 97%.

The problem seems to lie more at the level of concrete implementation of literacy experiences and related practices. Here is an apparent and potentially serious discontinuity – namely, that what is done in the home often is not the most effective thing for promoting literacy growth. The absence of literacy-promoting activities in the home, however, does not result from "low-academic-effort syndrome" or from the belief that schooling does not play an instrumental role in later jobs and earnings, as some have argued (Ogbu, 1982; Ogbu & Matute-Bianchi, 1986). Rather, it is the result of parents not knowing that certain activities, materials, and interactions in the home can play important roles in children's literacy development.

How parents respond to children's emerging literacy seems to influence the course of language and literacy development (Snow, 1983). Parents (or other competent individuals) can enhance language and literacy development if they respond to children's early reading and writing attempts in ways that are semantically contingent and assist higher levels of performance. Snow (1983) has hypothesized that experiences with "decontextualized language" might also be critical for school success. Such language is more abstract, less rooted in the immediate context of a situation, and is used to recall previous experiences and relate them to present situations. It is the type of language children must develop if they are to be successful in school. Children who have neither this kind of language nor emergent literacy experiences will require, as we argued earlier, language- and literacy-development conversations as a routine in the classroom activity setting.

The transition of language and literacy in schooling

The development of literacy is inseparable from the development of language. Among native speakers of English, there is a relationship between mastery of standard English grammar and standard English reading achievement (Clay, 1968; Guthrie, 1973; Vogel, 1975). Development of understanding requires "the ability to understand language and through that ability to acquire new knowledge" (Carroll, 1972, p. 1). If children are not familiar with the language that they are asked to read, if they are unfamiliar with the network of word meanings, if they are unfamiliar with the way that words modify and relate to each other, then learning to decode print in that language will be difficult, and an understanding of what has been decoded will be virtually impossible. Language and literacy are Siamese twins with one heart.

However, when language splits from an exclusively verbal stream to form a written branch as well, certain profound changes occur in the relationship between speaking and thinking. Presumably these developmental changes in the relationship may be observed both on a sociohistorical level (Ong, 1982) and on an ontogenetic level. For our purposes, it is pertinent that when children learn to read, there are major alterations in the entire form of thinking and in the relationship between language and thinking. Thus, the teaching of reading is inevitably implicated in the development of thinking, and no sensible program of reading instruction may proceed without a keen consciousness of these developmental and functional relationships.

How does the development of literacy alter verbal thinking? In order to examine this question, it is necessary first to distinguish between "everyday" concepts and "schooled" concepts. Minick translated the Russian *nauchnoe ponyatie* (Vygotsky, 1987) as "scientific concepts" (N. J. Minick, personal communication, 1986). It translates equally well as "scholarly concepts." The kernel of the issue is that these concepts, unlike everyday concepts, are schooled and systematic. The connotations of both "scientific" and "scholarly" are not quite correct for the realities of the phenomena, regardless of the translatability issues. Furthermore, science as it is practiced is not described accurately by Vygotsky's "scientific concepts" (M. Wilson, personal communication, 1986). Thus, the most accurate English word for the concept as we understand it today may be neither "scientific" nor "scholarly," but "schooled." We shall therefore use the term "schooled concepts" as the term to be opposed to "everyday concepts." Though he does not suggest any revision in the term "scientific concepts," Leont'ev (1935/1983) discusses the term in language consistent with our proposed usage. He urges that the social interactions that produce scientific concepts must be understood as arising from the social and historical development of formal education and its related and supporting social institutions.

It is also to be understood that concepts develop through joint activity, but those of the everyday context are closely tied to reality and to the objects and conditions that their names represent. A word that represents an everyday concept is seen as an integral part of the object, an attribute such as color, smell, or size. Words, in the realm of the everyday, can no more be detached from their designata than colors can be detached from the rainbow. Therefore, though the word "rainbow" has the everyday meaning of the sky's color curve, the word cannot be detached and manipulated in the young child's mind separate from the image of the sky phenomenon.

Then comes school, and verbal-conceptual thinking is never again the same. In schooled concepts, words are wrested from their designata and manipulated in the mind independent of their images. Many of these new schooled words are themselves imageless and serve to link and manipulate other words. The child's attention shifts from sign–object relationships to sign–sign relationships (Wertsch, 1985a). A system of words develops, and this system – with its units of detached, decontextualized words, with its rules of use and transformation, with its emphasis on internal relationships – floats free of its sensory moorings and rides over the world, parsing and discussing.

How does this detachment come about? Vygotsky discusses a limited number of conditions and activities that lead to the "decontextualiza-tion" of language. For example, he mentions that learning a second language illustrates to the child that a thing can have more than one name, and *pari passu* that names are arbitrary. Vygotsky appears to argue, how-ever, that the unique route to higher-order verbal thinking is the experi-ence of schooling. Schooling detaches the word from its designatum and attaches it to a generalization. This shift is of profound importance, because only if the word is freed of its sensory impedimenta can it be manipulated voluntarily and with conscious awareness. Once awareness of the decimal system *qua* system is acquired, the thinker is freed to use it in the solution of problems in domains far beyond the one in which it was orginally demonstrated.

Although Vygotsky mentions only a few, Minick argues that there are limitless ways that one can learn this detachment of representation from designata (Minick, 1985). In a late paper, Vygotsky expands his discus-sion of experiential routes by which language is freed from its objects and applied to the activities of early play. When a child adopts a stick as a horse and calls it "horse," the bondage of that word to the specific animal is broken. Thereafter, the word "horse" is available for voluntary attach-ment to other objects that can be "ridden" (Vygotsky, 1978).

Vygotsky discusses the effects of schooling only monolithically and in abstract terms; in no works known to us does he provide any useful treat-ment of instructional practice or in any way attempt a differentiated description of schooling processes. However, it is clear from our own data that reading is the main gate to the castle of schooling. Vygotsky points out that written speech must have more words, be more precise, and be more expanded than verbal speech, because it cannot rely on paralin-guistic elements such as tone of voice, gestures, and supplements from other modalities. This enforces an experience of language as system. This systematicity – self-contained and self-sufficient – is what allows language to be unhooked from the sensory world, to be taken in hand by the thinker, to be used as a tool for thought.

In our own work, it is evident that first-grade children who begin school in relative innocence of written language – children who have not been taught text and its uses in the homes of schooled parents – first experience written text as unconnected to reality. These marks on paper or chalk-board are meaningful – if at all – only in their mysterious internal relationships. Written language appears to have no relationship to speaking, nor to the concepts that are symbolized in speech. Written language, the system of schooled concepts, stands unconnected to speech, the system of everyday concepts. These relationships must be taught, and must be taught by bringing everyday concepts into connection with the system of writing in a context of joint social use. The "system" of writing is far different from the everyday concepts that have been learned through practical activity in activity settings of the home and community.

Vygotsky emphasizes this discongruence. He points out that everyday concepts are learned "upward," from sensory experience to generalization. Schooled concepts, however, are learned "downward," from generalization to palpable example. Everyday concepts are learned primarily through speech; schooled examples are learned primarily through written symbols. In spite of these discongruities, in spite of the reversal of developmental direction, in spite of the different relationship to the sensed world, the course of development of higher mental processes lies in bringing the two together, in allowing a synthesis of the opposites.

Everyday concepts stand between schooled concepts and the experienced world. Schooled concepts, in Jovian detachment, can connect with the world below only through the everyday concepts that have risen through practical activity. For example, it is well enough to understand theoretical economics in its internal relationships, but it can be used as a tool for verbal thought and problem-solving only if concepts like supply and demand are reified through the everydayness of eggs and butter, trucks and taxes. The constant relating of schooled with everyday concepts enriches and saves schooling from aridity, but this relating also profoundly changes the nature of the everyday concepts that are touched, making them ever more systemic, autonomous, and tool-like. Of course, everyday thinking does not disappear. It continues, permanently. But the relationship between the domains of everyday concepts and the system of schooled concepts is much like that between a native language and a learned second language. The experience requires the learner "to attend to aspects of linguistic activity that had earlier been mastered without conscious awareness" (Minick, 1985, p. 365). Their conjunction illuminates both, and frees both.

However, the development of consciousness itself, as a general capacity, is not dependent on schooling, on learning a second language, or on any other specific symbol system. Vygotsky argues that consciousness of the system of symbols that is learned gives rise to consciousness and voluntary use of that system specifically. Learning to write, for example, will be associated with the development of consciousness of only those aspects of speech that are required by the acts of writing. The power of the verbal symbols of schooling arises because their references are both broad and continually expanding.

The tension, the dialectic between everydayness and detached systemic tools of schooled verbal symbols, is what gives rise to consciousness of these symbols and makes possible their use in practical thinking. Therefore, the instructional task of the school is to facilitate that developmental process by teaching the schooled language of reading and writing and facilitating the constant conjunction of these systems with those of everyday concepts. "Effective instruction with young children involves a continuous integration of language and action" (Wood, 1980, p. 290).

Vygotskian theory, as it is represented by the texts now available in English, is incomplete and suffers from errors in emphasis. For example, he appears to believe that higher-order mental functions can develop *only* through schooled systems of language. This is clearly erroneous, because many of the most experienced thinkers of schooled society operate in systems of symbols that are nonverbal (John-Steiner, 1985), not to mention legions of nonschooled cultures whose socialization for their most complex skills is in symbol systems that are primarily visual (Cazden & John, 1971; John-Steiner & Oesterreich, 1975; Jordan et al., 1985).

The basic Vygotskian argument, however, is difficult to contravene – that schooling does free the symbol systems of reading, writing, mathematics, and science for use as tools, thus allowing forms of thinking different from those of the everyday. This conception is also consistent with an emerging consensus in cognitive psychology and education that language development, reading, writing, and thinking are profoundly interconnected, and so must be their instructional programs.

In a neo-Vygotskian instructional approach, it will be necessary to ensure that the interface between emergent schooled concepts and everyday concepts is provided. It is on that interface that the highest order of meaning is achieved, ensuring that tools of verbal thought can be manipulated for the solution of practical problems in the experienced world. Reading and writing prepare the child for receiving schooled concepts, thus preparing the child's mind for building an interconnected system of schooled word meanings and discourse meanings. Reading is both the condition and the process of acquiring meaning.

Therefore, to learn to read is to learn to comprehend, and to teach reading means to teach comprehension.

Teaching reading and comprehension

As a practical matter of instruction, we have adopted a simple definition of "comprehension": *the weaving of new information into existing mental structures*. To comprehend text – whether to read it, to write it, or to listen to it – involves the weaving of new and old information. In many instances, this means the weaving of new, schooled concepts with those of everyday life, a process that Wittrock (1974) described as generative. In Wittrock's conception, comprehension is "a function of the abstract and distinctive, concrete associations which the learner generates between his prior experience, as it is stored in long-term memory, and the stimuli" (1974, p. 89). When we say, "Now I understand," the material in question has become meaningful because it has become woven into our *system* of meanings and understandings.

This metaphor of "weaving" is deeply connected to the basic processes of literacy. Consider the etymology of the word "text." Deriving from the Latin verb *texere* (to weave), "text" has come to mean the woven narrative, a fabric *(textile)* constructed by the relating of many elements. In the instruction of comprehension, the teacher herself is weaving a "text" composed of written and memorial materials. What we study, as researchers and students of the process, is that text created by the teacher–child interchange. That instructional conversation (the text that is continually becoming) – the fabric of book, memory, talk, and imagination that is being woven – that instructional conversation is the medium, the occasion, the instrument for rousing the mind to life.

In all likelihood, the basic capacities for this cognitive weaving process are phylogenetically provided. However, the capacities for comprehending text are developed ontogenetically and, indeed, culturally. Extracting information from text, arraying and preparing it for weaving into existing cognitive systems – these are competences that literate societies transmit, both through families and through schools. This enterprise – the school-based instruction in comprehension of written text – is indeed the main route toward establishing societal systems of discourse meanings that create both the intermental and intramental capacities for verbal thinking (Vygotsky, 1987).

Therefore, even though this cognitive act of weaving is not taught (Wittrock, 1978, p. 15), the task of instruction is a serious task, with two basic features. First, the competence for arraying the material of text and the material of the existing system can be instructed, because there are protocols, heuristics, and metacognitive rules available as tools for preparing the material. It is as though weaving need not be taught, but "carding" must be. Second, reading for meaning can be strengthened through practice – directly, through repetition, and indirectly through the increasing complexity of the system of word meanings that each text and its discussion provides.

At the earliest levels of instruction – for children whose emergent literacy experiences in the home have been limited – it is necessary to build those cognitive competences that are foundational to eventual text comprehension. For the very young child, or for the child without early interactions with schooled parents, it is necessary first to build word meanings on the everyday, verbal level and to gradually introduce the linguistic stream of writing itself.

Thus, comprehension is established by the weaving of new, schooled concepts with the concepts of everyday life. Textual material becomes meaningful because it has gained a new attachment – it is now hooked by *sense* to everyday concepts and hooked by *system* to the whole structure of meaning given by schooling. The homely weaving heuristic used by reading teachers is not only a short-term instructional strategy. Indeed, it is used consistently in the highest reaches of scientific and philosophical thought. Theoretical thought and discussion require a continual freshening by example and a testing against sensory data. This constant connecting of schooled concepts and everyday concepts is the basic process of understanding the world used by mature schooled thinkers.

The weaving of the schooled with the everyday is not only enhancing to the dialectical growth of concepts but also motivating. For example, we know that the discourse of science occurs in a particular register, with its distinct rules and formalities. In the teaching of science, however, these conventions frequently are violated by the interpolation of everyday discourse. These alternations are unmistakable, ordinarily being marked by tone of voice, laughter, asides, and so forth. During these times, the attention of students is at its highest (Cazden, 1987; Lemke, 1982).

"Formal schooling is a place where the child is drawn into unique modes of social interaction and thinking that have their roots in the history of Western science and philosophy" (Minick, 1985, pp. 367–368). From kindergarten to graduate seminars, the small discussion group in which text and personal understandings can be compared, discussed, and related is the prime opportunity for this unique social interaction.

In contemporary schools, this social interaction is rare indeed (Goodlad, 1984; Hoetker & Ahlbrand, 1969; Sarason, 1983). For example, Durkin (1978–1979) observed 18,000 min of reading-comprehension instruction and found that less than 1% dealt with units of meaning larger than the single word. Hiebert (1983) has compared instruction patterns for higher- and lower-ability groups. Children in the lowest reading groups receive more word-list drill, but less reading of connected text; they are asked more simple, factual questions and fewer questions that require inference or synthesis. Opportunities for participation in the unique social interaction we call literate discourse are virtually nonexistent. Such patterns of instruction will only reinforce the problems of poor readers. It is known that poor readers are unlikely to make the inferences required to weave information in a text into a coherent overall mental model.

Poor readers' beliefs about knowledge do not lead them to suppose that consistent interpretations of events are generally possible, or even desirable. For the poor reader, knowledge is a basket of facts (Anderson, 1984).

A group discussion, around a text, is a reflection of the larger society for which children are to be educated, in which pairs and groups of people in the workplace and at play interact around a text, the meaning of which influences their actions. When Minick (1985) argues that society, as the larger social context, influences schools to adopt relevant activity settings, he is arguing the ideal rather than the actual instance. Perhaps the fact that schools have not been reflective of the larger context of society is the reason for society's impatience with the schools. Society depends on the school to prepare students in ways more profound than learning baskets of facts. For the child, the educational design of activity settings produces more than habits of action, more even than cognitive transformation. The school's activity settings bring about a fundamental restructuring in which all are transformed: actions, relationships, and thinking (El'konin, 1972).

Responsive teaching and the instructional conversation

Discourse, in which teacher and students weave together spoken and written language with previous understanding, has appeared in this volume in several guises. It was discussed first as responsive teaching. It appeared as literacy experiences in the activity settings in successful students' homes. It is the way that mothers teach their children language and letters. It is disguised in many activity settings as the chat that accompanies action. We heard it as the natural conversational method of language instruction. In Chapter 10, it will be the medium for teacher training. It can wear the mask of a third-grade reading lesson or a graduate seminar. Its generic name is the *instructional conversation.*

The task of schooling can be seen as one of creating and supporting instructional conversations, among students, teachers, administrators, program developers, and researchers. It is through the instructional conversation that babies learn to speak, children to read, teachers to teach, researchers to discover, and all to become literate.

The concept itself contains a paradox: "Instruction" and "conversation" appear contrary, the one implying authority and planning, the other equality and responsiveness. The task of teaching is to resolve this paradox. To most truly teach, one must converse; to truly converse is to teach.

The second half of this book presents in detail the many levels of instructional conversation that occur in the activity settings of a school where everyone learns.

Part II

Practice

In the first half of this book we have discussed theoretical considerations that can guide the organization of a school designed for teaching. In the second half, we turn to a close examination of the principal activity settings required to realize a fully teaching school organization. The principles we have described have found expression in a school organization known as the Kamehameha Elementary Education Program (KEEP). Schools in the KEEP network will serve as our principal (though not exclusive) examples. The KEEP educational system, for a number of years, exemplified most of the principles suggested in this volume. From our opportunity to participate in this unusual experiment we have learned much, both from mistakes and from their correction.

A major lesson learned is this: Teaching transactions in the classroom are organically related to organizational transactions throughout the school administrative and authority lines. The advantage of our KEEP "case study" is that during the years described here, the entire organization consistently operated on principles of maximizing assisted performance for all members of the institution. Therefore, we can now discuss the processes, advantages, and disadvantages of a particular activity setting, and that activity setting can be seen in its relationships to the activity settings that supported it. This dialectic between the teaching/learning interactions and their organizational context must be appreciated, or else the theoretical principles and operational admonitions of this book will be deceptive. No activity setting, however exemplary, will shine long if alone in a black night. For teaching excellence to survive, it must be supported systemically. It is for that reason that we now present a rapid overview of the entire KEEP educational system, described in terms of its major activity settings, so that the context can be understood before presenting the details of its many elements.

Chapter 6 gives an overview of the KEEP system. Subsequent chapters examine the major activity settings of that system – from classroom to program development.

6   A school organized for teaching: the Kamehameha Elementary Education Program

The Kamehameha Elementary Education Program (KEEP) developed from a 15-year continuous research-and-development program for improving the cognitive and educational development of a group of educationally at-risk ethnic-minority children. At the time of this writing, KEEP consisted of a laboratory-and-demonstration school in Honolulu enrolling about 500 Hawaiian and part-Hawaiian children in kindergarten through the sixth grade, an organization for exporting and supporting the program into the public schools of Hawaii, some 60 classrooms serving about 2,000 public school students of many ethnicities in five public elementary schools on three of Hawaii's islands. In addition, schools on a Navajo reservation in Arizona and schools in Los Angeles were part of the research and program development enterprise, a strategy of inquiry that expanded the experience base to include students and faculties of many other cultures and settings.

KEEP was first a research-and-development program, involving psychologists, anthropologists, linguists, and educators. Interdisciplinary and multimethodological, the program was based firmly on inquiry, but was dedicated simultaneously to producing educational success for large numbers of children according to strict evaluation.

A complex organization was required for these multiple goals: administrators, principals, consultants, site managers, curriculum specialists, trainers, teachers, aides – all the usual school roles and positions, in addition to the researchers who operated as program developers. For greater clarity, the levels of operation will be presented as four positions in the supervisory chain: program developers, consultant/trainers, teachers, and students (Figure 6.1).

The purpose of this chapter is to sketch an overview of the institution, illustrating the interrelationships of the various operational levels, from program design to student performance. For each major activity setting of the program, dyadic and triadic analyses will be presented. The major

115

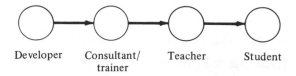

Developer   Consultant/   Teacher   Student
              trainer

Figure 6.1. Developer, consultant/trainer, teacher, student.

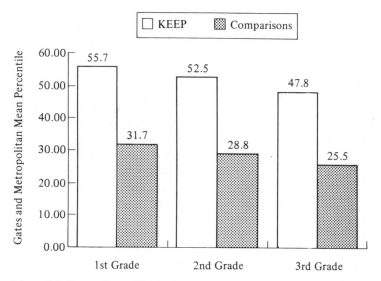

Figure 6.2. Comparison of KEEP-instructed and non-KEEP-instructed classes.

processes of the program will be discussed in detail in following chapters. First, however, we briefly present an evaluation of the effects of the KEEP system on students' reading achievements.

Evaluation of KEEP

In general, it can be said that the effects on school achievement by the at-risk children whom the program served were most felicitous. For over a decade, the largely at-risk minority children enrolled in the Kamehameha Schools KEEP system performed at national-norm levels in reading achievement.

Figure 6.2 compares the scores for children taught in the KEEP reading program and those taught in a standard public schools curriculum. The KEEP-instructed classes all attended the KEEP research-and-demonstration school.

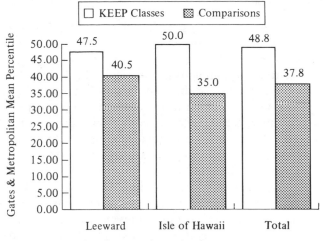

Figure 6.3. Results of export-site evaluations.

The mean percentiles presented in Figures 6.2 and 6.3 are based on a combination of two widely used and standardized measures of reading achievement. Statistical analysis of end-of-year differences between KEEP-instructed and non-KEEP-instructed classes yielded highly significant *p* values (Gallimore, Tharp, Sloat, Klein, & Troy, 1982; Tharp, 1982).

Statistically superior performance by KEEP-instructed first-graders was also obtained in a comparison of *public* school classrooms (Figure 6.3) taught by experienced KEEP teachers. In this instance, KEEP and comparison classes were formed at the beginning of the school year by random assignment of all entering first-graders to either a KEEP-instructed class or a conventional-program class. Statistical analysis of end-of-year differences revealed an overall superior performance by the KEEP-instructed children.

Following this result, KEEP training and support were offered widely to a number of public schools serving underachieving Hawaiian children. Even with problems of implementation integrity and enormous student and teacher transience, a 10-year study of 3,345 public school students taught in KEEP classrooms showed a statistically significant positive relationship between number of years in the KEEP system and academic achievement (Klein, 1988).

Details on sampling, populations, and other technical matters are available in several publications evaluating the KEEP reading program (Calfee et al., 1981; Gallimore et al., 1982; Klein, 1988; Tharp, 1982).

Classroom description

The most visible element of any school program is the classroom itself.
The KEEP classroom is an open area that is functionally divided into
several activity settings, or "centers." The classroom is a group of articulated activity settings, not an activity setting itself. A rotational system
schedules each child into five of these centers each day for about 20 min
each. Over a week's time, each child may attend as many as 12 different
centers – library center, game center, listening-skills center, and so forth.
In describing the classroom, we concentrate first on the interactions
between teacher and student. Then we turn to a discussion of assistance
provided by students to one another.

The focal activity setting for teacher–child interaction is Center One,
the instructional conversation in which the teacher instructs groups of
five or six children of a homogeneous achievement level in reading and
language development. Every child attends Center One every day. After
a brief period of early morning orientation for the whole class, the teacher
works entirely in Center One. Groups of children rotate to her in Center
One every 20 min; all other children are working in the other activity
settings, largely on their own recognizance, on materials that support each
child's instructional objectives.

An account of a brief section of a KEEP classroom day may help to
communicate the flavor of the classroom. The following describes the
typical first half-hour of each day:

As the morning opens, the children, on the floor and in chairs, cluster around the
teacher, who chats quietly with them about things personal or general. They are
soon calm and attentive; the teacher then opens the daily flag and anthem ceremonies. Immediately after, she explains to the whole group any new tasks for the
day. After these ten or so minutes, every child gets their own individual folder,
and refers therein to the personal daily schedule which indicates each learning
center to be attended during the morning's six portions. The children quickly dis-
perse into some of the 10 or 12 "centers" of the room – which are usually tables,
but sometimes consist of floor pillows or audio-cassette cubicles. Two to five children share centers, so not all centers are active at all times. Center One is always
filled. There the reading lesson takes place. The teacher is seated so that she can
easily scan the entire room, but her attention is focused on the semi-circle of five
or six children who have taken their places before her. This first reading group is
ordinarily composed of the lowest achieving students. As the teacher passes out
the text materials for the lesson, the other children at other centers are sorting out
the worksheets or materials they have found there and are getting to work. Children at the nearest centers often keep an ear half-cocked to the lesson at Center
One, but they are never allowed to interrupt or join the discussion. The teacher
is concentrating on the active instruction of that one reading group.

The reading lesson revolves around the discussion of a story. If the day's story
is a new one, the teacher begins with a general discussion of the characters or

themes. Her questions draw out the children's previous experience – through life or text – which they can bring to bear in achieving comprehension of the new material. "This story is about a frog. Has anyone ever seen a frog?" "Yes!" the children may chorus. "Have you ever touched a frog?" "Ick!" or "Yeah!" Some child may volunteer a frog-touching incident. At the third-grade level, this joining of the children's experience to the upcoming text may occur at such abstract levels as forms of government or themes of jealousy or loyalty. Then the teacher, based on or prompted by the discussion, sets a reason-to-read, a general question to bear in mind during the silent reading to come. "Why does Freddie want to have a frog? Read page 1 to page 3 and then stop."

As the children read silently, for perhaps two or three minutes, the teacher scans the room, where there is a high rate of task engagement at the centers and a drone of muted conversation as the children discuss their work, assist each other, or sometimes just gossip. On rare occasions of boisterousness or wandering, the teacher may call out an offender's name. More often, she will respond to infractions by praising a diligent center.

During some silent reading times, the teacher may refer to her master record book, in which a continuous individual record of criterion-referenced testing is displayed. There she can see the current level of each child's accomplishments – in word identification strategies, sight vocabulary, and comprehension. Each objective of instruction is tested at several levels, and so recorded. Thus she can focus teaching of this lesson on those objectives next in order for each child. When the teacher estimates that a child has mastered an objective, an aide immediately administers the corresponding test. (Routine class-wide testing also occurs five times yearly.) The reading groups are homogeneous in achievement levels, but individualization of instruction can and does occur.

Now the children have read to page 3 and the teacher begins to discuss the text. Questions often begin at a recall-of-detail level: "What is the boy's name, Malia? Where is he when the story begins? Who is the man he's working with?" And, of course, the thematic question previously set, "Why does Freddie want a frog?" As the discussion continues, it becomes more vigorous, with much overlapping and volunteered speech. The children supplement one another's remarks; several children contribute before the teacher refocuses with another question. The teacher encourages this pattern but ensures equal time over a week's period by inviting contributions from more reticent children. Teacher questions are preponderantly of a higher order: "Can Freddie really hide that frog? How could he do that? How do you think he feels now? Why is his uncle taking the frog? What do you think he will do now?" The questions repeatedly return to the child's own experience as it can be related to the text material: "Does anyone have an uncle like that? Do you remember last month's science lesson? What will Freddie's frog want to eat? What would you do if you were Freddie?" She then sets another theme-question, the children silently read the next text segment, and the teacher again scans the other centers.

After about 15 minutes of alternating reading and discussion, the books are closed and other aspects of reading skills are taught – phonics, drill in sight vocabulary, and, at the higher grades, instruction in bibliographic skills. The teacher may work at the blackboard or from printed sheets. This part of the lesson is brisk and chorused responses are characteristic (although some touch-up individual work is frequently inserted). The content of this part of the lesson is drawn whenever possible from words or issues in the current story. The teacher may announce that John and Malia are ready to take a criterion-referenced test on, for example, digraphs; and the whole group may applaud the news that Henry passed *two* tests yesterday.

The reading lesson has now lasted about 20 minutes, and the teacher sets off some signal (often a kitchen timer) which cues the whole class to rotate. The first reading group disperses to the centers specified in their folders; ordinarily they all go to Center Two, where they find work directly drawn from that morning's reading instruction. During later rotations, the members scatter, perhaps to the listening center, or art center, or the library center. John and Malia will report to the aide for their tests.

Within three minutes, the children have all relocated. The next group is at Center One with the teacher. In 15 to 25 minutes another rotation will occur. By lunch time, every child will have been face to face with active instruction in comprehension of the selection for that day. (Tharp, 1982, pp. 516–518)

Teacher assistance of student performance

The teacher assists children through the ZPD by co-participating actively with them. In Center One, children do not perform individually for the teacher in one-to-one or large-group patterns; rather, a small group of children engages in an instructional conversation jointly with the adult. Within this group context, each child's contribution is voluntary. There is mutual participation by teacher and children in the task, rather than the children performing while the teacher observes. This mutuality of enterprise is an attitude constantly demonstrated by the teacher. She will even occasionally feign errors; as children correct her, the mutuality of task engagement is reconfirmed. Learning takes place in joint productive activity; that is, children and teacher actually engage, in whole-task form, in the enterprise that is to be learned (e.g., decoding, comprehending, and integrating with previous knowledge the information carried by text), rather than the teacher trying to teach small out-of-context pieces of the task or rules for how to go about it (Jordan, 1981a, 1981b).

Program goals and curriculum

The overall goal of the instructional program is the teaching of general literacy. The active teaching of comprehension is the basic intent of the reading program; instruction in the mechanics of reading is seen as supportive of the basic goal of understanding text. Thus, two-thirds of face-to-face instructional time is allocated to comprehension. The remaining one-third is divided between sight vocabulary and analytic phonics. However, in earlier levels of instruction (kindergarten and beginning of first grade), the proportions are 50%–67% comprehension and 33%–50% sight vocabulary and decoding. For all levels, supportive center work is about 50% comprehension, 25% phonics and sight vocabulary, and 25% other language arts (Hao, 1980).

Active instruction for language development is a second basic goal. This includes increased facility with standard English and general linguistic/cognitive skills. The particular teaching strategies for language development are discussed in detail in Chapter 7.

In all stages, integrated instruction occurs. For example, during discussions of the text, the teacher will offer assistance in language development as well as in cognitive processing. At another level of integration, sight-vocabulary and decoding instruction takes place in the context of meaningful material that is being taught for comprehension. Integration of instruction is synchronized by a curriculum with specific objectives and levels – those of the Kamehameha Reading Objective System (KROS) (Crowell, 1979). There are three "strands" (comprehension, sight vocabulary, decoding), with specific objectives at each level. This integration is present not only in direct instruction but also in work done in the independent center. This "seatwork" is supportive of the same objectives emphasized by the teacher in direct teaching. The supportive materials are designed by the classroom teachers or selected by them from a variety of commercially available sources.

Continuous monitoring and feeding-back of student achievement are provided by criterion-referenced tests, each of which is linked to the objectives specified by the integrated curriculum. These tests are administered no fewer than five times per year. A continuous individual record for each child is maintained. These data are displayed and fed back to the teacher, and by the teacher to each child (Au & Hao, 1980; Crowell, 1976). The passing of objectives is celebrated by both children and teacher, in ways ranging from "high-fives" to applause. Careful assessment is necessary in order to delineate two points relative to the ZPD: the "developmental" level of individual competence and the "instructional" level of assisted competence. This assessment information allows the next program feature.

Individualized, diagnostic/prescriptive instruction is characteristic. Although the prescriptions generally are for the homogeneous groups, daily individualization of prescription is possible in the center work. The more able teachers often can attend to individual needs even in the vigorous direct group instructions. This assessment provides an ongoing estimate of the position in the ZPD for each child's objectives and allows the teacher to set the points at which further assistance is needed.

The activity settings

Assistance of child learning is accomplished by creating activity settings in the classroom that maximize opportunities for co-participation and instructional conversation with the teacher, and frequently with peers.

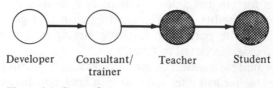

Figure 6.4. Center One.

Center One

The focal point of teacher–child interaction is the event called Center One. The specific activities vary from one group to another and from day to day, but in each group the children and teacher are engaged in a lively instructional conversation. The Center One lesson teaches not only reading but also listening, speaking, and thinking: The basic goal of instruction is the development of cognitive/linguistic abilities (Figure 6.4). This direct daily instruction occurs in homogeneous-ability groups of five to six children. Four characteristics of these instructional groups have been identified:

1. The form of co-participation depends on the objectives (Au & Mason, 1981). The more common pattern, however, is highly informal mutual participation by the teacher and students, co-narration, volunteered speech, instant feedback, and lack of penalty for "wrong" answers. However, for vocabulary and decoding teaching, the pattern may be highly teacher-dominated, almost drill-like.

2. Instruction in comprehension follows, in general, a pattern of repeated thematic routines, labeled "E-T-R sequences" (Au, 1979, 1981). The teacher introduces content drawn from the child's experience (E), followed by text (T) material, followed by establishing relationships (R) between the two. These sequences may last from a few sentences up to several minutes. E-T-R analysis is discussed in detail in Chapter 7.

3. The teacher relies heavily on questioning that samples from the various levels of cognitive operations, extending from recall of specific detail through the higher orders of inference and extension (Crowell & Au, 1979; White & Tharp, 1987).

4. Responsive instruction is characteristic, so that the teacher plays off, and builds on, the children's responses. This requires flexibility; the teacher maintains goals for the discussion, but often alters or even abandons the anticipated "script" for a given lesson (Baird & Bogert, 1978). When all these characteristics are present, the result is a vigorous, enthusiastic lesson with lots of teacher–student interchange of ideas.

This activity setting, Center One, occupies the preponderance of the

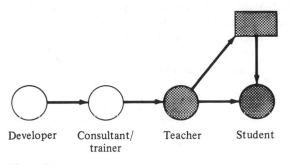

Figure 6.5.

teacher's time in interactive teaching. The teacher only occasionally monitors the other 20 or so children who are busy working at their other independent activity settings.

The independent learning centers

As each group moves into and out of the direct-instruction area, each child rotates to the next activity setting. The independent centers are either assigned by the teacher or selected at the beginning of each week by the child from a menu of choices. Each independent center has a characteristic activity that is supportive of the individualized instructional objectives. Typically, each classroom's Center Two is a "follow-up" center, where the objectives of that day's Center One instruction are reinforced by practice. A library center, an art center, a phonics center, a listening (oral-comprehension) center, and a game center are also common activity settings in KEEP classrooms. The centers are numbered, and a series of these numbers, written in each student's folder, guides the child through the daily and weekly schedule of rotations.

Moving through the complex schedule and remaining diligent in the independent centers require fine levels of child responsibility. These skills and values are taught to the children by specific procedures and means of assistance (Figure 6.5).

Contingency management assists children; maintaining independent work is assisted by the teacher's provision of a high rate of praise and other forms of positive interpersonal reinforcement. The overall effect is one of teacher warmth and an unusually positive atmosphere. This system and its felicitous effects on child industriousness are described in detail in Chapter 8.

There is a vigorous rate of interaction in the independent activity settings. KEEP kindergartners are engaged in peer interactions 50% of the time, and first-graders 70% of the time (Jordan, 1978a). Rates of peer interaction in KEEP's first, second, and third grades have proved remarkably stable across teacher, grade-level, subject-area, and time-of-day variables. These activity settings are designed to harness peer interaction for learning purposes. These centers are organized to keep the children working in the ZPD, to ensure the availability of necessary assistance, and to make the children receptive to the assistance. Learning centers differ from the Center One lesson, however, in this respect: In the reading lesson, the child works in that part of the ZPD where moderate to major levels of assistance are needed; at Center One, the teacher can ensure the provision of that assistance. In the independent centers, children work most of the time at the edge of the ZPD that is closest to the child's independent competence; there, performance requires only the assistance of peers who have perhaps only slightly different competences. This means that much of the time the group of children can perform the assigned activities by plying their individual competences in a complementary fashion. Children "practice" skills at centers – not skills in which they are fully, independently competent, or there would be no need for practice, but rather those skills in which feedback and some instructing can be provided by peers. Also, in centers, the children not only get assistance but also give it, and through these trials at independent performance they gain fuller control and become more confident of their own skills (Tharp, Jordan, et al., 1984). Further discussion of this activity setting is presented in Chapter 8.

Assisting the performance of teachers

This curriculum and classroom organization requires a high level of teacher skill. A central commitment of the KEEP system is to provide assistance to the teachers in developing and maintaining these necessary and highly refined teaching skills. Teacher performance is assisted through a wide range of activity settings that allow self-assistance, peer assistance, and assistance from administrators, consultants, trainers, and specialists. The full range of the means of assistance is provided. For novice and preservice teachers, assisting activities are scheduled as frequently as the system will bear. For skillful teachers, assistance is reduced, because "assistance" for teachers, just as for students, can interfere with smooth performance. But even for the skillful teacher, new competences are always needed and wanted. The assisting school should and can pro-

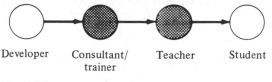

Figure 6.6.

vide activity settings in which needed assistance can be delivered (Figure 6.6).

Observation-and-conference activity settings

Each teacher is observed at least once a week by an assigned consultant (or other supervisor), and some assessment is made of the teacher's performance on a teaching skill of current focus. An example is an observation of the proportion of time spent by the teacher on comprehension instruction, as opposed to decoding or sight-vocabulary objectives. The results are fed back to the teachers immediately. Measurements of student on-task rates (or engaged time) are taken periodically, or on request by the teachers or their supervisors. Rates of reinforcement are also measured, especially for beginning teachers. Sample lessons or videotapes of direct-instruction sessions are periodically reviewed by supervisors, and feedback is provided.

The activity setting for consultant–teacher interaction is also an instructional conversation, that of the "weekly conference," where the two meet to discuss the feedback, to decide on the next goals for the teacher's own learning, and to work cooperatively in planning for the children in the classroom.

In the weekly conference, a frequent event is reviewing a videotape of one of the teacher's lessons. Both participants comment on the tape, and the consultant uses this stimulus to provide feedback, instructions, reinforcement, questioning, or cognitive structuring. In the later stages of the ZPD, the teacher herself provides most of this assistance, in a pattern of "self-collaboration."

Peer coaching

For some topics and purposes, peer consultation is more appropriate and more readily available. Peer coaching groups are formed as "interest groups," grade-level colleague groups are organized to provide peer counseling on issues of professional growth and decision making, and ad hoc peer coaching arrangements are often made by consultants.

Self-examination of videotapes

An activity setting in which this self-collaboration is the specific purpose is the private viewing of these videotapes by the teacher alone. This "microteaching" activity is most effective when used in the middle or advanced stages of the ZPD for the skill goal. Once the teacher's need for external assistance is reduced and self-assistance has begun to appear, self-examination of tapes provides the setting in which self-assistance can occur in an atmosphere of calm reflection and concentration.

Floor training

In the earlier levels of the teacher's ZPD, an activity setting that we may call "floor training" is arranged as needed. The physical setting is the classroom itself. The consultant herself may teach a demonstration lesson in the teacher's class, emphasizing some new skill or a skill of particular focus. The teacher will observe this, and discussion follows. Even more effective is floor training that involves three adults as well as the students. A demonstration teacher – who might be the consultant herself, a more competent peer of the teacher, or some specialist – conducts the lesson, while the consultant guides the teacher's observation of the demonstration.

Workshops and courses

The "workshop" is a typical activity setting in which teachers are assisted, and it is also present in the KEEP system. Workshops are useful for introducing new skills to teachers and for providing cognitive structuring. The valuation of workshops at KEEP is consistent with that of the field in general – workshops, as sole forms of assistance, are of limited utility. When workshops are followed up by other activity settings, they can be economical introductory activities. In the absence of additional settings, little classroom change can be expected to be maintained. The same may be said of the university class as an activity setting for teacher training. At one stage of development of KEEP, the university course was frequently used as a setting for trying to assist teachers to improve their skills, and it is still occasionally prescribed. However, when either workshops or courses are unsupplemented by continuing forms of teacher

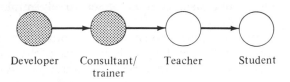

Figure 6.7.

assistance, little continuing profit can be expected. These activity settings at KEEP have been carefully researched and reported in detail (Johnson & Sloat, 1980; Sloat, Tharp, & Gallimore, 1977; Speidel & Tharp, 1978; Tanaka-Matsumi & Tharp, 1977).

Project consultation

The most powerful model of assistance is that of the project collaboration (Vogt, 1985). Detailed discussion of this process is delayed until Chapter 9. Here, we observe only that when program developers or researchers and consultants form a project team with the teacher, and the entire group operates in joint productive activity for the purpose of solving a particular problem, powerful assistance is offered to the teacher, but it is less formal "teaching" than collegial work.

In this model, the consultant's interaction with the teacher is virtually confined to the project-team-related activities. Each member of the team has different skills, and each contributes assistance to the others as well as receiving it. *In this model, it is acknowledged that none of the members yet possesses the cognitive structures that are the goal of the enterprise.* It is not necessary to be "superior" in order to assist; the supervisory line is transcended, and for the purpose of the joint productive activity, participants are partners.

Assistance to consultants/trainers

Program developers and researchers assist the performances of consultants, trainers, and supervisors in a variety of settings. Before, during, and after such participation, program developers also provide assistance to consultants in a variety or other settings (Figure 6.7).

The consultant/trainer training program

Assisting the performances of teachers requires a high degree of competence in consultant/trainers. Knowledge of curriculum, of teaching methods, and of the techniques of assistance must be sensitively employed in assisting teachers to assist students.

The first activity setting that a new consultant encounters is a specific "consultant training program." Over the year-long course of that training, each beginning consultant is involved in a variety of activity sub-settings: instructional conversations with the trainers, seminar presentations, tutorials, role-playing, guided observation, guided practice, and finally assignment as an assistant consultant to actual classrooms. During this training program, all the means of assistance are provided by the training staff, which consists of two coordinators and a participating staff of experienced consultants, researchers, and program developers.

The workshop and retreat

Workshops and retreats are provided for consultants on a variety of topics, particularly on new developments in instructional goals and methods. These are the settings in which program developers introduce new material, interpret it, provide instructions and cognitive structuring, and offer occasions for guided observation and practice.

Producing training materials

Program developers frequently produce materials for the use of consultants in assisting teachers. Demonstration videotapes of a new classroom method are most often produced by a team including an expert developer of the method and a consultant who represents the "users." Through the collaborative process of joint activity with the researcher, the consultant also becomes an expert. In fact, through this activity, the product may well be changed or refined through the assistance provided by the consultant to the program developer.

Such training materials are important means of assistance, through video modeling, that program developers provide to consultants.

The project team as a setting for assisting consultants

This collegial, joint-activity mode is even more effective in the "project team" already described. When the consultant and the program developer work together with the teacher in a project for problem solution, the assisted performance occurs in each permutation of interaction. This project-team model, for the researcher/developer also, is the highest form of assisted performance that can be offered to trainers. All that has been said in describing the project team from the point of view of the teacher and consultant can be said from the point of view of the researcher and consultant. Participating in this activity – the "highest" setting – does require a good level of basic competence in the consultant and equally high levels of competence and confidence in the researcher.

7 The activity setting of the instructional conversation: developing word and discourse meaning

Assistance to the developing child occurs in activity settings: Who is with the child to provide assistance, what they are doing (and the rules or scripts that govern how participants conduct themselves), and when, where, and why they are doing it – these define the activities in which cognition develops. Assisted performance occurs in these activity settings' interpersonal transactions and in the context of their intersubjectivity. The task of designing systems for assistance is that of designing activity settings. The criterion for an educationally effective activity setting is that it should allow a maximum of assistance in the performance of the tasks at hand. The activity setting is a unit of analysis that transcends individuals and provides a meaningful way to integrate culture, local contexts, and individual function (Cole, 1985; Rogoff, 1982; Weisner, 1984; Weisner & Gallimore, 1985; Weisner et al., 1986).

Like all institutions, schools are constituted of activity settings: The classroom, playground, cafeteria, nurse's office, and auditorium evoke, even in aging graduates, images of place and event. These shared memories reflect school activity settings that have been as stable as a rock and have been sources of dismay to succeeding generations of reformers. To secure change requires that the school's activity settings be understood and be altered so that they will give rise to the desired assistance of performance.

We begin our analysis of the school's activity settings with those that are closest to education's final common pathway – those of the classroom itself. To analyze the KEEP school, we consider three activity settings, nested within the classroom: Center One, the independent learning centers, and the whole-group setting. The present chapter treats the most fundamental setting, the "instructional conversation," known in the KEEP system as Center One.

130

The development of language, literacy, and thinking in conversation

Language, cognition, and reading are intimately related. As language develops, capacities for concept development increase apace. With each new vocabulary item, a new concept for generalization is available to the expanding word-meaning system. With each advance in the complexity of the system, there is the possibility for more complex operations. With greater capacity for speaking, there is available greater capacity for the self-directed speech of verbal thinking.

Likewise, the development of reading comprehension is inseparable from the development of language. The development of understanding requires "the ability to understand language and through that ability to acquire new knowledge" (Carroll, 1972, p. 1). If children are not familiar with the language that they are asked to read, if they are unfamiliar with the network of word meanings, if they are unfamiliar with the way that words modify and relate to each other, then learning to decode print in that language will be difficult, and an understanding of what has been decoded will be virtually impossible.

The development of spoken language is a requisite for the development of verbally mediated concepts, both everyday and schooled concepts. In this chapter we describe instructional procedures in which schooled and everyday concepts are carefully related. This relating enriches and makes useful the schooled concepts and simultaneously transforms the nature of everyday verbal thinking, making it more voluntary, systemic, and flexible.

Natural, contextualized procedures for language development are characteristic of the KEEP system. In brief, this natural-context approach is strongly influenced by the ways that language is acquired in natural speech communities of home, community, and culture (for detailed discussion, see Chapter 5). Language, according to Vygotsky, is acquired through interaction with more competent speakers. The nature of the language environment and interactions become critical for acquisition. This is the "emergent interactionism" discussed by Kohlberg and Wertsch (in press). Initially the competent speaker provides maximum support for the communication, filling in words for which she believes the learner is struggling (Rogoff et al., 1984). As the child becomes more competent in the conversation, the adult gradually phases out the assistance (Cazden, 1979, 1981). In natural speech communities, adults probably are unaware of this process; they are concerned only with understanding the child, and in that effort they will make the child's utterances more elaborate and precise.

Of course, the KEEP language-development program is a good deal more self-conscious than that. The natural-context approach is effectuated in the instructional conversation. The activity setting for this instructional conversation is known in the KEEP system as Center One. In the earliest years, from kindergarten to third grade, the surface goal of this small-group, teacher-led activity setting appears as the teaching of reading. In upper elementary through high school classes it may appear as teaching science or social studies. At every level, however, the instructional conversation has a higher and more general purpose, which is conceptual and linguistic growth.

These goals are achieved through the group discussions that create discourse-meaning structures that are both intermental and intramental. The entire group of teacher and students shares both verbal language and written text, and so is intermental. Simultaneously, these meanings are internalized for each member and become the stuff of the thought system of each individual. That which is first social, in Center One, becomes psychological in the higher cognitive processes of each member. The processes of this internalization were discussed in detail in Chapters 2 and 5, in which it was emphasized that the conditions for the development of cognitive processes are those of joint productive activity. Those conditions are vital to Center One. There is mutual participation by teacher and children in the task, rather than the children performing while the teacher observes. This mutuality of enterprise is an attitude constantly demonstrated by the teacher. She will even occasionally feign errors; as children correct her, the mutuality of task engagement is reconfirmed. Learning takes place in a mode of enterprise engagement; that is, children and teacher actually engage, in whole-task form, in the enterprise that is to be learned, rather than the teacher trying to teach small out-of-context pieces of the task or rules for how to go about it (Jordan, 1981a, 1981b).

Our discussion focuses on teaching oral language and next on teaching text comprehension, but it must be understood that the teaching of language and the teaching of the comprehension of text are united in the Center One lesson. This close harnessing of speaking and reading pulls forward the capacities for verbal thought.

The instructional conversation: who, when, where, what, and why

Who

Those present in the instructional conversation of Center One are three to six students and the teacher. Homogeneous grouping for achievement level has been the typical pattern, though some experimentation with heterogeneous groups has been conducted. Groups of gifted children have been effectively taught in like manner (Schneider et al. , 1985), as well as groups of retarded children (Zetlin & Gallimore, 1980, 1983) and all ability levels in between, from preschool to graduate school.

When

The basic template of the KEEP system for kindergarten through third grade calls for a meeting of Center One each day for about 20 min. Longer sessions (meeting three or four times per week) appear to be more appropriate for upper grades. A wide variety of time formats has been used experimentally; the ideal continues to be for each child to be present in at least one instructional conversation with the teacher each day.

Where

In the typical KEEP classroom, Center One is conducted by the teacher from her seat near a chalkboard, with three to six children facing her across a semicircular table. (From this position, she is also able to monitor the rest of the classroom. For a discussion of the other, simultaneous activities in the classroom, see Chapter 8.)

Among the interesting variations of the instructional conversation – in both kindergarten and junior high school – is that in which the teacher "floats" from table to table of children, creating impromptu discussion sessions over the work being created by the children there. Whether the work is the children's own writing, artwork of clay or paper, science experiment, or even the routine worksheets, the work at hand creates the condition of joint productive activity so essential for involvement and the development of discourse meaning. Impromptu Center Ones have been successfully operated at preschool around play materials, on field trips, in a "pull-out" classroom for Title One students, and in almost any conceivable place where work or experience is centered.

Scheduling of the instructional conversation, however, is highly recommended, so that it will not be slighted in favor of less demanding activity. The typical setting, therefore, is at the "conversation table" or around the active work space of studio or laboratory.

What

What the activity setting does is infinitely variable: It may be forming clay, heating beakers, laying out a newspaper, inventing a puzzle. Most often, it involves reading some text, although this "text" can be presented orally.

The essential feature of the activity is very simple and very common-place: to read the text and talk together about it. The text may be of the students' own writing, it may be an early storybook, or it may be the Con-stitution of the United States. Whatever the text, the structure of the instructional conversation is for students and teacher to talk together in the presence of text. This task is distinctively designed and orchestrated. It requires a conjunction of the student's everyday style of participation and discourse with the emerging schooled type of participation and discourse.

The action of the teacher in the instructional conversation is to elicit from the students their emergent understanding of the text, to do so in ways that assist comprehension beyond the level students can achieve alone, and thereby to develop increasing competency in schooled discourse.

Why

The purpose of this small-group conversation is to develop language, lit-eracy, and thinking. Some teachers, for some purposes, in some class-rooms, may refer to this conversation as the "reading lesson." Others describe it as the "language-development" lesson. For others it is "the writing group," and for older students it may be the science lesson. Although the content of instruction changes with grade, teacher prefer-ence, and school district requirements, the instructional practices follow closely the theory of instruction elaborated in Chapter 5. The reason for the conversation, from the point of view of the teacher and the school, is to develop word meaning, discourse meaning, and higher cognitive processes.

As emphasized in Chapter 4, neither the motive force nor the meanings of activities are necessarily the same for all participants. In the example of the reading lesson, Au and Jordan (1981), following Wallace (1961), have pointed out that the meaning of the lesson in the mind of the teacher is substantially different from that of beginning readers, who understand the activity setting as story-talking. Over time, children will understand the events in ways more congruent with those of their teachers, because the tendency of activity settings and their accompanying language is to develop a mutual meaning structure, an evolving, developing, and con-verging understanding.

There is a second consideration in a discussion of why an activity set-ting continues – its product. As the canoe motivates the canoe carvers,

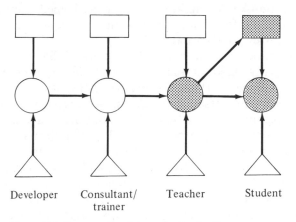

Developer   Consultant/   Teacher   Student
trainer

Figure 7.1. Sources of assistance in Center One.

so some product of joint activity is eventually necessary to drive the continuation and interaction of the group. The instructional conversation works best when Center One is focused on some product. In early years, when children experience the activity as another form of story-telling, some minimum product (even the routine worksheets that follow up the instructional goals of the conversation) can suffice. Even for these younger children, though, a real product of a mural, a bulletin board, a painting, or a play will energize the activity immeasurably. And for content-area instruction and more mature students, it becomes necessary to arrange some use of the acquired knowledge, some application of the concepts, some product to either follow the conversation or accompany it. All carvers must have a canoe – idle talk palls.

Assisting performance in the instructional conversation

The sources of assistance in Center One are primarily the teacher, but the student peers also provide a vigorous source of influence and assistance for one another (Figure 7.1).

Conducting this conversation requires of teachers a finely tuned attention to the utterances of students. Too much distraction, or too many students, and the crucial opportunities to assist performance are lost, because responsive teaching in this context means that teacher assistance and instruction are contingent on student productions, rather than being preplanned, scripted, or didactic. Because student productions are not predictable, responsive teaching involves thoughtful, reflective tailoring of assistance to learners as instructional opportunity and need arise.

Through conversation-like interactions, children are helped to relate personal experience to text information. Digressions, incomplete child utterances, and differing viewpoints are the norm.

Discourse-meaning learning opportunities at KEEP have been integrated into the daily instructional conversations of Center One (Dowhower-Vuyk & Speidel, 1982; Speidel, 1982; 1983a, 1984, 1987a). Center One lessons are conversational and topic-centered, and they provide speakers opportunities to participate without artificial turn-taking rules. Teachers take children's perspectives and recall information about the children's backgrounds and interests in order to comprehend and clarify intended communications. By attending carefully to what children are trying to say, the teacher is better able to tailor responses in ways that assist the children to make more complete and elaborated utterances. It is these qualities of the Center One interaction that make it conversation-like, more like natal caregiver contexts than is typical of most "language-teaching" programs in public schools.

However spontaneous and ad hoc the teacher–student exchanges in Center One, there is in fact an underlying structure. The structure is provided by an explicit set of instructional objectives, devised by the teacher from the specific subject matter of the lesson, and the ever-present meta-objective, to increase comprehension and competence in discourse in the domain of instruction.

The continuum of discourse-teaching stages and strategies

The instructional conversation of Center One changes character, of course, depending on the age of the pupils, and especially on their increasing sophistication about written text. As a rough guide to the progress through several strategies, KEEP system developers have described a continuum of discourse-teaching stages and strategies (Figure 7.2) (Hao, 1983; Tharp, Jordan, et al., 1984; Vogt, 1982).

In the earliest stage, called concept/experience, group discussion is almost exclusively centered on shared experiences, usually with concrete objects. Drawing children into discussion is the primary objective; the route is by way of performance skills: handling, shaping, moving, arranging some object or product. The goal is to assist the children to develop word meanings and systems of word meanings. Although some illustrative written words are used, the primary concentration is on establishing language competence by teaching verbal discourse. For educationally at-risk children, this is particularly important, because their speaking competences may limit the development of everyday verbal concepts.

The second stage is word play. Though this is similar to the previous

Concept/ experience	Word play	Language- experience approach	Experience- text relationship	Concept- text application

Figure 7.2. The continuum of instructional strategies: I.

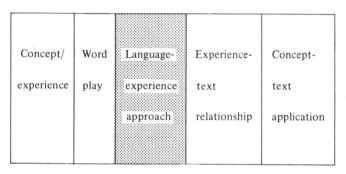

Concept/ experience	Word play	Language- experience approach	Experience- text relationship	Concept- text application

Figure 7.3. The continuum of instructional strategies: II.

stage, printed words are more salient. Posters, pictures, and objects are used for discussion; the children then label various parts of these charts. The labeled charts are used for a variety of word-finding and other verbal games. Word play is a first step along the road to freeing words from their sensual connectedness to designata. It is often a necessary precursor to the first introduction of written language, which occurs in the next phase. Word games are a particular delight to young children and have been an apt way to bridge from verbal word meaning to print familiarity.

The third stage is that of the language-experience approach (LEA) (Figure 7.3) (Allen, 1976; Hall, 1976; Stauffer, 1970). LEA involves oral dictation of stories by children concerning some joint experience or activity, transcription of those stories by the teacher onto a chalkboard or chart paper, publication of the stories on typewritten sheets, and use of these sheets of "texts" for instruction in elementary principles of reading. For dialect-speaking children, these texts are written in dialect, just as they are spoken, not "improved" into standard or adult English. This faithful transcription assists children to learn the relationships between orthography and oral language (Vogt, 1982).

Language-experience lessons are joint productive activities. Because the teacher is engaged with them, and because there is a tangible product, the children are engaged by Center One, and because of their active participation, language-learning opportunities are created.

At this point, we pause for an extended example and discussion of assisting language development in the language-experience lesson. We shall resume the discussion of the continuum of discourse-teaching strategies immediately following.

Teacher assistance in the instructional conversation

The means of assistance used by the teacher run the gamut of all six available means, as we saw from the extended example of the Center One conversation in Chapter 3. In this chapter, we shall see that phenomenon again, although the most common means of assistance, when language development is the primary purpose of the conversation, are modeling, feedback, and questioning.

The following transcript is excerpted from a Honolulu KEEP kindergarten lesson with a teacher and six students. In this lesson, as is common in LEA, the teacher has arranged a joint activity for the children that will form the basis for their dictated story. The joint activity itself is prime time for language development. In this example, the activity is one guaranteed to engage the energy of all young children.

Means of assistance: questioning, modeling, and feedback

The teacher, who is seated facing six kindergartners across a table, leads them in a rhythmic chant about peanut butter and jelly sandwiches: "Peanut, peanut butter and jelly!" When she reaches beneath the table and produces a jar of each and a sack of bread slices, the children squeal in approval.

Verbal	Nonverbal
T: We're gonna make our peanut butter sandwich. What is the first thing I'm going to need?	[Produces a jar of peanut butter, a jar of jelly, and and a loaf of sliced bread in a bag]
J: Get the bread!	[C points to bread; reaches across table and pats the bag of bread]
T: I need to get a piece of the bread. What am I going to do with it?	[Reaches into bag and retrieves a slice; J nods approval]
J: Put this first . . . and put this second . . .	[Touches peanut butter jar; touches jelly jar]
T: Put it . . .	[Hesitates]

J: Oh, no. Put this first . . . and this second . . . [Touches jelly jar; touches peanut butter]

R: Get the knife first, no, get the knife in and spread it.

Jk: Put the jelly on the sandwich, then that on the sandwich, and then you eat it. [Points to peanut butter]

T: I put the jelly on top of the sandwich . . . ? [Places jar of jelly on top of the bread slice]

Children: [Chorus] No! No! No! [Two stand up; another points; they laugh and smile with surprise and amusement]

R: You *open* it. [Takes jelly jar from teacher and removes lid]

Jk: Then you put it on!

R: You open it. [Reaches jelly jar and removes lid]

Jk: Then you put it in.

T: Oh! I need to twist the lid off the jar?

Children: [Chorus] Yeah. Yes. And make like that, and put it on . . .

R: First you have to do peanut butter . . .

J: No, that! [Gestures toward jelly, disagreeing about which ingredient is applied first]

R: [Shakes head in disagreement and frustration]

T: I have to spread the peanut butter first? Are you sure?

R: Yeah, cause I tried it, that's, that's [the truth], everybody's [looking at it]

T: How do I spread it? Do I take my finger, stick it in, and rub it all over the bread?

J: No, this! You stick that in . . . [Picks up knife; makes spreading motion with knife over bread]

T: [Takes knife] You stick the knife into the jar? [Acts out instruction given by child by placing large lump of peanut butter on bread]

T: There, it's spread. What do I have to do?

J: You gotta mix 'em around. [Takes knife; shakes head in disbelief at the teacher's incompetence]

T: I have to spread it around on top of the bread with a knife.

The children's participation in Center One lessons creates many opportunities to teach language without making the children conscious that they are learning language (Speidel, 1984; Speidel & Dowhower-Vuyk,

1981). In what appears to the children to be a sandwich-making session, the teacher is able to assist their language performance by the use of the three means of assistance most common in language-developing conversations: questioning, modeling, and feedback.

Through regular *questioning,* the teacher solicits verbal responses that assist the children to express themselves to the maximum of their ability.

Through *feedback,* she prompts a child to rephrase an utterance in order to communicate a message, without drawing attention to language forms per se. This is illustrated when a boy says "Put the jelly on the sandwich . . . then you eat it," and the teacher responds by placing the unopened jelly jar on top of the bread. All the children shout "No!" recognizing at once that the teacher took the boy's directive literally. The child amends the directive to be more explicit about the next step ("You *open* it"), to which Jk (the original communicator) adds an additional detail ("Then you put it on"). In this assisting interaction, the teacher provides feedback to the child that his utterance did not convey his intended message. This stimulates subsequent efforts by the child to communicate more precisely. If the child suspected the teacher really understood, it did not seem to matter; the teacher's response was taken to be playful, and the children immediately engaged in an exchange as if it were a serious situation or at least a game-like situation. This response of children to communication "games" is not unusual (Conant et al., 1983). Even if the children suspect that the teacher already knows what to do, the tenor and atmosphere of this kind of exchange are dramatically different from the sometimes disruptive effects of "known information" questions (Mehan, 1979).

The transcript also illustrates how teachers in Center One assist by *modeling.* This means of assistance occurs whenever the teacher rewords or elaborates portions of a child's utterance into what linguists call an *expansion:* "an utterance of a caregiver that follows an utterance or a series of utterances of a child in which a child's utterance or utterance series is recouched in more appropriate, that is, adult grammatical terms" (Ochs, 1982).

Thus, when a child shouts "Get the bread!" the teacher expands by saying "I need to get a piece of the bread." By modeling these alternatives and vocabulary words, she assists each of the children to form similar utterances later. She acts on the statement by retrieving a slice of bread, and she pulls forward the dialogue by asking some questions. In a like manner, the teacher works through the task of building a sandwich; at each step she assists the children to make more complete, precise statements about sandwiches. All the statements of assistance are embedded in the instructional conversation. All assisting techniques obey the overarching rule: They are used only when they facilitate communication. Overuse will quickly stiffen the discussion's required fluidity.

For many KEEP classrooms, particularly in the earlier years, this instructional conversation may well be bidialectal (as in Hawaii, when children offer Hawaiian English) or bilingual (as at Navajo, when the Navajo language is offered, and in Los Angeles, where Spanish is many students' first language). Routinely, the teacher speaks in standard English. One of the main goals for this conversation is the development of language ability in general, and standard English in particular, which the teacher assists by modeling, feeding-back, and questioning. But the context of the conversation is communication, and the teacher keeps communication going, encourages the children to communicate, and accepts whatever language they use in order to communicate. Her assistance is through questioning and the modeling-plus-feedback that expansions provide. She does not suppress the children's comfortable language expressions; she models alternatives. Above all, her assistance is responsive.

Several variations of modeling were described by Speidel (1987b) in her study of Center One conversations in KEEP Honolulu classrooms. She reported that 87.6% of the teacher's utterances were responsive to a student's message or behaviors. However, not all the responsive utterances of the teacher were linguistically related. For example:

Means of assistance: none
John: Maybe the, the guys that supposed to drive the plane . . .
Teacher: Just a second, Sean . . . [Attends to something else]

Or:

Mileka: Because the mother wen buy her toy.
Teacher: All right.

However, 54.2% were both responsive and linguistically related to the students' utterances. In almost every such instance, some means of assistance could be seen as influencing the children in their ZPD for discourse competence. Because the focus of the teacher was on communication, the most frequent means of assistance was the modeling provided by the teacher's own more elaborate speech. She also provided feedback and set standards for that feedback by frequently restating the children's utterances in more complex and precise forms.

In assisting performance in small groups of children, what is feedback to a speaker is a model for a listener. Separating out the feedback and modeling functions of teachers' utterances probably is not possible. Such a conception of modeling and feedback is well beyond the earlier views that such means of assistance played no role in language development. As Speidel (1987b) noted, the earlier views were based on an oversimplified conception of modeling and feedback.

These means of assistance were modulated by the amounts of the children's own speech that the teacher incorporated into her responses. Speidel discussed this modulation in terms of four levels:

1   The teacher repeated everything or parts of what the student had said without adding any of her own words, called *exact repetition.*
2   The teacher repeated parts or all of a student's words, but with *addition or substitution* of her own words.
3   The teacher used *extensive rewording or elaboration,* as well as repetition.
4   A student's message was *reworded or elaborated with minimal or no repetition* by the teacher.

The first category, exact repetitions, constituted only 8% of the linguistically related utterances in Speidel's study. She suggested that extensive use of exact repetitions would fail to produce language development, as well as grind the conversation to boredom and silence.

The most frequent kind of teacher expansion was repetition with some addition or rewording, which occurred in about one-fourth of the utterances coded. For example:

Means of assistance: modeling

Mileka: Probably wen trip.
Teacher: He probably tripped.

In this example, the child's use is acknowledged for the words "probably" and "trip" and for the proper sequence. But, in addition, the teacher expands the child's utterance in two ways: She models the use of the pronoun "he" and the past tense in standard English (marked by "ed" added to the verb stem, rather than by "wen" as in Hawaiian English). She assists the child by feeding-back that some elements are correct and then assists by modeling a new standard for additional forms.

In the next example, the teacher rewords or expands the child's effort by providing the label "plane" for the Hawaiian English indefinite "om." She also models the preposition "on" as an alternative to "inside" in reference to the "news."

Means of assistance: questioning and modeling

Jude: Maybe they was going . . . maybe, maybe the wind. The wind wen go push 'om down. Maybe the wind wen push 'om down like inside the news.
Teacher: Oh, like on the news? Like maybe the wind was too strong and pushed the plane down?

The third level of teacher expansion, repetition with many additions or rewordings, was used by the teacher in 13.6% of utterances.

Means of assistance: modeling

John: Probably, probably have snow on the ... stuff and ... thing, thing was heavy and thing fall.
Teacher: Oh, you mean there might be so much snow and ice on the plane that it couldn't fly?

In this excerpt, there is little use of the child's wording. The teacher recasts the intended communication into one that provides feedback and sets a model. It also introduces new word meanings. It is cast in a form ("Oh, [do] you mean") that invites rebuttal if the child is dissatisfied with the teacher's version of his intended message. These stratagems all work together to advance the discussion.

The final level involves rewording and elaboration that involve minimal or no repetition (7.8% of utterances). In rewording, the student's language is paraphrased into clearer, more condensed, or more standard expression.

Means of assistance: modeling

John: Maybe the guys that 'sposed to drive the plane went to look at something and they, they felt the plane go down and then they just run to there and the plane was on the ground already.
Teacher: Oh, you mean perhaps the pilots weren't watching what they were doing?

Even with such little overlap, "the student will probably be able to map the structure and lexicon of the teacher's rewording onto the internal image of the situation he was trying to describe, because he already has the concept in his mind [given that the teacher paraphrased him correctly]. This type of meaning induction is probably typical for children who already have a fair amount of competence in the language. It might be too difficult for ... those who are less knowledgeable" (Speidel, 1987b, p. 117). Again, the teacher invites continuing dialogue; there is no hint of disapproval, despite the teacher's substantial rewording.

In elaboration, the teacher adds information to the student's message without using any of the student's words. The following example contains elaboration and also includes an instance of cognitive structuring as a means of assistance: The teacher clearly explains a concept and provides a word meaning.

Means of assistance: cognitive structuring, questioning, feedback

Teacher: What do we put in our mouth underneath our tongue?
Jude: A temperature.

Jason: A temperature.
Teacher: No, that's what we find out. Your temperature goes up. That means your
    body gets hot.

What kinds of linguistic information are provided by the teacher's modeling expansions? Speidel (1987b) examined these same transcripts and
classified this linguistic information into three types: lexical, morpholog-
ical, and syntactic. Language does not fall into three such discrete categories, and Speidel rightly urges caution in interpretation. Nevertheless,
her data do give a rough indication: About 40% of teacher expansions
contained grammatical morphemes, about 40% contained syntactical
information, and about 20% contained lexical information. The variability across lessons suggests that the nature of linguistic information is a
function of story and lesson purpose, among other factors. But even using
these crude measures, we can see that instructional conversations of this
sort can contain rich models for language development, in all its
complexity.

These excerpts are accurate snapshots of the Center One interactions.
There is no attempt by the teacher to control turn-taking. Children are
largely free to contribute at times of their own choosing, without raising
their hands or using other conventions of turn-taking. The teacher's high
rate of assistance, in the form of models and feedback, "disappears" into
the students' excitement about the topics of their Center One conversations, and the teacher uses only mild means to maintain topic continuity.
Nevertheless, the means do assist.

This can be seen by examining the developing utterances of the students. Speidel coded students' speech in a manner similar to the teacher's. The students were highly responsive, and their utterances were linguistically related to those of the other speakers 73.3% to 92% of the time.

The models are imitated. Like the teacher, the students frequently
adopted preceding speakers' words and phrases. Of the words used by
students in the lessons, 52.8% had been spoken before. Not only did the
students repeat many of the words already used in the conversation, but
also they frequently incorporated fairly large phrases of others' speech.
For example:

Means of assistance: modeling, questioning

Teacher: Do you think the money is going to run away?
Jude: I don't *think* it's *going to run away.* [Repetition of six words]

The number of instances in which each child used chunks of speech
containing three or more repeated words is substantial: On the average,
20% of students' utterances were constructed of two or more chunks of

speech containing three or more repeated words adopted from preceding speakers' utterances. For example:

Means of assistance: modeling

Lei: But maybe. . . . maybe he was riding his bike and then he wen go fall down.
John: Probably he fell off his bike and skin his knee.
Mileka: Prob. . . . *probably he wen* scrape and *riding his* skateboard and, um, he, um, *he wen fall* and *wen scrape his knee*

Peers as sources of assistance in the instructional conversation

These data suggest that there is substantial use by students of peers as well as teachers as sources of assistance. However, clear identification of the utterance source is virtually impossible. Speidel (1983b) attempted to trace sources and concluded that students repeated words used by each other twice as often as they repeated teacher words. However, the process is similar for both peer and teacher sources of assistance, as can be seen in another "peanut butter" lesson:

Means of assistance: modeling and questioning (by teacher)

Mileka: Rub it on the bread.
Teacher: Rub it on the bread. Or I could say, "I would spread it on the bread. I am spreading it on the bread."

A moment later:

Teacher: And then what'll I do with it?
Jude: Put it on top the bread.
Mileka: Rub it.
Teacher: Okay, you said rub it. Now what's the other word we were using for . . .
    [Jude, Mileka, and Lynn simultaneously]:
Jude: Spread it on top the bread.
Mileka: Spread out.
Lynn: Spread it out.

Later the students were asked to dictate story sentences.

Means of assistance: instructing (by teacher and peer)

Teacher: Lei, give me a sentence about that.
Lei: Put, the, peanut butter . . .
Jason: [Whispers] Spread. [To prompt Lei]
Lei: . . . spread . . . on the bread.

In another example from the study of six children, a child (Mileka) uses "that" and "om" instead of "it," a pattern common in Hawaiian English. After the teacher and his peers use "it" several times, Mileka adopts their usage.

Means of assistance: modeling (by all)

Mileka: No, get the knife and put *that* in.
Teacher: Oh, all right. I stuck *it* in the peanut butter. [Replaced "that" with "it"]
Mileka: Then put *'om* in on there.
Teacher: You have to tell me what to do with the knife.
Jude: Put *it* in. [Peer model]
Teacher: I did put *it* in. [Teacher model]
Keala: Put *it* in. [Peer model]
Mileka: Now put *it* on the bread. [Uses "it" to refer to knife]

A moment later:

Mileka: Rub *it* on the bread. [Uses "it" following a different verb, with no immediate model]

These excerpts suggest that the children are assisted to use new language forms and features through the provisions of models and feedback. Mileka's adoption of "it" is effortless and is achieved with no direct attention called to the alternative forms used at first. There is no reason to believe, of course, that complete mastery of the third-person pronoun has been achieved. But as in the case of toddlers, it is participation in hundreds of mundane, goal-directed activities of everyday life that provides the context for learning language. There is every reason to believe that a similar process for teacher–student interactions is desirable.

Among these reasons are the evaluation studies of the effects of this form of responsive, conversational language-development program (Speidel, 1981b, 1982, 1984, 1987a,b). These effects are favorable, although the effects of the language-development portion are impossible to disentangle from the effects of the other forms of instruction – reading, writing, and thinking – that also occur at Center One.

In conclusion, we may say that both the transcript analyses and the evaluation studies suggest that it is important for teachers to maximize interactions in the ZPD of language (Speidel & Dowhower-Vuyk, 1981). Sadly, there is little evidence that children are taught in U.S. schools through interaction in the ZPD (Duffy et al., 1980; Goodlad, 1984). The typical condition is far removed from what we have described to be the typical reading lesson in Center One at KEEP, in which nonstandard dialect speakers have many opportunities to converse during goal-oriented activities with a responsive, noncritical standard-English-speaking teacher.

Teaching literacy in Center One

The language-experience lesson is the fulcrum balancing language development and literacy development. It is fitting to exemplify the beginnings

of learning to read with a continuation of the peanut butter lesson into
the dictation of text phase:

T: Kc, can you tell me something about making peanut butter and jelly sand-
    wiches? In a whole sentence?
Kc: I like the bread.
T: You like the bread with peanut butter?
Kc: [Nods yes]
T: I . . . like . . . the . . . [Teacher directs the children to keep their eyes on her as
    she writes the sentence on the chart paper]
R: I like the peanut butter and jelly sandwich.
T: I like the bread? [Still addressing Kc]
R: You should say, "I like the peanut butter and jelly sandwich."
T: I like the bread. Wait. Is that okay?
Kc: [Nods yes]
T: Okay, R. Let's hear your sentence.
R: I like the peanut butter and jelly sandwich.
T: You like the peanut butter and jelly sandwich? [Writing on the chart paper]
    What do you like to do with your peanut butter and jelly sandwich?
Children: Eat 'em!
T: Everybody, altogether, your last sentence, from the whole group.
Children and Teacher: [Chorus] We got the bread out. I like to eat the jelly peanut
    butter. I like to put jelly guava kine on top the bread. I like the bread. I like
    the peanut butter and jelly sandwich. I like to eat the peanut butter and
    jelly. The end. The Red Group. [The guava kind of jelly: "kine" is
    Hawaiian English usage]

That small, self-created text becomes the focus of instruction for the reading portion of the lesson for the next few meetings of the Red Group's
Center One. The children will learn that these marks on the paper contain
meaning, and that meaning will be the same tomorrow as it is today. The
words in the story will become rudiments of their sight vocabulary. They
will learn that text is a record of speech and a repository of meaning. The
everyday concepts of their sandwich making will find another form of
expression in the system of schooled, literate language. Center One has
smoothly moved into an instructional conversation in the presence of
text. The system for discourse in schooled concepts has begun to connect
with the everyday concepts that have risen through practical activity.

The continuum of discourse-teaching stages and strategies (resumed)

We have described, thus far, three parts of the continuum of discourse-
teaching stages and strategies: concept/experience, word play, and the
language-experience approach (LEA). We now resume our presentation
of the continuum of instructional strategies by considering the instruc-

Concept/ experience	Word play	Language- experience approach	Experience- text relationship	Concept- text application

Figure 7.4. The continuum of instructional strategies: III.

tional conversation as it takes place when focused specifically on the reading of written text. That instructional strategy is described as the experience-text-relationship heuristic (Figure 7.4).

Even educationally at-risk children, through LEA, can be brought to readiness for the printed text of other authors by the middle of the first grade. When the text expresses ideas, events, and words that are not the children's own, the instructional task changes. The teacher must assist the children to make them their own. To do so, the teacher assists the students to weave together the next text with materials called up from their memory.

In Chapter 5, we discussed the issues involved in comprehending text. Whether to read it, to write it, or to listen to it, understanding text involves the weaving of new and old information, the weaving of new, schooled concepts with those of everyday life. Textual material becomes meaningful when it is hooked by *sense* to everyday concepts, and hooked by *system* to the whole structure of meaning given by schooling. The homely "weaving" heuristic used by reading teachers is not only a short-term instructional strategy but also the basic cognitive process for understanding the world used by mature schooled thinkers.

On the level of practical activity, teachers realize the weaving metaphor through a heuristic called the experience-text-relationship method, or E-T-R (Au, 1979; Mason & Au, 1986), which is particularly suited to a Vygotskian analysis (Au & Kawakami, 1984).

In the first phase of the E-T-R reading lesson, the teacher assists the child to prepare the existing relevant systems of understanding: Relevant prior knowledge and experiences are arrayed and sorted. Our practitioners refer to this stage of instruction as the *experience* (E) phase.

Next, the information in the text is "carded" by reading, discussing, and verifying the students' accuracy of recall of text material and by bringing different elements of the text into some systemic relationship with each other. The teacher provides various forms of assistance for this performance. Our practitioners refer to this as the stage of discussion of the *text* (T).

The third stage is the weaving proper, in which the experience (or previous knowledge) is brought into relationship with the text information. This stage is the *relationship* (R) stage. The teacher assists the children to bring the E and the T elements close enough together that they attach and are woven into the larger structure of discourse meaning that has both intramental and intermental planes.

Mason and Au (1986), Tharp, Jordan, and associates (1984), and Au and Kawakami (1984) have provided descriptions of this E-T-R process in some detail. During the experience (E) phases, before the text is encountered, the teacher has the children call up prior knowledge relevant to the text to be read. She then moves them toward the text by asking for predictions, usually on the basis of the title or pictures accompanying the text ("What will this story be about?" "Where will Susan find a rock painting?"). The students' relevant experience is also prepared ("carded") by vocabulary and classification operations. The teacher assists by grouping relevant experiences, providing words for these experiences, and developing word meanings through the discussion ("Are petroglyphs also rock paintings?" "What does 'charge admission' mean?" "Have you ever bought tickets for something?").

A period of silent reading signals the start of the text (T) phase. Students are then asked to evaluate the predictions made earlier and to discuss supporting details in the text ("Where did she find the painting?" "Was that the first place she looked?"). The teacher may have the students clarify nonpredicted text information and make connections among text ideas. Students are also asked to make inferences about the feelings and motives of story characters. Gradually, as students respond to text-implicit as well as text-explicit questions, their attention is shifted from text information back toward previous knowledge and experience (E).

During the relationship (R) phase, the teacher may ask questions that lead the students to relate text information to their own experiences ("How would you feel if people came to your back yard to see rock paintings?" "Would you charge admission?"). This step involves the use of text information to enhance, reorganize, or change existing meaning structures. Finally, the teacher asks questions leading students to make predictions about the next sections to be read ("What do you think Susan will do?"). The text and relationship phases of instruction continue in alternation until the end of the lesson.

In this way, the teacher assists the children through the steps required to comprehend narrative text. If instruction is to be effective, the teacher must provide neither too much nor too little assistance for student performance. The degree of teacher assistance required depends on the stage of students' metacognitive mastery of particular steps and phases in the model, with respect to a given text. That is, the E-T-R sequence is itself a metacognitive strategy that third-grade children have begun to master. Students' learning is assumed to have two aspects, cognitive and metacognitive (Au & Kawakami, 1984), and students move through both ZPDs with teacher assistance. Teachers assist performance of the metacognitive aspect with the same means of assistance ("What is the next thing to do? Right! Combine what you already know with what you just read.").

Teachers' questions that assist performance include a variety of levels that encourage speculation and relational statements that tie the text to previous experience, previous learning, and previous systems of meaning. In addition, teacher questions range from a narrow, factual focus to those involving generalization, analogy, and main idea.

Teacher assistance is responsive in terms of working at appropriate levels of difficulty. That is, teacher questioning should be challenging, but not discouragingly difficult. In fact, substantial proportions of teacher questions seem to strike this balance, being eventually but not immediately answered correctly by the children (Au & Kawakami, 1986).

Not only this semantic competence but also the students' systemic knowledge of written language, such as grammar, must be taught. Each Center One lesson devotes approximately one-third of its time to instruction of the systemic aspects of written language: sight vocabulary, phonics rules, spelling, and/or grammar. The ideal lesson draws its content from the text under study at the time.

A lengthy example of a third-grade E-T-R lesson on the social studies topic of the astronauts was presented in Chapter 3. In the interest of saving space, we shall reserve our final example for the next stage in the continuum. The lesson in Chapter 3 was a KEEP lesson taught to Navajo children by a Navajo teacher at a community school on a reservation in Arizona. Certain features of that example differ from those in such lessons taught to Hawaiian children in Honolulu or to Latino children in Los Angeles. These features involve the concept of participation structures.

Participation structures: culturally congruent conversation

Participation structures are differentiated by the nature of the rules governing speaking, listening, and turn-taking at different times in a speech event (Erickson & Schultz, 1977; Phillips, 1972; Schultz, Erickson, & Florio, 1982). Participation structures at home and school may well differ. For example, Heath (1982, 1983) studied black and white communities in the rural South. She reported little congruence between the black communities and their classrooms, but greater congruence between home and school participation structures in her white, middle-class sample, which practiced similar literacy-preparation routines at home and school.

The participation structures of American blacks, Native Americans, Hispanics, and Hawaiians have all been studied, and this work suggests that variations among cultures in participation structures may account for some minority-student problems in public schools (Cazden, 1986, p. 445). Specifically, it has been widely suggested that incongruent natal-culture and school-type participation structures confuse and disrupt minority-child participation and interest, so that children may not participate to the degree necessary for assistance to be provided in the ZPD. KEEP data and experience support this hypothesis.

The participation structures of the KEEP Center One lesson conducted in Hawaii are specifically designed to resemble those in "talk-story," a frequent and favorite informal conversation among adult members of Hawaiian culture (Au, 1980; Au & Jordan, 1981; Jordan, 1981a, 1981b, 1983). Center One and talk-story are both characterized by *overlapping speech, joint performance* (the cooperative production of responses) by a group, and *informal turn-taking*. The group-discussion pattern for Hawaiian children's instructional conversations is characterized by rapid-fire responses, liveliness, mutual participation, interruptions, overlapping volunteered speech, and joint narration. Children build on one another's responses to create a pattern of "group-speech." Teachers in the KEEP lesson do not require the children to speak one at a time, but allow them to cooperate with one another to frame answers to questions. These lessons encourage learning by allowing the children to engage in text discussion in participation structures compatible with those of the natal culture.

Au and Mason (1981) assessed the probable effects of culturally congruent participation structures on student learning. In a microanalysis of sample lessons, they found lessons incorporating congruent participation structures to be associated with higher rates of academically productive student behavior than lessons without such structures. Furthermore, within the congruent lessons, there were higher rates of academically productive student behavior at times when interaction was judged to be most congruent than when it was judged to be less so.

Of course, there are also differences between the Center One interactions and talk-story in the natal environment:

For example, the teacher ensures equal opportunities for each child to speak, over a period of days. However, she does not enforce a rigid turn-taking system, nor demand responses from a child who is not ready to participate, thus preserving the child-experienced informality of the enterprise that is necessary for the child's continued engagement with the lesson. (Jordan, 1981b, p. 18)

This combination of features means that during the reading lessons, children are able to engage in discussions in a *culturally compatible* if not culturally isomorphic participation structure (Au, 1980; Au & Jordan, 1981; Jordan, 1981b).

Navajo teachers with Navajo students conduct Center One lessons in quite a different structure of participation (Jordan et al., 1985; Tharp, in press). In the experimental Navajo school, each student speaks for longer periods in a more discursive manner. The other students wait courteously until a clear end is communicated; then another will take a similar turn. This pattern is readily observable in many formal Navajo events – school board or chapter meetings, faculty meetings, and indeed informal conversations and friendly chatting and gossip. A discussion pattern involving long, patient turn-taking has been the standard description of Native American meetings from the earliest recorded powwows to the contemporary Native American Church.

Native American story-telling is conducted with participation structures quite different from the talk-story of the Native Hawaiians. Wyatt (1978–1979) observes that among the Mt. Currie band (British Columbia), as opposed to usual school practices, "Story-telling in a community setting is . . . quite different. . . . It would be considered stifling to limit a story-teller to 20-minute sessions. . . . Children are expected to listen quietly, . . . not asked to recite the names of the main characters or to answer questions about plot, motivation, and moral" (Wyatt, 1978–1979, p. 23). Teachers who frequently interrupt narrative events with assessment questions produce a sharp cultural discongruity, a point also made by Phillips (1972, 1983) for the community and children of the Warm Springs Confederated Tribes (Oregon).

Very different participation structures characterize KEEP Center One lessons in these two cultures because very different participation structures characterize speech events in their homes and communities. This gives different textures to the surface of the lesson, and these two textures are highly important for reducing any friction between the styles of the students and the enterprise of the conversation. But underneath this surface there are the same load-bearing beams and trestles: the same means of assistance and the same processes of intersubjectivity, development of word meaning, E-T-R sequences, and the cognitive weaving of meaning and text.

The instructional conversation: variety in texts, contents, and grade levels

The instructional conversation, with its guiding metaphor of weaving, is by no means restricted to narrative, to young children, or even to written text. KEEP system developers have also sought to increase divergent or creative verbal thinking through conversation conducted during instruction in art. Such a prototype paint-and-clay art-instruction program has been tested for a number of semesters. By this instruction, divergent or creative thinking is increased and does generalize across modalities (Speidel & Pickens, 1979).

Content-area expository text should also be introduced to children in the early years and will come to dominate their reading time during the upper grades and into university levels. The weaving metaphor holds as well for expository text teaching as for narratives, and as well for eighth-graders as for kindergartners, as can be illustrated by the following transcript.

The transition to complex expository text: concept-text-application

The students in the lesson were in an eighth-grade remedial social science class, 90% Latino, and were reading four to five grade levels under the norm for their age group. The teacher was very new to the KEEP responsive-teaching patterns, but managed to make his assistance responsive and nicely within the ZPD. Shuy (1986) has praised the published excerpts of this lesson (Schneider et al., 1985) as a rare instance in which responsive teaching actually takes place. The teacher's achievements were in spite of the context: The school had been demonstrated by previous extensive observation to be dominated by the typical recitation-script pattern of nonteaching (Hyland, 1984).

The problems that develop in this lesson are those from which we can advance our understanding. Following the E-T-R heuristic, the teacher attempts to evoke the students' relevant experience (E) before turning to the text (T). His difficulties illustrate the problems that can arise when expository text involves the use of concepts that students have not yet crystallized sufficiently to use as warp on which new information can be woven.

Means of assistance: questioning

This lesson is based on part of an account of a Supreme Court decision in the case of *Minersville School District v. Gobitis* (Starr, 1978). The case involved a flag-salute controversy in which two children whose religious beliefs prohibited them from pledging allegiance were expelled from public school and forced to enroll in and pay fees to a private school.

Teacher: First of all, who could help us to review a little bit? I was here five days
        ago or last Friday – more than five days ago. What were some of the things
        that we got into?
Arturo: Freedom.
Teacher: Freedom. Dante, what else? Give me some examples of things we talked
        about.
        [Silence]
Teacher: Marcia?
Marcia: Religion.
Teacher: That was something we talked about. What was it all about?
Marcia: About church.
Teacher: Okay. What about church? I'm not sure what you have in mind. Give
        me an example.
Marcia: Religion. What they have to do.
Teacher: Tell me a little bit more. Give me an example.
Marcia: Like when they went to stand up for the flag.
Teacher: Okay. Dante, what does that have to do with the problem? Marcia
        reminded us that we talked about the idea of the flag salute and religion.
        What's that all about? What does that have to do with?
Dante: [Pause] They don't have to do things that other people do. If you're in a
        different religion . . .
Teacher: Dante, if you think back during all your years in school, do you know
        of anybody from a religion that might do some things differently?
Dante: [Shakes head no]
Teacher: Anybody familiar with a student or friend who might do things
        differently?
        [Silence]
Teacher: Marcia brought up the flag salute, but what are some other examples of
        things that are related to religion?
        [Inaudible from student]
Teacher: I think it was Pacita that talked about parties. What does that have to
        do with freedom? I'd like to talk about freedom.
        [Inaudible from student; apparently from Salina]
Teacher: Parties. You go to parties.
Salina: Yes.
Teacher: Oh, I thought you were going to say something. You were just telling me
        you go to parties. Well, okay, is there anything else that anybody wants to

Concept/	Word	Language-	Experience-	Concept-
experience	play	experience	text	text
		approach	relationship	application

Figure 7.5. The continuum of instructional strategies: IV.

bring up here about what we talked about last time? Everybody's clear? No questions? Louis, you got any questions?

Louis: No.

Teacher: You sure?

Louis: No.

Teacher: All right. I'm going to come back to this stuff, but it sounds like you want to get ahead. I have a feeling you guys want to push ahead into the next step, so . . . now I'm going to hand out a story to you.

The teacher may well be the one who wants to push into the next step, because this E phase is going nowhere. Two concepts needed for this lesson are listed by the students – religion and freedom – but there is no personal experience elicited that will assist the children to understand this complex case, with its implications for society and personal values. Indeed, the concept of "freedom" is degraded, through the students' limited everyday concept of freedom, into one of going to parties.

To deal with more complex text for which we cannot presume adequate everyday concepts already to be available to students, KEEP system developers have suggested a slightly different heuristic for the weaving of comprehension that they have labeled the concept-text-application method, or C-T-A (Figure 7.5) (Wong & Au, 1985). Although similar to E-T-R, the C-T-A heuristic suggests that the first stage (which is "experience" in the teaching of narratives) should be spent in calling up, introducing, and arraying the *concepts* that the expository text will require. The second, or text phase, is substantially the same as in the E-T-R; the text is reviewed and assimilated to the concepts.

Following this heuristic, the teacher would have presented the concepts of "religion" and "freedom" and "law" in more abstract terms, drawing on possible common knowledge from public events, as well as any personal knowledge.

In any event, the group has now completed reading a three-page section, and the instructional conversation resumes:

Means of assistance: questioning

Teacher: So . . . who can . . . what is this story about? What is this story about? Vincent?

Vincent: People from another religion didn't do the flag salute.

Teacher: Okay. Tell me something about the story. . . . You say "people". . . . Tell us some . . .

Vincent: Students from the school.

Teacher: Students from school? What's their names?

Vincent: Lillian Gobitis . . . and the brother William.

Teacher: Pensie, tell us something else about this story.

Pensie: [Pause; laughs] They got expelled for not . . . not saying the flag salute.

Teacher: Okay . . . Arturo, how many people got expelled? We're just trying to get the details out here, class. How many people are we talking about?

Arturo: Two.

Teacher: Two? Who can tell me something else about the story? [Pause] Salina?

Salina: They were Jehovah's Witnesses.

Teacher: Okay. And what does that mean?

Salina: They can't participate in some things . . . or . . .

Teacher: They can't participate in some things? Like what? What's the obvious thing they can't participate in?

Salina: Doing the flag salute.

Teacher: The flag salute. Okay. Something else about the story. [Pause] For example, Gordon . . . why can't they do the flag salute? What's that all about?

Gordon: Cause they're from a different religion.

Teacher: Uh huh. Okay, but there's lots of different religions. What's that all about? Why is it that they wouldn't be able to do the flag salute? What's involved there?

Gordon: I don't know.

Teacher: Anybody? Why is it they can't do the flag salute? According to the story . . .

Jamie: Because they broke the law.

Teacher: How's that?

Jamie: [Shrugs; pause]

Teacher: Jamie says they broke a law. Did they break a law?

Arturo: Yes.

Teacher: How's that?

Arturo: Cause everybody is supposed to do the flag salute, and they didn't do it.

Teacher: So according to the story, what happened to them in the story?

Jamie: They had to go to a private school.

Through careful, narrow-band questioning, the teacher is assembling a group comprehension of the text. They have reached a ceiling, however, and the teacher (correctly) decides that the students cannot go much further until they improve their inadequate memory of the facts in the matter. Therefore, he soon returns the students to the text to retrieve more information:

Teacher: Tell us more about that. Who told them to go to a private school?
Jamie: [Inaudible] Kicked them out and expelled them.
Teacher: Who did that to them? According to what you read in the story, who did that?
Students: [Chorus] Teachers. Parents. Courts.
Teacher: I got teachers, parents, courts. . . . Did everybody read the same story here? Pensie?
Pensie: From the school . . .
Teacher: A school. Pensie was correct. I think she was looking for . . .
Pensie: I can't pronounce it.
Teacher: Spell me the word, so I can know what you're looking at. What is it?
Pensie: It's spelled M-i-n-e-r-s-v-i-l-l-e.
Teacher: Okay. That's the name of the town. Good. Minersville. Louis, tell me something else about the story. We know there are two kids. We know they didn't say the flag salute. We know they lived in Minersville. What else?
Louis: They went to court.
Teacher: They went to court. What happened in the court?
Louis: They were talking about how come they didn't do the flag salute.

After about 15 turns, during which the teacher tries with little success to clarify the motivations of the various characters in the drama, the teacher moves to assist the students' understanding by a series of narrowly focused questions that take the students forward a small step at a time. In this instance, the teacher also uses some feedback and contingency management:

> *Means of assistance: questioning, feeding-back, contingency management*

Teacher: Okay. I think you're on the trail here. Marta, what does it mean, supreme authority? What are they talking about there? [Pause, silence] You guys have read a story, right? I'm asking what this story is about? So far, I know it's about two kids. I know these two kids didn't do what?
Students: [Chorus] The flag salute.
Unidentified student: Religious people.
Teacher: About religious people. Okay. Right? Is everybody with me? Now my question to you is, what's the problem?
Arturo: The problem is they didn't do the flag salute.
Teacher: But what's the problem about that? Lot of people don't do the flag salute.
Arturo: Cause there was a law in school.
Teacher: OHHHH! RIGHT! You got a law in the school. And where else do you have a law?
Arturo: In the church.
Teacher: A law in the church. Thank you, Arturo. You're pushing us forward here. So we got two laws here. What does that mean? What's the problem?

Pensie: They don't know which one . . .
Teacher: What?
Pensie: They don't know which one to um . . .
Teacher: Pensie, you gotta finish your sentence, I know you're saying something.
    I'm not sure . . .
Pensie: Uh, they don't know which one to obey.

This is a gratifying example of a group of students and teacher, none of whom is accustomed to instructional conversation as a means of instruction, gradually building a common understanding and the schooled concepts of law, religion, and freedom.

We now leave this example and briefly conclude the discussion of the C-T-A heuristic for the instructional conversation around complex expository text. At the juncture between the text and application phases, it is worthwhile to include some summarizing, synthesizing, and speculating about the text. During the final stage, application, students apply their new knowledge in follow-up activities:

These may be very simple, taking perhaps only a half hour of class time, or more elaborate, stretching across several weeks. Possibilities include writing group or individual reports incorporating information from tradebooks and the encyclopedia, making a display or mural, or sharing information learned orally with the rest of the class. In our example, the children polled their classmates to see how many thought the Loch Ness monster was real. They then made a bar graph to display the results. (Mason & Au, 1986, p. 202)

These follow-up activities that affirm, practice, expand, and strengthen the new knowledge are vital to the maturation of discourse competence in the domain. Follow-up applications are emphasized in the KEEP heuristic of C-T-A, not in E-T-R. However, the embedding of the instructional conversation, even around story text, in joint productive activity is the ideal condition for teaching language, literacy, and thinking skills. Expository text may lend itself more readily than narrative text to such application. For these reasons, among others, we believe that the KEEP system has emphasized story text over expository text unduly in grades from kindergarten through third grade – an opinion shared by external evaluators (Calfee et al., 1981), the Navajo teaching corps of KEEP, and other KEEP system developers (e.g., Mason & Au, 1986, p. 195):

Seen only as a laundry list of theorems in a workbook, science can be a bore. *But as a "hands-on" adventure guided by a knowledgeable teacher,* it can sweep children up in the excitement of discovery. Taught by the regular classroom teacher, it can illustrate the point that science is for everyone – not just scientists. (Bennett, 1986, p. 27; emphasis added)

These principles apply not only to science but also to every domain of concern in the schools' curricula. The thinking-skills movement, for example, will succeed in the long run only if prescribed student work can be incorporated into an instructional conversation, modified to suit individual needs, redirected in flight by a responsive teacher, and followed by meaningful joint productive activity. In the KEEP system, the instructional conversation has been used as the setting for teaching the CoRT system (Crowell, Aka, Blake, Choy, & Mai-Chun, in press; de Bono, 1973). Many newly developed thinking-skills programs allow for conversational instruction; those that do not are likely to be soon discarded, as has been the eventual fate of all previous "teacher-proof" drill systems. The source of strength in existing thinking-skills programs probably lies in the productive activities designed to support them.

Whatever the subject matter, the materials, the content, or the nature of the text, the productive activity that incorporates new knowledge is the final stage in the activity settings for teaching word and discourse meanings. The activity lets the discourse be used, and this completes the weaving metaphor: What was woven can now be worn.

The continuing conversation: discourse with texts

In considering the instructional conversation, there is one last activity setting still to be discussed: the individual reader with a book. The self is a major source of assistance for all performances, and so it is with comprehending text. Thinking about text is an instance of Vygotsky's "unique social interaction" of discourse with the self (see Chapter 2). In the KEEP system, time, space, and resources are made available for the activity setting that contains only a child and an author speaking through a book.

In these settings, the conversation is not only with the self but also with the book. In all ages and stages of human development, the literate life can be seen as continuing discourse with text. Learning to carry out discourse with text can begin early, and it should. Eventually, it becomes the most common activity setting for learning; in graduate school and beyond, individual learning from text is the occasion for lifetime acquisition of new information and analytic tools. That learning, too, is through discourse. We dispute text, we praise it, we may throw it to the floor, we write on it, so intense is the urge to engage it in conversation. Good text is like a conversational companion; it does speak back to us and is responsive to our available schemas of understanding. Flaubert and Thomas Jefferson do not say the same things to us at age 50 as they urged at 25.

Some years ago, two of our fine students, who were at that time quite young, during an audience with the revered Buddhist spiritual leader the Dalai Lama, asked (Hilgers & Molloy, 1981, p. 195):

Student: I wonder if you have in your past any people who were important . . . teachers . . . or a kind of master that you think about now?
The Dalai Lama: Those Indian pundits! Many centuries back . . .
Student: No, I mean someone who influenced you when you were a child or a younger man, who was a master to you, and you his disciple.
The Dalai Lama: Yes . . . the great Indian pundits of the past many centuries.
Student: But no one living? I mean, not an actual person?
The Dalai Lama: No. You see, those living persons, they are just carrying the messages of the great Indian pundits . . .

Through text, the pundits speak to us through many centuries. More important, they speak *with* us. We venture to say that the conversation among the pundits and the Dalai Lama continues and grows in depth.

Assisted performance in the instructional conversation appears first on the interpersonal plane, between people; it then appears on the intrapsychological plane, as cognitive process. We are taught to speak with text by speaking with others about text, and in this way we are taught how to learn by speaking with text.

That instructional conversation continues until we ourselves each fall silent. Literate men and women continue to experience the world anew, and they do not cease to read. The woven understanding is a constantly changing cloth.

8   The orchestration of activity settings: learning and social interaction in the whole group and independent centers

If the instructional conversation is so essential for cognitive growth during schooling, why is it so seldom implemented? Why does the ubiquitous recitation script continue?

Shuy goes to the root of the matter by suggesting that these matters have "little to do with learning and or teaching as such, but instead grow out of economic interests. Teachers faced with thirty or more students in one classroom find it difficult to dialogue in an effective way with one student in any developmentally productive way" (Shuy, 1986, p. 3).

Again we see that effective teaching can occur only in a context of effective schooling. Effective schooling means the design of productive activity settings, and that requires major additions of resources, or major changes in their deployment. Although we all know that more teaching personnel are needed by schools, there are also improvements available if better priorities are adopted and better design of classrooms is achieved. For example, even with typical resources, if the teacher dialogues with a small group of students, many of the benefits of the instructional conversation will accrue. The teacher can be freed to engage in small-group discussions only if the other students are meanwhile engaged in productive activity settings.

Activity settings of the classroom must be orchestrated to allow instructional conversations, joint productive activity, and assistance to performance in the ZPD. In this chapter we discuss the other two activity-setting types that are necessary in the conduct of effective schooling: whole-group settings and independent-group settings.

Orchestration of the settings is vital because each setting is dependent on the others. Each activity setting gives rise to important teaching opportunities and, at the same time, to particular management problems. For example, behavior-management issues most often arise in the whole-group setting because the larger numbers of children are more difficult to control by topics of individual interest or by intense teacher attention.

161

Thus, it is necessary to systematically manage student deportment. This increases the burden on adults who assist; they must maintain order at the same time that they secure student participation in learning tasks.

The whole-group setting is also the setting in which the proclivity of peers to engage and assist each other is not helpful, but disruptive. Peer-oriented behaviors must be kept in check until they can be channeled into the proper activity setting – peer learning centers, where behaviors that are troublesome in the whole-group setting can be encouraged.

"Independent centers" are activity settings with enormous potential for assisting the performance of students through the involvement of peers. But however significant peer assistance becomes in a school program, it cannot substitute entirely for assistance by teachers. Educational research is clear on this point: Effective instruction requires teacher-assisted lessons (Brophy & Good, 1986; Ellis & Rogoff, 1982), in which the teacher sets the agenda and ensures that students learn and practice through assisted performance. Independent learning centers and teacher-led small groups are the two activity settings with maximum potential for assistance in the ZPD. But for their potential to be realized, the third activity setting – the whole group of children with one teacher – must function smoothly.

In each setting, students are moved through their ZPDs by the means of assistance and the sources of assistance that have been discussed throughout this volume. However, each setting is characterized by different patterns of means and sources, and each must orchestrate them differently to achieve the educational goals.

The whole group

Who

The "whole group" encompasses the teacher and all the children of the class.

What

The whole-group setting is used to orient the children to their independent-center activities for the day and to instruct them in any new skills and procedures required to perform their independent tasks. The whole-group setting is also used for music or theater instruction, ceremonies, and the like. On an ad hoc basis, it is used for class-wide problem-solving on a social or value level. Among the most frequent uses of the whole-group setting are opening the classroom's morning and opening home-work review.

The most typical pattern is a group of children all of whom are facing the teacher, who is lecturing – explaining, modeling, or instructing. Sometimes the whole group of children will recite; sometimes the teacher will engage members of the group in dialogue. More rarely, there is a whole-group discussion, but full participation is as hard to manage for children as for any adult large group. The teacher may also dismiss the large group by assigning everyone some task and then observing them and commenting on their performance.

When

At KEEP, the 20-min whole-group activity begins each day and ends it. The ad hoc problem-solving sessions are scheduled most often in midafternoon. But for many schools, the whole-group setting is the only activity setting, and it lasts the entire instructional day.

Where

The whole group meets in the classroom, but there may be considerable variation. Younger children often sit on the floor, with the teacher facing them, but they may also sit in chairs at their different tables. For special purposes, the whole group may improvise appropriate locations, as on field trips.

Why

On the good functioning of the whole group rests the prospects of the entire day. This is because no teacher can conduct the small-group lessons of Center One unless the independent centers operate smoothly. But for the peers of the independent centers to function smoothly, they must know each day's tasks and goals. They must know and accept the basic system of rotation through different centers and tasks. They must be able to function both independently and cooperatively as need arises. Each must operate as a member with the shared values and goals of the entire class membership.

To create this intersubjectivity – as well as foster an understanding of general instructions, the use of listening skills, the development of artistic expression, and the building of group solidarity, cooperation, identity, and values – teachers depend on the activity setting of the whole-class group.

Problems in the whole group

In many public schools, teacher–pupil ratios may be 30 to 1, or worse. In such whole groups, success depends heavily on the teacher's ability to manage student behavior. Independent centers and Center One have their own challenges for student management, but as we shall discuss later, they are quite different from those required in the whole group.

Few teachers have been trained specifically to manage whole groups in ways that assist performance and learning. The following descriptions, drawn from our field notes, illustrate the problems that can arise in whole-group settings. One teacher is in her first year, but the other is a veteran.

1. A first grade in an urban community

The noise level is high – children's chattering punctuated by "pow pow," "varoom," and the whacking of sticks on the work tables. Each child appears to own a little stick with a tiny pennant on one end; the other end fits into a soft clay ball. Few children are on task. They talk, try to balance their sticks on their noses, and leave their chairs for destinations unknown.

"Allright, freeze! Freeze, one two three!" the teacher calls out smartly over the din. The cacophony drops slightly in volume, but the children continue with their activities as if no directive has been issued. One boy continues to walk across the floor, chin forward, sneaking up on some prey.

"Remember, this is quiet," comments the teacher giving encouragement to the decreased amount of noise. "I want . . . ," she continues, but her words cannot be distinguished over the din. A chunky boy waves his stick, seeking the teacher's attention while conferring with a classmate. The clay ball thuds onto the table.

"I want you to work quietly," the teacher admonishes everyone again. Replacing the clay ball, the boy resumes flagging for help, but down falls the clay again. The teacher's voice stops. The lad gives up waving for attention: He has become distracted by the activities of his buddy. The noise level is back to what it was before the teacher tried to stop it.

2. A kindergarten class in a rural community

According to the teacher, a few of the 28 kindergartners in her class were well behaved, but the majority – from the first bell in the morning to the end of the school day – ignored her so completely that she was unable to complete a single lesson. During one observation session, the teacher began by singing a song to gain the interest and attention of the children; they were to respond with a chorus. The students' responses varied: one boy continued to circle the room on a skateboard; one girl threw blocks at her tablemates; two boys continued to play on the lawn just outside the room, ignoring the teacher's demands to come and sit down; four other boys were totally absorbed in a contest to determine who could scoot across the room without leaving their chairs. Under a portable chalkboard, a boy was fending off a long stick expertly wielded by a small girl who punctuated her thrusts with loud taunts.

During these episodes, many of the classmates were attentive and ready to begin. But, when the teacher went to retrieve the boys on the lawn, two of the attentive children began to fight so vigorously that the teacher returned immediately to stop them. The boys on the lawn stayed there. While the teacher scolded the pugilists, the skateboard boy crashed into a table, sending a half dozen classmates fleeing for safety. The teacher abandoned the fighters to physically move the skateboarder into a circle of children, all the while reprimanding him.

This pattern continued for the entire 30 minutes of observation, during which time the teacher conducted no lessons, praised no child, and delivered one reprimand per minute.

These episodes, adapted from MacDonald & Gallimore (1971), may sound extreme, but we have repeatedly observed similar "activity settings" (Gallimore, Boggs, & Jordan, 1974; Lenz & Gallimore, 1973; MacDonald & Gallimore, 1971; Tharp & Wetzel, 1969). Like those many others, neither of the teachers in these two excerpts had had training in classroom management, and neither conceived of their control problems in terms of the strategies and tactics they personally employed.

Virtually every teacher with whom we have worked has had problems gaining control and managing student behavior, particularly with at-risk children. Many have found it the single most difficult task of their first year. Many have felt guilt and failure because so much time and energy had to be given over to "discipline."

A majority of young teachers report that they were ill-prepared for this aspect of teaching by their university education and preservice training. Veenman (1984), even though confining his review of young teachers' complaints to work published after 1960, located 83 studies (of which 55 were from the United States). Twenty-four different problems were reported in these 83 studies. Ranked first was *classroom discipline*; 85% of the studies reported it to be a problem for beginning teachers. Ranked second, and reported in 53% of the studies, was *student motivation*, which, as we shall see, is merely the problem's obverse.

In Hawaii, we studied a group of 81 teachers of Hawaiian children, who listed 552 discipline problems that they wanted to solve. Of the 552, 160 involved class rules (keep class clean, have pencil and paper, follow directions, etc.), 113 involved work rules (attend and complete lessons), and 85 involved class etiquette (avoid rudeness to teachers and other students, do not destroy work of others, do not steal). Only 13 teachers (in a low-income, minority school district) mentioned academic or learning-related issues. The vast majority of complaints involved problems in managing students in whole-group situations. Few teachers made any use of peer centers or small groups (MacDonald & Gallimore, 1971, p. 153).

Improving the situation through in-service training has not been simple to arrange. In many schools it has been the course of prudence for a teacher to tolerate difficulties in a classroom, because admitting the problem to the principal has brought punishment more often than assistance. To researchers who offered consultation, teachers were less reluctant to admit management problems, which were then most often blamed on working conditions or on the students' families and cultural backgrounds.

Even brief training in behavior management can have an effect. After 10 weeks of classroom- and behavior-management training, the same teachers of Hawaiian children were again asked to list the problems they wished to work on. This time, nearly half the problems were related to academic matters (MacDonald & Gallimore, 1971).

This sequence has been repeated many times, in many places, with many teachers, including those in the KEEP system. First, teachers are reluctant to detail their management problems. Once they admit them, the problems for which they want help are very similar. The solution is the development of a repertoire of behavior-management strategies based on the sources and means of assisting student performance. Once these abilities are acquired, the teachers are able to turn their attention to teaching the curriculum, and they do.

It is ironic that the details of this effective repertoire of management strategies have been known for some time (Tharp & Wetzel, 1969) and indeed have become standard treatment for individual problem children. Yet when such preservice or in-service training is offered, it is likely to be to special education, not general elementary teachers. How general classroom teachers can be assisted in gaining a repertoire of behavior-management strategies is the topic of Chapters 9–11. Our immediate purpose is to insist that teachers be listened to: They desperately need these skills, and until training and support are provided, education will continue its "dirty little secret" – too many classrooms, and especially those of minority at-risk children, are filled with daydreams, drug dreams, or chaos.

Assisting performance in the whole group

In assisting students to adapt to the classroom and to the whole group, KEEP teachers use the full range of the means of assistance: verbal instruction, cognitive structuring, modeling of desirable behaviors by teacher and peers, questioning, feeding-back, and contingency management, yielding positive (and occasionally negative) consequences both to groups and individuals. The behavior-management repertoire includes frequent and accurate visual scanning of the classroom (Sloat, Tharp, & Gallimore, 1977; Tharp & Gallimore, 1976b).

The behavior-management strategy provides teachers with the tools to feel confidence in their ability to deal with disruption, inattention, and other common behavior problems. At the same time, the emphasis is on maintaining a positive atmosphere, keeping the task rate high, and minimizing the need for management actions by the teacher.

The patterns of assistance are somewhat different according to the age of the students and the time of the year. For entering kindergarten children, an extended period of socialization is a regular part of the program. Children need an orderly framework in which to pursue their learning. The children are not expected to arrive at school already displaying the complex array of cooperative and individually managed sequences of actions necessary to the smooth operation of a center-based classroom. It is the teacher's task to assist them to learn those understandings and habits, rather than demand them. Thus, for example, in the first few days of their school lives, children are taught the rules and the rest of the social system that make up the classroom and school:

Means of assistance: instructing, modeling, managing contingencies

Mrs. Ah Ho has instructed each of the new kindergartners to find the cubby hole with his or her name on it, in which to place the bag full of belongings each has brought from home. Bending over, hands on her knees, so that she is at same height as the children, Mrs. Ah Ho smiles encouragingly as she watches their efforts with interest.

"Good! Dean found his," she says quietly but enthusiastically, as she moves to help the boy. While standing behind him, gently assisting his small arms to rearrange his paper bag so it will fit into the hole, Mrs. Ah Ho monitors the activities of two little girls nearby who are shoving their sacks into cubby holes.

"Good girl, Jackie, you found yours," Mrs. Ah Ho says as the girl approaches her.

Means of assistance: questioning, managing contingencies

"Jim David," the teacher calls out. Jim David immediately rises from his chair and strides toward her.

"Ooooooooh," she warns in a stage whisper. "What did you forget?" The boy slows down. After he arrives by her side, the teacher bends down and cups the back of his head gently in her hand.

"What did you forget?" she asks him softly. "You forgot something. What did you forget?" He pauses thoughtfully, faces about, and returns to his table to push in his chair. When he turns to look, the teacher smiles, and when he comes back to her side she touches him on the back.

After the first few weeks, the amount of time spent on socialization diminishes sharply. During the first 2 to 5 weeks of each school year, KEEP teachers attend, as needed, to developing desirable classroom comportment. The proportion of academic content is gradually increased as the children learn and relearn classroom rules and routines. All the means of assistance are employed, including for younger children a heavy reliance on feedback and various forms of contingent reinforcement, notably verbal praise and physical affection (hugs, etc.).

The KEEP behavior management system's goal is to make children responsible for themselves and their actions by enabling them to become independent learners. The positive motivational system creates a cooperative social climate, reinforces desirable performance, and minimizes the negative learning processes. Teacher attention is a powerful reinforcer for children ... when teachers direct their attention to desirable behavior, they increase the likelihood of that behavior being repeated. Similarly, the negative attention of punishment is likely to increase undesirable behavior ... interfere with learning, and lower children's self-esteem.

Example: A first strategy for meeting milder forms of undesirable behavior is to ignore it. A second strategy is to praise the desirable alternative that can be seen in another child or children. A third strategy is to use a desist statement and re-instructions, followed by reinforcement for a return to compliance. Desists should be, in ordinary circumstances, used only if strategies one and two have failed. Behavior maintained by other students' reactions is not likely to be affected by ignoring it; immediate intervention is sometimes necessary. ...

Example: A teacher may find hugs, pats, smiles & winks, and expressions of affection are effective for younger children. Older students, especially boys, may respond more to smiles, jokes, and winks. (Center for Development of Early Education, 1986, pp. 49–51)

For older children, the use of praise for deportment drops to trace levels and is observed only when a disruption occurs. For the older children, positive teacher comments are more likely addressed to academic performance. For these children and for older students into junior high and high school, means of assistance other than contingency management become more prominent.

Prominent among these other means of assistance are instructing and cognitive structuring. For example, KEEP-influenced studies in junior high school confirm the importance of instructing as a principal means of assisting students in classroom activity settings. Teachers who provide a clear instruction at the beginning of a history period, for instance, have much less trouble engaging students in the daily assignments (Hyland, Gallimore, & Schneider, in press). Studies of opening homework review (Berliner, 1986; Leinhardt & Greeno, 1986) found that visual scanning and well-scripted routines were important features used by experts. In their study of classroom openings that characterize experienced effective teachers of the seventh grade, Brooks and Hawke (1985) find the same two features; they suggest that an important feature used by effective teachers is to include in the address to the students critical behavioral and academic expectations.

When described as abstract principles, this calculated use of praise, structuring, instructing, and other forms of performance assistance may

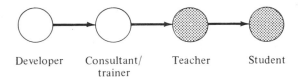

Developer Consultant/ Teacher Student
trainer

Figure 8.1. Sources of assistance.

convey a mechanistic tone that is not, in fact, felt in the classroom. Some illustrations:

Means of assistance: modeling and managing contingencies

"I like the way Center 3 is doing their work," the teacher says from her seat at the reading group. Children at other centers turn to look at Center 3, a ripple of heads turn back to tasks, and some children who were daydreaming begin to work.

Means of assistance: instructions and managing contingencies

The teacher looks sternly at a kindergarten boy. She turns her head as if to signal. He looks at her, puzzled. She points. He continues to stare, as if by returning her gaze it will come to him. Finally, she says, "Joseph, put your leg back on. Someone can trip on it."

He smiles, and moves toward the artificial limb he had left by Center 4. A little later, she approaches Joseph, smiles, and says, "Good." This teacher usually remembers, somehow, to acknowledge a child's efforts to comply after a reprimand.

Means of assistance: managing contingencies

Ms. Bogert looks up from the text she is reading with Center One. She looks around at the independent work centers. Two boys who have been talking loudly enough to attract her attention make eye contact with the teacher. She smiles. Both look down at their papers and resume work. A few moments later they are talking again, this time one is asking the other about the assigned task. A few moments later, the teacher calls the boys by name, and says, "Thanks for getting back to work!" The boys smile.

Sources of assistance in the whole group

In the whole-group activity setting, the teacher is the predominant source of assistance (Figure 8.1). Aides may sometimes be present and participate in instruction, but the sources of assistance are almost entirely the teacher-folk; much less often is assistance provided by books, manuals, or peers. Very rarely we have observed some peer assistance, but this ordinarily has been in periods of transition into or out of the whole group or when each member of the whole group has been working independently under the teacher's floating supervision. Here is a nice, if rare, example of the exception, when a peer provided assistance, unsolicited by the teacher:

Means of assistance: instructions, modeling, managing contingencies

A teacher is struggling to explain to a boy how to get his partner to ask a series of questions so he can complete his assignment. "Ask your partner, 'what color is my hair?'"

"Black," he says quietly.

"No, you ask *her* what color is your hair. Ask her: 'What color is my hair?',", insists the teacher.

The boy mumbles something. The teacher repeats her instruction, but he still cannot comprehend what he is to do.

Laura, a girl from another table, has been observing the proceedings and now springs into action.

"Like dis," as she taps him on the shoulder to get his attention. When he turns, she demonstrates the proper action by speaking to Kelly, who is sitting across from him. To Kelly, Laura says, "What color is my hair?" Kelly says "Black." Then the boy understands, and he also asks, "What color is my hair?"

The teacher smiles, thanks the helpful girl, pats her on the back, and says "good job!"

The deliberate management of classroom behavior

Much of the objection to planned, deliberate classroom management is based on an extreme Orwellian vision that has sometimes been stimulated by behavior-modification texts. We see the teacher's deliberate, strategic use of performance assistance as a means of eliciting capacities and behaviors that are a part of a child's natural repertoire developed in the natal culture. Tharp (1979) has argued that one of the principal errors of the early applications of behavior modification was its presumption that new behaviors were to be created whenever a problem arose. Thus, if a group of children displayed inattention to schoolwork, the standard practice was to use a *universal* (or *etic*) definition of attention, arrange the contingencies, apply the consequences, and count the responses. In the case of cultural minorities, the odor of imperialism was unmistakable. In counterpoint, Tharp made a case of observing children in their natal activity settings and identifying existing cultural repertoires that could be elicited through designing activity settings and using the means of assistance within them:

Careful, personal, participating observation is the method that can lead to understanding of children. . . . We must not make the mistake of thinking we have to *create* behaviors, our task is rather to *find* them . . . ethnography allowed us to *find* the repertoires of work, responsibility-taking, and participation, and to *find* the setting events which allow them to occur. Then, the behavior-change strategy is to change the school-environment to more resemble those natural setting-events. The desirable behaviors will then, naturally and lawfully, occur. (Tharp, 1979, p. 15; italics in original)

Tharp discussed Hawaiian children who come to school unaccustomed to attending to a single adult, but not lacking the attentional and motivational capacities needed to learn from assisted performance (Gallimore et al., 1974). The trick is to elicit these capacities by using patterns of teacher assistance that are compatible with their natal culture (see Jordan, 1985, for a general discussion of cultural compatibilities in educational program design). One form of assistance, not common in the Hawaiian culture, but compatible with it, is adult praise of child behavior. The responsiveness of Hawaiian students to teacher praise and other positive acts is among the most widely documented findings of our 20 years of research (see reviews by Gallimore et al., 1974; Tharp & Gallimore, 1976b; Tharp, Jordan, et al., 1984).

But there is more to this praising of children than mechanical dispensation of positive words. For the deliberate use of praise to be effective, it must rest on a personal, affective link between child and adult. The praises must be genuine, and they must be dispensed fairly and consistently. To use the children's own terminology, the teacher must prove to be both "nice" and "tough" for Hawaiian children to judge that teacher worthy of respect and obedience (D'Amato, 1981b).

To be "nice" means being warm and nurturant. It means dispensing social reinforcement such as touches, hugs, and pats to younger children, and praise and approval to older children (D'Amato, 1981b; Jordan & Tharp, 1979). Help must be provided when needed, but without being "bossy" (D'Amato, 1981b). The teacher must avoid punishing minor offenses and allow a touch of rascality (Jordan & Tharp, 1979). It is important that teachers, like Hawaiian parents, allow their children to "win" a little; when they must lose, it must not cost too much of their pride or status (D'Amato, 1981b, 1982). The temptation to overcontrol must be resisted, and children must be allowed some measure of that independence in their own activity that they have been socialized in the natal culture to expect and manage.

To be "tough" means to be firm, clear, and consistent in insisting that children obey prescriptions for classroom conduct and comply with teacher directions and requests (D'Amato, 1981b; Jordan & Tharp, 1979). It is especially important that sanctions and negative consequences applied to rule-breakers be carried out without loss of teacher emotional control.

More recently, Jordan and associates (1985) have demonstrated that behavior management among other cultural groups must be retailored. For example, the frequency and intensity of teacher responses must be

toned down for Navajo children, for whom a wider range of uncoopera-
tive behavior may be best left ignored. Classroom-management skills, to
be effective, must be sensitive to individual children as well as to their
cultures. Such techniques are not mechanistic or manipulative. On the
contrary, these teacher skills create an atmosphere of positive regard,
teacher affection, and classroom warmth.

The effects of systematic classroom management

The impact of teacher praise (and other positive responses) on student
industriousness was thoroughly evaluated early in the KEEP system
(Tharp & Gallimore, 1976b). On average, KEEP teachers have been
observed to give significantly more praise and less criticism as compared
with groups of teachers in local schools and on the mainland (Tharp &
Gallimore, 1976b). Although some stars, tokens, and privileges are dispensed contingently, the KEEP management system relies in the earlier
grades on the reinforcing effects of hugs, smiles, and praises, and, as the
children grow older, on public, verbal recognition of progress and
diligence.

To conduct our systematic evaluations of behavior management, we
used a nine-category teacher-behavior observation schedule. In most conditions, only three of those categories occurred with sufficient frequency
and variance to be analyzed. These are (a) *management praise* for
"deportment" behaviors, (b) *academic praise* for learning-task-related
behaviors, and (c) *verbal negatives* (scolds or desists) for unacceptable
behaviors.

Over the years, interobserver reliabilities varied, but were overall .81
for observers located in the classrooms or behind one-way glass. We
believe observations of our own teachers to be externally valid: Observers
stood unseen in an observation deck equipped with a one-way mirror and
an extensive ceiling microphone system. Most often, teachers were
unaware of the exact times of observation. They worked continuously in
this fishbowl, and the reactivity effects provided a constant condition.

For control-group teachers, we observed within the classroom, and
reactivity effects were undoubtedly strong. Presuming that reactivity
worked in the usual way (increasing socially approved behaviors and
decreasing socially disapproved behaviors), its effects would serve to
reduce the differences between control and KEEP teachers. Therefore, the
differences we obtained are likely to err toward underestimates.

Control subjects were selected at random. The necessary *quid pro quo*
arrangements with these teachers limited both the numbers and locations
available. However, they ranged in distance from near neighbors to teach-

Table 8.1. *Overall means of teacher approval and disapproval per 15 min of observation*

School	Academic praise	Comportment praise	Total praise	Verbal negative
KEEP				
Mean	21.80	13.87	35.67	2.07
SD	15.27	16.06		3.10
Comparison schools				
Mean	6.03	.65	6.68	6.01
SD	4.93	.54		3.81

ers on other islands in the Hawaiian chain, from rural to urban, from large to small classrooms. However, all had largely Hawaiian pupils of the same ages as our own. Praise rates by teachers varied by age of child (White, 1975), by time of year, by subject matter, and so forth. Therefore, when making comparisons, we paired control-subject data with observations on KEEP teachers taken on the same day (or, when those data were unavailable, the nearest adjacent day), during similar activities, and with children of the same age. More details are available in two technical reports (Antill & Tharp, 1975; Tharp & Gallimore, 1976b).

For economy's sake, we present here only a summary of all available comparisons of KEEP and control data. The unit of analysis is the frequency of three types of teacher behavior during 15-min intervals.

On average, KEEP teachers gave significantly more praise than did teachers in local comparison schools (Table 8.1); in comparison with "mainland" normative data (White, 1975), the KEEP rates were notably higher (Tharp & Gallimore, 1976b). The preponderance of social reinforcement and other forms of performance assistance was directed toward groups of children rather than individuals. Statistical analysis confirmed the differences between KEEP and the comparison schools. KEEP teachers displayed significantly higher rates of academic praise [$t(6) = 3.15$, $p < .025$], management praise [$t(6) = 3.55$, $p < .01$], and total praise [$t(6) = 3.72$, $p < .01$].

The appropriate use of teacher praise should result in increases in those behaviors praised by the teacher. This proposition is difficult to demonstrate in a normal classroom setting, but in our reseach-and-development program it was possible to collect both contingency-management data and data on children's performance of behaviors that the teachers valued.

These valued behaviors vary and can include completing math sheets, reading a story, listening attentively, and even standing in line. We describe children who are engaging in these teacher-valued behaviors as being "on task." Our on-task measure is closer to what has been described as "academic engaged time," in contrast to "academic allocated time" (Rosenshine & Berliner, 1978). The overall category is "doing what the teacher values at this moment." In other words, on-task behavior consists in following the prescribed curriculum. In common language, it is called *industriousness.* Our hypothesis was that appropriate teacher praise causes the pupil on-task rate to increase. Although causality could not be proved, covariation between teacher praise and child on-task rates could be examined.

On-task observations were made by searching for each child in turn by name and recording his/her behavior as on task, off task, or disruptive (defined as interfering with the work of others). This enabled us to keep longitudinal data for each child. Typically, there were three observation sessions per day, with three consecutive searches per observation, yielding nine data points per day per child.

On-task rates for the KEEP students have averaged about 85%, about 20% higher than for average comparison classrooms (Tharp & Gallimore, 1976b). Data from four comparison schools are available. The range for KEEP was from 84% to 92% of children on task. At the comparison schools, the range was from 60% to 82%. The difference between the combined KEEP and comparison schools was statistically significant. In 1985–86, on-task rates in kindergarten classes throughout the KEEP system exceeded 90% (Farran & Cunningham, 1987).

Learning to assist performance in the whole-group setting is a difficult task. In the next three chapters of this volume, which deal with assisting teachers to develop, we use as a principal example the development of behavior-management skills.

The disadvantages of whole-group activity settings

The whole group is probably the most frequent activity setting in American and Canadian classrooms. The whole-group setting is well suited to the recitation script, which is so highly characteristic of "instruction." The most familiar and often the most comfortable for teachers, the whole-group setting is not the most comfortable for children. In KEEP kindergarten classrooms, for example, data taken in 1986 indicate that the whole-group setting entails about twice the amount of control talk by the teacher as the small-group setting. The necessity to engage in such frequent control of children indicates their restiveness and reflects a situation surely more stressful for teacher and children alike (D'Amato & Inn, 1987).

The whole-group setting is also inequitable in its opportunities for participation. In the whole group, the lower-ability children suffer from insufficient opportunity to speak; such individual opportunities as do exist for teaching/learning interactions with the teacher fall disproportionately to the more able students (Herreshoff & Speidel, 1987).

Finally, responsiveness is less likely to occur in the whole-group setting. It is evident that there is less opportunity to relate individually to children when there is a sea of faces before the teacher. But the problem compounds: Individual contact with children, so unlikely and so unfairly distributed in the whole group, is necessary for the teacher even to maintain accurate assessment. In the whole group, therefore, she cannot respond responsively to children even when she gets an opportunity, because she interacts with them too seldom to really know them (Farran, 1987).

Although whole-group settings are indispensable for certain tasks, exclusive reliance on them prevents accurate assessment and denies opportunities to provide assistance. To maximize assisted performance, other activity settings must be provided.

Independent centers

Students have a proclivity to interact. Independent centers channel this desire into activity settings that attempt to use social and cooperation skills and to expand them. There have been several extensive efforts to capitalize upon these proclivities – Teams-Games-Tournament, Learning Together, Student Teams/Achievement Divisions, Jigsaw I and II, Group Investigation, and Team-Assisted Individualization, among many others. In general, these various programs and their collective research base are known as the cooperative-learning movement (Leming & Hollifield, 1985).

Among the leading figures in this movement are Dansereau and his associates (Dansereau, in press) and Johnson and Johnson (Brandt, 1987b); a recent entire issue of *Educational Leadership* was devoted to the subject (Brandt, 1987a). The research base is extensive: In 1981, Johnson, Maruyama, Johnson, Nelson, and Skon cited 122 relevant studies; Slavin (1983) cited 66, of which 41 treated effects on student achievement (Leming & Hollifield, 1985), and continuing outcome evaluations of cooperative research have been convincingly positive (Joyce, Showers, & Rolheiser-Bennett, 1987). The cooperative-learning literature would be even more impressive if it did not largely ignore the vigorous anthropology-and-education movement that encourages cooperative formats for many cultural groups (Erickson & Mohatt, 1982; Jordan, 1978a).

Evidence has also been accumulating that cooperative peer activity set-

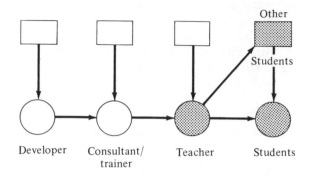

Figure 8.2. Sources of assistance: independent centers.

tings not only can increase achievement but also can bring more general cognitive benefits. Forman and Cazden (1985) have recently provided a detailed discussion:

Two Russian researchers, Lomov [1978] and Kol'tsova [1978], and two Japanese investigators, Inagaki and Hatano [Inagaki, 1981; Inagaki & Hatano, 1968, 1977], have reached similar conclusions – that peer interaction helps individuals acknowledge and integrate a variety of perspectives on a problem, and that this process of coordination, in turn, produces superior intellectual results. For Kol'tsova, the results are precise, rich and logically rigorous definitions of a social science concept. For Inagaki and Hatano, the results are generalizable and stable conservation concepts. For Perret-Clermont [1980], the results are increased ability to use concrete operational logic. (Forman & Cazden, 1985, p. 330)

By what process are these cognitive gains achieved? Forman and Cazden offer this explanation:

By assuming complementary problem-solving roles, peers could perform tasks together before they could perform them alone. . . . One way to achieve a shared task perspective is to assume complementary problem-solving roles. Then each child learns to use speech to guide the actions of her or his partner and, in turn, to be guided by the partner's speech. Exposure to this form of social regulation can enable children to master difficult problems together before they are capable of solving them alone. More importantly, experience with social forms of regulation can provide children with just the tools they need to master problems on their own. (Forman & Cazden, 1985, p. 343)

As indicated in Figure 8.2, peers themselves become the primary sources of assistance for one another in the interactions over tasks of independent learning centers. But the teacher's influence is not absent; it is merely exercised at a greater distance and indirectly.

For example, A. B. Champagne (1985), of the American Association for the Advancement of Science, has discussed a model for teaching science to learners (from middle school to university) through the use of peer interactions:

The teacher in setting the task and the conditions under which it will be completed has a learning outcome in mind. The interactions are highly disciplined goal directed activities, not free wheeling sharing of ignorance. . . .
The use of structured peer interactions is particularly effective in refining students' spontaneous notions about the motion of objects. The interactions are structured around simple physical situations, falling blocks, trucks rolling down an incline, a block suspended from a spring immersed in water. Discussion about the situation is initiated by the teacher with the description of a demonstration. Students are asked to make predictions about the outcome of the demonstration and give reasons for the prediction . . . to resolve the differences in their predictions [or] make the differences among points of view explicit. The teacher's role is to help the students communicate their ideas to each other, and moderate the quality of the discussions. . . . After observing the demonstration, the students are asked to reach consensus on *what* they observed. . . . When consensus on the observation is reached, student explanations that support the incorrect observation are examined to try to identify the fallacies in them. . . . [Then] the teacher presents the canonical explanation for the observed motion of the objects. The student-generated explanations are contrasted with the canonical explanation to identify essential differences. (Champagne, 1985, pp. 25–26)

Among the pleasing outcomes of Champagne's study was the students' reconciliation of their formal knowledge of physics with their observations of the motions of the objects used in the demonstrations. It may well be that this peer-interaction instructional activity setting produces ideal conditions for generating the continued dialectic between everyday and schooled concepts that is characteristic of continued learning (see Chapter 5). Students "became more introspective about their own learning and thinking processes" (Champagne, 1985, p. 27). The latter outcome is predictable from Vygotsky's assertion that schooled thinking produces meta-level awareness of cognitive processes. The experience requires the learner to examine previously held everyday concepts – in Minick's words, "to attend to aspects of linguistic activity that had earlier been mastered without conscious awareness" (Minick, 1985, p. 365).

The use of independent centers increases exponentially the amount of communication and assisted performance available in the classroom. The teacher is not the only fountain of knowledge; the student's 20 to 30 peers are rivers of potential assistance.

Independent centers as activity settings

Who. Groups of 3 to 7 children work together, with the teacher providing only distant general supervision. At KEEP, schedules are arranged so that children of a variety of ability levels are present in each independent center.

What. Various activities are conducted in the centers, including paper-and-pencil tasks, listening activities, bibliographic work, artwork, experiments and demonstrations, creative writing, and indeed almost any instructional activity of the school day. For example, on most days the children will be asked to complete comprehension activities that are intended to reinforce what was done in the teacher-assisted small-group reading lesson. The children are also likely to do word decoding and sight-vocabulary work. Depending on the grade level, they might also work on dictionary skills, writing, or free-choice reading.

The center work is teacher-assigned, but the tasks often are designed by the teachers and students together during Center One (Dalton & Cramer, 1987). Tasks range from independent paper-and-pencil tasks to group projects. Tasks may be the same for each student in the center, or different.

When. Beginning as early as preschool, and certainly by kindergarten, and through the third grade, children in the Honolulu KEEP program spend at least half of the day in independent centers. In upper elementary grades, this proportion decreases in favor of more individual activity, but small-group project work can – and in our view should – constitute a portion of the school day throughout the educational career. Each center rotation lasts about 20 min for younger children, and up to 40 min, depending on children and task.

Where. The independent centers are located in designated areas of the classroom and may be areas of the floor, specific tables, a pile of pillows, or other space that is appropriate to the center's activity and product. For older children, work need not be tied to a permanent location, but the group may shift from library to bulletin board to garden, as the task shifts.

Why. The tasks of the independent centers are designed to support, reinforce, practice, extend, and generalize the instructional goals that are pursued in all the activity settings of the classroom.

Assisting performance in the independent centers

At KEEP, children in the independent centers are encouraged to help each other, and no specific guidelines are enforced for patterns or frequency of assistance. The children are allowed, and if necessary encouraged, to discuss their work with one another in the peer centers. As a consequence, children look for opportunities to assist. Jordan (1984) has described this phenomenon as "scanning," which comes in two varieties: Children scan the classroom environment for a possible source of assistance when they encounter difficulty, and they also scan for indications that others need help. Many peer-assistance sequences begin by one child volunteering help to another.

Means of assistance: feeding-back and instructing

As at home, children will scan the group for help and may announce to the group as a whole that they are having difficulty. Two first-grade girls, Page and April, sitting at a table with four other children, have been interacting intermittently with each other and with the others at the table while working in their workbooks.

April slouched down in her seat and said, "Oh, give up! Trouble, trouble, trouble!" Page looked through April's book and said, "Oh, you *pau* [finished] already. Give to teacher. All pau [finished]." (Jordan, 1984, p. 67)

Means of assistance: feeding-back and instructing

Children also scan their environment for evidence that others are in need of help. Much peer teaching-learning is cued by errors perceived by the "teaching" child.

Four kindergarten children were seated together at a work table. All had the same tasks – to circle all the "A's" on a work paper and then to complete a dot-to-dot picture by connecting the letters of the alphabet. Wanda finished her first task very quickly. She then went on to the dot-to-dot picture. Grant looked at her picture and commented, "Hit the ball crooked with the bat. Good!" He was referring to the fact that Wanda has drawn the bat in the dot-to-dot picture crooked. Grant then said, "That's A, C . . . A, B!" He repeated this several times. He was telling Wanda that she had connected A to C when she should have connected A to B. That's why her bat was crooked. (Jordan, 1984, p. 67)

Jordan's study of peer learning at the KEEP primary school indicates that a peer teaching–learning interaction occurs every 3 min per child in kindergarten (about half of which involve academic tasks). In the first grade, these interactions occur about once every 2.5 min, with academic matters the topic in two-thirds of the cases observed (Jordan, 1977, 1978a, 1978b).

Regardless of task or ability levels, these assisting interactions exhibit two characteristic features:

The first is *contextuality*; that is, teaching/learning interactions usually took place as part of ongoing attempts to perform an activity to which the content of the teaching/learning interaction was related. While a great deal of verbalization might be part of a teaching/learning interaction, and the enterprise itself might be a verbal one, such as an insult rhyme, the children seldom simply talked about how to do something, without at least one of them being actually involved in doing it. This links up with the second major characteristic of such interactions, which is *mutual participation*. In most peer teaching/learning interactions, the teacher as well as the learner became involved in the enterprise at hand. (Jordan, D'Amato, & Joesting, 1981, pp. 33–34; emphasis added)

Means of assistance: modeling, feeding-back

Three first-grade children (Edgar, Felix, and Katie) were seated at the "follow-up" center. An observer (C. J.) was seated about two feet away from their table, closest to Edgar. Edgar turned toward C. J. and, as he pointed at his work paper, said, "Only this way?" C. J. made no response. Edgar turned back to the group of children. Felix attempted to sound out the word that Edgar asked about, "Ch ch, chimney." Edgar wrote on his paper as Felix watched. Felix then pointed to Edgar's paper and said, "C-h, c-h, c-h. . . . " Slightly later Edgar, pointing to his paper, said to Felix, "Look at this." Felix made a short "e" sound, saying, "Eh, eh, eh, elephant." Edgar wrote on his paper and asked, "Is this right, Felix? Is this all right?" Felix nodded and Edgar said, "Now we all finish." (Jordan, 1984, p. 67)

There is considerable shifting between the role of the assisted and the role of assistor. Assistance does not flow only from high-ability children to those of lower ability. Children often can perform different portions of the same task and will assist one another by pooling their knowledge. Shifts between the teacher role and the learner role are frequent.

Means of assistance: instructing, questioning, feeding-back

In the following incident, Amanda, Sally, and Lyle, first graders, are all working on the same exercise, which involves reading a sentence, choosing the appropriate word to complete the sentence from a given list, and marking the chosen word. Sally is reading the sentences aloud as she works. . . .
Sally hesitates in choosing the right word. Lyle looks at her paper and reads the sentence slowly, pointing to and repeating the word he chooses, saying, "He will go on a bike . . . !" Sally says, "He will. Right. He." She looks at Amanda and says, "He." Amanda nods. Then Lyle looks at the girls and repeats the whole sentence again. (Jordan, 1984, pp. 67–68)

Children may switch back and forth between teacher and learner roles as confidence and perceived competence of others in the group vary. In the following example, Lyle, Sally, and Amanda are working at a center together. All have been assigned the same phonics task. Lyle, who was in a teacher-helper role earlier, encounters a task he feels unable to handle and switches to the "being helped" role.

Lyle asked, "You know how make one five-square, Amanda?" Amanda counted the squares. The task was to fold a piece of paper in such a way as to produce a certain number of boxes into which answers would be written. Lyle asked again, "You know how make one five-square for me, Amanda?" Amanda answered, "Yes. How much squares was that?" Lyle answered, "Five squares." Amanda and Sally both looked at the assignment and Amanda said "Six," meaning there should be six squares. Sally repeated, "Six," Lyle counted the squares. Amanda said to Lyle, "You can make six squares." Lyle passed his paper to

Amanda, "Do dat" [make the six squares]. Sally grabbed the paper, "Here! I make 'em." (Jordan, 1984, p. 68)

Cultural issues in designing independent-center activity settings: Hawaiians

In the KEEP system, designed on and for native Hawaiian children, the use of independent centers was one of the first features to emerge and has been the most visible of the several cultural compatibilities of the KEEP system with the natal culture of its pupils. Hawaiian children take to cooperative learning like fish to the ocean; it is their native habitat. For general discussions of cultural compatibility in the KEEP system, the authoritative sources are by Jordan and her associates (Jordan, 1978a, 1978b, 1981a, 1981b, 1983, 1984, 1985; Tharp, in press).

First of all, the proclivity to orient to peers is strong among the Hawaiian children at KEEP, even in early kindergarten. The origins of the proclivity are rooted in the natal culture (Gallimore et al., 1974). Hawaiian children are socialized in a context that involves role flexibility and joint responsibility. Teaching of children takes place in the context of goal-directed activities in which teacher and learner share responsibility for the work and the product. Collaboration, cooperation, and assisted performance are therefore commonplace in the everyday experience of Hawaiian children.

One of the features of a joint-responsibility/role-flexibility system is the shared caretaking of toddlers and infants. Hawaiian children learn early the direct care of infants and toddlers, as well as ordinary domestic skills and routines.

Hawaiian households emphasize, in child socialization, the learning of appropriate control strategies, selection of activities on the basis of self-managed sequences of activities, voluntary social activities, and enterprise-engaged activities (Jordan, 1985). By age 3 years, children operate as part of the sibling group and turn to siblings for help with many things, including teaching (Gallimore et al., 1974; Jordan, 1978a; Weisner et al., 1986; Weisner, Gallimore, & Tharp, 1982). The sibling group, in some contexts, is permeable and in many activity settings expands to become a diffuse peer-companion group (D'Amato, 1981a).

Home observations reveal children who shape their own styles of communication and language use with parents, siblings, and peers. They have a great deal of influence over the sorts of interactions, verbal and otherwise, that occur in their daily routine. They actively explore the allowable range permitted in their local niche. They create their own activities, and then are shaped by them (Boggs, 1985; Gallimore et al., 1974).

It is not surprising that children accustomed to self-managed activities in peer-companion groups have problems adjusting to classrooms that emphasize whole-group activity settings, in which they are expected to orient to a single adult. Teachers have often complained that Hawaiian students are inattentive and peer-oriented to a fault. Initial classroom studies by our team indicated a low level of Hawaiian child attention to teachers and classwork and a high level of attention to peers (Gallimore et al., 1974; MacDonald & Gallimore, 1971; Tharp & Gallimore, 1976b). These attentional patterns often were classified by school personnel as disruptive and a product of low academic motivation.

The creation of independent peer learning centers provides a context in which the peer orientation of these students is channeled into settings that allow home-developed repertoires of productive and cooperative activity to transfer to school. These repertoires include productive action in the absence of moment-to-moment adult regulation. They also include the self-managed interaction scripts observed in the peer-companion groups in the natal setting by Boggs (1985). As at home, the independent-center activity settings provide an opportunity for the children to "creatively" use a context, relying on self-regulated and mutually co-regulated sequences of activity.

Although there are many differences between home activity settings and those of independent centers, they share the following elements (Weisner et al., 1986):

1. flexible access to peers of equal, greater, or lesser skill
2. influence over the sorts of interactions, verbal and otherwise, that occur in the daily routine
3. opportunities to actively explore the allowable range of activities permitted in both settings
4. opportunities to create and redesign their activities and respond to their self-generated changes
5. low levels of adult direction and monitoring and considerable latitude in what children do and how they do it

Cultural issues in designing independent-center activity settings: Navajos

In exploring the appropriateness for Navajo children of the KEEP systems, all program-team members predicted that the independent-centers activity settings would work in roughly the same way for Navajo children as for Hawaiians. Navajo children also are given a good deal of responsibility at an early age, are accustomed to operating independent of adults, and engage in high levels of sibling caretaking.

But with Navajo children, the independent centers did not function well. In the first place, the level of peer assistance in the centers was low. Children worked on their own papers and paid little attention to anyone else. Whereas Hawaiian children ventured to help if they thought somebody else had gotten something wrong or did not know what to do, the Navajo children largely ignored each other. Whereas Hawaiian children sought the assistance of others when they were stumped, Navajo children sat it out alone, patient, but not doing or learning much. Second, the Navajo children often seemed uncomfortable in the centers. They were restless; squabbling was frequent. The centers were not running comfortably, and they were not producing peer assistance.

A lengthy quotation from Jordan and associates (1985) details the problem, its consequences, and its solution:

The Navajo children's interaction [pattern] was a source of much puzzlement to all. The Navajo staff insisted that there were many instances of peer caretaking and mutual helping in the community. . . . It is a fundamental value and custom in Navajo society to work together in family, clan, ceremonial and friendship events. Even in the school context, there was good evidence for the theme of family – and even sibling – assistance [which did not transfer into the independent centers]. Several possible explanations were explored. Perhaps the students would more readily interpret a situation as calling for cooperation if it were a group-produced task rather than separate assignments for different levels of students. Some improvement resulted, in that the task demands did enforce some cooperative work. But the tenuous cooperation was interspersed with blatantly territorial behavior. One center was given a huge piece of chart paper, and the children there were asked to fill it with drawings of animals. They immediately partitioned the chart paper into 5 separate boxes, and each drew his animals into a separate pen. The Navajo teachers were as puzzled by this as were the KEEP staff; they joked that the behavior couldn't be cultural, because there were no fences on the reservation. . . . A second question arose: Had the *school* succeeded in teaching the children its conventional rule, "Do your own work!". . . . To test this explanation, center situations were created which *demanded* that the children work together. Credit for having done the center work was not given unless it was done cooperatively. . . . But one group held out: they would not work cooperatively.

[As the next resort], an out-of-classroom training session was set up, in which the teacher described, modelled, prompted and reinforced helping behavior. While this group of children was able to perform these tasks in the training sessions, no appreciable change in their classroom behaviors occurred.

As a continuation of the training sessions, the teacher finally took them off into the office, sat them on the floor and said, "You simply have to work together. What can we do to help you do it?" The children told her very clearly and explicitly, "Well, first we have to have smaller groups. We could work in pairs. . . . Then the girls could work together and the boys could work together." And that in fact was the key: smaller groups of the same sex. . . . There is a sharp separation of the sexes in Navajo culture, both in roles and for purposes of interaction. By puberty this is extremely important, and by adulthood, male and female roles are clearly defined and separate. . . . This cultural feature . . . is salient in the ethnographic literature on Navajos, as well as a part of daily life of the Navajo staff themselves.

However, we had not expected it to be a controlling parameter of behavior in eight-year-old children. But boys and girls at that age are beginning to expect and be expected to operate in same sex groups. They are becoming uncomfortable together, and they are not accustomed to working together. Boys this age are admonished not to "play with" their sisters, and girls told to stay separate from their brothers or opposite-sex clan-mates.

For Hawaiian children, 4 to 5 students of mixed sex and ability produce the maximum peer interaction and assistance at centers. In Navajo, this combination effectively annihilated interaction. [Our] early data suggest that Navajo children will indeed help and interact in groups of 2–3 students of the same sex, working at the same task. . . . Through similar processes of inquiry, we have concluded that peer assistance will be fostered also by having children of about the same achievement level working on the same task.

There is a major difference between Navajo and Hawaiian children's experiences that now seems obviously linked to the necessity for smaller classroom groups. Navajos live in widely dispersed dwellings. . . . Ordinarily a child would have close access only to siblings. . . . Among Navajo children in traditional home settings [there is] little occasion to engage in activity settings made up of same-age mates. On the other hand, Navajo children traditionally take on individual responsibilities at very early ages; many of the children in our class had begun sheepherding, alone, at five years of age. (Jordan et al., 1985, pp. 12–16)

These two cultures, Navajo and Hawaiian, are extreme contrasts in many respects and were chosen for study for that reason. The lesson they teach, however, is a critical one for all schools: *Independent centers will be influenced by the cultural repertoires of students more strongly than will any other activity setting.* Because the teacher's influence is more distant and indirect, the students themselves will operate in the centers with the repertoires they have developed in comparable activity settings in home and community.

This is well illustrated by a short independent-center interaction between some third-grade Navajo children and their only Anglo class-mate, named Kyle. Kyle is quite teacherly in these interactions, assisting his classmates through questioning much as a teacher would, with a role repertoire quite common among Anglo adults and children.

Means of assistance: questioning

[Kyle points to an item in Ermile's booklet]
Kyle: Okay, now this one.
Victoria: Together.
[Kyle is giving directions; Victoria is suggesting joint performance]
Kyle: I'll tell you how this one works. This one I know how this one works. It says . . .
[Kyle has attracted the attention of Charlie, Velma, and Ermile, who all look over to Kyle's book, where he begins to read; Ermile has found the place in her own book, and reads along with Kyle; they point to the words as they chorus the two alternative answers]

Kyle & Ermile: Fish do, do not . . .
Kyle: . . . have eyelids.
Ermile: . . . have eyelids.
Kyle: Do fish have eyelids?
Ermile: A fish can . . .
     [But Kyle is firmly in the role of teacher]
Ermile: No.
Velma: No.
Charlie: No.
     [Kyle points at Ermile's booklet]
Kyle: So, "Do not."
Ermile: Where, "do not"? [Ermile looks to Kyle]
Kyle: "Do not." This one says, not that one. Okay.
     [Charlie watches as Kyle points out the "do not" in Ermile's booklet]

We have had few observations among Hawaiian or Navajo children in which such a perfected "little teacher" sequence of assistance has occurred. On the other hand, Kyle was not so comfortable and effective in less structured general-conversation sequences of sharing knowledge among his Navajo classmates.

No groups of children with whom we have worked have been prepared for all forms of cooperative activity settings. Cultural variations are crucial for anticipating child behavior in independent centers and for planning how to assist children to assist each other.

Assisting and training cooperation in independent centers

The structural elements of independent centers (who, what, when, where, and why) must all be considered by teachers and designers and selected so as to maximize cooperative interactions.

In the standard, mainstream culture of the school, the repertoires necessary for cooperative learning in independent centers cannot be assumed. In fact, typical schools, with their recitation scripts and whole-group organizations, actively suppress and even punish cooperative learning. Before independent centers can be expected to function well, teachers will need to structure the activities and settings to foster mutual assistance. Active training may be necessary. It is naive to suppose that independent centers are Gardens of Eden in which children will automatically recover some prelapsarian cooperativeness.

Champagne, in continuing her discussion of structured peer interactions and physical science learning, observes that her intermediate school and college students must be taught to learn with and from one another:

The teacher must motivate students to interact with each other and teach them the rules for academic discourse. Motivating students to communicate with their

peers is no easy task. Students have been socialized to a form of classroom interaction where all communication goes through the teacher. The teacher asks questions, the student called upon to answer it responds to the teacher, and the teacher
tells the student if the answer is correct or not. All the students' verbalizations are
designed to communicate effectively with the teacher. Since the communications
are primarily between a student and the teacher and the teacher is the authority
on what is to be learned, students typically do not listen to what their peers are
saying. Consequently, a first task facing a teacher who wishes to apply the method
of peer interaction is to structure the classroom in a way that encourages students
to communicate with each other. The teacher also instructs the students on how
to monitor the quality of an interaction. How does one determine if others in a
group understand what has been said? Can the recipient of the communication
restate the sender's message to the sender's satisfaction?. . . . The development of
the communication skills necessary to answer these questions is an important part
of the learning that takes place when peer interactions are used in formal schooling. (Champagne, 1985, pp. 22–23)

Certainly the precise skills needed in independent centers vary according to the culture, the age of the children, the nature of the subject matter,
the nature of the task, and the experiences of the students in other kinds
of schooling. All needed repertoires can be trained, and it is not naive to
expect pleasure in learning, self-satisfaction, and cognitive growth to
increase as effective functioning in independent centers is achieved.

Tasks can be designed to foster group product and group process.
Teachers can assist pupils toward cooperative skill development in the
same way that teachers assist the development of other capacities: by
instructing, managing contingencies, modeling, feeding-back, questioning, and providing cognitive structuring.

For our final example, we print without comment a longer section of
children's interaction in an independent center. This transcript was taken
in the midst of the Navajo research, when the training sessions were
under way, but the gender separation had not yet been carried out. It is
typical in many ways – not ideal, but still illustrative of the ways that the
interpersonal plane in peer joint activity can be gained. Here we see the
performance assistance occurring not so much in teacher–learner dyads
but in free-form dynamic conversation in which an intersubjectivity is
being built from shared work and expanding word meanings. The performance of each member is assisted and assisting.

> *Building the intermental plane: mutual assistance through sharing of
> knowledge and speech*
>
> [In independent center 6, some third-grade children are working on a joint
> project. First they were to write all their names on the chart paper. While
> they were finishing that task, Victoria jumped the gun]
>
> *Jimmie:* How is Victoria spelled?
> *Victoria:* [Finishing before the group and opening her folder] I'm going to start
> now.

Ermile: Don't you do it!

Victoria: Well, hurry then!

Ermile: [Looking up at Victoria] How do you spell your name?

Victoria: V-I-C

Annie-Bear: You draw right here. [Indicating where Jimmie is supposed to write]

Victoria: [To Annie-Bear] Do you know how to spell my name?

Annie-Bear: Yes, I have it written down already!

Ermile: C-what?

Jimmie: [Tries to spell Victoria's name, but garbles it]

Victoria: Annie-Bear, spell it for Ermile.

Jimmie: Spell it slow.

Victoria: [Walks around the table toward Ermile] No, he's wrong. It's like this.

Jimmie: [Places folder down] Here, copy this.

Annie-Bear: [Speaking about the first page in her own folder] Mine is a pencil and eraser. [Goes to her own seat] Are you ready now?

Jimmie: [Opens his folder] I'm going to start anyway. You don't have to stay together.

Victoria: Yes [we do]!

Annie-Bear: No! [She looks at the stand on the center of the table where the teacher's instructions are pinned] Let me see.

Victoria: [Looking at the instructions and pointing] It says "together" here. [She reads the entire instructions] Now we all do it together. Next you go to another place. A place over there.

Ermile: Yes! If you do a good job and work together you get to go first!

Melissa: [Already beginning to work] What's right here?

Victoria: Now, let's go ahead and start now.

[The entire group read the first paragraph in chorus; then they must answer questions about it; they read the first question, and look at one another; Victoria gives the answer]

Victoria: It's frog eggs. Now who is [the next answer], Sam or Bill?

Dora: Sam! It's Sam!

[After an inaudible exchange of several turns]

Charlie: Where shall we draw it?

Victoria: [Turns the page] Right here! I'll draw a pencil.

Annie-Bear: Is it this one?

Victoria: No. It's this one. [Turns page for Annie-Bear]

Ermile: I'm going to draw a pen. I'm drawing a pen.

Jimmie: Do snakes come out of eggs?

Annie-Bear: Yes! Some eggs are spotted.

Charlie: Yes, some are black too.

Jimmie: I said I was going to draw a pencil first and you copied me.

Victoria: I'm going to draw a bag too.

Annie-Bear: I'm going to draw a bag too.

Ermile: I drew a pen. I'll do paper too.

Annie-Bear: [Showing her book to Victoria] Look, I did this!

9   The interpsychological plane of teacher training

The pertinacious recitation script: why?

Why does the recitation script persist in the face of repeated evidence that it is insupportable on either theoretical or practical grounds? The brief answer is simply because teachers are not trained to do anything different. As we described in Chapter 4, the entire system of schooling merely directs and assesses teachers; it does not teach and support them. Schools hire teachers, drop them in classrooms, and subsequently attend to them only to perform assessment. This is wrongheaded and destructive for every member of the school community. Teaching is as crucial as any social role in contemporary life, and teachers should be held accountable and recognized for their performances through their careers. But how should this accountability and recognition be accomplished? Bird and Little (1986) point to two ways, the first conventional, and the second reformist:

> Consider two views of how [accountability and recognition] might be done. In one view . . . teaching can be reduced to a few days of standard in-service training that teachers can implement on their own. Such teaching can be assessed with an observation form [and] the results of teaching can be checked by standardized achievement tests. Teachers are moved primarily by hope for a pension, fear that their incompetence will be detected, or respect for authority. This is a caricature of talk about teachers; as a description of behavior towards teachers, however, it is more accurate.
> In another view, teaching is a complex, humane activity at which a teacher can grow steadily more proficient over years by disciplined curiosity, continuous training, and skillful assistance. Teachers can be supported and evaluated by persons – including principals – who join with them in mastering and advancing the craft. . . . In this view, one influences teachers primarily by organizing the support and recognition that permit them to realize the higher motives of service that bring them to teaching. (Bird & Little, 1986, pp. 507–508)

The absence of continuous training and skillful assistance not only frustrates and stunts the growth potential of teachers but also precludes the introduction of new curriculum and instructional goals. So long as

188

there is only the recitation script in the classroom, and an analogous system of schooling supporting it, there can be no real movement even in the content of instruction.

A case example: the New Math

One of the better-documented efforts to improve American education was the "New Math" reform of the post-Sputnik era (Sarason, 1971). What the reformers actually believed about teaching and teaching reform is not clear, because their views on the reform process and teacher training were never made explicit. Judging from the logic of their proceeding, the New Math reformers apparently believed that the persistence of recitation and other forms of automatic teaching was an artifact of textbooks that featured computational skills and memorization of times tables.

They made classic errors: They misjudged the time it would take; they underestimated the difficulty of reforming the nature of teacher–student interaction, and in the most telling error, they failed to conceptualize explicitly the process of achieving change in teaching and schooling practices (Sarason, 1971).

Although it was never articulated, the assumption of the New Math reformers seems to have been that the change problem was getting a new curriculum officially adopted; once teachers were assigned a new curriculum (new textbooks), they would as a matter of course adopt or develop a new style of teaching. The reformers did not recognize there is no vehicle in public schools through which a fundamental change in teaching can be transported and that there never has been (Sarason, 1971, p.78). They did not know that most teachers report negatively on their training and believe they were virtually abandoned during their initial teaching experiences (Joyce, Bush, & McKibbin, 1981; Joyce, Howey, & Yarger, 1977a, 1977b). They did not realize that what teachers do with a curriculum, once adopted, is more crucial than the nature of the curriculum itself (Rosenholtz, 1986).

They also failed to appreciate that no mechanism of effective staff training exists as a part of ordinary school district operation. Most staff-development efforts rely on extremely weak forms of training, mainly college courses, workshops, and the like. The workshop and the university class may assist teachers, through cognitive structuring, to learn new ideas and concepts and employ new materials; they can excite, but they cannot provide the means needed to assist fundamental changes in teaching behavior. On average, in-service teachers receive less than 3 days of "staff development" per year, and not all of it deals with teaching and instruction (Joyce et al., 1981).

The factors that make changes in teaching so difficult to achieve were summarized by Joyce and Clift (1984). It is clear from their review that in either preservice or in-service programs, no mechanism presently exists for reforming teaching or for reducing recitation to its proper role. Teachers sorely feel this lack:

A survey was recently conducted by *Instructor* magazine, which questioned its teacher readership. . . . Of the 8,000 mostly elementary teachers responding . . . forty-seven percent said they make "none" of the important decisions related to inservice training in their schools. Sixty-one percent had no opportunities to observe their colleagues teaching . . . only 16 percent "frequently" received useful guidance from the principal on instructional matters. (Bennett, 1986, p. 47)

Assisting the performance of teachers

The choke-point of change that defied earlier reformers can be restated in the terms we have used in this book: The problem now, and during earlier reform movements like that for the New Math, is the lack of a *social context* of training and professional development. There has been no theory or model of schooling that has presumed the responsibility for assisting (rather than merely assessing) teachers' performances. The activity settings common in most schools contribute to the resistance to change inherent in current practices (Joyce & Clift, 1984). If the recitation script is to be changed to responsive teaching, we must construct activity settings that will assist teachers to perform the new script – to adopt a role in which teachers assist students in the ZPD.

Current means of staff development cannot provide for the development of teaching skills required to meet this criterion of assisting performance in the ZPD. The major barrier to change in teaching practices is the absence of activity settings in public schools that would provide for assisted performance of those acts that must be employed in the classroom in the presence of students. Teachers, like their students, have ZPDs; they, too, require assisted performance. As with students, activity settings for teachers must create opportunities for them to receive all the six means of assistance.

With this perspective on teacher support, the fundamental problem is immediately identified: Most teachers work alone, in splendid isolation (Jackson, 1968; Knoblock & Goldstein, 1971; Sarason, 1971). The current joke is that of all adult acts, teaching is the second most private.

[Teachers] meet with the same groups of students in a classroom for all or most of a school day in elementary schools and with classes of students who move on to other teachers in secondary schools. Students observe one another and their teachers: teachers usually observe only their students, not one another. Also, groups of teachers seldom engage in problem solving. Rather, they often talk with one another only in the lunchroom or the teachers' lounge, when talk about the activities of teaching is, not surprisingly, anecdotal and brief. (Griffin, 1985, p. 3)

The social isolation of teachers accounts for much of the problem encountered in trying to achieve the changes that would have been required to carry out the New Math and other earlier reforms. Isolated teachers have limited opportunities for receiving assistance through modeling and feedback, two means of assistance crucial to acquisition of complex social repertoires. Workshops and coursework can provide cognitive structuring, but alone will not assist teachers to develop new repertoires of complex social behavior necessary for responsive teaching. This argument is consistent with reports that field experience is the most valued aspect of preservice training (Lortie, 1975; Mason, 1961; Watts, 1982).

Reducing the isolation of teachers and building collaborative activity settings in which teachers are provided assisted performance are neither simple nor pain-free endeavors, as Fullan's evaluation (1985) of successful teaching innovations clearly indicates. Even in successful programs, innovation and change always cost time, anxiety, and uncertainty. To develop competences and programs under this stress, it is essential that teachers have supportive interaction with peers, technical advisors, and administrators.

The components of successful school innovation can be mapped onto those concepts we have used throughout this volume to discuss activity settings in the classroom. Schools trying to innovate must construct activity settings with certain personnel present, personnel who share common goals, work at relevant instrumental tasks, and interact in particular ways that reduce anxiety, encourage persistence in the face of difficulty, and employ all the means of assisted performance.

The useful concept of activity setting can "unpackage" school contexts and provide a unit for analysis of teacher training and development. It is a unit of analysis that brings the social context into focus and thus attacks directly the isolation of teachers from the means of assisted performance. We shall illustrate with material and data from KEEP.

The problem

In the early days of building KEEP, we found ourselves doing to teachers the same things that we are now decrying. We, like schools in general, were ignorant about how to proceed in developing teacher skills, and we know from firsthand experience that a well-intentioned staff can be clumsy and destructive. Teacher #11 recounted her early experiences, which were unusual only in that some effort was made to prepare her:

Teacher #11: You don't give two weeks of workshop and have someone walk into a new classroom and a new situation, and then expect them to teach reading. . . . You gotta' give them more than that. Plus, I had been sick that summer and . . . I was physically run down. Even then the first week was beautiful. But the beginning of the second week, the problems started. The kids started acting up, Mikea wouldn't cooperate, and Dolph started throwing his abuses.

When the problems started, all I got was criticism. I didn't get much support. I'll never forget the day. [Two consultants] took me up to the observation deck and say, I want you to watch Mabel teach. I had never seen anybody teach the program, ever, ever. So I took down word for word everything she said, and [the consultant] turned to me and she says, "Now can you go in and do that?" She said, "after recess, you go in and teach. You go in and do what Mabel just did." It was a large group, and at that point I was so flustered and upset . . . I couldn't even get the words out of my mouth. . . .

Interviewer: She told you that just before a recess? You only had recess time to think about it, then you. . . .

T: Yes. It was just a nightmare. It was very, very poorly handled. I will never forget it as long as I live. Anyway, I was very, very upset. Later, I started thinking "[three other teachers] are off in corners whispering about me." You know how that affects you. . . . It was awful and unfortunately, [that consultant] and I have never really repaired that damage. If it wasn't for [my subsequent consultant] who took the bull by the horns, and said, "Okay, now we're going to sit down . . . and [help you work on this, beginning with step 1]". It was partially my fault and partially their fault. It stripped me of all my self-confidence. . . .

There were a couple of times I even vomited before I taught. It was not easy. . . . I'd just say, "Dear Lord, please don't let anybody kill themselves today, or me either. Please give me patience." [So] I figured a class could never get any worse. (excerpted from interview with teacher #11)

These first inept efforts to assist teachers did not differ markedly from the experiences all beginning teachers have with difficult classes, except that here there was someone watching and, later, someone listened to her story.

Means of assisting teachers: experimental results

The activity settings used at KEEP for supporting teacher professional growth were not developed in a day. A fully realized system for schooling in which all staff members assisted learning was not available to us for study, and our own efforts to design effective assistance often stumbled forward rather than racing.

An early effort to understand the means of assisting teacher performance included an experiment that compared incremental degrees of effectiveness for various concatenations of the means of assistance (Sloat,

Tharp, & Gallimore, 1977). The main focus of the study was attempting to influence teachers toward one effective teacher repertoire: increasing the positive classroom-management behaviors of praises, hugs, and other forms of positive reinforcement described in Chapter 8. Five newly hired KEEP teachers spent 16 weeks learning to use praise effectively. Six 1-week training experiences were provided, each followed by a week of practice and observation. The six components of training were employed in the same sequence for all trainees.

Components were selected and ordered by reconciling two goals: steadily increasing the amount of information to trainees to enable them to identify, discriminate, and increase positive acts toward their students; increasing the cost (time and money) of the components. These goals could not be achieved simultaneously; the chosen order represented the best judgment. The sequential-components design is clearly limited in that any change of order can be expected to change the relative effects of all components. However, because the components employed are rather typical of teacher-training activities, the results bear on the planning of in-service programs.

Each of the six training components lasted 1 week (5 teaching days). There was a break between components, with a "baseline" week before and after each component. Total elapsed time for the training was 16 weeks. The six training experiences were as follows:

1. Didactic instruction. This component focused on principles of behavior management. It was conducted in five 1-hour sessions. Trainees were given reading assignments from books and journals. Sessions with the training consultant were devoted to discussion of the readings and their application in the classroom. There was also an activity assignment (e.g., all teachers observed a child in another class for 15 min and wrote a narrative description of the child's behavior).

2. Modeling and role-playing. Videotapes showing teachers in classroom situations were used to demonstrate behavior-management skills presented during didactic training. The teachers coded each tape for occurrence of teacher skills and target behaviors of children. In four of the sessions, each teacher practiced for 5 min the management skills she had observed on the tapes.

3. Feedback (via videotape). During this component, each trainee was videotaped for 15 min during her regular classroom teaching time. Later in the same day, each teacher observed her own tape and coded the frequencies of praise and negative comments directed at students. The group met as a whole to examine the data collected by each trainee from the coding of the tapes. Portions of each trainee's tape were reviewed by the group and discussed.

4. Direct coaching in the classroom (via a "mike" in the ear). Each of the sessions in this component lasted 15 min. The training consultant sat on the observation deck (behind one-way glass) viewing the classroom and listening via a wireless microphone worn by the trainee teacher. He also had a wireless transmitter through which he could talk to the teacher, who had a portable FM receiver with an earphone. The consultant praised and commented on trainee use of behavior-management skills.

5. Feedback (via graphs of classroom performance). Each day, each trainee teacher was provided a graph based on her frequency of use of the behavior-management skills. The graphs included data on frequency of praise (for academics and deportment), rule statements, and ratio of positive to negative statements directed at students. No specific instructions were provided in relation to the data.

6. Feedback graphed with explicit goals to match. The final component was the same as the fifth, except that individuals' goals were marked on each graph, showing clearly the extent to which the observed rate of behavior matched the goal. The individual goals were based on the high weekly frequency a teacher had attained at some point in the training. Generally, trainees had not attained their peak rates for both academic and deportment praise during the same week; thus, the goals during this component were higher frequencies of praise in total than they had ever exhibited.

The teacher trainees were observed daily during regular teaching activities. In brief, the results were as follows: Following didactic training, there was little change over the initial baseline (Figure 9.1). Following the modeling component, there was an average increase of 38% in total praise rate. With the exception of the final component, the highest mean total praise rate occurred after videotape feedback, with an increase of 53% over the initial baseline. A substantial increase in rate occurred when graph feedback was combined with specific goals. The other training experiences [didactic instruction, graph feedback (no goals), and mike-in-the-ear coaching] had minimal or no effect on praise rate.

The lack of effect for "bug-in-the-ear" coaching must be interpreted with care: the trainees reported that hearing the voice in the ear was so distracting that it disrupted them:

Teacher #28: I remember one thing that stands out. [The experimenter] put an ear-piece in our ears. He was up on the observation deck. He could talk to us and we could hear him. He would tell us what to look for and where to go in the classroom. I always thought that was really strange. It was a really unusual experience, because half the time I was tapping the ear-piece and saying, "I can't hear you." The sound quality was very bad. The kids would look at me like, "It's God talking to Mrs. A." (excerpted from interview with teacher #28)

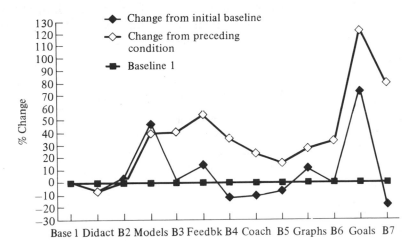

Figure 9.1. Percentage change in total praise rate from initial baseline and preceding conditions. (Adapted from Sloat, Tharp, & Gallimore, 1977.)

Although the most dramatic effect was achieved during feedback with explicit goals stated by the trainer, the teachers responded negatively to the procedure: They reported feeling great pressure to "crank out the praises" to reach criterion. They believed that because of having to achieve the goal, they were unable to concentrate on other aspects of their teaching. Indeed, the teachers were right: The praise rates requested of them during the graphs-with-goals component were much higher than needed to maintain a positive classroom atmosphere and interfered with other vital teaching functions.

Though graphed feedback with goals is a powerful means of assisting performance, it will not assist if it is arbitrarily and bureaucratically imposed. Allowing the teachers a voice in goal-setting was an obvious improvement suggested by these results; we learned to make joint goal-setting a routine part of the consultant–teacher interaction. In this way, both can capitalize on the powerful effects of explicit goals.

There was considerable variability among the five trainees. One teacher trainee began with a total praise rate (36%) that was probably near her optimal rate. Except for the demand of the research design, it would have been possible to accelerate her training and expand the range of teaching skills covered. For others whose rates were considerably lower, more extended periods of modeling and video feedback would have been desirable.

This suggests that training should be individualized as much as possible, and indeed individualization became one of the hallmarks of the KEEP consultant–teacher interaction system. Chapter 10 demonstrates in a full case study the careful, responsive individualization characteristic of effective teacher assistance.

Activity settings for assisting the performance of teachers

Only after much research, many errors, hard self-examination, and harder effort did the staff evolve an integrated system of teacher assistance that blends individualization, teacher involvement, a full range of the means of assistance, and a variety of activity settings. A central commitment of the KEEP system is to provide assistance to its teachers in developing and maintaining highly refined teaching skills. Teacher performance is assisted through a wide range of activity settings that allow self-assistance, peer assistance, and assistance from administrators, consultants, trainers, and specialists. The full range of the means of assistance is provided. For novice and preservice teachers, assisting activities are scheduled as frequently as the system will bear. For skillful teachers, assistance is reduced, because "assistance" for teachers, just as for students, can interfere with smooth performance. But even for the skillful teacher, new competences are always needed and wanted. The assisting school should and can provide activity settings in which needed assistance can be delivered.

The KEEP activity settings for the training and development of teaching skills are described in the following sections.

Observation-and-conference activity settings: individualized assistance

An indispensable activity setting for assisting teacher performance is the conference, in which a consultant and teacher confer over negotiated goals for professional improvement (Figure 9.2). Mutually choosing goals for development, through conversation and negotiation, is necessary for teachers to perceive supervisory assistance as helpful (Levin, Hoffman, & Badiali, 1986). These authors also report that teachers need to be observed often enough that they will feel the consultant's impressions to be representative. In the KEEP system, teachers are observed at least once a week initially by an assigned consultant (or other supervisor). Sample lessons or videotapes of teaching sessions can be used by the observer to make some assessment of the teacher's performance. Examples of features assessed include the proportion of time spent by the teacher on *comprehension instruction,* measurements of student on-task rate (or engaged time) and rates of reinforcement (especially for beginning

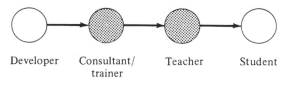

Figure 9.2.

teachers), effective use of the means of assistance, adequate familiarity with subject matter, and teaching in students' ZPDs.

During the conference, the teacher and consultant meet to discuss the feedback based on the consultant's observations, to decide on the next goals for the teacher's own learning, to arrange opportunities for the teacher to view other teachers (live or on tape), and to work cooperatively in planning for the children in the classroom. In a conference, a frequent event is reviewing a videotape of one of the teacher's lessons. Both participants comment on the tape, and the consultant uses this stimulus to provide feedback, instructions, reinforcement, questioning, or cognitive structuring. In the later stages of the ZPD, the teacher herself provides most of this assistance, in a pattern of "self-collaboration." An extended account of this process is presented in Chapter 10 via a case study of a consultant and teacher who met regularly for several months. A frequent outcome of this conferencing is the planning of additional activity settings, such as arranging for teachers to observe additional live or videotaped models, as the need arises. Teacher #11, who had such a disastrous beginning, did become extremely competent in the program. She mentioned particularly the efficacy of these arranged observations:

Teacher #11: The thing that helped me most to get started in the program [after the disaster] was to observe classrooms operating. I did a lot of observing of Ruth's classroom. I think modeling is the best way to show somebody the program, and um, you know observing and watching a teacher do it.

Of course, simply establishing a policy on using observation and conferences is not enough. The outcome will be determined by the manner in which such settings are implemented. A teacher consultant must establish a working relationship, be sensitive to feedback from the trainee (that is not always explicit), and be flexible in arranging for training experiences.

A negative outcome can also follow from a consultant's efforts to be too sensitive and understanding and thus inadvertently failing to treat teachers as professionals:

Teacher #26: When I kept asking the consultant questions, she would say, her excuse was that she didn't want to overwhelm me with giving me too much responsibility. She was being too overprotective, cause if I knew where I was going, if I knew what was supposed to be happening, I could participate in the planning. But I didn't know where I was going, I wasn't going to branch out and I wasn't going to be brave. I was going to be a chicken and hide.

Effective consultation demands many abilities and skills, including the capacity to explain and direct an effective consultation. For example, one teacher complained that her consultant was unable to explain adequately what she wanted to happen:

Teacher #27: I began to feel more comfortable when I got a new consultant. The new one made things a little bit clearer, and she was a little bit more relaxed and open than the first one. That first one was kind of pressured herself to get us going with the program. . . . But I didn't know how to do it, because she didn't really explain where do I go from here.

I just went home in a state of confusion [starts to cry]. I guess . . . it didn't slow down. It seemed like the pace was getting faster and faster, and things were just getting thrown on us.

Around Christmas time, my team member asked for a new consultant. She couldn't take the confusion that was going on, so she wanted another person to clear it up. But I felt maybe it was me that couldn't understand what was going on. So it took me a little while to see it wasn't me. I felt because I was new to the program, that's why I feel so stupid [crying]. I would ask the consultant, and her answers made me feel as if I should know the answers – I felt dumb because I would ask questions but the answers she gave were to different questions.

For example, one time I said I thought some materials we were putting in a Center were too hard for the children. She said, just try it and see. She didn't take into consideration what I had said. She just said do it and see how it comes out. It was like, do it and fail. That's alright. But I am the one that is going to be feeling bad not her, because I'm the one that put it out there. So before I do, I wanted to tell her that it's not going to work with them. But she said, "You don't know, try it."

When observation and conferences were properly implemented, an entirely new picture emerged from the teacher interviews. The following excerpts provide an illustration of the variety of reactions to consultation and the kinds of experiences teachers reported. We begin again with teacher #11, who finally did receive competent assistance:

Teacher #11: When I get feedback from the consultant, I think about the situation in much more detail. I look at it much more objectively. Day to day it's all subjective. Lots of things come into my mind. If you talk to somebody about one particular lesson, you can go through the steps one at a time. I can select some of the details that happen; she [the consultant] pointed out, for example, that one particular statement I said to the children. Or she noticed that I was monitoring out there, or looking at the clock. At the end of the day, I don't remember that I've done that. I remember the lesson I taught, the objectives I covered, how the kids did on their work, and how they reacted to it. But I don't remember the other behaviors I'm doing, because it's so involved, and I don't pull it out. I'm really more concerned about moving the lesson ahead and how's the work going instead of how I'm actually behaving.

Interviewer: So she's like a mirror for you?

Teacher #11: Yes. The consultant makes you be more objective about it.

Teacher #18: Before I had a regular consultant, they arranged that I could observe. I learned to teach comprehension from observing Sally. She's really good at questioning the kids. I used to observe her, and mainly from hearing and seeing what she does, I started using more of it. At that time, we didn't have a consultant coming in all the time. So if we had a question, it had to wait a week or two or whenever the consultants could come down. Sally didn't have time to talk to me except after school; and then we would usually discuss things like if you had a problem with a child. We never got to talk about teaching comprehension and things like that.

This year is really good. Because we are now working in the KEEP program, we have the consultants and then if something goes wrong they [talk to us] right away. If you have a problem, you had somebody to talk to and ask what you could do.

Teacher #20: I used to be a lot more critical of the students. I would tell them they were wrong and directly confront them. Now that I've gone through the KEEP training, I present myself in a more positive way. I still pinpoint it when something is wrong, but I am more positive. It was the consultant's reaction to the videotapes that I have seen at KEEP, showing the teacher as a model. We also went into the classroom and observed how the teachers handled the children as well.

I started copying what the teacher model did on the tapes. Just using their way to switch over from my old way. I remember starting to do it with two boys in my class who were quite naughty about different things and they interrupt a lot. They tease a lot, and cause a lot of trouble. Rather than being negative, I started to try to praise them a little more for what they did do that was good.

It did take some straining myself to look for something good. But when I found some little thing, I would pounce right away and say how nice – I'm glad you did that. Thank you very much.

When I saw the child's reaction – feeling good about himself and smiling, then I said to myself, well, once in while I'll be able to do this when he does nice things.

Teacher #21: One group was very rowdy. I needed my consultant to come in and observe, and help me out in this area. I was really frustrated with this one group. Once I got them into independent centers, they quieted down and did their work; it was just heaven as compared to the first time I did it.

A big help was sitting down with my consultant and having her look at it objectively. She told me, "Hey, wait a minute. It's not only you." She put me back into perspective. That's one of the greatest things of this program – having a consultant here. Somebody to see it from the outside. When you're in your own classroom, usually there's no one there so it's all on you. I think it's very important to have someone else. A lot of times we as teachers need someone else to help us put things back into perspective [describes how she was taking problems home, and consultation helped end that].

I felt pressure when we were first observed and coded. But towards the end, I didn't feel the pressure as much.

Sometimes when the consultant came in to observe, things would go haywire. Then I realized these things were going to happen. We're not doing it for her. I just have to accept it. . . . It's more natural, because things don't go smoothly every day. So it's like she is actually not there, because she is seeing what really goes on – because some days things do go haywire. I shouldn't be worried; I shouldn't be aware of things that should or should not be happening. I should just let things happen naturally.

Peer coaching

Peer coaching, in which teachers assist one another in professional development, has rightly received much recent attention. Nearly 70% of teachers want to observe other teachers at work; yet most have never had any systematic opportunity to do so (Goodlad, 1984). In a national survey of teachers, their salient needs for in-service assistance included pleas for more time to exchange and examine ideas with colleagues (Yarger, Howey, & Joyce, 1976).

In the KEEP schools, the consultant occupies a specific paid position – a system that is highly desirable, but expensive. Peer coaching is an attempt to reorganize schooling to maximize opportunities for assisted performance in the most cost-effective way:

Improvements in education will increasingly depend upon more fully using and improving the human resources presently available to schools rather than upon introducing substantial new human, material, and economic resources. (Sergiovanni, 1975, p. 1)

Peer coaching is one obvious way of achieving activity settings that will provide for joint productive activity, for the sharing of ideas to create intersubjectivity, and for assisted performance of all participants, while requiring very little additional staff.

There are advantages in peer assistance other than economy. Frequently teachers can respond more openly and accurately to one another than can paid consultants or line supervisors:

Teacher #27: The consultant didn't fully explain it like my team member could explain it. I would understand what my team member said even though she was not the consultant. I got more help from my team member because the work was made clearer by her.

For both these reasons, peer coaching has been investigated in a number of settings, including our own. As desirable as such a system clearly would be, it is infrequent, and most installation efforts have failed. Why is this so? Goldsberry suggests that colleague consultation does cost time, and time is money; however,

the first obstacle is not time but structure. Nothing about the way schools are typically structured, from their isolated classrooms to their modular, clock-driven work day is conducive to colleague consultation. For one teacher to witness the teaching of another, someone generally has to juggle administrative details so that a class of youngsters is not left alone. For two teachers to confer, either both must donate a mutually free time or more administrative juggling is required. For teachers simply to find time to learn and practice the skills of colleague consultation someone generally has to organize, to create a structure which permits it. Alas, these someones, those managers who have the knack for such organizing, seem rare in schools. (Goldsberry, 1986, p. 5)

Researchers at the University of British Columbia have studied a district-wide effort to install peer coaching in 24 schools over a 3-year period. The model for implementation was much like the triadic model described here and used at KEEP: District supervisors coached the principals, who coached the teachers in how to conduct peer coaching. Later, some teachers were "promoted" to coaches, and the principals then coached them. Grimmett, Housego, and Suddaby (1986) reported on this ambitious and optimistic program and in general terms documented a failed implementation in the broad context of the district.

In our view, the most valuable discussion of this project is the Grimmett, Moody, and Balasubramaniam report (1986) on the one school that achieved quite a successful level of implementation. It is clear that the indispensable condition for success is not the technical ability of the staff to conduct the assisting interactions. *Rather, the linchpin condition is the success of the principals in creating and maintaining activity settings in which the coaching can occur.* In the successful school, the principal arranged a series of interconnected activity settings: Not only was time made for the peers to meet together, but another activity setting was created in which the groups reported back to him and to the faculty about their experiences. This principal exhibited determination and flexibility in providing the colleagues their activity settings; he himself substituted for teachers, taking more than one class at a time to the gym, so that the teachers could actually meet!

Such a jury-rigged system is testimony to the excellence of that principal, but it also bears witness to the recalcitrance of the social organization of schooling. Society simply must recognize that more resources must be deployed to ensure opportunities for teachers to continue to learn. Even one "substituting" teacher could have freed classes and thus freed teachers. A minimum additional (or redeployed) resource could have allowed this superior principal to do more of what he did so well: plan and support activity settings for teachers' professional growth.

A further resistance to the peer coaching model is the unfamiliarity of teachers themselves with a system of giving and receiving coaching (Figure 9.3). Showers reported on a chained model of coaching in which she

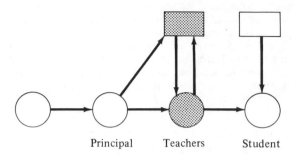

Figure 9.3. Peer-coaching activity setting supported by principal.

served as expert coach; coached teachers improved, as compared with the uncoached. When the coached teachers themselves took on a coaching role, 4 of 6 teachers resisted receiving this kind of assistance (Showers, 1984a, 1984b). It may be that these coaches were asked to perform in domains where they lacked sufficient expertise; it may be that all teachers need a new vision of schooling in which mutual assistance does not seem peculiar.

Finally, as valuable as is peer coaching, we suggest that it cannot be a total substitute for all expert consultation. Particularly in implementing an innovation, teachers need joint activity with program developers and supervisors (Ellis, 1986). In steady-state conditions, when some particular identified new expertise is not at issue, peer coaching is at its most useful.

Self-examination of videotapes

An activity setting in which self-collaboration is the specific purpose is the private viewing of these videotapes by the teacher alone. This "micro-teaching" activity is most effective when used in the middle to advanced stages of the ZPD for the skill goal. Once the teacher's need for external assistance is reduced, and self-assistance has begun to appear, self-examination of tapes provides the setting in which self-assistance can occur in an atmosphere of calm reflection and concentration.

Teacher #32: Watching videotapes of my lessons helped me see things going wrong that I never noticed while I was teaching. I was aware I should be looking at things, but I did not know what to look for. I made 16 tapes, watched them, and tried new things. The consultants were not consulting with me. I was already trying all the things they thought I should try. I don't know where the strategies came from. They don't come from some package you learn in ed. school or in training. I guess an organism in a bad uncomfortable position has ways to adapt. . . . I thought, studied, evaluated, analyzed a lot. I went over my 16 tapes exhaustively. Eventually I didn't need to tape myself to figure out what to do, but at first I did because things went so fast I couldn't respond. The taping helped me a lot in that.

Self-examination can also be assisted directly by a consultant. This is sometimes required when a teacher has difficulty focusing on relevant aspects of teaching. If a teacher chooses a useful focus at the outset of self-examination, the consultant's contributions are minimal. But if the teacher chooses a focus too broad, chooses an inconsequential topic, or focuses on problems attributable to students or their families, then consultant intervention is required – even specific directions, such as choosing a particular problem and requesting that the teacher do narrative recordings of the child's behavior. Assistance can be tailored to the individual: The consultant "can use a somewhat clinical approach in which the teacher comes to define a problem area and conduct the [self-examination] by herself, with only gentle questions and suggestions from the consultant. On the other hand, the consultant can take more of an instructor's role and state the goals" (Speidel, Tharp, & Gallimore, 1974, p. 9).

Sometimes, in order to be effective, self-examination must include training in observation skills. At one point, the KEEP training program included 8 hr of observation training in which teachers were taught to describe and record behavior in objective terms. Before observing children, seals and parrots were the objects, because their simpler behavior provided less difficulty for novice observers and because teachers were likely to be influenced by their customary ways of observation (Speidel et al., 1974, p. 5). In some instances, substantial changes in performance were obtained through observation training. The teachers involved reported learning to distinguish important cues in student behavior as a result of improved observation skills. Discriminating such cues allowed for more effective performance assistance.

Until a teacher has learned to observe the self more accurately, there is a possibility of gross error in estimating how much time is spent on various aspects of teaching. This inability to observe oneself accurately while teaching was evident early in the training for two teachers:

Teacher #30 [after viewing tape of herself teaching a reading lesson]: It didn't seem like I was spending so much time on behavior management. I would have estimated a lot more time on instruction. But I really did only five or six minutes [out of a 20-min reading lesson in Center One]. There's lots I didn't remember doing. I guess I am pretty unconscious while I'm teaching.

I repeated one question four times. I don't remember doing that. I know I spend time on behavior management, but I leave the lesson with the impression that it is minimal. Then I watch the tape, and it seems that's all I am doing.

Teacher #31 [after viewing tape of herself teaching a reading lesson]: There is this one child I have had a lot of trouble with. He loses his temper and is hard to control. On a day I taped myself, I was very concerned. I was expecting problems with him all that day. I noticed he was looking very unhappy. It was really bothering me while I was teaching: I'm sure it was affecting my lesson. But then I went to look at the tape, and I was amazed to discover that the boy was very attentive, very responsive, and gave me no trouble. I can't understand why I didn't see that at the time. I think the reason was past experience. In the past when he looked unhappy like that, it meant big trouble was coming. This past experience kept me from seeing how he was actually behaving. I had to look at the tape before I saw what was happening.

One of the consequences of self-examination is a growing willingness to explore new approaches to the improvement of teaching. It can lead to increased sharing among teachers who work together:

Teacher #23: We were working with being more positive with the children. We were videotaped. Each one had to go in and view the tapes by ourselves [sic]. That really helped us a lot. After that the consultant would come in once in a while, not to code, but to talk with us about things we were working on. The teachers also talked among themselves how to work on the positive with the children. We remind each other.

This is the nicest thing about the program. We are all close, and we can really share ideas and talk about things, our problems. It's really nice because six of us ride in a car pool. So, going and coming to school we let out all of our problems. We help each other; if we need materials we run over and borrow it. Everybody's willing to share. Last year, before we got into the KEEP program, we had to collect all of our own materials. But since there were teachers who had been in KEEP last year, they were willing to share with the rest of us who were new to KEEP.

Of course, this activity setting of tape viewing is a direct descendant of *microteaching,* as it was formulated some years ago based on foundational research on modeling by Bandura. Yet now, the use of microteaching and interest in it have faded (Walberg, 1986), despite evidence of its impact (Butcher, 1981; Walberg, 1986). The microteaching movement never succeeded in embedding self-observation in the routine of public schools. This is because even microteaching requires the time, place, persons, equipment, supervisory support, and other elements that all teacher-assisting activity settings must have.

Floor training

In the earlier levels of the teacher's ZPD, an activity setting that we may call "floor training" is arranged as needed. The physical setting is the classroom. The consultant may teach a demonstration lesson in the teacher's class, emphasizing some new skill or a skill of particular focus. The teacher will observe this, and discussion will follow. Even more effective is floor training that involves three adults as well as the students. A demonstration teacher (who might be the consultant, a more competent peer of the teacher, or some specialist) conducts the lesson, while the consultant guides the teacher's observation of the demonstration.

University courses

University courses frequently are used as settings for assisting teachers to improve their skills. MacDonald and Gallimore (1971) enrolled 81 public school teachers in a university extension course, for which they received credits for an advanced degree, a new credential, or salary increments. The teachers were asked to develop a project designed to solve some problem in their own classrooms or improve academic performance of their students. Ninety percent of the teachers took less than 3 weeks to conclude their observations, record a baseline, select a goal, and develop a plan.

The most difficult step in the process was the implementation of an intervention. Implementation required an average of 4 weeks for the teachers to achieve criterion. Ninety-three percent eventually achieved the criterion; this figure excludes 6 teachers, of the original 81, who refused to participate in the intervention phase on the grounds that being systematic, as the process required, violated their philosophy of teaching.

Wide-ranging innovative projects were developed and implemented. Direct observation of one-third of the participants suggested only one case of discrepancy from the written teacher reports on which the evaluation of projects was based. In addition, a majority of participants expressed favorable opinions about the course at the end of the semester.

A notable finding was the range of interesting ideas the teachers suggested and the speed with which they acquired the "action research" skills needed to develop, implement, and refine their innovations. Whether or not they were as affected by the experience as they reported was not fully documented. One qualitative finding: A majority of the teachers lacked the confidence (and some skills) needed to experiment in their classrooms. The course and the support of peers and a supportive "authority" (university professors who drove from an urban area to a rural area each week) compensated in part for their lack of confidence and encouraged teachers to try new approaches. Several years later, teachers who participated in that course reported that they were still practicing "action research" to solve problems and improve instruction; however, these claims were not objectively verified.

The success of the "action research" course was, in part, due to the emphasis on translating research into practice in each teacher's own classroom. This is consistent with prior research showing that effective inservice programs must offer teacher assistance that can be efficiently used in their own classrooms; training activities conducted in isolation from teachers' immediate responsibilities seldom have an impact on teacher practices (Guskey, 1986).

Another factor in the success of this effort was the provision of explicit instruction in implementation of teacher-designed innovations. The lack of training in implementation has been well documented as one of the major barriers to most innovation efforts undertaken by local school personnel (Berman & McLaughlin, 1978).

Teacher workshops

The workshop is a typical activity setting in which teachers are assisted. Workshops are useful for introducing new skills to teachers and for providing cognitive structuring. The evaluation of workshops at KEEP is consistent with that of the field in general – workshops, as sole forms of assistance, are of limited utility. For example, Sloat, Tharp, and Gallimore (1977) found no change in teacher behavior from baseline values following a workshop devoted entirely to didactic presentations (lecture, readings, and discussion). Other studies have shown that changes are short-lived, for example, when data are collected some weeks after the workshop has ended (Speidel & Tharp, 1978).

Of even more limited value are workshops whose purpose is to change teacher attitudes and beliefs (Guskey, 1986). Such a strategy is based on the assumption that attitude change necessarily precedes behavior change. In fact, Guskey's review suggests that the opposite is true: Changes in teaching practices precede changes in teachers' attitudes and beliefs. Guskey cited a study of dissemination efforts supporting school improvements (Crandall et al., 1982) that examined efforts to implement 61 innovations in 146 school districts nationwide. Outcomes were poor in those cases where teacher commitment to innovative practice was sought prior to implementation. "The new practices typically lost their effectiveness because they were altered by teachers beyond recognition" (Crandall et al., 1982, p. 8). In the successful cases, teachers became committed to the practices only after implementation: In effect, the attitudes of veteran teachers are shaped by experience with practice in the classroom. When innovations work, they are liked.

If the standard workshop format is expanded to include activity settings and a broader range of the means of assistance, the effects can be increased. Among the more important elements to be added to the workshop are observation of videotapes, feedback, and the floor-training elements described earlier.

This conclusion was supported by follow-up data collected 5 months after a 3-day workshop (Speidel & Tharp, 1978). This study is reviewed in detail, because several others to be reviewed later in this chapter used similar methods and procedures. Speidel and Tharp recruited 6 experienced teachers (teacher trainees, or TTs) from two Hawaiian public elementary schools. The 6 participated in a 3-day workshop at KEEP that was conducted by a psychologist and 3 demonstration teachers (DTs).

Before the workshop began, each teacher was observed in her home classroom on three different mornings during the week preceding the workshop. Six behavioral categories were recorded: frequency of praise (for work and comportment), positive and negative body contact, delivery of material rewards, and scolding.

The workshop opened with a 1-hr lecture on social-reinforcement principles that included videotaped examples from the KEEP classrooms. Following the lecture, the TTs were trained to observe and record pupil on-task, off-task, and disruptive behaviors from videotapes. These observations were followed by discussion and replays of incidents about which the TTs disagreed.

The next step in the training was observation, by the TTs, of a DT praising students for working. The TTs were then asked to enter the classroom and practice giving as many praises for work as they could – without regard to quality of student work.

After the practice session, the teachers were introduced to four types of effective praise: general verbal praise, general praise for good deportment, praise for sustained academic work, and specific praise that focused on precision of praise.

The TTs were told that they would eventually practice the four kinds of praise, but first they were to observe a DT and record each time one of the four types of praise was delivered. Two TTs were assigned to each DT. After recording, the TTs entered the classroom with a DT and practiced praising while the class was conducted as usual by the DT (who was monitoring work in learning centers). Each DT first modeled praise several times and then asked the TT to praise various children for practice. DTs gave brief comments on TTs' performances, emphasizing aspects well done.

The practice episodes were videotaped and subsequently viewed (in pairs) by the TTs. Under the guidance of their DT, each pair of TTs counted the number of times they praised correctly. The training workshop ended with a discussion among the TTs, the DTs, and the workshop leader (a psychologist).

A week after the workshop ended, the TTs were again observed in their home classrooms, on four different mornings. Five months later, they were again visited and observed for two different mornings. At both the 1-week post-workshop visit and the 5-month follow-up, the same observation procedure was used that had been applied during the pre-workshop visits to the home classrooms.

The mean frequency of incidents of praise for academic work increased from 3.77 (per 15-min intervals) during pre-workshop observations to 13.63 at the post-workshop phase and to 12.00 at the follow-up [$F(12, 10)$ = 15.12, $p < .001$].

Praise for comportment displayed a similar pattern. The mean frequency prior to the workshop was 1.72 (per 15-min intervals); it increased to 6.93 at post-workshop visit, and 8.57 during follow-up visit [$F(2, 10) = 11.14, p < .01$].

These results suggest that workshops can be an effective setting for assisting teacher performance. However, changes are not permanent.

A second study (Johnson & Sloat, 1980) was conducted in public schools. This study indicated that the workshop format can vary from that employed by Speidel and Tharp and still achieve changes in teaching practices. Thirteen public school teachers enrolled in an extension course. The sequence of training stages was: didactic instruction, instructions to practice, guided practice, discrimination training, and performance feedback. The guided practice was similar to the procedure used by Speidel and Tharp (1978), except that it was conducted during a 1-day visit to KEEP. As before, the major variable of interest was effective use of praise. Only performance feedback had any effect on the praise rate.

In a third study, Sloat (1981) selected the most powerful elements from the preceding studies and combined them into a single training package. The training consisted of a 1-day guided-practice session. No didactic instruction was provided, except for a brief statement of purpose. The trainer then demonstrated the techniques in the classroom, prompted the trainees to use the techniques, and reinforced proper use. Three teachers were coded for praise rates prior to training; 2 of the 3 completed the training. After training, recording of praise rates indicated that the 2 trainees doubled their praise rates, while the third nonparticipant showed no change. This suggested that didactic instruction, videotape models, and elaborate feedback could be curtailed if the goal was a simple increase in praise rate.

A fourth study (Sloat, Tanaka-Matsumi, Ah Ho, & Sueoka, 1977) used a two-part training sequence. First, a session was conducted after school on one afternoon, during which participants discussed expected student behavior and appropriate management techniques; this was followed by viewing and coding of videotapes for discrimination training. The second part consisted of 2 days of guided practice in participants' home classrooms using the same procedure described by Sloat and Hao (1980). Rates of praise approximately doubled after the two-stage training session.

Overall, this series of studies indicates that augmented workshops that include modeling, practice, and feedback can affect teaching behavior. Although the focus in these studies was on teacher praise and its effects on deportment, a number of other domains of teaching behavior can be influenced through similar procedures (see the next two chapters for training of responsive teaching). However satisfying these results, they should not obscure the importance of the activity settings and assisted-performance opportunities that await teachers after workshop training.

Workshop training does not ensure that what is learned will be routinely used in a teacher's home classroom. As Sloat has noted, such an approach "ignores the effect the environment has in supporting the behavior, and assumes that once a person has demonstrated mastery of a behavior, he will continue to use it" (Sloat, 1981, p. 40). In fact, only one of three follow-up studies at KEEP has shown maintenance of praise rates following training. Speidel and Tharp (1978) observed no difference in teacher praise rates immediately after training and 5 months later. However, Johnson and Sloat (1980), in follow-ups of 5 months and 1 year, and Tanaka-Matsumi (Sloat, Tharp, & Gallimore, 1977; Tanaka-Matsumi, 1977), following up after 11 months, found that praise rates had reverted to pretraining levels.

None of the studies described earlier demonstrated that trainees acquired new knowledge or behaviors. All that was measured were changes in rate of various behaviors. Often dramatic changes in rate were obtained. However, in most cases the behaviors were already being performed (albeit at low levels) prior to "training." It is possible that trainees did acquire new skills ... but such acquisition cannot be shown on the basis of data available. (Sloat, 1981, p. 40).

Workshops are notorious in educational institutions, providing short cycles of enthusiasm, followed by loss of interest and rushing off to the next fad. The workshop circuit is analogous to a carnival midway: A teacher collects plaster dolls and puts them in the closet, and has wasted months of Saturday mornings.

When workshops are followed up by other activity settings, they can be economical introductory activities. However, when either workshops or courses are not supplemented by continuing forms of teacher assistance, little continuing profit can be expected. For such assistance to be provided, changes in the activity settings of the sort outlined earlier in this chapter are required.

The project team as a model of "consultation"

The fully teaching school must provide opportunities for continuous learning, for professional growth and development, even for exemplary teachers (Rosenholtz, 1986). Often, for skillful teachers, some next appropriate goal for professional development is not experienced as some lack of skill, but rather as a problem that needs solving. Such situations are ideal for the activity setting that provides the most powerful source of assistance – the activity setting of project collaboration (Vogt, 1985). The Project Model of Consultation (PMC) involves collaborative problem-solving or research in which the teacher is a full partner with the consultant or researcher, or sometimes a member of a committee or project team. Teachers will change if they play a role in shaping curricula and if they help determine values embodied in curricula (Fullan & Pomfret, 1977; Rosenholtz, 1986). Because of the powerful intersubjectivities developed during the joint productive activity of the project team, cognition and motivation themselves are transformed.

There are many examples of this consultation model operating at KEEP sites. Sometimes the consultant is directly involved and considers the project a major staff development goal for the teacher and herself. Sometimes the teacher works primarily with a researcher or project team.

In the project-team model of assisted performance, the activity-setting members consist, as a minimum, of the teacher, the consultant, and a researcher, although several of each of these may be involved. Solving the problem is the goal of the activity, and collaborative work is the style. The creation of the intersubjectivity is the process, and mutual assistance is the outcome. In this model, the consultant's interaction with the teacher is virtually confined to the project-team-related activities. Each member of the team has different skills, and each contributes assistance to the others, as well as receiving it. In this model, it is acknowledged that none of the members yet possesses the cognitive strtuctures that are the goal of the enterprise.

Lynn Vogt, a senior consultant at KEEP, has described the PMC using this example:

Last year I "supervised" one of our expert teachers by engaging with her in a Project Team. The project began by having the teacher articulate a goal to focus our interaction for the year. She wanted to expand her comfort and skill in using student contributions to develop higher level themes in ETR lessons.

Over the course of the year, we read and studied articles, viewed many video-taped ETR lessons, devised and revised a responsive questioning checklist, and wrote a paper describing how to use it when observing and giving feedback on ETR lessons. From the early stages of the project the teacher's lessons began to improve. In striving to articulate the complexity of the ETR process for the observation forms, she began to integrate the teaching skills herself. The form may be moderately useful for other sets of teachers and consultants, but the most important factor is that the Project itself resulted in a developmental leap for the teacher (and for me as well).

The project had the following characteristics: (a) The teacher was a full collaborator, from the moment of setting the goal that would focus our work. (b) Defined program standards guided the project, but the process and outcome were totally open-ended. (c) Reflection and analysis accompanied trial and error as we developed the observation form and checklist. (d) Observation, feedback, and discussion tracked the effect of the project on the teacher's lessons. And (e) the project operated flexibly and responsively as we juggled the events of daily school life and worked together to better comprehend and articulate the ETR strategy. (Vogt, 1985)

Providing assistance to consultant/trainers

Program developers and researchers assist the performances of consultants, trainers, and supervisors in a variety of settings, not only in the project-team model, but directly. Before, during, and after such participation, researchers and program developers also provide assistance to consultants in a variety of other settings.

The consultant/trainer training program

Assisting the performance of teachers requires a high degree of competence in consultant/trainers. Knowledge of curriculum, of teaching methods, and of the techniques of assistance must be sensitively employed in assisting teachers to assist students.

The first activity setting that a new consultant encounters is a specific *consultant-training program*. Over the year-long course of that training, each beginning consultant is involved in a variety of activity "sub-settings": seminar presentations, tutorials, role-playing, guided observation, guided practice, and finally assignment as an assistant consultant to actual classrooms. During this training program, all the means of assistance are provided by the training staff (Figure 9.4), which consists of two coordinators and a participating staff of experienced consultants, researchers, and program developers.

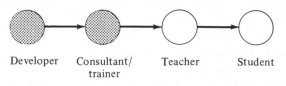

Figure 9.4.

The workshop/retreat

Workshops and their somewhat more extensive versions, retreats, are provided to consultants on a variety of topics, particularly in new developments in instructional goals and methods. These are the settings in which program developers introduce new material, interpret it, provide instructions and cognitive structuring, and offer occasions for guided observation and practice.

We have already discussed the workshop format in the section on providing assistance to teachers. The same principles apply when the recipients are trainers/consultants. Workshops, as vehicles for in-service training, are notoriously ineffective – at least in their traditional formats, which resemble selling snake oil from the back of a wagon through hyperbole and entertainment. The limited time available for most workshops imposes constraints that prevent the most careful, patient, and individualized teaching. It is small wonder that the best estimates of the long-term effectiveness of workshops have predicted poor results.

However, workshops can be better than they usually are. The most effective short presentations at KEEP have involved (a) extensive use of modeling as a means of assistance, with either live demonstrations or videotaped exemplars, and (b) involvement of workshop participants in some form of action, such as practicing segments, with immediate feedback, or some presentation of the materials in the formats that are being advocated. For example, a workshop on the instructional conversations should include some small-group conversational activity settings. For workshops on "innovations" to use activity settings of lecture, text presentation, and assessment merely perpetuates the old script.

Producing training materials

Program developers at KEEP frequently produce materials for the use of consultants in assisting teachers. Demonstration videotapes of a new classroom method are most often produced by a team including an expert developer of the method and a consultant. The latter represents the "users," those consultants who will eventually use these videotapes as models for their teachers. Through the collaborative process of joint activity with the researcher, the consultant also becomes an expert. In fact, through this activity, the product may well be changed or refined because of the assistance provided by the consultant to the program developer.

Such training materials provide the video models that are such important means of assistance to teachers. In this section, however, we are focusing on the performance assistance provided *to the consultants* during their interaction with program developers as they produce the training materials together.

Myra Kent is the consultant at KEEP's Honolulu office who works most often in producing training tapes. Here she discusses the process with the authors:

Myra: The discussions that arise during the production of training materials make the products better since it makes the construction of the tapes a part of the research debates. It is actually a participation of researchers and trainers in the process of dissemination and training. We will never agree on all points – if that happens it only means our research is dead or dying!

One example is the work I did with Gisela Speidel to develop a tape to train teachers to promote language development. Gisela was very interested, since our language development methods are largely the product of her research. And the consultants felt that the teachers needed a better set of model tapes for language development.

I first asked the consultants what teachers they might recommend to help in creating a new set of tapes. Julie was recommended, and she agreed . . . then she taught a lesson. We edited the tape in the preliminary form and then at a consultant in-service retreat on vocabulary development, I showed it and got feedback. They felt it was rather confusing in the initial edit. So, we re-edited. That's how we did that one.

I have learned a lot about language and vocabulary from working with Gisela on the tapes. I've learned a tremendous amount about how she looks at things and what she considers to be important. . . . She is very specific, very clear and precise, which helped us identify ways of editing the tape, to show the teacher doing exactly this, and this, and that.

But what I get from the [researchers like Gisela] gets a little diffused as it goes down the line, from me to the consultants and then to the teachers. If all the consultants could work as I was able to do with Gisela, and really pin down some of those ideas, then perhaps they could transmit them more. But I've done it much better since working with Gisela on these tapes – I found when I did the in-service workshops on vocabulary they finally understood it! What made the difference was the specificity.

Authors: This is an example of learning through the joint activity of producing the tape. And the learning wasn't confined to the tape. What you learned in interaction with Gisela generalized. It's a lovely example of joint productive activity which produces growth, which is internalized and becomes part of our problem-solving skills. You can be sure that Gisela learned as much as you did.

Myra: I think Gisela was very aware that she can overpower consultants with too much technical information. She relied on my judgment and asked others how much we should include. We opted to focus very narrowly on Julie, on one aspect of what she was doing because I thought that was enough for consultants to try and convey to teachers. I wanted to focus on what I would want out of the tape to train teachers. In all of this, Gisela was bringing her expertise and I was bringing my practitioner's knowledge.

Authors: That's why we organize these activity settings as we do. They require that shared concepts be developed and that's the whole purpose of it. It's the same as we do in teaching at all levels: we bring the technical concepts into conjunction with the practical ones, and refresh both and make them useful tools for thinking. Developing concepts, establishing word meaning – these are as important for us here as it is for the children in Center One. Can you think of one particular example, some concept you two had to discuss and come to agreement on?

Myra: She used the word "labels" to represent something a little different from my idea of what "labels" meant. I knew the teachers would have a meaning of the word more like mine – it's a technical term in the Word Play stage of instructional strategies [see Chapter 7]. Gisela was using the term's common everyday meaning, like pasting a label on something like we do at the art center. So when Gisela used the word "label" in that way, it would be misleading to them. We really had to thrash that out and really had to come to an agreement about how we could use that word in the context of the tapes. She yielded and was willing to accept what I was arguing for. We used "label" in the sense that the teachers do, and "naming" for the technical concept that Gisela wanted to teach in the tape.

Authors: Vygotsky speaks of a constant tension between everyday concepts and what he calls scientific concepts. You knew that "label" was already a technical or scientific concept for the teachers, and Gisela knew that a new technical term was needed for language development – so you two agreed on using "naming." Now has Gisela revised her own terminology?

Myra: I don't know. That would be interesting.

Authors: Gisela, how do you use the word "labeling"?

Dr. Speidel: Just in the everyday way, though when I'm talking to teachers and consultants I'm careful, because I know they use it to talk about a Word Play activity. For me though, this "naming" has become strictly as a technical term in language development, just as Myra and I worked out.

The project team as a setting for mutual assistance

Collegial joint activity and its intersubjectivities are even more effective in "project-team" activities. When the consultant and the program developer work together with the teacher in a project for problem solution, assisted performance occurs in each permutation of interaction. The project-team model, for the researcher/developer also, is the highest form of assisted performance that can be offered to trainers. All that has been said in describing the project team from the point of view of the teacher and consultant can be said from the point of view of the researcher and consultant. Participating in this activity – the "highest" setting – does require a good level of basic competence in the consultant and an equally high level of competence and confidence in the researcher.

Our experience is consistent with that of the many current authors who advocate collaboration among researchers and teachers; for example, Bird and Little (1986) have pointed out that both teachers and researchers have a stake in the disciplined inquiry of teachers into their own work. "By sharing their knowledge of research methods and by engaging teachers and administrators in their research, researchers can contribute to a faculty's capacity to study its own work and to employ the researcher's product. . . . Teachers can guide researchers to the issues and problems that vex them most" (Bird & Little, 1986, p. 508).

It is through team research that program developers and researchers are able to provide the richest assistance to educational personnel, and it is through this same team research that researchers are assisted most to perform effective research. In the KEEP system, the most useful research – in the sense of the most influential, pertinent, and problem-solving inquiries – has invariably been conducted in some partnership of researchers, trainers, and teachers.

Often, particularly for skillful teachers, the next goal for professional development is experienced as a problem that needs solving, and the specific behaviors needed to solve the problem are not clearly seen by anyone in the system. Recent examples from the KEEP system include these two problems:

1. More responsibility for planning center work could be assumed by the children themselves. A project team was organized that consisted of a researcher, consultant, and one teacher with her classroom. Together this group invented, experimented, and evaluated different methods of assisting children to better assist themselves (Dalton & Cramer, 1987).

2. More writing needed to be included in the language arts curriculum. But how to articulate it with the demonstrated effectiveness of the reading program? Two separate project teams were created, each containing a different researcher, consultant, and teachers; each project team approached the problem solution in a different way, and the ultimate program development was enriched by having this variety of experiences.

This setting can be considered the highest level of activity setting. The highest "entry" level of competence for the teacher, for the consultant, and indeed for the researcher/developer is required, and the highest level of skill advancement is produced. It is the highest instantiation of the theory of teaching. It provides the purest form of intersubjectivity, arising from cooperative work to solve a jointly valued problem-goal. It produces a coordinated set of intrapsychological planes – jointly acquired and coordinated cognitive structures. It demonstrates that assistance can

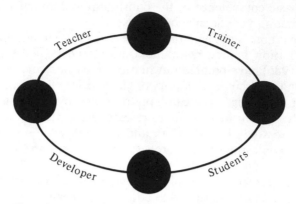

Figure 9.5. The project team: mutual assistance through joint productive activity.

be provided through ZPDs *mutually. One need not be "superior" in order to assist.* Mutual assistance is provided by the task orientation of joint productive activity.

As Figure 9.5 illustrates, the project-team activity completes the circle of assistance because it involves the students as well, and the linear model of assisted performance is transcended. When research-and-development activities are carried out by teacher, researcher, and trainer, there is another major participant as well: the student body of the classroom where the problems are being solved. The students in such activity are more than "subjects" of scrutiny. Their performance, as feedback to the research team, provides an indispensable form of assistance to the problem-solvers. When such a team works together for solving the problem of improving education for the students, the ideal is most nearly met: The educational institution becomes a learning environment for all.

10   Assisting teacher performance through the ZPD: a case study

The management of activity settings and the orchestration of assistance to teachers are complex tasks, with endless opportunities for error, delay, confusion, anxiety, and all the other problems that can arise in human social transactions. Cast as a set of propositions about teacher training, the theoretical structure presented thus far has all the advantage of the "schooled' or "scientific" or "systematic" set of concepts – and all the disadvantage: "Propositions are remarkably economical in form, containing and simplifying a great deal of complexity. . . . They gain their economy precisely because they are decontextualized, stripped down to their essentials, devoid of detail, emotion, or ambience" (Shulman, 1986, p. 11).

The liability of this "schooled" propositional knowledge is its inability to convey how the structures and processes appear and function in concert, in particular circumstances of everyday life (Shulman, 1986, p. 11). In practice, the means and sources of assistance to teachers – in given activity settings – are inevitably concatenated and interpenetrated. Their complexities are further compounded by the personalities of the actors, the particularities of a given school, and other features of the local eco-cultural niche. Knowing only the propositions of Chapter 9 would provide little assistance to any who sought to implement them.

Shulman offered one remedy for the liability of propositional knowledge: *case* knowledge:

A case, properly understood, is not simply the report of an event or incident. To call something a case is to make a theoretical claim – to argue that it is a "case of something," or to argue that it is an instance of a larger class. . . . Case knowledge is knowledge of specific, well-documented, and richly described events. . . . Cases exemplify, illustrate, and bring alive the theoretical propositions that are potentially the most powerful tools teachers can have. (Shulman, 1986, pp. 11–12)

"Case knowledge" is much like "everyday" concepts, described in Chapter 5 as being in constant dialectical tension with schooled concepts. We argued that the good instructional conversation will bring these levels

217

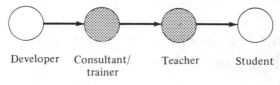

Developer   Consultant/   Teacher   Student
             trainer

Figure 10.1.

into conjunction, enriching both and precipitating useful cognitive skills. Likewise, we here present the everydayness of an extended case study in assisting teacher performance, with the goal of enriching the propositional knowledge of the theoretical structures.

This is the case of a teacher learning to teach the KEEP reading program, in particular learning to conduct comprehension lessons in the instructional conversation of Center One and to assist students' text comprehension through the use of responsive questioning. The principal activity setting for her training was the observation-and-conference activity setting, and the primary source of assistance was a consultant. The teacher-in-training and her consultant conducted an extended, months-long instructional conversation (Figure 10.1).

However, in the course of the 4-month consultation, other activity settings and sources of assistance were mobilized: a teaching peer who provided a decisive model in her own classroom, a supervising teacher of high status who offered praise for progress during an informal conversation, and, finally, that source characteristically depended on by truly professional teachers – the self.

With this case, in Shulman's terms, we are making "a theoretical claim . . . that it is a 'case of something,' . . . that it is an instance of a larger class." It portrays and documents, through a connected narrative, the workings and concomitants of our teacher-training model:

1. the interplay of different sources of assistance, and the six means of assistance.
2. the instructional conversation, complex and extended, in which the means of assistance are embedded.
3. the importance of teacher and consultant intersubjectivity that permits the latter to assist the former in her ZPD.
4. the decisive importance of intellectual grasp of subject matter by the teacher who is learning to assist the performance of students.
5. the potential for stress and anxiety that participants in such training activities must accept and that consultants must learn how to manage without compromising training goals.
6. the stages of development through which teachers proceed in their ZPDs, from reliance on assistance by the consultant and others, to grow-

ing dependence on self, to the approach of fully internalized and integrated skill – these stages of teacher development are presented in propositional form in Chapter 11 and illustrated by case knowledge in this chapter.

Participants and context

The teacher (Grace) whose training serves as a case example was a KEEP first-grade teacher in her first year of training. She had completed a workshop phase of training and had worked in the classroom for a few months when the initial consultation sessions began.

The consultant (Stephanie) had worked at KEEP for 3 years and had completed a training course in consultation skills. Her work with Grace was one of her first full-fledged consultations.

The sessions were informal. For each session, the teacher had videotaped a recent reading-comprehension lesson. The playback of the tape focused the discussion between teacher and consultant. On most occasions the teacher controlled the tape and chose points at which to stop for discussion, comment, or other reaction. She also stopped the tape to talk about episodes at the consultant's suggestion.

Eight consultation sessions were conducted from January to May. All these sessions were audiotaped and transcribed. We also transcribed all videotapes discussed in the consulting sessions. Of the eight consultation sessions, seven are presented here in the form of excerpts and summaries. The eighth session dealt with details of institutional procedures; the content was unrelated to the training and is not included here.

In the weeks prior to the sessions described here, Grace had been provided a limited number of consultation sessions that were terminated when she was judged to be making excellent progress. During these initial months in the classroom, she had easily mastered the classroom- and behavior-management skills that all KEEP teachers are taught. She was also learning the KEEP reading program.

The first goal: building responsive teaching in the instructional conversation

In the beginning, the consultation sessions revealed that the teacher, Grace, had already developed a certain level of skill in the KEEP reading program acquired in workshop sessions. For example, early in the first consultation session with Stephanie, she discussed the value of selecting a *theme* to guide her interactions with the students in Center One. This theme would link the children's available concepts with the narrative of the text, according to the experience-text-relationship (E-T-R) model (see earlier chapters describing this model). In general, Grace's idea was that the theme would provide a goal toward which she could assist student comprehension. This theme could also serve to guide choices among alternative lines of discussion during the lesson.

As Stephanie and Grace discussed a lesson on the folk tale *Billy Goat Gruff*, Grace reported that she had selected the "greediness of the troll" (who kept waiting for a bigger goat to come by) as the central theme for her lesson preparation. In this first consultation session, Stephanie and Grace were watching the videotape of Grace's first lesson about the troll and goats. But the conduct of the lesson did not come up to Grace's standards. Here is a short excerpt from the lesson they were watching.

Grace: Why, why, what was the problem with the troll?
Kanani: He wanted to eat. . . . He was greedy.
Grace: Greedy. Are you greedy?
Chorus: No.
Grace: What happens to you if you're greedy?
Louise: You going to come mean and you going to get spanking from your mommy.
Grace: Does the troll have a mommy?
Louise: No. [giggles]
Sheida: He's all by himself. He's lonely. He can't find an equal, with nobody.
Kanani: His mom dies. He killed his mom.
Summie: He doesn't have food.
Grace: All right, so we know we think. . . . You're thinking, that's your idea.
Kanani: He killed his mom.
Grace: He's that greedy and that mean? All right, we learned something about the troll yesterday. We did find out one thing about him. What did we find out about him from our reading yesterday?

In this excerpt, Grace's questions are responsive, in the literal sense, but to no clear purpose. She produces a string of questions and answers that are linked to one another, but they are not tied by a line of thought, and certainly not tied to the preselected theme of "greediness." For example, Grace asks if the troll has a mommy in response to the child's connecting of greediness and parental punishment. The child responds with an elaboration that adds details not found in the text, nor in the usual versions of the myth. Grace recognizes that she has elicited some original thought, but she does not know what to do with it. She comments once on the child's idea, and then changes the topic. This series of questions has the form but not the substance of assisting performance through questioning.

Nearing the end of the session, Grace and Stephanie have discussed a number of issues, but Stephanie has made no comments about the quality of the comprehension questioning, although her goal at this point was to assist Grace to see that literal responsiveness was not enough – the children needed assistance in linking their existing knowledge with the text's information.

Stephanie reported later that she was waiting for an exchange (on the videotape) between Grace and the students that had some positive elements; she did not want to bring up problems in this first session until there was something positive to build on. She wanted to assist Grace first by some contingent – and deserved – praise. And now, though the session had almost ended, Grace had produced little that her trainer could compliment.

Why? Though a newcomer to this program, Grace was a highly motivated and dedicated professional. She had completed workshop training and knew the program principles well enough to talk about them intelligently. How did this aimlessness come about?

Later in this first consultation session, an answer began to emerge: A major issue is Grace's approach to the text itself. She treats the text as consisting of the literal details presented in the primer, organized by her single theme of greediness. Grace herself needed a deeper understanding of the text. The opportunity for Stephanie to provide some assistance arose with the following exchange on the tape:

Grace: Okay. We know that it has something to do with ...
Chorus: The troll.
Grace: The troll, and what belongs to the troll?
Chorus: The bridge.
Grace: The bridge. Okay, we know something ...
Sheida: What belongs to the goats?
Grace: What belongs to the goats?
Tosufa: The grass.
Grace: The grass belongs to the goats.
Sheida: Not all of it. The village has ... you got to share the grass.
Grace: Who has to share the grass?
Chorus: The goats.

The tape is stopped, because Stephanie has found her opportunity. She begins her assistance by recognizing a positive achievement and follows that up by instructing with a mild suggestion:

Stephanie: That seems to be a moment of responsiveness, Grace. Where you picked up on when the child said "all that belongs to the troll"...
Grace: [Responds favorably and at length] I thought it was kinda neat when Sheida brought up what belongs [to the characters]. I think it's neat when the kids can start asking questions about what they're [reading] and that we are trying to ... take the purpose from them. ... I thought it was a good

question for her to bring up. . . . I thought it was kind of neat to pick up on what she was saying.
Stephanie: Yeah. It's because it could relate to some bigger concepts in the story. In fact, [you could begin] the investigation of the character of the troll in terms of why is he acting this way. One reason may be that he is plain hungry. Another reason might be that he is [being territorial] and they are invading his place. And [there are] other things that you know about animal behavior that make them operate in certain ways [but] his nature may not be exactly as they see here. There may be other things that are making him act the way he does. [You're] starting to touch on some items that later you might want [to use].

Grace, however, does not think so. She objects by complaining about the story.

Grace: The story is very. . . . it's very shallow. All it says is, the goat comes along and is going to eat grass. [The troll says], "No, I am going to eat you." [The goat says], "Don't eat me. Wait for the bigger one who's coming behind me." [Grace continues paraphrasing text] And this is all the kids get . . .

Stephanie mildly challenged the assertion that "greediness" – Grace's chosen theme – was necessarily a full interpretation of the troll's motivation. Grace initially resisted this line of discussion by commenting that the story was "very shallow." She quoted the text as proof that it offers little on which to build a discussion.

Grace's comment that the story is "very shallow" is a key to understanding the early phases of the consultation. Her initial problem in conducting the comprehension lessons had more to do with subject-matter knowledge than pedagogical method.

Integrating the two domains of knowledge

We have decided from observation and reflection that two large domains of knowledge must be readily accessed to be an expert pedagogue. We have stipulated those two domains of knowledge to be subject matter knowledge and knowledge of organization and management of classrooms. (Berliner, 1986, p. 9)

Only an effective integration of these two domains will produce the expert pedagogue, and a precondition is an adequate knowledge of both domains.

The study of literature, for English majors as well as "English-methods" students, provides some basic skills in literary structual analysis. Grace exhibits some ability by perceiving one potential theme in the story of the troll and goats and pronouncing the story "shallow."

Stephanie now faces a training problem. Grace must be brought to a higher level of skill regarding content – for example, to be able to perceive more than one theme in the story and to relate themes structurally. In addition, Grace also needs more skill development in pedagogy. However, there is evidence that content knowledge and pedagogical knowledge do not separate as simply as it seems. Grace must also learn to encourage and elicit theme identification in students. This latter ability – a hybrid of pedagogy and content – is usually bred in teacher-role socialization experiences and in courses on methods of teaching English (Clift & Morgan, 1986). Stephanie must assist Grace to develop this hybrid skill, but Stephanie makes the (correct) training decision to address first the content knowledge: She assists Grace through a theme-and-structure analysis of *Billy Goat Gruff*. After that basic skill is acquired, she will be in position to address Grace's need to shift from the role of *analyzer of themes* to the role of *assistor of children who analyze themes*.

Stephanie's first goal became to assist Grace in developing a higher knowledge of the subject matter – literary qualities and possibilities inherent in simple texts. Their discussion began to sound more like a seminar on children's literature than a consultation on questioning technique. This is entirely appropriate, because Grace will not be able to assist the children until she can recognize in the story multiple opportunities to link schemata, concepts, and text details; only after that point can knowledge of questioning technique be joined effectively to subject-matter knowledge.

So Stephanie persists. Through a series of questions and comments about character interpretation, she leads Grace to the appreciation that the troll and goats have in common that they are hungry as well as territorial, that in fact the troll's behavior may be complexly motivated. The conversation continues:

Stephanie: So, do they [goats and troll] have similar needs? The animals in the story seem to have similar needs. They are all hungry. The troll's going to eat the goats. The goats [are] coming over [the bridge] to eat the grass.

Stephanie's questions and challenges have an effect, and Grace begins to engage in the intellectual process of literary analysis, which she apparently had not considered applicable to simple texts.

Grace: I never even thought about the troll being hungry. I just thought the thing was mean. . . . "If you cross my bridge, I'm going to eat you." . . . It's an awfully difficult way to earn a meal!

Now firmly in the role of literary critic, Stephanie notes the ironic outcome of the story:

Stephanie: [The troll] is so strong and so adamant in his position and so assured of himself and he is the guy that ends up with nothing in the end. [Stephanie then points out that Grace could draw a parallel between these

animals and the experiences of the children in her group] Especially those
from families with older children . . . where the older ones use [the troll's]
strategy [and] the younger ones come out on top.
Grace: Oh, how interesting . . .

The session continues at some length, with Stephanie elaborating an
interpretation of the text that goes well beyond Grace's initial greediness
theme:

Stephanie: So maybe they have a lot more to share about what's happening with
these goats from their own experience. But you've already started thinking
about that, because of looking at what this troll is. He is mean. And because
he is so one-dimensional, he's made himself be that way. He is going to
miss a lot. So that in your life if you just get into something, you . . . life is
going to pass you by while you are paying attention to this one stupid thing.
So I think there are some ways to talk about your characters as you have
been, and continuing on looking at what they are doing and what's making
them do that and what it's saying about them . . . and then asking the kids
to do the human analogy thing.

Stephanie's immediate goal (she reported later) was to assist Grace
toward the idea that there is more to these texts than what is literally
presented. She focused on the case at hand and discussed the parallels
between the character and circumstances of the troll and of people – especially those in the world of the students. She wanted to assist Grace to
consider more than a single preselected theme. A single theme places a
severe limit on how responsive a teacher can be to the ideas and interpretations that a topic or text elicits from children. If the teacher insists
on being guided solely by preselected goals, a lesson will inevitably take
on more of the quality of a directed rather than responsive interaction.

Directing them to an interpretation provided or imposed by the teacher
can have merit, but the ultimate goal is to teach students to construct an
understanding without assistance:

It's important to distinguish between help that somehow gets a child to produce
the right answer, and help from which the child might learn how to answer similar
questions in the future [without the assistance of a more capable other]. . . . If, for
example, when a child cannot read the word *bus* on a word card, the teacher
prompts the answer with the question, "what do you ride to school on?" the child
may answer correctly . . . say "bus." But that is not a prompt the child could give
to herself the next time, because the prompt depends on the very knowledge of
the word that it is supposed to cue. (Cazden, 1981, p. 5)

Analogously, students must be assisted through the steps of meaning construction so that they can eventually self-manage comprehension by
themselves, in the absence of someone who provides an interpretation to
be memorized.

The first consultation session ended with an agreement to tape the next day's lesson and to meet again. In concluding, Stephanie reminded Grace of the steps of E-T-R and urged her to focus on the R phase in her thinking so that she would be better able to respond to child contributions.

Integrating text and student experience

In their first interaction, Grace and Stephanie dealt with the issue of text interpretation and the importance of having alternative themes in mind. But even with alternatives at the ready, children's speech cannot always be quickly understood and related to the text. The integration of student ideas and experience with the text is a fundamental cognitive goal of teaching comprehension; the importance of this goal is matched by its difficulty of achievement!

These difficulties are well illustrated in the second consultation session, which occurred the following day. Stephanie opens the session by questioning Grace about her objectives for the lesson:

Grace: So I said [to myself], "Ok, I'll take your suggestion about developing the character of the troll and further developing the goats and why the goats are doing such things." It was interesting to see what they came up with
. . .

Grace turned on the videocassette recorder (VCR), and the tape began as Kanani commented that he had a noisemaker that could make sounds like footsteps. Stephanie and Grace listen to Grace's lesson, in which Grace acknowledges Kanani's comment, but does not pursue it. Rather, Grace jumps into the lesson that she had planned in response to Stephanie's suggestions. Grace asks: "What do we know about trolls?" Marvela mentions that trolls are "ugly. They so stink." Stephanie asks to stop the tape and makes the point that Grace has missed a chance to build on Kanani's mention of a noisemaker and footsteps.

Stephanie: You had the footsteps thing and I thought maybe you'd start "and would it make any sounds like troop, troop, trip, trap, or whatever sounds the goats make on the bridge?" . . . and use that information to gain your opening into the story. . . . [by] being responsive to what they share, you work it in to create these real smooth transitions into the lesson.

Stephanie commends Grace for letting the "stink" comment go, because it would not relate to story details. But she suggests that the soundmaker was a good opportunity, because "you were in the same sensory area" as the text details.

Grace makes a case for why she dropped Kanani's comments on soundmakers and footsteps. First, she doubted the boy in fact had a noisemaker at home, because he had a reputation for "inventing" possessions identical with those mentioned by classmates. "I hate to always think it, but maybe that kid is putting one over on me." Second, she found the idea of "smelly troll" interesting and connected to background knowledge of the children, which she believed could be explored.

However, Grace acknowledges that Stephanie has a good point and comments that "I felt like . . . [laughs]. On some days I think I'm much more responsive than others, and today I was not responsive."

Stephanie disagrees that responsiveness is a generalized state of attentiveness to students, which Grace has implied in her remarks. Stephanie defines responsiveness for Grace in this way:

Stephanie: You're [assisting] him when you respond to it, then take what he says, and use it for your own purposes too. [When a child says something, you should say to yourself] "I am going to find out what it is you are trying to say and then while you are saying that, I'm going to think about how I can use that to bridge the gap and start my agenda." That kid may have been inventing the noisemaker. But the idea he introduced can be used to build on anyway.

Grace: That's something good to remember. Because I know some days I just feel like, "Oh my God, I want to do this for the kid," and I think that that's part of not being totally comfortable with this responsiveness yet. . . . It's very easy to let them lead me down the little path. . . . I've got to give the kid the benefit of the doubt. Maybe he does have one, you know. If I am going to go into it, I might as well go full cycle.

Stephanie: And you may as well get your own agenda working too, right? So [you say to yourself] "I'm going to do this with you [students] and I'm going to find out what you're trying to tell me and it may be relevant and in that case you have really made a contribution, but if it isn't relevant, then [I'll ask myself] what can I do to make use of it?"

The development of intersubjectivity in the consulting activity setting

At this point, a new stage of cognitive development had been reached by Grace, although Stephanie did not know it and indeed did not realize it until almost 2 years later, when Grace and Stephanie were both interviewed by the authors and asked to comment on these tapes.

In the second session, Grace had acceded to Stephanie's point about the potential usefulness of the noisemaker remark at some cost in surface pride, because that child and that noisemaker had a problematic recent history. Not only was Kanani Grace's number-one management problem, but also he had a consistent history of attention-seeking, fantasizing, and dominating classroom discussions. The very day before, Grace had been preparing a dramatic presentation of *Billy Goat Gruff* with the children, and Kanani had been disruptive and inappropriate with his story about his noisemaker. Grace had forbidden him to mention it further. Kanani waited until the next day; then, at the first opportunity, he introduced the (probably) imaginary toy again. This noisemaker carried more emotional meaning than Stephanie imagined.

In the retrospective interviews conducted 2 years later, Stephanie reported that she had not understood. If she had, she might have been more sympathetic, but she still would have returned to the point that even problem children's contributions can be used for the teacher's purposes, and indeed such children can best be managed by incorporating their speech into the group conversation. But Stephanie expressed admiration for Grace, who attended to this main point of the program's values, rather than insisting on details that were, at that moment, tangential.

And that is what Grace did. She accepted Stephanie's *consulting* theme: responsiveness for the teacher's purpose. This moved the two of them into a joint understanding, an achieved and emergent concept, and a foundation for their developing intersubjectivity. This action displays Grace's excellent maturity and self-control. The emerging intersubjectivity, created by building and refining joint concepts, moves both toward mutual trust.

But in the second consultation session, there is still work to be done. The tape is started again. Grace and Stephanie watch a long sequence in which the students discuss what trolls really are (monsters? real?). One child suggests they lived in the time of the dinosaurs. By now Grace seems to be wandering (a point she confirms herself when the tape is stopped). She is again responding to children's comments, but she has lost purpose.

Kanani: Hawaii doesn't have any trolls.
Grace: Hawaii doesn't have any trolls? Oh. Is there a real . . . are there real live trolls?
Children: No. They not. They like giants.
Grace: They're like giants?
Sheida: When the . . . you know, when the dinosaurs, when they alive, trolls was alive.
Grace: Oh, so dinosaurs and trolls were alive at the same time?
Kanani: Trolls and dragons.
Grace: Trolls and dragons were alive at the same time?
Tosufa: And the trolls . . .
Louise: Dragons . . . we don't have any dragons.
Grace: Do we have any trolls?
Tosufa: No. The trolls was stepping one little bit and he fell in the tar.
Grace: So let's get this straight. Are trolls like us?

Her questions are again literally responsive, but not goal-directed, in the sense of being guided by a theme – neither her own nor ones she gleans through careful attention to interpretations offered by the students.

Many interesting ideas are mentioned by the students, but none are exploited in ways that assist understanding or push the interpretation forward. For example, a child connects trolls to dinosaurs, but Grace lets another child change the subject to trolls and dragons without making use of the dinosaur connection. And then a child offers a correction that there are no dragons in the story and introduces the idea of the troll "stepping in tar." Later, this same child implies that she has seen tar pits with remains of dinosaurs, another idea not pursued. Grace is eliciting good material from the students, but does little to exploit the opportunities it presents.

The problems in this sequence are recognized as clearly by Grace as by her consultant:

Grace: Oh my God. What I am going to do with all this information. . . . I did not expect to get myself in this direction. I'm really amazed with what these kids give me. I didn't expect that much. . . . I think that's my one problem. . . . I'm not experienced enough to make the most out of the situation while I'm in it right then. [I get a lot out of just watching my tapes along with you] but I really need your feedback. Because there's tons I would have missed, really, without you. . . . I feel more comfortable . . . with the stories . . . and I think I'm giving those kids more, because each time I read the story I see a little bit more. Maybe I'm reading it slower and slower as I go down the line with these kids, or maybe I'm taking more time to bringing, figuring things out. But I can see that I go right over a whole lot of stuff.

In this exchange Grace "discovers" that she has misjudged what the texts portray and also underestimated the children's reactions to them. One important insight for her is the value of more careful study of the text, so that she can "see a little bit more." She also realizes that without the consultation sessions and video feedback, she would have missed "tons."

She also recognizes that she cannot yet make use of all that the children say. One reason has been her lack of consideration of the literary qualities of these simple primary texts. Lacking that, no teacher can hope to conduct effective comprehension lessons. She cannot anticipate all lines of discussion that the topic and text provoke, for example, the dinosaur connection. But with sufficient literary consideration, she can be ready to respond and build on what a child contributes. To be responsive means that a teacher does not attempt to fully anticipate what students will say, what ideas and experiences will be provoked by the discussion and the text itself. This, in turn, means that the teacher must be intellectually prepared to respond. A full consideration of alternative interpretations of the text is one form of that preparation. Teachers' interpretations of stories, on the level of plot and theme, have been shown to influence their instructional decisions, both in comprehension questioning and in the choice of topics for concept building (Shiel, 1987).

This second consultation session was a pivotal session. It was one in which Grace moved toward an intersubjectivity with her consultant. She developed a finer understanding of critical concepts. Consequently, she moved toward a new set of standards by which to judge her own teaching. She discovered how important it is to be attentive to text and student utterances and to observe, accurately and conscientiously, not only the text but also her own behavior. She discovered and acknowledged that she needs improvement at "in-flight" thinking, recognizing themes and choosing alternatives while in the midst of conducting a lesson. Although she is eliciting valuable information, she realizes she does not know what to do with it and that the line of discussion takes directions she never anticipated. When this happens, she cannot react effectively and purposively. Text understanding is vital, but that knowledge alone is not sufficient to enable Grace to conduct lessons that are responsive enough to child utterances to provide for assisted performance. She must also be able to capitalize on the ideas and knowledge the children bring to the task of comprehension.

In the next consultation session, the initial focus is on the substantive content of the story being read, but this time another problem arises. This time the problem is Grace's skill in eliciting ideas from students and engaging in responsive interactions that assist performance. That this becomes the focus of the consultation is a testament to Grace's intellectual growth and to her development as a teacher. She now knows the value of being prepared in a literary sense. And now she must work on pedagogy.

Responsive teaching in context

This next session occurs several weeks later. Schedule conflicts, special events, and illness have prevented Stephanie and Grace from meeting. The session begins with viewing the first-graders' lesson tape for an extended period. The story in the text being read concerns Ira, who is staying overnight with a friend named Reggie. Ira's sister often teases him about sleeping with a teddy bear, and now she creates a problem by asking if he will take the bear with him to Reggie's. From fear of being teased, Ira leaves the bear behind. Once there, he is unhappy that he does not have his teddy bear to sleep with, but is afraid he will be teased if he admits his wish. Ira asks his friend Reggie several leading questions about teddy bears that Reggie either ignores or seems not to hear. But at bedtime, Reggie takes a bear to bed! Which prompts Ira to go home for his teddy. Ira learns that Reggie is also afraid of being teased about needing a bear to sleep with.

After viewing the tape, Grace and Stephanie discuss the text at some length. Grace has begun to use a richer appreciation of text in her conduct of comprehension lessons. She notes that the author of the story sets up the conclusion in advance. The visiting boy asks his host several times about teddy bears. The host does not respond. Grace leads a line of discussion with the students on this point, prompting them to speculate about Reggie's reasons for ignoring questions about bears. Grace assists them to examine the text and pictures for evidence. Stephanie expresses approval of this work.

Stephanie notes that this early part of the taped lesson involves a focus on the T or next phase of E-T-R. She asks Grace if she had an R in mind. Grace reports her initial intention for a theme, but in contrast to the first consultation session, now displays a richer appreciation of the text's possibilities and of the value of listening to child contributions.

Grace: Yes. At the beginning of my story, I had planned "if you believe it's right, stick with it." At the end of the story, I asked them what could Ira have done at the very beginning to alleviate this problem? Then Aaron brought up that had Ira had the courage to voice his opinion on what he really believed, there wouldn't have been any problem!. . . . I didn't think Ira was [brave] . . . somehow brave didn't quite fit in. But having the courage to speak up to say . . . it went along with what I was thinking of – "sticking to your convictions" – but I'd never thought about it in terms of having the *courage* to stick with your convictions. So I thought it was so neat when he brought that up.
Stephanie: So actually he validated [the theme] that you selected?
Grace: He is *thinking.* . . . He is able to generalize it, broaden from what I could bring. I was so shocked at that child. . . . And I think that he may be able to relate a little bit more to this story because Aaron has a lot of fears. He really has a lot of fears. And I think his parents talk to him a lot about being brave and trying new things.

Grace has begun to see, in the children's comments and in her knowledge about them, information to use in guiding their analysis of text. However, she is not yet able to translate this understanding into action.

Stephanie: Did you modify your R statement with your children or your questioning or anything as a result of Aaron broadening your . . . [Grace: Gosh, I can't remember] . . . view of what the R would be? Why don't you think about or see if you were thinking about anything like that at the time [while we look at the tape some more].
Grace: Like broadening or . . .
Stephanie: Well, it doesn't have to be especially on that. But as we go on [trying to find place on tape] see if there's anything that the children say that changes the direction of your questioning or changes the direction of your thinking about where you're going in the lesson.

As they watched the tape, it became obvious to both Grace and Stephanie that it was Grace, not the student, who had introduced the idea of courage into the discussion. Stephanie noted that it was "great . . . that Aaron held it and gave it back – but he didn't really generate it."

The fact that Grace could not remember if she had modified her line of questioning is also important. She recognized an important child contribution, and she appreciated alternative interpretations of this simple primer text. But she still could not, "in flight," regulate her interactions using this recognition and appreciation. She was not yet being guided by what the children offered in the course of the lesson. When she becomes so guided, she will remember it.

The struggle to be responsive

This exchange in session three also reveals a limitation in Grace's pedagogy, one that becomes the focus of many of the subsequent consultation sessions. Because she is not being guided by student contributions, Grace dominates the lessons. She is telling them about the story, rather than assisting them to understand. She is not yet assisting students to do what they cannot do without her collaboration. Instead, she relies on two styles of interaction that, at best, assess but do not teach. The first pattern is yes/no questions:

Grace: Okay, was Reggie's sister able to change his mind?
Chorus: No.
Grace: No. Why? Why was Ira going to stand firm? What did he find out?
    [Inaudible]
Grace: He knew that Reggie wouldn't laugh at him. So did that give him the courage to go through with what he wanted to do?
Chorus: Yes.
Grace: Did it matter if his sister was going to tease him?
Chorus: No.
Grace: Okay. So it's not important to him any more.

The second pattern is highly directive and recitation-oriented:

Grace: Look at Ira on page 105. What's he saying to Reggie?
Sheida: Wake up.
Grace: Why does he want him to get up?
Isaac and Sheida: Because he wants to show him his teddy bear.
Grace: Because he wants to show his teddy bear and what else? Okay. Why else would he want him to get up? What were they doing before he fell asleep?
Summie: Telling ghost stories.

Stephanie stops the tape and intervenes. She is concerned that Grace is misled by the apparent success of the yes/no questions and the directed/recitation questions. Stephanie comments that it is easy to be fooled by feeling "in sync" with the students when the yes/no answers flow smoothly. But Stephanie notes that Grace may find later that the students do not understand the text, that she has inadvertently "fed" them lines, rather than assisted comprehension.

Grace responds by saying that she is using yes/no and recitation questions to check for understanding, to ensure that the group is together – that sometimes it is necessary to do so.

Stephanie then challenges Grace's belief that assessment can be conducted best by yes/no questions. Stephanie tells her that these simplified questions can cause a teacher to make unwarranted assumptions about children's understanding, because in fact the children are merely picking up the cues from the questions themselves.

Stephanie: And so a way to check on that is to go back and ask them . . . to explain why . . . get them to let you know what they're thinking, make them finish the statement or at least give you whatever incomplete utterances are going to be their description. . . . Never assume that the kids know [unless they've] given . . . a real clear understanding of [their] thinking and background. . . . And then as we move along [they] can find and read . . . in the story what it is that supports that. . . . By keeping these [yes/no] questions to a minimum you're forcing yourself to actually improve the questioning. Because then you turn it around. You say, "Well, am I going to get a yes or no from this?" And if you are, then you turn it around . . .

Stephanie then gives examples of good questioning, offering models drawn from a lesson that Grace herself had taught and Stephanie had observed live earlier that same morning. These questions required that the children think and provided just enough information to help them do it.

Stephanie: And that's the kind of thing that will help you avoid feeding them any of this information, and also [help you avoid] making assumptions about where they are. When these kinds of questions start happening . . . the teacher–student ratio gets heavier on [the student] side, so that the kids are giving you more, more talk. [There's] less teacher talk, more student talk. That's when you get these pieces of information from them that make you think "Wow. I didn't even think of that. Now where is he going? And how does that relate to what I'm trying to do in this lesson, where I'm going?"

For the first time since the consultation sessions began, Stephanie has described for Grace, in direct terms, some of the fundamental elements of responsive teaching. It is a succinct and appealing description. It attempts to assist Grace by cognitive structuring. Grace's initial response is one of confusion, but she engages the issue and struggles to understand the concept and its relationship to the tape. She asks Stephanie how one can maintain the E-T-R instructional strategy and at the same time remain responsive to student contributions.

Grace: But then that brings up another point. What if you have your R planned and you've been building it [and] at the end ... the kids come up with a totally different one? Now, does that invalidate your R?

Stephanie: No, that's great. That's responsive teaching. Then you listen to what they say, and you put it together with yours.

Grace: But then, but then you keep thinking, "Wait a minute. What about all those littler tracers I left with the kids along the way?" What happens to that?

Stephanie: Then you can go back and think about it, right? And say, "Well, isn't that interesting it came out that way." Like all the ...

Grace: Oh, okay. Because I would almost think of it as being less responsive. Being successful in being responsive to the kids, but maybe being unsuccessful in not, in not having foreseen it. So I don't ...

Stephanie: I think that being unsuccessful [in that sense] can be one of the most exhilarating experiences! Because it's a completely different way [of teaching].

Grace: I thought I was doing with the kids [one thing] and they went this [other] way, which is neat, but. ... No. I thought they were with me the whole time. I mean it wasn't way off in left field, but it was a slightly different slant as to what I thought I was leading them to.

Stephanie: If you think you're going along here, and you're doing a lot of [assuming], and you're doing a lot of explaining, then you don't know where they are, so that they may not have been here, they may have been over there, or they may have been anywhere. But if you constantly have these check points along your way ... asking them to explain what they're thinking, asking them to find and read the evidence that supports that thinking as you move away ... from pure E, then you're going to know where they are. ... You can take what they're saying and then adjust your lesson outcome, or you can bring them back to you through topic control and asking them to ... read and find [in text], and use that evidence.

Stephanie then suggests an important clue to checking on responsiveness: the ratio of teacher/student talk. She tells Grace that if she finds herself talking a lot or getting a lot of yes/no answers, she knows that she may be in for trouble down the road. But Grace has to leave and rushes through the last point.

Grace: Okay. I gotta sum this up real fast. Let me see, to work on this teacher–student ratio of talk ... and to be more aware of whether I'm feeding them [telling them] or whether I'm enticing [assisting] them [to comprehend].

This extended exchange of teacher and consultant reflects a problem that is familiar in the literature on teacher cognition. To what extent can a teacher be expected to revise and adjust lesson plans based on student responses to material presented? The literature suggests that teachers follow preselected scripts and activities and seldom alter lesson plans "in flight." Some writers on the subject go further and suggest that teachers cannot be expected to think and decide "in flight" because of the information load they bear in typical classrooms.

Yet, by definition, the responsive teaching that Grace is learning to conduct requires that in-flight adjustments become commonplace. In fact, they are necessary if the teacher is to assist performance in the ZPD, because it is not always possible to anticipate what ideas and knowledge students will bring to a text.

In her question about students introducing "totally different R's," Grace raises a fundamental problem. The research literature suggests that most teachers occasionally handle this problem by making some effort to adjust, but mostly they handle it by terminating the lesson (Shavelson & Stern, 1981). How, indeed, should the teacher respond? How can one move toward instructional objectives and at the same time be responsive to students? Getting these two aims in balance is not easy, and at this point Grace doesn't see how to do it.

Grace decides to work on her ratio of teacher/student talk. She found Stephanie's points (cognitive structuring) about responsiveness interesting, but too vague a basis on which to continue. She is impressed by the idea of monitoring the ratio of student/teacher talk, because it is a concrete guidepost to judge performance. The ratio of talk idea turned out in the subsequent consultation sessions, and in her own thinking, to be an important concept for Grace.

But there is some irony here, in that Grace chose to reduce teacher talk after her own "teacher" – Stephanie – had begun to rely somewhat heavily on "talk" as a means of assistance in the consultation session. Stephanie's cognitive structuring had increasingly resolved into attempts to "tell" Grace what responsive teaching is and how to do it. Stephanie began to feel the frustration of her own excessive talk and the futility of "telling" a teacher about a complex set of social acts.

Now a critical incident in the consultation occurs: Stephanie arranges an entirely new activity setting for the consultation and an entirely new means of assistance for Grace (Figure 10.2). She arranges for Grace to observe another teacher (Janet) who is extremely competent in the skills of responsiveness and elicitation of student contributions with minimal teacher talk. Assisting Grace's performance through modeling turns out to have a dramatic impact, as the next consultation session reveals.

A new activity setting, another means of assistance

The observation of Janet was arranged by Stephanie as a follow-up to the discussion of "teacher–student ratio of talk." Grace was lecturing too much to her students. Although she could talk about an alternative way of responding to limited student knowledge, Stephanie believed that Grace needed an "image" of what that could be like in action.

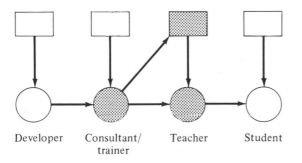

Figure 10.2. The consultant arranges for others to assist the teacher.

To provide that image, Stephanie created a new, short-term activity setting. This was not simple to arrange, because negotiating the time, place, goal, explanation, and personnel, even for one guided observation session, required considerable organizational maneuvering.

Stephanie and Grace observed together one lesson taught by Janet, who was working on stories with social science themes at a higher grade (third) than Grace (first). In the lesson they observed, the topic was municipal government – a topic for which it was clear that the students had little relevant background information. Stephanie judged that it was particularly appropriate for Grace to observe Janet dealing with limited child E because of Grace's assertion that when children had no relevant experience, the teacher had to provide it. Providing the E seemed to be the motive behind Grace's frequent long lectures.

It was immediately obvious to Grace that Janet's students began the lesson not knowing much about municipal government: What is a mayor? A petition? Grace watched Janet elicit the few "tiny E's" the children could contribute about city government – some had seen city hall, and some had watched election returns on television. Janet was able to provide a bridge from these tiny E's to the new vocabulary and constructs in the social science lesson by using several techniques – visual displays, discussions, semantic maps on the chalkboard, and the like. These techniques were identified and labeled by Stephanie and Grace as they watched Janet's 20-min lesson. After they left the room, Janet and Grace discussed the lesson for less than 10 min. This total of some 30 min of observation and discussion was judged by Stephanie to be a "major event" in the consultation process.

This visit and the focus on the ratio of student/teacher talk proved a powerful combination for assisting Grace's advancement through her ZPD.

Advancing through the ZPD

Ordinary complexities of school and teacher life intervened. A month has passed since the last consultation. As their new session begins, Grace and Stephanie are watching a tape of Grace and her students reading a story about characters who cannot stop eating cookies.

Grace: In the beginning of the story there is not a whole lot until they come across this thing called "willpower." That's where the big deal is because the kids don't know what willpower is. We spent a lot of time talking about it. I had anticipated it, but I didn't want to bring it up in the beginning of the story.

In this session, it seems clear that Grace had studied the story and correctly identified the concept of "willpower" as a crucial theme. Grace reported that she had learned much about eliciting from kids their "tiny E's" and that she had applied her new understanding to the taped lesson they were now reviewing. According to Grace, it was the Janet visit that helped her anticipate the importance of "willpower" in the story. That visit had also taught her that it may not be a good idea to bring up such concepts too early – because the teacher ends up "telling" the students about the concept, which may not help them comprehend or use the concept to process the text.

Grace: When we went to visit Janet, I saw that she could have mentioned "housing project" at the beginning, but instead she waited until the children read it, and then she chose to talk about it at that time. . . . [Before the visit] I would have been inclined to [start today's lesson by asking], "Who knows what willpower is?" right at the beginning. And I would have thought, "Oh, yes, I'm laying the groundwork for the R [relationship or theme]," but really it would be too farfetched, I think, at the very beginning of the story . . . [smiles] "Have you ever heard of willpower?" [Instead, today I was] planting these little R's: "Who decides how many cookies you eat? Does *mom* say, 'You can eat only 3'? or do *you tell yourself* 'I better not eat more than 3 because I didn't eat my dinner yet'?"
Stephanie: Were you trying to elicit . . .
Grace: . . . from them. You know, just laying it out and then have them tell me what they would do. And most of them said that *mom* would say [how many cookies to eat].

Implied in Grace's comments is the assumption that this line of discussion will eventually lead to the question of "telling yourself" to eat only three cookies, which is just a short step from an understanding of "willpower." This tactic is in response to the model presented by Janet. It represents a major shift from her thinking observed in earlier consultation sessions. Previously, Grace expressed some doubts about the value of eliciting from the children rather than "telling" them. Her impulse to "tell them things" arose from an accurate recognition that often they did not know certain facts or definitions that would be crucial for understanding a story. Her doubts in the earlier session were expressed in terms of the problem of reconciling elicitation (from students) and working with a preselected lesson objective.

In this session, she is beginning to appreciate that elicitation of child utterances actually assists the development of comprehension and that the goal is to assist students to engage in such cognitive activity, rather than "feed" them the lines. As a result of observing Janet, Grace seems now to see the value of being patient and building comprehension on a foundation composed of students' experiences, their initial responses to discussion topics and to the text itself. Grace appreciates that the new understandings will emerge from collaborative text analysis. Grace's understanding of comprehension instruction is developing rapidly, and it looks as though the need for Stephanie's assistance is diminishing.

A crisis of development

In the next exchange in this session, we see that Grace has learned an important distinction. She has learned that announcing to children the meaning of a word, concept, idea, or theme does not mean that they can then use it to comprehend what they read. As Vygotsky (1987) has pointed out, the acquisition of word meaning proceeds well in advance of the ability to control the concept on the level of production. Although the children have the definition of "willpower," they cannot use the concept as a tool of thought.

A startling parallel between Grace's learning and the children's learning also reveals itself: Grace has grasped the concept of elicitation, but she cannot yet control it as a tool of teaching, just as the children can discuss the concept of "willpower," but cannot yet use it as a tool:

Grace: Okay. Do frog and toad have a problem?
Chorus: Yeah.
Summie: They can't stop eating cookies . . .
Grace: They can't stop eating cookies. And what is one of the solutions they gave for their problem?
Isaac: Willpower.
Grace: Willpower. Willpower is one solution. Have you any idea what willpower is?
Unidentified child: Superman.
Grace: Okay. What do you mean Superman? What kind of power?
Isaac: Exercise!
Grace: Exercise would be willpower? Okay. If you have . . . okay, let me use it in a sentence. If you have willpower and you know that exercise helps you to

lose weight, you have willpower if you exercise every day. If mom says you can have one scoop of ice cream when you come home, and you really want three, if you eat only one, you have willpower. Does that give you an idea of what willpower is?

At this point, Grace stops the videotape and says, sharply:

Grace: No! . . . it was like blank stares [on faces of children]. It just went [over their heads]. I thought I had brought it down to the point that they could understand, but they still couldn't get it. . . . I was hoping that since I had given them several examples that they should be able to tell me, because then I would think that they know.
Stephanie: It seems that you really didn't get enough [of their E]. You got some but not enough to sustain discussion. If we look at this section in terms of the student/teacher ratio of talk, it is heavy on teacher talk all the way to the end. At the end of the teacher talk, you've got deadpan silence, which says that it's got to come from them. So, you've got to turn it around into elicitation. . . . On this long run of teacher talk, as soon as you hear yourself starting the declarative statements or ending sentences with periods, ask yourself, "What is the effect on these [kids]?" Look at their eyes and their body language.

On the tape, Grace's "long run of teacher talk" has the form of a minilecture.

Grace: I thought: "These kids don't know anything about it [willpower]. If these kids don't know anything about it, you've got to teach them about it."
Stephanie: Well, that's true in the case of what Janet did with the city government lesson we observed. But how did she do that? What did she say? She elicited everything from them, through oral language discussion, to put on the chart [visual display she used in the lesson]. She had to plan how to question them about their background of knowledge of city government. She had to anticipate how she could get the children to generate the terms she wanted. That's what you do here. Get the background out of them. You anticipate what you can get from them. Then you have to fish until you hook it. . . . They may not be able to label [their experiences]. But you [should] expect them to talk about experience that they have had, so that the experience is out on the table. Then later they cap it when they see what happens to frog and toad. Then they think, "Well, yeah, that's what I do. I've done that." That's the coming together of the E and T – they make the R.
Grace: But what I feel is that if the kids don't have any E with [the topic or concept], then you have to supply it.
Stephanie: Or somehow find out what E is [for them]. [In some cases you may have to provide content background, like Janet did with texts]. But in the case of the stories at [your grade level], it's human experience. So you fish and fish and fish until you come up with whatever experience it is that they have that is going to relate to what's going to happen in the story.

As this exchange reveals, knowing the meaning and accepting the value of elicitation do not translate into its effective application. However, Grace's growing sophistication is revealed in this exchange. Her response reveals her developing skills of self-observation and analysis; she can now "see" more clearly what she is doing and what needs repair. But again, she cannot observe and repair "in flight"; until she saw the tape, Grace did not know that this lesson failed to match her advancing standards – standards that were internalized from earlier interactions with Stephanie and Janet.

And she cannot yet express her understanding in action in the lesson context. A growing ability to self-analyze does not produce an instant change in the ability to conduct lessons. Though Grace has gradually identified all the necessary components of good teaching, she cannot yet integrate them into a performance that matches the standard that she has now internalized.

This is an extremely frustrating point for the learning of any competence: the acceptance of higher standards, the discrimination required to identify good performance, and the awareness that one's skill is not yet there. Grace's discomfort is entirely human.

Stephanie: How about this . . . [I think you've got to go: the kids are coming back.] How about if you film your Blue Group lesson tomorrow?
Grace: No. I don't want to film anymore. . . . I won't. Maybe I'll [audio] tape it. I don't want to film it.
Stephanie: Because of the . . . is it easier to audiotape?
Grace: No. I just don't want to go through this tomorrow.
Stephanie: [Recounts her own complex schedule of the week, but offers to tape the lesson and make the meeting]. . . . If you were really, really . . .
Grace: No.
Stephanie: . . . hot to do it . . .
Grace: No.
Stephanie: . . . I could [delay some work I have] . . .
Grace: Yeah, maybe I should, Steph, . . . but I felt, you know, I felt really good about my lesson this morning. When I came to school today, I thought, "Well Grace, [today you finally start to do responsive teaching right]. . . . I felt, last night I felt, "Oh good, you've got it." Because some days I walk in and go, "God, what am I going to do?" I was feeling really good about this today. [Stephanie is offering supportive comments.] . . . Actually, I should audio. Audio would be easier for me to do because then I could listen to it at home. Because you know, I don't . . . I think I'll audio it. It would be easier all around.

Despite her frustration and disappointment, Grace nonetheless agrees to audiotape her lesson and to meet again. She is at the point in the ZPD that is most stressful, but that heralds the coming of a new level of competence.

Grace breaks through

The next session occurs about 1 week later. Stephanie begins by asking Grace about her goals for the lesson. Again, Grace returns to the problem of student/teacher talk ratio and her responsiveness to what the students have to say.

> *Grace:* I'm focusing on not talking so much. . . . My goals for today were to cut back on teacher talk and to think about my questions for them. I am focusing on the same goals.

Each teacher utterance at the beginning of this lesson is a question. Grace is talking less and doing a better job of eliciting ideas from the students, rather than "announcing" to them as in prior lessons. As the tape rolls, it is obvious that an important change has occurred in Grace's conduct of the lessons. A highlight of the entire series of consultations is about to occur.

> *Grace:* Okay, what did Cucullan say when he came over to Fin McCool's home?
> *Summie and Louise:* "Is Fin McCool at home?"
> *Grace:* Ammm.
> *Kanani:* She said, "No, Fin McCool is not home."
> *Isaac:* "He went out to look for a giant named Cucullan."
> *Grace:* Ahum.
> *Summie:* His wife said "Fin McCool is stronger," but he said, "I'll show you who's strong."
> *Grace:* Okay. What could he do to show his strength?
> *Kanani:* Lif' up the house.
> *Grace:* Alright. How is he going to do this?
> *Isaac:* Use his magic fingers.
> *Grace:* Aha. Using that . . . okay. What else could he do to show his strength?
> *Isaac:* By sweating.
> *Grace:* You show your strength by sweating? How do you show your strength by sweating?
> *Tosufa:* You go like this [child flexes her muscles].
> *Grace:* Okay. What do you call it when you do that?
> *Louise:* Show his muscles.
> *Grace:* Yes. Show his muscles. But does that show how strong you are?
> *Isaac:* Soft muscles.
> *Grace:* That you have soft or hard muscles? What could he do to show his strength?
> *Kanani:* Lift up a tree.
> *Grace:* Lift up a tree. Sure. What else?
> *Summie:* Lift up somebody's house.
> *Grace:* Alright. Turn to the next two pages . . .
> *Summie:* Wow. He lift up the house.
>   [Tape stopped]
> *Stephanie:* I just can't help but applaud, because that is such a good series of questions.

Grace: Bite my tongue! Did you see that? I almost felt like I was just really biting my tongue: "Don't say anything else, Grace. Don't you dare say anything else." . . . I was really concentrating on listening to them; I almost practically bit my tongue. I was, hmmm, I mean, that's about as . . . shut down as [a teacher] can be. . . . I really wanted to listen to what they had to say, and it was, it's true. I just . . . didn't say anything, and they keep feeding me more and more. And I thought, this is kinda' neat that they kept doing all this!

Stephanie: That was really apparent. That was real good. Not a single wasted utterance on your part. . . . It has got the ratio changed for sure.

Grace: Finally!

The frustration and disappointment of the preceding session are now gone, and in their place is Grace's deserved satisfaction with what she sees on the tape. The dialogues with the students are smooth and conversational. There are no more abrupt changes of topic. Gone is the failure to pick up on what the students are saying. The aimless sequences of questions have disappeared. Also, notably absent are efforts to "tell" the students about the text. This change is clearly revealed: At various points in the lesson, Grace begins declarative statements and then changes them into questions. Does she remember Stephanie's instruction from a previous session?

Grace: What's so special about Fin's wife?

Isaac, Louise, Tosufa: She can fool a giant.

Grace: So what might she say to fool him into lifting her house?

[No response from students]

Grace: She knows that Fin is in. . . . [stops and rephrases declarative statement as question]. What does she know when she has him move the house?

Isaac: He can't, because Fin is there.

Grace: What could she do to make the, the giant want to move her house? What would she tell him that would make him want to move the house?

In the next chapter, we discuss in detail the developmental stages typical of teacher training, particularly their advance through the ZPD from Stage I (where assistance comes from more capable others) into Stage II (where assistance comes from the self). But it should be noted here that Grace is now showing clear evidence of self-assistance in her frequent self-correction from declarative to interrogative forms. Grace has now enlisted a strong ally: herself. She has begun to engage in that "unique form of social behavior that is volition: the interaction with the self" (Figure 10.3). Grace's self-assistance is not restricted to substituting questions for declaratives. She is also reducing repetitions:

Grace: Another thing I'm trying to do is not repeat what the children keep saying. Because I noticed that on some of the last videotapes, the children will say something, and I'll repeat it. And that increases the teacher talk. . . . And

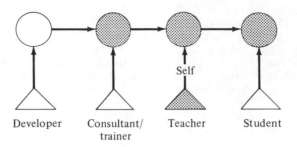

Figure 10.3. Two sources of assistance to the teacher: the consultant and the self.

then I thought that, well, if I keep repeating myself, then the children will learn "I don't need to listen to what Suzie is saying, because the teacher is going to repeat it anyway."

Another of Grace's comments reveals clearly her remarkable improvement in working with the literary and life-experience themes in the simple text stories. She is now able to respond to the unpredictable utterances of the children in ways that scaffold their understanding. The quality of her analysis and the progress it reflects speak clearly in Grace's voice here:

Grace: [After viewing a tape segment, Grace says that her questioning was guided by] this idea of *challenge.* . . . . I kinda' wanted them to get the idea that [the giant is] being challenged. His strength is being challenged. That's why he's [lifting the lady's house] – to show off that he can do that. . . . I presented them with the word "challenge," and somebody said, "Yeah, Pepsi challenge!" and that's what I was hoping they would click on. . . . And I said "Why do they have the Pepsi challenge?" [A student says] "To see which one is better." And that's it. That's what I wanted them to see. That she's challenging Cucullan on this thing. Then he gets beaten. This is a challenge that [the giant] accepts, and he gets beaten. And it's like he is beating himself. Because she's just challenged and he has lost.

Toward the end of the session, Grace expresses satisfaction about the amount of information she has elicited from the students through questions and about her movement away from "announcing" information to the students. Grace reports that Claire [another consultant of high repute] came by the day before and complimented her on the quality of her teaching, to which Grace replied, "I have been working on this. . . . I said we went to see Janet [the teacher who provided a model of elicitation], and I've had a lot of help from Janet. I said we had been working on this, and I was glad that she noticed it. I thought, 'Oh, great!'" Stephanie is delighted with Grace's progress and gives her a long praise that serves as a summary of progress to date:

Stephanie: I think that's really apparent here. If we could go through this tape and make a script, every single statement is either responsive to them or turned into a question to move them to the next increment of comprehension. At one point they were not responding well to your questions about the size of the wife relative to the giant. Then you "personalized" the idea by asking them how they felt if they were "real little," as a way of getting the kids to come back with the next little bit of knowledge form their own experience.

You've cut the amount of teacher talk, and that ties into eliciting from them, giving them the responsibility for getting facts and ideas out on the table. You're providing the links, but not feeding the facts and ideas to them. What you are doing is helping them to see how their experience relates to the text.

And sometimes you did right by bringing in some information for them. Like when you brought in the word "challenge," which got them to bring in "Pepsi challenge." From then on, you were really listening to what [they were] saying, asking them for their rationale, and finding out if you need to think about going off in a little different direction, or expand the idea in this lesson. You were doing a main objective: Development of students' ideas into a valid link to the lesson. That's what you're doing in these sequences of questions where you're getting a little bitty utterance from them. You restate. You ask another question, "Give me a little bit more of your ideas, your thinking. A few more questions down the pike from here, [you] might get what I'm referring to!"

If you get off-the-wall response, you back up and ask them, "Where did that come from? What does that mean? Why are you saying that? And how does that relate to what we're doing here?" And then if it's valid, which is a judgment you make at that time, then you can build it up, then you become involved in the valid link that develops the germ of the student's idea in a valid link to the lesson.
Grace: Is that scaffolding?

Grace has come full cycle. She can discuss the various elements of a responsive comprehension lesson. She can execute them with a fair degree of skill, and she can now link her understanding to her own performances and to Stephanie's efforts to instruct her.

Later in this same session, her comments identify a major barrier that teachers must overcome if they are to learn to be responsive in their teaching. Grace introduces a topic familiar to researchers, especially those who have examined teacher planning, decision making, and cognition (Hyland, 1984; Shavelson & Stern, 1981): completion of lessons and coverage of material. Grace's drive to meet time lines has not been extreme, and indeed she has had rational reasons for her concerns – for example, to finish a topic on Friday, so that her young pupils won't have the task of carrying complex memory across the weekend. But now Grace is willing to make this a lesser priority, as she comes to understand that the process of establishing comprehension is more important than memory of all the details. And that gave Grace a successful day:

Grace: I think it was partly because I didn't feel like "Oh, God, I want to finish this story today." . . . That's when I think I get impatient and I [stop listening and] start feeding the kids [ideas] because I want to finish this story this *Friday,* and today I [knew] we weren't going to finish the story.
Stephanie: So you just relaxed and enjoyed it.
Grace: There's not that urgency to "I gotta get it through. I gotta finish this all the way today." . . . I'm sure that's what it was today [that helped me do a better job].

The final chapter

Stephanie and Grace met three more times during the academic year. In two of the sessions, many of the same topics and issues were discussed as in the preceding sessions. For example, there is one sequence in which Grace analyzes why a lesson went slowly and why the students seemed bored. Stephanie assists her by questions, and Grace offers an alternative approach to the story that she was prepared to use and that she now thinks might have been preferable. Having these alternatives at hand depends on her having read the story carefully and thought about it herself. In contrast to the opening consultation sessions, she no longer complains that the stories are "shallow." She now sees the possibilities, in part because she spends more time analyzing the texts and because of the growth in her intellectual appreciation of the primers as literature.

In another one of these final three sessions with Stephanie, she again describes her attempts to stop "feeding kids ideas." She gives several forceful statements about her determination not to repeat this pattern of teaching.

In late May, Stephanie and Grace conduct the last consultation session. By coincidence, Grace is again teaching the lesson *(Ira Sleeps Over)* that she taught in the third consultation session some months earlier. This time, it is taught to a lower reading group. In every respect, the quality is improved. The contrast between Grace's conduct of the "Ira and his bear" story in January and that in May is a clear testament to Grace's growing competence. The lesson opens with a short exchange that briskly establishes Ira's fear of being teased. The tape is stopped, and Grace discusses the theme she is using to guide her elicitation at this point. In this commentary and lesson excerpt, it is clear that Grace now can recognize students' failure to comprehend, and she knows how to skillfully guide them in the creation of understanding. Stephanie and Grace have begun to develop a concept that they call "backing up" to lay a foundation on which comprehension can be constructed.

Grace: [I was hoping that somebody would say that] boys don't sleep with teddy bears the way that girls do. . . . [Girls] see nothing wrong with sleeping with a teddy bear, because they all do it. Or with a doll. And so I was hoping they would say that "Oh, [Reggie] might tease him because boys don't sleep with teddy bears." . . . That has never come up, and I didn't want to bring it up. . . . [So] I decided to go back a little bit, and I thought, well, maybe that would get at it.

Stephanie: Okay, so you were actually backing up to build at that point.

Grace: Yes. Did you see? Did you see the, like [Grace touches her head]. You could see me backing up. [She starts the tape.]

Grace: Why would Reggie want to tease him if he brought his teddy bear? Why did Ira want to take his bear?
   [Stops tape]

Grace: Before that, I think I did something like [Grace touches her head to denote that she is talking to herself while she is teaching the lesson on the tape. She reports saying to herself], "I'm not getting anything from these girls. So what do I have to do?" [This self-assistance, by means of questioning, indicates that Grace is close to the development of full competence.]
   [Now Grace starts the tape again]

Grace: So what is Ira afraid will happen if he doesn't take his teddy bear?

Racy: That Reggie might not tease him?

Grace: He's afraid that Reggie might not tease him?
   [Grace stops the tape; she and Stephanie smile at each other]

Stephanie: Now that looked like another "back up, build up."

Grace: Yes. Because Racy was [saying something that] doesn't make much sense. . . . [so I thought] okay, back it up again, start where we are, and let's take a little bit smaller steps, and take 'um up that way.
   [Starts tape]

Grace: If he didn't have his teddy bear, what might happen?

Racy: He might not sleep.

Grace: Okay. So he was afraid he [wouldn't] be able to get to sleep without his teddy bear. Boy, Racy, you're really hot today. You're really paying attention. Okay. But he's afraid that he won't take it because . . .

Racy and Mooki: Because Reggie might tease him.

Grace: Reggie might tease him. Is anybody else causing him a problem?

Mooki: Yeah.

Racy: His sister.

Grace: And what about his sister?

Racy and Mooki: She's teasing him.

Grace: Okay. She's teasing him too. But we know that deep down inside of his heart, Ira wants to take his teddy bear. You know awhile back when you were [inaudible], he talked about pilots, people being pilots. Your own pilot. Remember what we read? What did we mean about that?

Mooki: You're keeping your hands to yourself.

Grace: Okay. What would it mean if you were your own pilot?

Racy: You don't listen to anybody else.

Grace: Yeah, but how do you know what to do?

Racy: Just ignore them.

Grace: You ignore when they tell you to do things? See, but then how do you decide what to do?

[Stephanie can restrain herself no longer, and reaches out to stop the tape]

Stephanie: Grace, I just have to stop, because I think that, that is just outstanding elicitation.

Grace: There's a conscious effort [on my part] to eliminate these simple yes/no questions. I mean, that is first of all in my mind. Or if I do ask a yes/no question, I always come up with "Why?" and "How do you know?" Whereas in the past I would say "da, de, da, de, da," and they would say "yes," and I would say, "okay, let's go to the next. . . ." So that's one thing that this [consultation process] has brought about – this awareness of trying to rephrase a question so that it's not a yes/no question. . . . And it's a lot more satisfying now that I know what kind of things . . . I can get from the children if I delve deeper. And I think it's taken a few times of . . . *assuming* that they know, and then when we get to the big part where I'm ready to summarize it, then they kinda' go "ah, wait a minute." . . . I've lost them several miles down the road. So . . . I think that I would know now, maybe, have my feelers out to see if that is happening again. . . . I think that the awareness is up. That's why I keep backing up to where the common ground is, because I now know [children] will nod and say yes to anything. But when I ask [them why, that's the hard part].

Postscript: Grace 3 years later

Three years later, Grace examines the transcripts of the consultation sessions she had with Stephanie. She recalls the time spent with Stephanie as being "very good." This judgment has remained unchanged during the intervening years.

However, her construction of what happened adds some additional facets to the picture that emerges from our analysis of the transcripts and from Stephanie's consultation notes that were written at the time.

Though she had learned the principles of KEEP teaching from the academic workshop portion of the training program, Grace reports she never really learned how until she began trying to do it. In fact, until the consultation sessions began, she did not know what "it" should look or feel like in action.

As she examined the transcripts, she expressed amazement at the way she had approached each piece of the teaching in a "stair-step" fashion, whereas now in her teaching, things "flow."

However, she recalls that she "felt progress" only in the fall semester (the beginning of her second year at KEEP), following the consultation sessions with Stephanie. Then she began to feel that it "really worked for me – I didn't stop and think about the pieces any more."

Grace reports that before and during the consultation sessions, she was often distracted by her own emotional responses to whatever the children said. These feelings would send her off on tangents. Now she has the experience of control over the conversational flow. The children no longer distract her from the organization of the lesson. Now, she says, "I have a discriminating ear."

Discussion

This case study provides dramatic evidence that even at the level of beginning reading, teachers must develop professional-level skills if they are to move beyond recitation, if they are to overcome the assumption that children should learn on their own.

Neither pedagogy nor substantive knowledge is sufficient by itself. Grace made little progress until she developed an intellectual appreciation of the primers as literature. With this capacity developed, she was able to take on the next task of developing competence – the development of pedagogical techniques of questioning, responsiveness, and assisting performance.

There followed a long, intensive, and personally difficult series of consultations during which she had to confront repeated disappointment. As the intersubjectivity between teacher and consultant began to develop, their concepts were internalized by Grace, but that is a stage of development prior to mastery of performance. At the point of raising her standards, Grace was able to discriminate her shortcomings. Earlier, she had not seen what the consultant saw. When her eyes were opened, she reacted so strongly that she adamantly refused to tape another lesson: It was too painful; she was too disappointed in herself. But her pain signaled a rousing of the new consciousness that is required of those who would truly teach.

A timely use of a model proved decisive, as did the consultant's decision to directly address the teacher's problems with her tendency to "lead" the children rather than assisting them to comprehend.

We do not suggest that this individual, extended, and intense form of training is the only effective activity setting for developing teacher skills. The preceding and the following chapters urge that schools create a variety of activity settings in which teachers may engage in joint productive activity with others.

However, this case study does reveal the complexity and difficulty to be expected when even a dedicated, able teacher attempts to learn responsiveness to children's ZPDs. It took a wide range of assistance by the consultant, involving the full battery of means of assistance, and the cre-

ation of ad hoc activity settings. It required an extended, complex, sometimes frustrating instructional conversation. The sessions also reveal the
joys accompanying Grace's achievements and the two women's pleasure
in their developing intersubjectivity.

Grace Omura became an expert teacher in the KEEP system and 4
years later was herself a consultant, with extensive responsibility for
training teachers in public schools. Stephanie Dalton was by then a
research teacher and a program developer with responsibilities for assisting the performances of consultants of the next generation.

11 The intrapsychological plane of teacher training: the internalization of higher-order teaching skills

The theory of education developed in this volume sets a demanding standard for teachers: Teaching occurs only when assisted performance is provided to the learner in the ZPD. To achieve this ideal requires, of those who would be teachers, a transformation of mind. This transformation consists in the development of new, higher-order cognitive processes, new values, and new motives and is achieved by the same psychosocial processes that we have detailed in discussing the developmental progression that occurs in children.

The stages of development of higher-order teaching skills

The developmental progression of a performance capacity, for people of all ages, can be conceptualized in four stages, as described in Chapter 2 (Tharp, Gallimore, & Calkins, 1984; Watson & Tharp, 1985; Wertsch, 1979, 1985b). These developmental progressions have been studied mostly in children (Berk & Garvin, 1984; Rogoff & Gardener, 1984; Tharp, Gallimore, & Calkins, 1984; Wertsch, 1979), but can also be seen in adults during skill acquisition (Gallimore et al., 1986; Watson & Tharp, 1985). In this chapter, we use the theory to illuminate the development of higher-order teaching skills.

In Stage I, teacher behavior is regulated by more capable others in social transactions. In Stage II, it is regulated by self-directed speech and other forms of self-directed assistance by the learner. In Stage III, self-directed speech goes "underground," becomes silent, rapid, and shorthand, and disappears as performance becomes internalized, automatized, smooth, and integrated. Stage IV is recursive and may be observed when the automaticity of Stage III is disrupted by environmental changes or individual stress (Figure 11.1).

249

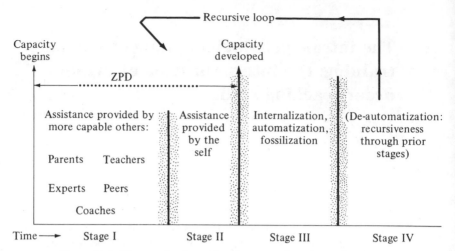

Figure 11.1. The genesis of a performance capacity: progression through the ZPD and beyond.

Stage I: assistance provided by more capable others

The transit from other-regulation to self-regulation begins in Stage I. In the beginning, the apprentice may only vaguely appreciate the goal toward which the collaborating pair is moving. Indeed, the predominant experience of the apprentice is likely to involve confusion, anxiety, and self-doubt. Attention is focused almost exclusively on small portions of the capacity to be acquired. Only gradually does the apprentice come to understand the way that the parts of an activity relate to one another and to understand the meaning of the performance. Ordinarily, in training a teacher, this understanding develops through conversation about the task to be performed or modeling of the skill in question. When some conception of the overall performance has been acquired through language or other semiotic processes, the apprentice can be assisted by other means – questioning, feeding-back, and further cognitive structuring.

We have already described in detail the transactions and dynamics of Stage I of teacher development in the case study in Chapter 10, which is largely an account of Stage I in Grace's development of teaching expertise. Some of the major facets illustrated in Chapter 10 are:

1. *The assisting expert teaches by providing several means of assistance.* Throughout the sessions, Stephanie used all the means of assistance, such as the arrangement for modeling in the visit to another teacher's classroom.

2. *The assisting expert provides assistance by organizing the task into*

appropriate goals and subgoals. Stephanie graded the task for Grace; the immediate sub-goals of the consultation session were selected according to Grace's developing understanding and progress in skills. Stephanie (correctly) made little attempt to relate the early sub-goals of the training to the overall structure of the ultimate teaching competence; attempts to explain the goals and related concepts may be confusing at early points in the developmental progression. This was the case, for example, when Stephanie attempted to assist by prematurely explaining some of the fundamental elements of responsive teaching. Grace's initial response was one of confusion.

During Stage I, the apprentice may not conceptualize the goal of the activity in the way that the expert does. Intersubjectivity must evolve. At the beginning of the consultation sessions, Grace did not conceive of responsive teaching in the same terms as Stephanie. With the increasing experience of working together, intersubjectivity was achieved, and Grace came to "see" the same things as Stephanie. "Working" concepts and terms arose from their interaction, such as their mutually developed concepts of "backing-up" and "teacher–student talk ratio." This shifting of goals and sub-goals – toward increasing intersubjectivity – is essentially the same in parent–child interaction (Saxe et al., 1984).

3. *The expert's responsibility for task performance steadily declines, with a corresponding increase in the apprentice's proportion of responsibility.* Toward the end of the consultation sessions, Grace acquired many of the skills needed to examine and critique her lessons: She was beginning to function as her own consultant. Stephanie's role shifted from providing directions and feedback to providing cognitive structuring of Grace's analyses and emergent conceptualizations of lesson activity. For example, in one of the last sessions, Stephanie offered a compliment and a conception of Grace's newly developed teaching skill, to which Grace responded by asking, "Is that scaffolding?" A new cognitive structure was emerging for Grace, one that had been in Stephanie's "mind" from the beginning and that had guided her efforts to assist performance. Other cognitive structures had also emerged at earlier stages, as when Grace accepted Stephanie's *consulting* theme: responsiveness for the teacher's purpose. These achievements provided a foundation for intersubjectivity.

Dramatic evidence of the shift from Stage I to Stage II surfaced in the session in which Grace described herself "as shut down as a teacher can be." In that instance, she described telling herself "Bite my tongue! Did you see that? I almost felt like I was just really biting my tongue: [I was telling myself] 'Don't say anything else, Grace. Don't you dare say anything else.'"

But before Grace's advance to a higher level of functioning, she experienced considerable stress and anxiety – at one point refusing to continue. This is to be expected: Self-regulatory cognition was predicted by Vygotsky to occur under conditions of learning, stress, and disruption.

In a series of interviews conducted with teachers throughout the KEEP system, many gave vivid accounts of the stress and anxiety they experienced while learning the program and the style of teaching it demands. A pervasive theme was the feeling of pressure to fulfill the expectations of the KEEP program. Several reported that considerable stress was experienced. One teacher said, "Compared to the old program, this new program involves a whole lot of work . . . you know the preparation is great, I mean it's tremendous" (teacher #17). Another commented that the program was "threatening because it is so highly structured . . . what skills to be covered, in what order . . . this time I had to be teaching something, where the kids would be tested" (teacher #18).

In other reports, the stress was described more graphically: "I don't see how one can stay married when you're in this program because it's very, very demanding of you as a teacher. I'm sure it takes away from your home life" (teacher #20). A few mentioned that during the first days of training, they were "taking their frustrations out on family members," and some teachers detailed psychosomatic complaints. There was much talk about pre-active planning and post-active review and evaluation. There were also complaints about particular consultants, criticism of specific KEEP policies, negative comments about aspects of training (context and sequence), and so forth. Although most of the teachers were favorable toward KEEP, more than half expressed displeasure about some aspect of the program and their participation, past or present.

Although many teachers eventually endorsed the KEEP system, they (like Grace in Chapter 10) experienced moments of extreme difficulty before they advanced to a high level of competence. During the early stages of training, when trainers provide – even impose – an unfamiliar pattern of teaching, teachers will feel stress, anxiety, and often resentment. Gradually the new patterns and strategies will become internalized, personalized, adapted, and owned.

Stage II: assistance provided by the self

In Stage II, the responsibility for task performance is shifted from others (and the environment) to the self (Figure 11.2). However, performance is not fully developed or automatized, because the regulating function remains with overt verbalization, often in the form of self-directed speech. Emergence of self-assistance marks a significant point in the development of a performance capacity. Performance that was assisted

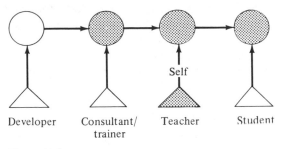

Figure 11.2.

by external means is now beginning to be assisted, guided, and directed by the self. What was regulated by the environment (and by more capable others) is now self-regulated.

Before the automaticity of Stage III emerges, self-assistance is typical. Self-assistance can take a variety of forms, including using standards and acquiring feedback, envisioning models of good performance, seeking and constructing cognitive structures to explain events, and arranging contingencies to reward one's own advances.

However, the most common form of self-assistance reported by teachers with whom we have worked appears to be self-talk: self-instruction, self-praise, self-scolding, self-questioning. The use of self-controlling language or self-directed speech should be seen as a form of assisted performance, the source of which is the self. This is a stage intermediate between external regulation and full individual competence (automaticity). It may also be seen as a stage in which the "voice" of the regulating other is gradually acquired by the learner, so that the regulations may be stated by the self to the self, gradually taken "underground," transmuted into thought, and eventually discarded as the behavior becomes fully developed and adaptively automatic. In daily life, this process is easily observed, as individuals "talk themselves through" some new skill, often in the very words of coaches and instructors (Gallimore et al., 1986, Watson & Tharp, 1985).

Accounts of self-directed speech were obtained in interviews of 27 teachers working in the KEEP system who were interviewed near the end of the school year. Seventeen of the 27 teachers had 1 year of experience in the KEEP system; of the remaining 10 teachers in the sample, 4 had 2 years, and 6 had 3 years of experience. Nearly all were natives of the Hawaiian Islands who received their training in local institutions; approximately half were working in public schools in which the KEEP system was being implemented. The rest worked at one KEEP R&D school or at a nearby private elementary school that was part of the foundation (Kamehameha Schools/B. P. Bishop Estate) that supported KEEP. Full details of the method and data analysis have been presented (Gallimore et al., 1986).

The interviews were informal and individual and focused mainly on behavior management and responsive questioning. Both strategies were described in detail in earlier chapters. Because of their prominence in the training, much of the teachers' talk concerned their problems in learning and implementing these two strategies.

No direct questions were asked about being monitored by KEEP consultants, the effects of the explicit KEEP criteria or standards, or self-directed speech. If the teacher spontaneously mentioned these topics, appropriate probes were used to get as full an account as possible. Because we did not ask directly about topics of interest, we have increased the risk of false negatives. By not asking about interactive cognition, teachers who did not spontaneously mention such activity cannot be distinguished from those who would have said "no" to a direct question. Thus, our procedure may have underestimated the rate of the phenomena of interest, but it certainly did not inflate reports of self-regulating cognition, as more direct questioning might have done.

Despite the conservative nature of our interview questions, half the KEEP teachers (15 of 27) spontaneously reported some form of self-directed speech. One additional teacher reported self-talk, but did not elaborate in response to probes. The teachers who reported self-directed speech associated with the behavior-management strategy ($N = 10$) tended to provide elaborate accounts, with dramatic examples. In contrast, the 9 teachers who reported self-directed speech in relation to the responsive teaching of reading comprehension tended to describe self-regulatory cognition more briefly; also, these descriptions were mostly of a different sort, which we shall discuss in a later section. Only 4 teachers mentioned both strategies in their accounts of self-directed speech. This may reflect levels of experience, because behavior-management strategies are taught before the questioning strategies.

A variety of metaphors was used by the teachers to describe self-directed speech. They included "my mental mind," "a tape-recorder in my head," "one part of my mind," "learning to be schizophrenic, with two voices in my head," "a little mental niche in my head," "my internal conversation," "divided consciousness," "having two levels of consciousness," and "double-think." The following excerpts illustrate some of the variety in these accounts:

There's a little mental niche in my head that says I've criticized somebody, or come down [hard] on somebody, now go find what they're doing good. (teacher #11)

I rarely used positive reinforcement before. You see all this negative behavior, and so you kind of scold the children for it. . . . I really had to make myself aware and remind myself about it because it doesn't come naturally. . . . I'd hear [teachers in the next room], and say [to myself], "I better do that [positive reinforcement]." (teacher #24)

I could see that positive reinforcement was definitely the way, and it made me feel good about myself, rather than yelling and screaming and scolding and being negative. I still have [to remind myself] to be positive. I have to remember to look up and look around the room, and what I try to do is point out somebody doing something good at that time [rather than scold the child who is misbehaving]. My initial tendency is to look up [and scold], but instead I say: "Look, Alohalani is making good use of her time!" It's a battle with myself, because [before] I was very much the enforcer because of the discipline problems. (teacher #9)

I used to get infuriated at some student's behavior, but I would tell myself to look for something positive; then I would go ahead and reinforce that. At first, it was so uncomfortable to do that. It was so unnatural – not like what we used to do, you know, just scolding the child and not looking for the positive things. As you work on it, it gets easier. (teacher #23)

Some teachers were embarrassed to talk about "talking to themselves." Others readily admitted "I talk to myself all the time," and sometimes they provided elaborate descriptions of the process and its benefits. Two reported that inner speech sometimes "slipped out," evoking puzzled looks from the children. In at least one case the teacher was unaware she had spoken "the inner thought" until a colleague asked about it later. Another teacher denied talking to herself – she said, "It's really more like thinking."

More than half of 27 teachers spontaneously mentioned specific classroom-management skills acquired through accompanying self-directed speech. For example, part of the behavior-management program involved learning to use praise effectively and frequently. For most trainees, remembering to praise was a problem at the beginning of the participation. Their consultants often would negotiate some specific number of praises to be delivered to the children in a training lesson. This number became the standard for the teacher's performance.

All the time, I know I was thinking, "You have to say something good, say something . . . say something, hurry up. You're not gonna get your mark, your quota [of praise]." (teacher #28)

Another (teacher #3) mentioned that the consultant had taught her to identify early warning signs of disruption, such as children beginning to tip their chairs. She could head off trouble by watchfulness and judicious use of praise, or she could provide more pencils in centers to reduce the number of trips to the sharpener and thus reduce unwanted, potentially disruptive interactions. She described telling herself to look for these warning signs and planning what actions to take.

Other teachers reported on self-assistance for the responsive-questioning strategy. One reported that she asked questions of herself during interactive teaching concerning the appropriateness of her questions and content; she claimed "I do that mentally." Another said: "[This is interesting], I hadn't realized until just now what was going on in my mind, like what I actually said at that time." (She was referring to "self-questioning" thoughts about content coverage, etc.) One teacher said she tells herself to remember to ask "the right things in the comprehension lessons." Four others gave short descriptions of self-directed speech in the context of discussions of the questioning strategy.

Thus, in this sample of teachers, self-directed speech was common enough, and reports related to behavior management could be obtained with a minimum of difficulty. This suggests that a more direct question might have produced even more accounts. Our indirect approach – not introducing the topic forthrightly – yielded a conservative estimate of approximately 50% reporting self-directed speech.

The transition from Stage II to Stage III was vividly described by some teachers. In these accounts, the need to "constantly remind" themselves eventually gave way to the automatic pattern of Stage III. The transitions to an "automatic" stage described by some teachers parallel Vygotsky's account. But before the automatic stage was reached, some teachers were acutely aware of the "voice" of the consultant:

T: I remember trying out these things in class and feeling very unsure of myself, and feeling like a robot.
Q: Did this make you feel phony?
T: Definitely! In the beginning, ummmh, it was almost like, well we'd hear these things on the tapes, and K would model some in the training sessions. It seemed like we were saying the same things as these people [on the training tapes].
Q: You were saying the same words [as the people on the tapes]?
T: The same words. I would remember these little phrases people would say: "You're doing a good job of sitting," or "You're sitting so nicely in your chair." You know, that kind of thing. You remember these little key phrases, and you go in and use them. And at first . . . it feels really strange, and really uncomfortable almost, to have these things come out of your mouth that you probably wouldn't have thought of all by your little old lonesome self. . . . It was just easier to say those things, things you'd heard other people say, and would use as examples. And it worked fine for those kids, and when you're at a loss and kind of on edge, "Oh, gosh, I'm supposed to say something to a kid; now what am I gonna' say?" It probably comes to mind a lot easier than to try and generate something yourself. (teacher #27)

Other teachers reported the same experience. When they were first introduced to the behavior-management strategy, they all tended to say the words or phrases spoken to them by the trainer. The parallel is the young child whose initial self-regulating statements are repeated words of the parent ("John, don't touch, hot"). With practice, the "voice in the head" becomes the teacher's own, in the sense that she has less of a "tendency to play someone else's tape than play my own," as one teacher put it.

Another teacher reported that the "voice in her head" became her own. In the course of learning the behavior-management strategy, she had wrongly concluded that only the modeled forms of praising and positive reinforcement were desirable. For 2 months she struggled in vain to control her class, "mouthing" the phrases she had learned, and telling herself constantly "Oh, God, I've gotta praise these kids." As she adopted her other-regulator voice from training to self-regulated inner speech, she said, the "tape in my head" was her own voice, using her own words. Once this transition occurred, some teachers reported that inner speech began to diminish in frequency – as far as behavior management was concerned. Such a development is, of course, the herald of full internalization and the automaticity of Stage III.

Stage III: internalization and automaticity

The processes leading to internalization can be seen through the window of self-directed speech and marked clearly by the transformation of the voice from trainer's to teacher's own that occurs in Stage II. But when the skill is internalized and automated, the window shuts, and the voice falls silent. Self-examining consciousness is also sharply reduced; as a consequence, so are descriptions of this stage in our interviews with the teachers. Viewed externally, Stage III teachers obviously have self-confidence and comfort with their skill; their enjoyment of their work is high, and the values and the understandings of their skills and the program are solid and readily available.

In theoretical terms, once self-directed assistance disappears, we may presume that the individual has emerged from the ZPD for the task at hand. Task execution is smooth and integrated, and its regulation has been internalized and automatized. Assistance, from others or the self, is no longer needed and would now be disruptive. Even self-consciousness itself can interfere with the smooth integration of all task components. Self-control and social control are no longer required. The performance capacity is now developed: Vygotsky used a vivid metaphor – "fossilized" – to describe its fixity and removal from the social and mental forces of change. This fixity, however, is not permanent.

Stage IV: de-automatization and recursion

These stages of development – from other-assistance to self-assistance – recur over and over again in the lifetime of an individual as new capacities are developed. At any point in time, the performances of an individual will reflect a mix of other-regulation, self-regulation, and automatized processes. Even the competent adult can profit from regulation for the enhancement and maintenance of performance.

Enhancement, improvement, and maintenance of performance provide a recurrent cycle of self-assistance to other-assistance. De-automatization and recursion occur so regularly that they constitute a Stage IV of the normal developmental process: What one formerly could do, one can no longer do. Slight environmental changes or individual stress, not to mention major upheavals or physical trauma, can affect the automaticity of a capacity.

At Stage IV, the first line of retreat is to the immediately prior self-regulating phase. Thus teacher #27 reported that self-directed speech was occasionally reactivated when the need arose, but her account suggested that it seldom happened. Her account also suggested that pre-active or post-active reflection was more important than interactive cognition at this stage of skill development:

T: Yeah, if somebody really stands out, then I'd probably do it more. And then I
    would also go over it, in my mind, some of the things we learned in train-
    ing: "Oh, what's he doing, why is he doing it? What am I doing to maybe
    encourage him to behave this way? What could I do different?"
Q: You do that right in class while it's going on? Or outside?
T: Uhmm, I do some of it in class, but not much of it. I think most of it takes
    place when I'm finished teaching and I can really sit down and think about
    it. (teacher #27)

In another case, the teacher had returned from summer vacation to find she had forgotten the behavior-management strategy: "It's so funny because I remember that first day [back to work], Gee, I guess I thought something was missing ... it's not the same. Then I guess, what it was, was about praising. I forgot how to praise and what to praise for and things like that." For some time it was necessary for her to do "self-reminders," in order to consistently use effective behavior-management techniques.

Another teacher reported that she "talked to herself" about behavior management only when things went wrong, and she had to remind herself to resume using the techniques she had been trained to use. But generally, once behavior management becomes "automatic," self-directed speech is not required. In general, these accounts are consistent with the prediction of Vygotskian theory that self-directed speech can be reactivated under conditions that require conscious self-regulatory cognition.

The eventual transition to automatic behavior management seems related to the characteristics of the strategy itself. Eleven of the 27 teachers described behavior management as a series of steps or a hierarchy of actions. The following are examples from these accounts that describe management in terms of steps or series of options:

[When I see a disruption coming], I'll count to ten first. [Then] we have, sort of have steps. [First] I look, and they look at me. They get the idea that maybe they should go back to work, and I don't even say anything, and for some kids I don't have to say anything. . . . With others, there's a hierarchy kind of thing, where they get a warning, and I try very carefully not to say a lot of things, and just what's wrong, or go back [to where I should be]. One thing I always do, is where I've given a kind of warning, and they've gone back to work. I always acknowledge that in some shape or form, whether it's verbal or not. (teacher #11)

First, I would, I would give a positive comment to those who are working very nicely, and see if that child will pick up the cue, and start doing his work. If he does, then I'd say, "So and so is now doing his work very nicely." If a child continues [to misbehave] . . . then I'd pull the child away from his table and have him work by himself. . . . I think about it first. If he, they continue doing it, [I act accordingly]. (teacher #7)

Thus, self-directed speech is a form of recursion often effective in restoring competence and one that our teachers reported in some detail. A further retreat, to remembering the voice of a teacher, may be required. Intentionally recurring to that point in the zone – consciously reconjuring the voice of a tutor – is an effective self-control technique.

But in some cases no form of self-regulation may be adequate to restore capacity, and a further recursion – the restitution of other-regulation – often is required. Just as the readiness of a teacher to repeat some earlier lesson for her pupils is one mark of excellent teaching, so one mark of excellent schooling is a system for providing opportunities to refresh teacher skills with occasional doses of assistance by others. The goal, again, is to re-proceed through assisted performance to self-regulation and to exit the ZPD again into a new automatization.

Responsive teaching and self-regulatory cognition

This account of the intrapsychological processes of teachers stands in some contrast to the existing research literature in the field of "teacher cognition." Because of the apparent contradictions, it is well that we now examine that literature in some detail. Most studies have suggested that most teachers reflect little on their classroom actions and seldom are guided by theories or principles of learning or child development. These studies suggest that many teachers are guided during interactive teaching by preselected activities and cultural or commonsense ideas about child development and educational practice (Duffy, 1981; Durkin, 1978–1979; Shavelson & Stern, 1981).

Although teachers report making decisions, they are of a limited nature; they seldom report being reflective, referring to educational theories, or engaging in pedagogical maneuvering (Duffy, 1981; Shavelson & Stern, 1981). The limited forms of interactive cognition that are reported seem primarily devoted to maintaining activity flow. The weight of the evidence prompted Shavelson and Stern to make a case that such teaching may be adaptive in most classroom contexts, given the heavy demands on teacher attention. Others have argued that existing data reflect training failures, limits of current pedagogical theory, overreliance on commercial materials, and the widespread use of the recitation script (Duffy, 1981).

Our data support the latter view. Recitation is the predominant pattern of interactive teaching observed in American classrooms, and for the most part recitation interactions proceed smoothly, requiring teachers to think only when interruptions occur (Shavelson & Stern, 1981). Thus, the successful execution of this ubiquitous strategy, with its limited options, should not activate reflective, dynamic, or pedagogically principled cognition by the teacher, and apparently it does not (Shavelson & Stern, 1981).

But train teachers to use a theory and practice of teaching that require them to think, choose, and reflect, and they will do it. Give them something more than the recitation script, and they will respond accordingly. Define teaching as assisted performance in the ZPD and provide effective training, and teachers' thinking will become strategic, driven by responses of students, and implicitly theory-based.

Further research in teacher cognition will reveal that teachers' thinking is in accord with the performance standards provided and modeled by program designers, trainers, and supervisors. If unresponsive and static teacher cognitions are found, the inertia is due to the theories and practices they are trained to use.

In contrast, in the assisting interactions of the instructional conversation, teachers are constantly thinking and constantly making decisions. Even in Stage III automatization, there is thinking. Teaching as assistance is an extremely complex skill that requires constant decision making, categorizing, structuring, and all manner of cognitive operations. Because the instructional conversation is responsive, and because children and their speech are so various, it is not possible to routinize these teaching acts.

For these complex cognitive skills, the transition to the automaticity of Stage III is accompanied by a silencing of *self-regulatory* cognition, but not of decision making and the execution of those cognitive operations of which the skill is composed. Thus, teachers, as they advance from Stage II to Stage III, will tell themselves less often to "remember E-T-R!" But they will *more often* consider whether to direct their next question toward the text or toward the child's experience. Making these decisions is the skill itself.

Therefore, long after they have become expert, with capacities internalized and automatic, teachers report that they continue to think about student utterances, what they mean, how they relate to a child's knowledge and background, and what response is appropriate. These cognitions are focused not on "directing self to execute to program standards," but on making sense of student utterances, trying to "pull" more complete, coherent ideas from the children, and tailoring a response using the questioning options (E, T, or R). Nine of our 27 teachers (33%) described such cognitions associated with responsive questioning. That is, responsive questioning may become automatic, but this automaticity includes active thinking while teaching. The following examples illustrate the phenomenon:

At first I relied on comprehension questions from the teacher's manual for the basal test. I stuck pretty close to it as far as comprehension. But once I became more confident and we were introduced to the E-T-R thing [KEEP questioning pattern], I started trying these different techniques, and it became more natural for me to ask my own questions. When I was sticking close to the manual, it was like someone else's questions. It was reading a speech someone else had written. If I got lost, then here I was; my mind would go blank, and they weren't responding, and [I would just] go onto the next question [in the manual] because my questions were not taken from where [the children] were coming from. (teacher #21)

I used to be very dependent on the teacher's manual for comprehension questions. [Now, with the KEEP approach], I just listen to what they're saying and from where they're coming. Sometimes, you know, it's really amazing [how they won't have the experiential background you expect], so [I say], "Just forget the story, and let's discuss this." Some days [I think] "Oh my, I thought they knew this," I have to rethink on the spot what I'm going to ask them. . . . It's a lot of changing. (teacher #26)

What do I think about [when the children are not responding]? *Why* they are not responding, what don't they understand? And then I try to rephrase my question [using the E-T-R thing]. . . . I have to backtrack to the E [experimental base] so they have enough E to understand the story. I always try to keep in mind the kinds of comprehension questions that we are expected to ask. (teacher #6)

I used to use a teacher's guide for comprehension questions. I used identical sequences of questions, rotely. But [after training], I would categorize the questions [into E, T, or R], and it would just flow out. .... I feel I can now expand spontaneously on my own; from the children's responses, you can continue questioning. It's constant interaction with the children. All I used to do was follow the manual. So there really was no interaction. I never got ideas from the kids. The kids just had to listen to me. ... [Now] I enjoy teaching. (teacher #14)

I think of times when the kids have been off on a tangent and I've been thinking ... trying to figure out why they have been saying those things and why they, why a majority of the group is feeling a certain way [about some aspect of the story], and it's really off base [to me]. Then all of a sudden it'll dawn on me, "Oh, I know why they're saying that" ... and so I might say something like, "Oh, I know." But I won't re-explain it to the kids. (teacher #27)

As these excerpts suggest, the responsive KEEP reading lessons create instructional conversations that *demand* reflective cognition. This is quite different from previous findings, which reported a paucity of teacher cognitions during interactive teaching.

When teachers – in previous studies – reported interactive cognition, it was likely to be in response to disruptions or breaks in the flow of the lesson – failures of the students to respond correctly (Shavelson & Stern, 1981). Failure of students to respond as expected was disruptive, because the teachers were using strategies that provided few options for pedagogical maneuvering. After a few efforts to get students back on track, most teachers responded to such disruptions by terminating the lesson. Because the majority of teachers – including those in previous studies – use a recitation style of teaching, students' inability to display information (known to the teacher) or produce convergent factual answers is experienced by teachers as a disruption, and they stop the lesson.

In the KEEP program, initial student comments, incomplete answers, and miscomprehensions are expected. They are expected in the sense that understanding of a text is conceived of as a gradual process that unfolds through a connected, cohesive discourse that is more like natural conversation than other forms of interactive teaching (Hoetker & Ahlbrand, 1969). The knowledge and experience that students bring to a text, and the meanings they derive after initial exposure, are used in the instructional conversation to develop interpretations, which are constructed through collaboration of students and teacher. Student miscomprehension becomes an opportunity to assist the child to a better understanding, to develop ideas, and to more fully express thoughts. Unexpected student comments or interpretive remarks are used to scaffold deeper and broader comprehension. These *expected* (even desirable) "disruptions" represent decision points at which teachers refer to the E-T-R strategy options.

"I have to rethink on the spot what I'm going to ask. ... It's a lot of changing" (teacher #26). Or teacher #6: "And then I try to rephrase my question [using the E-T-R thing]. . . . I have to backtrack to the E so they have enough E to understand the story. I always try to keep in mind the kinds of comprehension questions that we are expected to ask." In contrast, teacher #21 reported that before she was trained to use the E-T-R script, her "mind went blank" during interactive teaching, and she just went "on to the next question [in the manual]."

So, long after the internalization and automatization of some performance capacities, these teachers are reporting theory-driven, in-flight cognition, because the KEEP comprehension-teaching strategy does not dictate what they are to say or what they are to extract from the students concerning the text at hand. The options require continuing teacher reflection on which topics or ideas might aid comprehension and responsive assistance to students as they try to form their ideas and understandings. The teachers are engaged in *conversation*. It is an instructional conversation in which they have to think about what their student interlocutors are struggling to express.

Parental teaching and school teaching

These Stage III teachers' thoughts during their reading lessons yield important revelations. They are treating the sometimes halting, incomplete, even incoherent child attempts to interpret text *as expressions of a communicative intention*. In this way, at least, these teachers are behaving with their students as mothers behave with their children:

One of the most distinctive characteristics of middle-class Anglo caregivers is their willingness to engage in communicative exchanges [even] with the smallest infants. . . . Long before the child has actually produced its first word, it is treated as if it in fact does have something to say. . . . When young children actually begin producing words, this set of assumptions by the caregiver continues. The caregiver, typically the mother, considers the young child to be expressing somewhat imperfectly a communicative intention. (Ochs, 1982, pp. 88–89)

Later, a similar pattern is observed in storybook reading and other emergent literacy events (Heath, 1982; Teale, 1986).

In such exchanges among parents and children, and in the KEEP reading lessons, there is an assumption fundamentally different from that of traditional, recitation lessons (Mehan, 1979). Parents, and KEEP teachers, are assuming, as they do with their own offspring, that the child may have something to say beyond the "known answers" in the head of the adult. They occasionally extract from the child a "correct" answer, but to grasp the communicative intent of the child requires the adult to listen carefully, to make guesses about the meaning of the intended communication (based on the context and on knowledge of the child's interests and experiences), and to adjust responses to assist the child's efforts – in other words, to engage in discourse like the mothers cited by Ochs (1982).

This is not to say that teachers should act like parents in all ways. Schools are not homes, and teachers are not the students' parents. The large numbers of pupils, the restricted and technical curriculum, and the complexity of institutional restraints of schooling require that teaching be a highly deliberate, carefully structured, planful, professional activity. Unlike parents, teachers must systematically teach the accumulated knowledge and wisdom of civilization, as well as the skills required to grasp and use that accumulation.

So we do not mean that there is a simple transfer from natal to school activity settings. In contrast to conversations in natal settings, teachers have a deliberate agenda – the curriculum of schooling. Negotiating the goal structure (Saxe et al., 1984) of instructional conversations so that students engage that curriculum takes highly developed professional skills. Schooling as assisted performance requires a quite deliberate and self-controlled agenda in the mind of the teacher, who has specific curricular, cognitive, and conceptual goals. These instructional conversations appear to be "spontaneous," but they are not – even though young students may never realize that the conversation is pointed toward a goal by the teachers' intention, and even though the oldest learners may lose consciousness of the guiding goal, as they become absorbed in joint productive activity with the mentor. Nothing could be further from our intent than to advocate casual, drifting, "spontaneous" school chatter.

But within the curricular goals, *teachers can and must move closer to the communicative styles of parents with their own children.* They must assume that a student has something to say that is of value to a comprehension of the text at hand – something on which the teacher can base responses that will assist the child to higher levels of understanding.

Let us listen again to Grace (Chapter 10): "I'm really amazed with what these kids give me. I didn't expect that much. . . . I think that's my one problem. . . . I'm not experienced enough to make the most out of the situation while I'm in it right then." Here Grace was already appreciating that the children's knowledge, ideas, and sometimes incomplete understandings could be used to assist them in the evolution of a more complete understanding of a given text and, in the process, the development of more complete reading-comprehension skills. She and the other teachers then learned how to engage in instructional conversations.

A key element that can free classroom discourse from the tenacious hold of the recitation script can now be seen. KEEP teachers are taught that they do not know all that a child knows – they must inquire about it, and listen. This inquiring conversation entirely changes ordinary teaching interactions. Hawkins (1988) demonstrated the extraordinary effect on teaching style of a teacher's realization that she did not know what the children knew. Hawkins videotaped an ESL (English as second language) teacher who was discussing with Hispanic students something they had learned in another class – she needed to know what they had learned, in order to carry out her own day's lesson. In contrast to her ordinary recitation style of interaction, the need to discover what the children had learned in the other class prompted a conversational assisting interaction that was entirely untypical of her teaching practices.

This teacher recognized immediately that the lesson that followed was unusual in its high level of student participation, their evident enthusiasm and involvement, and the quality of the discourse. Though excited and pleased, she had no idea why it had happened. Therefore, she showed no inclination to return to an inquiring, conversational approach to instruction. No one had ever taught her that this is what teaching should be.

We know now that "teaching as assisted performance" and the arts of the instructional conversation can be taught. We know that these skills are acquired in the interpsychological plane, as Grace acquired these skills through her own instructional conversations with Stephanie. We have seen that these skills go through Stage II processes of self-assistance and that they are eventually internalized and automatized as intrapsychological cognitive processes. These thinking and decision-making skills may then be employed regularly and permanently throughout a teaching career.

In the intersubjectivities developed in instructional conversations, "teaching" takes on a different meaning. To produce these teacher-training conversations requires a different organization of schooling than is found in educational institutions today. To change toward that organization will require a change of mind.

12   The schools in mind and society

The meaning of the word "school"

Word meaning is acquired through the talk that accompanies joint productive activity. As people work together and use the same words to refer to their acts and experiences, they come to share the same lexicon, and they internalize the same meanings of those words. School is the one obligatory activity setting that is shared by all of our society. It is set in the formative years and lasts more than a decade; for many, it is the primary activity setting of youth and young adulthood. Because schools are so much the same, everywhere, and because they have been so much the same for so many generations, the word "school" has as deep, as shared, and as intractable a meaning as any other word in our language. In a century of bewildering changes, when grandparents and grandchildren seem born to different planets, there is one word and concept that is shared across the generations. All citizens know what "school" means.

When citizens and their leaders hear of places and things calling themselves "schools" and those places and things do not correspond to the nation's internalized and shared vision, a deep offense is experienced, an offense to all the components of basic *meaning* – the intellectual, emotional, activity, and historical components of the meaning of the word "school." The tendency of society is to gather back to the flock any errant geese. It is no accident that the political movement for greater emphasis on higher academic goals has labeled itself the back-to-basics movement. The New Math movement might have been better advised to label itself the Old Math. Any social system will attempt to recapture those who deviate from its shared and internalized symbols; schools wander off the well-worn path at their peril.

Nor is this innate conservatism countered by the socialization of young educators. Colleges of education offer far too few joint productive activities for university-based reformist concepts to ever take root. Students may memorize the new vocabulary of their lecturers, but these concepts

266

are not likely to be instantiated by meaningful work together with the faculty member. The "field-training" portion of teacher training takes place in schools very much like the schools in which the teachers were themselves pupils. Teachers themselves provide most of the guidance for their own teaching, and this self-assistance is based on the same vision of schools that society shares, a vision teachers internalized as children. Teachers and administrators are as deeply conservative and traditional in their view of the meaning of school as are average voters.

At the same time, the long-standing dissatisfaction with public education – attested by the recurrent calls for reform detailed in Chapter 1 – produces a deep ambivalence toward schools. This ambivalence is felt by political leaders, educators, concerned parents, business interests, and minority groups – few elements of society are satisfied with the *performance* of pupils or of schools. Educational reformers and researchers, including ourselves, point toward a deep flaw in the fundamental North American vision of schooling. But the citizenry and its leaders point out that schools have drifted from the vision of school they acquired in their own childhoods. Combine this with the idealistic glow from the remembered past – small wonder that educational "reform" devolves into an effort to make schools more like their "true" selves, more like "yours and grandma's." As in the old Minnesota gibe, "We're going to make it more like it was than it ever has been before."

Political school-bashing and teacher-bashing are almost always based on the assumption that schools are no longer adhering to their real purposes: Teachers are less knowledgeable than they should be; students are not as disciplined as they should be; the basic skills of reading, writing, and ciphering are not emphasized as they were in the good old schools. Some instruction in some schools is not even in English! Such deviation from the purpose of schooling is so offensive that it seems unpatriotic.

The intersubjectivity of the nation is the root problem – the shared meaning of school, the common history of schooling. Thus, the continual dousing of innovation and the restoration of the school to the comfortable conformity to the internalized image are reliable and reassuring political acts.

What is not understood by the populace at large, including many of its most powerful and best-educated speakers, is that the good old schools were no more effective than the current schools. The recitation script has never been sufficient and never will be. Schools that have not continually educated and refreshed their faculties have never been good schools, and they will not be improved by bashing them back closer to the old vision. The recitation script for teaching and the instruct-and-assess method of schooling were not developed in a state of awareness of developmental cognition, or of the principles of pedagogy, or of behavioral science. There were deep flaws, ambivalences, and dissatisfactions from the earliest days of the republic.

Before the Civil War, it was widely assumed that teachers in the common (elementary) schools needed to know only the subjects they were to teach: reading, writing, spelling, grammar, arithmetic, geography, and some theology. The idea that elementary school teachers should be as intellectually and academically prepared as high school teachers came much later, as did the notion that secondary and elementary teachers should be liberally educated in a college setting. Teachers, both elementary and secondary, were seen as technicians or artisans who did not make or even necessarily understand the bases of school or curricular policy. They were to teach from a prescribed syllabus, according to prescribed principles of instruction. Teachers were not professionals, nor, according to prevailing opinion, was it realistic to expect them to be (Borrowman, 1956; Warren, 1985).

The rise of science and secular society created a dilemma. If knowledge was no longer fixed and revealed through sacred sources, then education became more than dispensing facts and apprenticing skills. With industrialization and the growth of American democracy, more was expected of schools, and schools were required to serve more students for more years.

One of the emerging complaints was the poor preparation of the increasing numbers of students entering the nation's high schools. Common school teachers needed to get students ready for the higher subjects – which required that common school teachers themselves be better educated. Slowly a movement developed to provide a liberal education for all public school teachers.

Now we know that teachers must be engaged in lifelong learning and that schools themselves must provide it. Our insistence that schools be a place where all teach and all learn is the historical and logical extension of the slow dawning of awareness that common school teachers should go to college.

The point here is that North American schools have never fulfilled their highest aspirations, that the tensions now felt began in the beginning, and that true school reform can come about only with a radical change in the meaning of school. Schools will never improve if they are continually forced to try to become more like they always have been.

Ironically, schools will improve only when they are allowed to become what they have always been becoming – however slow, however halting the progress, schools have been moving toward more education for their teachers. Only when teachers are continually learning will they develop for themselves a new vision of schooling and teaching, one in which children will also learn.

The final irony is this: Because schools are not organized to allow continued learning by the faculty, the faculty can never learn anything truly new and thus can never change itself. Schools exist in a vacuum, and the seals are self-repairing.

The case study continued

For reformers, education is a long dark night in which innovations and optimism flicker alight, then gutter and die. The KEEP program, which has formed our central example here (with two exceptions, all KEEP materials in this book were from years prior to 1983), continues to be illustrative. At the time of this writing, a gradual infusion of a new generation of administrators and policymakers has made accelerating changes in the organization and management of KEEP, particularly in three respects. After 20 years, research-and-development functions are being phased out. In-service and staff-development programs, crucial activity settings for assisting teachers in continual learning, are being curtailed as "too expensive." Operational decisions have been moved to administrative control ever higher in the organizational chart. These changes have been undertaken in the face of continuing excellent evaluations of program effects. The changes are apparently in service of a goal that is all too familiar: a return to schools operated in traditional ways.

It is no news in American politics when educational reform and educational expense are attacked under the justification of a return to real schooling and realistic budgets. Such attacks and such cycles of reform and retrenchment are characteristic of American political life. Reform inches forward, and traditionalists haul it back. The public, deeply ambivalent itself – wanting its schools to excel by being more the same – surges back and forth on the tides created by its leaders, mistaking motion for progress. A return to simplicity and the old order never lacks for popular support, for it draws on shared cultural meanings and norms – which always feel "right."

When new policymakers decide that reforms and innovations are too expensive, when "control" is reestablished by a bureaucracy, who is there to gainsay such decisions? There are no protective institutional traditions, no accepted community standards for schooling, and no experience among the populace that would insulate the new culture from assaults.

As a contrary example, the universities of the nation have from time to time suffered repression, as politicians have made capital by punitive antiintellectualism. In every instance, however, the traditions and general expectations of society toward its universities – the meaning of the word "university" itself – have been deep and shared and have been strong enough to restore the university to its proper role. Whoever would permanently repress the intellectual life of the university must answer to a society whose members may be irritated with it from time to time, but who basically know exactly what "university" means.

When educational innovation is dismantled in public schools, however, there is nothing in tradition, in community understanding, or in the meaning of "school" to protect it. After all, the snuffing of innovation merely fits schools better to the template: the old vision that we have all shared. The culture of the school that KEEP created was at risk from the moment of its conception. It wasn't like a real school, and sooner or later someone would have to fix it.

Meanwhile, the KEEP ideal is alive and well in many schools, programs, and universities, including the University of Hawaii, and efforts are under way that may institutionalize some of its elements at UCLA and other locations. Public funds have been made available for wide-scale adoption of the curriculum and general teaching methods into the public schools in Hawaii. The KEEP model now forms one focus for reformist elements in Native American education, linguistic-minority education, multicultural education, comprehension-based teaching of reading, and many facets of the school-reform movement generally.

But a more important issue than the fate of this single innovative program remains to be addressed. Can *any* real innovation be sustained?

Producing and mastering a new script

Some specific changes in some schools do occur, and these exceptions can also inform our understanding of the more usual condition of stagnation. Fullan (1985) has discussed the conditions that may contribute to successful innovation, drawing on four cases published by Huberman (1981), Stallings (1981), Joyce and Showers (1980), and Little (1981). Conditions critical for the success of innovation as described by Fullan can be easily translated into the terms of the theory of education presented in this volume.

1. The choke-point that has defeated past efforts to substitute genuine teaching for recitation can be located by the analytic principles presented in this volume: American teaching practice has remained unchanged for a century because the means of assistance are not used during preservice and in-service teacher training.

2. For the performances of teachers to be assisted, activity settings must be created such that sources of assistance will be part of in-service and preservice experience. Until opportunities for assisted performance become a standard part of teacher education and training, no new conception or theory of teaching and instruction will supplant the ubiquitous recitation. Lacking this, no policy changes in teacher education and conditions of employment will open the choke-point.

3. "The most fundamental breakthrough occurs when people can cognitively understand the underlying conception and rationale with respect to 'why this new way works better'"(Fullan, 1985, p. 396). In our terms, this understanding comes about through discourse during joint productive activity. Assisted performance must occur in the context of productive tasks and the conversation that accompanies them.

Could schools provide these conditions, now, without a massive and budget-breaking infusion of additional tax dollars? Indeed they could. Joyce and Showers have pointed out vast improvements that could be made, even with current resources:

The workplace of teachers was organized long before anyone anticipated that the lifelong study of teaching would be necessary. Now educators must face the problem of arranging for time both for ongoing training and follow-up activities, such as peer coaching. (Joyce & Showers, 1987, p. 22)

They go on to suggest several practical ways that schools could now arrange activity settings in which teachers could learn: (1) Twenty-five percent of the needed time will be provided if administrators teach 1 hr per week each, freeing teachers for staff-development activities. (2) Students can occasionally be gathered together for larger classes than single-class instruction, thus freeing teachers for observation, peer coaching, or study. (3) Bringing in free or low-cost assistance to the school, through use of student teachers or volunteer aides, can free teachers for several hours per week. (4) Team teaching for some subject matter will allow each teacher some time to engage in joint learning activities with workshop leaders or peers. (5) Videotaping a teacher's lessons, for later viewing by peers, can solve many scheduling problems and make group discussions possible (Joyce & Showers, 1987).

These and many other suggestions advanced in this book and elsewhere could make immediate and massive changes in the climate of schooling and in its efficiency. But however obvious and rational it seems that schools should adopt such changes, questions of "technical efficiency," however easy to settle, are never the issues that cause reform to be adopted or rejected by institutions; institutions change or do not change according to the meanings associated with their practices (Reid, 1987). That schools have not already been reformed testifies to the controlling power of the meaning of "school" and the necessity to change that meaning.

Changing the meaning of "school"

We must come to understand that a school is not a school unless all learn. However great the obstacles, the path to changing that meaning is clear. "School" is an everyday concept, not, ironically, a schooled concept. In the lexicon of the average citizen and the average educator, "school" has no technical, scientific, elaborated, conceptualized, abstract, parametric definition that would establish quality and a standard against which various examples could be judged. Rather, school is the everyday, unconceptualized thing that we each went to. Because our schools have been so similar, it is possible to carry on everyday community discourse about schools in the same way that we can easily talk to one another about bridges or roofs. Fortunately, when it comes to spanning new rivers and covering new buildings, there is a technology and theory to guide new ventures. To span new educational needs, we have only the everyday concept of school, as comfortable and familiar and worn out as an old hat.

So we must establish a schooled meaning of "school." The processes of establishing schooled or scientific concepts have been discussed in the preceding chapters, and the principles for conducting such discourse are well established. There must be explanatory variables. There must be everyday examples, as well as general principles. There must be a schema, gradually made more complex by adding new concepts and new experience. Only with such discourse can the word "school" be released from its designatum – each speaker's own childhood days. Only then can "school" come to mean a set of standards, principles, values, and virtues.

Our own effort to participate in this discourse has been to offer a theory and technology of teaching, school, and literacy that can begin to establish a schooled concept of education. Our intention is to provide these not in the belief that our suggestions are final and definitive but with the clear hope of providing a framework in which discussion, debate, refining, and new examples can occur in schools, colleges of education, and halls of policy. The power of an idea is great, and in this instance there will be no educational reform until the idea of school and the idea of teaching are changed. Those new ideas must be elaborate and clear, based in sound theory and experience, and available for thorough discussion in the presence of examples.

The power of an idea is great indeed, but we also know that word meaning, on a social and intermental level, is not achieved until all this talk takes place in a context of joint productive activity. Talk in colleges of education and arts and sciences, in-service settings, school administrative settings, teacher committees, or school boards will be empty unless it is accompanied by action. For example, teaching a new theory of teaching will not change the meaning of the word "teaching" unless it is taught in a way that is consistent with that new theory. Long lectures on assisted performance will produce no new schema for schooling. Textbook presentations of imaginative classroom organization will not change the internal vision of the classroom; only students moving about a classroom will do that. Elaborate explanations to whole-faculty convocations concerning the principles of the instructional conversation will change no teacher's internal vision of what teaching can and should be. If we, as educators, are to change the vision of the next generation of teachers concerning schools, then we must exemplify that vision in joint productive activity with preservice teachers. If we want to hold out hope to today's teachers that there can be a better way to teach and learn, then we must stop the snake-oil workshops that entertain but do not produce, in which teachers listen and yawn; they must be replaced by joint productive exemplifications of a new culture of education, such as when teachers are trained for teaching in a climate of cooperative learning by activities of cooperative learning (Leggett & Hoyle, 1987; Sharan & Sharan, 1987).

Universities must take the lead to create joint research activities involving schools' personnel and researchers (Tharp & Gallimore, 1979, 1982). Crucial elements of such settings include a stable and viable problem focus that remains unchanged by the winds of fashion.

Longevity and stability of funding are other elements often unrecognized by funding authorities; many efforts to solve problems through research are doomed from the first because the team that starts is never allowed to learn from experience, because funding is terminated at the first sign of difficulty. Organization and funding must avoid the error all too often found in education projects – the search for a "quick fix" in a short time frame. "Hard" science and engineering learned long ago that combining research and action to solve a specific problem takes time, persistence, and stable funding.

An interdisciplinary perspective is also an essential element of joint research activity: The complexity of educational practice requires the broadest and most intense analysis possible. Many disciplines need to be represented, both in theory and method, if a sufficiently broad intersubjectivity is to be created.

Finally, the crucial aspect is joint productive activity itself in the form of schools/university collaboration. Teachers, administrators, researchers, and professors must be committed to sound science and objective evaluation. Such joint productive research activity must be created by universities and schools if educational, social, and behavioral sciences are ever to have any meaningful impact on public education. From the discourse of such joint work can arise the new vision of schools on which regeneration depends.

Schools in the context of society

Let us return for a moment to the basic theory of education presented in this book. We know that the intermental plane of discourse and meaning is inseparable from the social plane of shared activity. When we examine the shared activities that produce the shared vision of schools, we find immediately that schools do not exist in isolation. The larger society in which schools are embedded has a profound effect on them. The schools are incorporated into the larger society and have that as their context, so that some of their activity settings are determined by this larger contextuality:

> The links between dyadic or small group interactions and the broader socio-cultural system must be recognized and explored . . . actions are at one and the same time components of the life of the individual and the social system. . . . No less than the action of an individual, the action of a dyad or small group is a component in the social system. Correspondingly, the intermental action and the social interaction that makes that action possible will be defined and structured in certain respects by the broader social and cultural system. (Minick, 1985, p. 257)

Indeed, it would be possible to detail certain parallelisms among the recitation script, the instruct-and-assess methods of school management, and the typical treatment of schools by their directing political bodies. Just as teachers treat students in the recitation script, schools themselves are given certain "texts" to master, in the form of regulations and authorizations, and they are from time to time assessed or audited to determine if they are in correspondence with those texts. Little assistance, understanding, responsiveness, or genuine dialogue occurs between policymakers and the schools. Just as the recitation-script teacher responds to students, so the legislatures, school boards, and trustees respond to the administrators of their schools: If one "fails" the assessment, the text is reassigned; if the assessment is satisfactory, new texts are assigned (new laws or regulations passed), and another round of assessment, reward, and punishment rolls on.

Teaching is nested within the school which is nested within society, each differing in scale, but not in form, and each mutually supportive of the entire structure. Thus, the larger society is the context that hatches the activity setting of classrooms, but it is classrooms that produce the problem-solving styles and the discourse meanings that prepare new citizens to operate in mature society. This is a formidable structure indeed, and little wonder that it is conservative.

However, society itself is not a stable context, and although it continues to relate to schools in the pattern of expectations laid down in the schools of its childhood, society is not so happy with the effects. Society has changed, but not its conception of schools, which no longer provide activity settings that are microcosms of the contemporary and emerging workplaces of America. Indeed, schools' activity settings, lagging behind the workplace, do not prepare students with the problem-solving and literacy skills to allow North American society to continue to compete with others. The cooperative-learning movement, as one contemporary example of intended reform, has some credibility with business and industry leaders who know well that teamwork is a necessary skill for corporate success. The shifts in technology and management techniques demand a new complex of skills from today's school graduates, a complex not required by the society of half a century ago. Does this mean that the cooperative movement will institute genuine reform in American education? Not at all. Cooperative learning will encounter the same massive inertia that all violations of the meaning of "school" meet. Does that mean that it will fail? Not necessarily: To the extent that social pressures are consistent and broad, it is possible to nudge schools forward. To the extent that a new vision of schooling as cooperative can be brought into citizens' discourse, then it is possible to see education *streak* forward. For example, industry-sponsored schools, training and continuing-education programs, if they do indeed incorporate new cooperative activity settings, can help to change the vision of schooling held by those who participate in them.

A relevant historical example of genuine school reform has recently been discussed by William Reid (1987). In the late 19th century, the leading independent boarding schools of England replaced their traditional schoolrooms with the newly invented concept of the smaller and differentiated "classroom." In the large, crowded schoolroom that accommodated all of the school's pupils, only the most rudimentary form of the recitation script was possible – setting tasks and "hearing" students to assess their learning. In fact, little could be heard from one end of the schoolroom to another, and critics complained that the vast majority were learning nothing. The royal commissioners appointed to study the matter shrewdly recognized two things: There was a theory of education involved in whether or not classrooms should replace schoolrooms, and that theory was connected to the outside world. The commissioners observed that these crowded and noisy conditions were not unlike those of Parliament or the bar where these young lads would eventually do their mental work amidst similar distraction.

Yet within 20 years or so schoolrooms were extinct and all lessons were being taught in classrooms. And the reasons for this had a lot to do with the world at large. Conceptions of career had changed, methods of recruitment to the professions had changed, understanding of the qualities and virtues required for public success had changed. The schools did not have to move faster than the world. They just had to keep up with it. (Reid, 1987, pp. 11–12)

We have mentioned the emergence of cooperative work as a productive necessity in commercial success and its potential for affecting school practice. There are other changes under way in North American society with even more complex potential. Consider the massive demographic changes occurring in the ethnic and cultural composition of the United States; not far into the 21st century, European-Americans will be in the minority. There is no doubt whatsoever that this will eventually bring about changes in schooling. Those changes can be rapid, anticipatory, effective, and beneficial, or they can be slow, painful, grudging, and ineffective. We have detailed throughout this book instances of ways in which motivations, conventions of discourse, values, social organizational preferences, and cognitive preferences are different for different cultures. We have spoken at length here and elsewhere of the ways in which conventional schooling is not compatible with the natal cultures of many of the nation's people. This must and will be changed.

However, the course and pace of that change can vary widely. Blacks, Hispanics, Native Americans, Pacific islanders, Filipinos, and others have themselves experienced North American schools, and the meaning of "school" for them is by and large the same meaning held by majority-culture members. We have consulted with many schools in North America that are populated by minority students, and taught by minority-culture teachers, in which teaching and schooling are entirely conventional. All teachers have been taught in the same schools and trained in standard colleges of education. However unsatisfied these teachers may be with the effects of school on themselves and their children, they lack a clear alternative vision. For them, the meaning of "school" is much the same as for the minority communities they serve, and indeed for the majority culture.

Except in one important respect: The affective dimension is much more likely to be negative. Blacks, Hispanics, whites, and Indians together can hold a coherent discourse about school – the discourse composed of congruent, intermental symbolism and common images – but the bitterness or pleasure or satisfaction or boredom attached to the lexicon and images of that discourse will be predictable, distributed according to cultural group, and very highly correlated with school success and school frustration. This is not to say that all non-European cultures suffer underachievement in schools; they clearly do not, as attested by the astonishingly rapid adaptation to American schools accomplished by many Southeast Asian immigrants and the similar success achieved by Chinese immigrants decades earlier. But many cultural groups, now minorities, have patterns of natal life that do not provide the literacy and other training in the home on which American schools depend; the children of these cultures do not prosper in schools.

Our own work has been largely in schools for underachieving minority children, where this failure has been massive and frustrating. In this volume and elsewhere we have documented the success that is possible for minority children when schooling is designed to provide teaching and learning for all members of the educational institution.

This experience has led us to examine, in the same terms, schools for majority-culture children, even schools in several cities for the children of the most successful and affluent of American citizens. It is well known that the "best" and most able teachers often are recruited by the schools and districts of affluent communities, but we have found many able and dedicated teachers in remote or needful schools as well. In every school, there are some individual teachers who are responsive and who work jointly with pupils. But when comparing the typical scripts of teaching and the organizational structures of schooling, we find less difference than similarity. Wherever they are, schools are not designed to teach, and they tend to operate, largely without awareness, on the assumption spelled out in the Introduction to this volume: In American classrooms, now and since the 19th century, teachers generally act as if students are supposed to learn on their own.

Everywhere, schools assign the texts, assess the learning, and depend on the homes to do the teaching. In the Santa Monicas of the nation, many parents provide this teaching; on the Ute Mountain reservations of the country, most do not. In typical political rhetoric about minority education, the schools accuse the minority communities of "not caring," and the communities complain of "insensitive" teachers.

Are parents of nontraditional families, as well as minorities, able to provide the "parental involvement" that schools desire and on which teachers depend? Lareau (1986, p. 2) studied teachers' desires for parents' behaviors and reported that schools want parents to meet children's physical and emotional needs, of course, but they have very specific desires for parents' relationships to schooling, including

> socializing children to values espoused by schools
> responding to requests for signatures and attendance at school events
> monitoring and supporting academic achievement at home
> initiating contact with teachers on the school site

Lareau points out the difficulty this presents for the rising number of single-parent families. She suggests that there are great social-class differences in parental ability to perform these tasks. We might add that cultural differences, particularly for many parents of underachieving minority children, make these behaviors extremely unlikely, particularly for parents who have themselves been alienated from school, who have rightly felt the school to be a mysterious, supercilious, and formidable enemy. It is also critical to note that the three expectations concerning direct parental involvement in school work per se, even when well met by such families as those in Goldenberg's sample (1987), are not likely sufficient to ensure literacy at a competitive level. And the first expectation, socializing children to the values espoused by schools, is the problem itself. Here is a standoff; homes and schools look to each other, and neither is prepared.

The solution seems obvious: We must find ways to teach children literacy in school. But schools, as we observed at the beginning of this book, are not designed to teach. Therefore, the rising tide of "minorities" in America will destabilize standard schooling, because the inadequacy of schools for teaching will become visible, more widely frustrating, and indeed threatening to national self-interest.

Will this destabilization result in a forward movement of American education? The optimistic view is that dissatisfaction with schools, when it affects the emerging new majority of citizens, will reform education for us all; if society creates schools that teach, then all will benefit. However, dissatisfaction with schools is not a new emotion, and the impregnable nested egg of teaching, mind, and society has rocked on, complacent in a sea of discontent. Dissatisfaction alone will not penetrate the shell.

Can schools be saved? If so, it will be through a combination of forces. All are present now, but they must be bundled, focused, and consistent if schools are to become places of teaching and learning. The first of these is the force of *discourse,* guided by a new theoretical and practical vision of schools, discourse that must accompany action. The second is the force of new *educational activity settings outside schools,* in universities, inservice settings, business and industry. Such settings, accompanied by the new discourse, offer the opportunity for the action that can change the personal and social meanings of the word "school." The third force is that of *social change* itself, generated outside the educational establishment. Changes such as the lowered competitiveness of American commerce and the rise to majority status of the old minorities may awaken our society to the necessity to change the way it treats its young.

None of these forces in isolation will change schools. The discourse of this book will amount to nothing unless it is spoken in educational settings of joint productive activity. No workshops and courses and training institutes will change the image of education unless those activities are linked through discourse to educational reform. No social discontent itself will move education unless the spokesmen of commerce and minorities join in the discourse that insists that we must all learn and teach in our schools. We must teach, work, and speak together. Only in that way can we rouse the mind of society.

References

Abelson, R. P. (1981). Psychological status of the script concept. *American Psychologist, 36*(7), 715–729.

Adler, M. J. (1983). *Paideia: Problems and possibilities.* New York: Macmillan.

Adler, M. J. (1988, January 10). Learning disputes. *Los Angeles Times,* part 5, pp. 1, 6.

Allen, R. V. (1976). *Language experience in communication.* Boston: Houghton Mifflin.

Andersen, E. (1977). *Learning to speak with style.* Unpublished doctoral dissertation, Stanford University.

Anderson, L. M., Evertson, C. M., & Brophy, J. E. (1979). An experimental study of effective teaching in first-grade reading groups. *Elementary School Journal, 79,* 193–223.

Anderson, R. B., Hiebert, E. H., Scott, J. A., & Wilkinson, I. A. G. (1985). *Becoming a nation of readers: The report of the Commission on Reading.* Champaign, IL: Center for the Study of Reading.

Anderson, R. C. (1984). Some reflections on the acquisition of knowledge. *Educational Researcher, 13*(9), 5–10.

Antill, E., & Tharp, R. G. (1975). *A comparison of KEEP and public school teachers' rates of positive and negative feedback* (Technical Report No. 56). Honolulu: Kamehameha Schools/Bishop Estate, Kamehameha Early Education Program.

Arends, M. J. (1980). Beginning teachers as learners. *Journal of Educational Research, 76*(4), 235–242.

Armor, D. J., Conny-Oseguera, P., Cox, M., King, N., McDonnell, L., Pascal, A., Pauly, E., & Zellman, G. (1976). *Analysis of the school preferred reading program in selected Los Angeles minority schools.* Santa Monica, CA: Rand Corp.

Ashton, P. T., Webb, R. B., & Doda, N. (1983). *A study of teachers' sense of efficacy* (final report). University of Florida.

Au, K. H. (1979). Using the experience-text-relationship method with minority children. *Reading Teacher, 32*(6), 677–679.

Au, K. H. (1980). Participation structures in a reading lesson with Hawaiian children: Analysis of a culturally appropriate instructional event. *Anthropology and Education Quarterly, 11*(2), 91–115.

Au, K. H. (1981). The comprehension-oriented reading lesson: Relationships to proximal indices of achievement. *Educational Perspectives, 20,* 13–15.

Au, K. H., & Hao, R. K. (1980). *A quality control system for reading instruction* (Technical Report No. 89). Honolulu: Kamehameha Schools/Bishop Estate, Center for Development of Early Education.

Au, K. H., & Jordan, C. (1981). Teaching reading to Hawaiian children: Finding a culturally appropriate solution. In H. Trueba, G. P. Guthrie, & K. H. Au (Eds.), *Culture in the bilingual classroom: Studies in classroom ethnography* (pp. 139–152). Rowley, MA: Newbury House.

Au, K. H., & Kawakami, A. J. (1982). A conceptual framework for studying the long-term effects of comprehension instruction. *Quarterly Newsletter of the Laboratory of Comparative Human Cognition, 6*(4), 95–100.

Au, K. H., & Kawakami, A. J. (1984). Vygotskian perspectives on discussion processes in small-group reading lessons. In P. L. Peterson, L. C. Wilkinson, & M. Hallinan (Eds.), *The social context of instruction: Group organization and group processes* (pp. 204–225). New York: Academic Press.

Au, K. H., & Kawakami, A. J. (1986). The influence of the social organization of instruction on children's text comprehension ability. In T. E. Raphael (Ed.), *The contexts of school-based literacy* (pp. 63–77). New York: Random House.

Au, K. H., & Mason, J. M. (1981). Social organizational factors in learning to read: The balance of rights hypothesis. *Reading Research Quarterly, 17*(1), 115–152.

Baird, L. A., & Bogert, K. H. (1978). *The teaching of comprehension skills: A workshop for teachers* (working paper). Honolulu: Kamehameha Schools/Bishop Estate, Center for Development of Early Education.

Bandura, A. (1969). *Principles of behavior modification.* New York: Holt, Rinehart & Winston.

Bandura, A. (1977). *Social learning theory.* Englewood Cliffs, NJ: Prentice-Hall.

Baumrind, D. (1971). Current patterns of parental authority. *Developmental Psychology Monographs, 4,* 99–103.

Beck, R. H. (1985). Plato's views on teaching. *Educational Theory, 35*(2), 119–134.

Bell, R. Q. (1979). Parent, child, and reciprocal influences. *American Psychologist, 34,* 821–826.

Bennett, W. J. (1986). *First lessons: A report on elementary education in America.* Washington, DC: U.S. Department of Education.

Berk, L. E. (1986). Relationship of elementary school children's private speech to behavioral accompaniment to task, attention, and task performance. *Developmental Psychology, 22,* 671–680.

Berk, L. E., & Garvin, R. (1984). Development of private speech among low-income Appalachian children. *Developmental Psychology, 20,* 271–286.

Berliner, D. C. (1986). In pursuit of the expert pedagogue. *Educational Researcher, 15*(7), 5–13.

Berman, P., & McLaughlin, M. W. (1978). *Federal programs supporting educational change: Vol. 8: Implementing and sustaining innovations.* Santa Monica, CA: Rand Corp.

Bernstein, L. E. (1981). Language as a product of dialogue. *Discourse Processes, 4,* 117–147.

Bird, T., & Little, J. W. (1986). How schools organize the teaching profession. *Elementary School Journal, 86*(4), 493–512.

Bishop, J. M. (1977). Organizational influences on the work orientations of elementary teachers. *Sociology of Work and Occupation, 4*(2), 171–208.

Bloom, B. S. (1976). *Human characteristics and school learning.* New York: McGraw-Hill.

Boggs, S. T. (1985). *Speaking, relating, and learning: A study of Hawaiian children at home and at school.* New York: Ablex Publishing.

Borrowman, M. (1956). *The liberal and technical in teacher education: A historical survey of American thought.* New York: Teachers College, Columbia University.

Brandt, R. S. (Ed.). (1987a). *Educational Leadership, 45*(3).

Brandt, R. S. (1987b). On cooperation in schools: A conversation with David and Roger Johnson. *Educational Leadership, 45*(3), 14–19.

Brookover, W., Schweitzer, J., Schneider, J., Beady, C., Flood, P., & Wisenbaker, J. (1978).

Elementary school social climate and school achievement. *American Educational Research Journal, 15,* 301–318.

Brooks, D. M., & Hawke, G. (1985). *Effective and ineffective session-opening teacher activity and task structures.* Paper presented at the annual meeting of the American Educational Research Association, Chicago.

Brophy, J. E., & Evertson, C. (1976). *Learning from teaching: A developmental perspective.* Boston: Allyn & Bacon.

Brophy, J. E., & Good, T. L. (1986). Teacher behavior and student achievement. In M. C. Wittrock (Ed.), *Handbook of research on teaching* (3rd ed.) (pp. 328–375). New York: Macmillan.

Brown, A. L. (1978). Knowing when, where, and how to remember. A problem of metacognition. In R. Glaser (Ed.), *Advances in instructional psychology* (Vol. 1, pp. 77–165). Hillsdale, NJ: Lawrence Erlbaum Associates.

Brown, A. L., Bransford, J. D., Ferrara, R. A., & Campione, J. C. (1983). Learning, remembering, and understanding. In J. H. Flavell & E. M. Markman (Eds.), *Handbook of child psychology: Vol. 3. Cognitive development* (4th ed.) (pp. 77–166). New York: Wiley.

Brown, A. L., & Campione, J. C. (1986). Psychological theory and the study of learning disabilities. *American Psychologist, 41*(10), 1059–1068.

Brown, A. L., & Palinscar, A. M. (1987). Reciprocal teaching of comprehension strategies: A natural history of one program for enhancing learning. In J. Borkowski & J. D. Day (Eds.), *Intelligence and cognition in special children: Comparative studies of giftedness, mental retardation, and learning disabilities* (pp. 81–132). New York: Ablex Publishing.

Bruner, J. S. (1962). Preface. In L. S. Vygotsky, *Thought and language.* Cambridge, MA: MIT Press.

Bruner, J. S. (1966). *Toward a theory of instruction.* Cambridge, MA: Harvard University Press.

Bruner, J. S. (1973a). Organization of early skilled action. *Child Development, 44,* 1–11.

Bruner, J. S. (1973b). *Beyond the information given: Studies in the psychology of knowing* (J. M. Anglin, Ed.). New York: Norton.

Bruner, J. (1983). *Child's talk: Learning to use language.* New York: Norton.

Bruner, J. S. (1984). Vygotsky's zone of proximal development: The hidden agenda. In B. Rogoff & J. V. Wertsch (Eds.), *Children's learning in the "zone of proximal development,"* (pp. 93–97). San Francisco: Jossey-Bass.

Butcher, P. M. (1981). *An experimental investigation of the effectiveness of a value claim strategy unit for use in teacher education.* Unpublished doctoral dissertation, Macquarie University, Sydney, Australia.

Calfee, R. R., Cazden, C. B., Duran, R. P., Griffin, M. P., Martus, M., & Willis, H. D. (1981). *Designing reading instruction for cultural minorities: The case of the Kamehameha Early Education Project* (report to the Ford Foundation). Cambridge, MA: Harvard Graduate School of Education, and Honolulu: Kamehameha Schools/Bishop Estate. (ERIC Document Reproduction Service No. ED 215 039)

Calkins, R. P., & Tharp, R. G. (1984). Cognitive mediation of motoric responding. *Perceptual and Motor Skills, 59,* 51–60.

Carnegie Foundation Forum on Education and the Economy. (1986, May). *A nation prepared: Teachers for the 21st century.* Report of the Task Force on Teaching as a Profession.

Carroll, J. B. (1972). Defining language comprehension: Some speculations. In R. O. Freedle & J. B. Carroll (Eds.), *Language comprehension and the acquisition of knowledge* (pp. 1–29). New York: Wiley.

Carver, C. S., & Scheier, M. F. (1981). *Attention and self-regulation: A control-theory approach to human behavior.* New York: Springer-Verlag.

Cazden, C. B. (1979). Peekaboo as an instructional model: Discourse development at home and at school. *Papers and Reports on Child Language Development* (Stanford University), *17,* 1–29.

Cazden, C. B. (1981). Performance before competence: Assistance to child discourse in the zone of proximal development. *Quarterly Newsletter of the Laboratory of Comparative Human Cognition, 3*(1), 5–8.

Cazden, C. B. (1986). Classroom discourse. In M. C. Wittrock (Ed.), *Handbook of research on teaching* (3rd ed.) (pp. 432–464). New York: Macmillan.

Cazden, C. B. (1987, January). *Text and context in education.* Paper presented at the Third International Conference on Thinking, Honolulu.

Cazden, C. B., & John, V. P. (1971). Learning in American Indian children. In M. L. Wax, S. Diamond, & F. O. Gearing (Eds.), *Anthropological perspectives on education* (pp. 252–272). New York: Basic Books.

Center for Development of Early Education. (1986). *Description of the Kamehameha Elementary Education Program (KEEP): Principles of instruction* (Early Education Bulletin No. 22). Honolulu: Kamehameha Schools/Bishop Estate, Center for Development of Early Education.

Champagne, A. B. (1985). *Structured peer interactions and physical science learning.* Paper presented at the annual meeting of the American Educational Research Association, San Francisco.

Clark, E. (1978). Awareness of language: Some evidence from what children say and do. In A. Sinclair, R. J. Jarvella, & W. Levelt (Eds.), *The child's conception of language* (pp. 17–43). New York: Springer-Verlag.

Clay, M. M. (1966). *Emergent reading behavior.* Unpublished doctoral dissertation, University of Auckland, New Zealand.

Clay, M. M. (1968). A syntactic analysis of reading errors. *Journal of Verbal Learning and Verbal Behavior, 7,* 434–438.

Clift, R. T., & Morgan, P. (1986, April). *Future English teacher or English major? Exploring qualitative differences in subject matter knowledge.* Paper presented to the annual meeting of the American Educational Research Association, San Francisco.

Cole, M. (1985). The zone of proximal development: Where culture and cognition create each other. In J. V. Wertsch (Ed.), *Culture, communication, and cognition: Vygotskian perspectives* (pp. 146–161). Cambridge University Press.

Cole, M., & Scribner, S. (1974). *Culture and thought.* New York: Wiley.

Conant, S., Budoff, M., & Hecht, B. (1983). *Language intervention: A communication games approach.* Cambridge, MA: Brookline Books.

Conant, S., Budoff, M., Hecht, B., & Morse, R. (1984). Language intervention: A pragmatic approach. *Journal of Autism and Developmental Disorders, 14*(3), 301–317.

Corsaro, W. (1979). Sociolinguistic patterns in adult–child interaction. In E. Ochs & B. B. Schieffelin (Eds.), *Developmental pragmatics* (pp. 373–389). New York: Academic Press.

Crandall, D. P., Loucks-Horsley, S., Bauchner, J. E., Schmidt, W. B., Eiseman, J. W., Cox, P. L., Miles, M. B., Huberman, A. M., Taylor, B. L., Goldberg, J. A., Shive, G., Thompson, C. L., & Taylor, J. A. (1982). *People, policies, and practices: Examining the chain of school improvement.* Andover, MA: Network.

Cross, T. G. (1977). Mothers' speech adjustments: The contribution of selected child listener variables. In C. E. Snow & C. A. Ferguson (Eds.), *Talking to children: Language input and acquisition* (pp. 151–188). Cambridge University Press.

Crowell, D. C. (1976). *The use of minimum objectives in curriculum research and development, 1975–76* (Technical Report No. 45). Honolulu: Kamehameha Schools/Bishop Estate, Center for Development of Early Education. (ERIC Document Reproduction Service No. ED 158 858)

Crowell, D. C. (1979). *The Kamehameha Reading Objective System.* Honolulu: Kamehameha Schools/Bishop Estate, Center for Development of Early Education.

Crowell, D. C., Aka, K., Blake, K., Choy, K., & Mai-Chun, G. (in press). Teaching thinking strategies: An attempt to promote generalization in D. Topping, V. Kobayashi, & D. C. Crowell (Eds.), *Thinking: The Third International Conference.* Hillsdale, NJ: Lawrence Erlbaum Associates.

Crowell, D. C., & Au, K. H. (1979). Using a scale of questions to improve listening comprehension. *Language Arts, 56,* 38–43.

Dalton, S., & Cramer, J. (1987). *The participatory learner.* Paper presented at the annual meeting of the American Educational Research Association, Washington, DC.

D'Amato, J. (1981a). *Power in the classroom.* Paper presented at the annual meeting of the American Anthropological Association, Los Angeles.

D'Amato, J. (1981b). *Sibling groups, peer groups, and the problem of classroom rapport.* Paper presented at the meeting of the National Association on Asian- and Pacific-American Education, Honolulu.

D'Amato, J. (1982). *Contests and confrontations among Hawaiian schoolchildren.* Paper presented at the annual meeting of the American Anthropological Association, Washington, DC.

D'Amato, J., & Inn, K. (1987). Teacher control talk in models A and C. In D. C. Farran (Ed.), *Kindergarten project team research design 1985–86* (Technical Report No. 143). Honolulu: Kamehameha Schools/Bishop Estate, Center for Development of Early Education.

Dansereau, D. F. (in press). Cooperative learning strategies. In C. E. Weinstein, E. T. Goetz, & P. A. Alexander (Eds.), *Learning and study strategies: Issues in assessment, instruction, and evaluation.* New York: Academic Press.

Darling-Hammond, L. (1986). A proposal for evaluation in the teaching profession. *Elementary School Journal, 86,* 531–551.

deBono, E. (1973). *CoRT teachers notes.* New York: Pergamon Press.

Delgado-Gaitan, C. (1987, August). *Socializing Mexican children to literacy in the home.* Paper presented at the Santa Barbara Conference on Linguistic Minorities, University of California at Santa Barbara.

Diaz, R. M. (1986). The union of thought and language in children's private speech. *Quarterly Newsletter of the Laboratory of Comparative Human Cognition, 8*(3), 90–97.

Dodson, C. J. (1984, November). *Models for second language acquisition.* Paper presented at the Second International Conference on Language Acquisition: Language Contact–Language Conflict, Hamburg.

Donaldson, M. (1978). *Children's minds.* New York: Norton.

Dore, J. (1979). What's so conceptual about the acquisition of linguistic structures? *Journal of Child Language, 6,* 129–137.

Dowhower-Vuyk, S., & Speidel, G. E. (1982). The process of language learning and reading instruction. In G. E. Speidel (Ed.), *Oral language in a successful reading program for Hawaiian children* (pp. 59–73) (Technical Report No. 105). Honolulu: Kamehameha Schools/Bishop Estate, Kamehameha Early Education Program.

Duffy, G. G. (1981). Teacher effectiveness research: Implications for the reading profession. In M. Kamil (Ed.), *Directions in reading: Research and instruction: 30th yearbook of the National Reading Conference* (pp. 113–136). Washington, DC: National Reading Conference.

Duffy, G. G., Lanier, J. E., & Roehler, L. R. (1980). *On the need to consider instructional practice when looking for instructional implications.* Paper presented at the Conference on Reading Expository Materials, Wisconsin Research and Development Center, University of Wisconsin, Madison.

Duffy, G. G., & Roehler, L. R. (1980). *Classroom teaching is more than opportunity to learn.* East Lansing: Michigan State University, Institute for Research on Teaching.

Duffy, G. G., & Roehler, L. R. (1981, December). *An analysis of instruction in reading instructional research.* Paper presented at a meeting of a research session on reading instructional research, National Reading Conference, Dallas.

Duffy, G. G., Roehler, L. R., Meloth, M. S., & Vavrus, L. G. (1986). Conceptualizing instructional explanation. *Teaching and Teacher Education, 2,* 197–214.

Durkin, D. (1966). *Children who read early: Two longitudinal studies.* New York: Teachers College Press.

Durkin, D. (1978–1979). What classroom observations reveal about reading comprehension instruction. *Reading Research Quarterly, 14,* 481–533.

Educational Research Council of America. (1974). *John Glenn, Astronaut.* Boston: Allyn & Bacon.

El'konin, D. B. (1972). Toward the problem of stages in the mental development of the child. *Soviet Psychology, 10,* 225–251.

Ellis, N. (1986). *Collaborative interaction as support for teacher change.* Paper presented at the annual meeting of the American Education Research Association, San Francisco.

Ellis, S., & Rogoff, B. (1982). The strategies and efficacy of child vs. adult teachers. *Child Development, 53,* 730–735.

Elsasser, N., & John-Steiner, V. P. (1977). An interactionist approach to advancing literacy. *Harvard Educational Review, 47,* 355–369.

Erickson, F., & Mohatt, G. (1982). The cultural organization of participation structure in two classrooms of Indian students. In G. Spindler (Ed.), *Doing the ethnography of schooling* (pp. 132–174). New York: Holt, Rinehart & Winston.

Erickson, F., & Schultz, J. (1977). When is a context? Some issues and methods in the analysis of social competence. *Quarterly Newsletter of the Institute of Comparative Human Cognition, 1*(2), 5–10. [Reprinted in J. Green & C. Wallat (Eds.), *Ethnography and language in educational settings.* New York: Ablex Publishing, 1981.]

Ervin-Tripp, S. (1976). Is Sybil there? The structure of some American English directives. *Language in Society, 5,* 25–66.

Ervin-Tripp, S. (1977). Wait for me, roller skate! In S. Ervin-Tripp & C. Mitchell-Kernan (Eds.), *Child discourse* (pp. 165–188). New York: Academic Press.

Farran, D. C. (1987). *Kindergarten project team research design, 1985–86* (Technical Report No. 143). Honolulu: Kamehameha Schools/Bishop Estate, Center for Development of Early Education.

Farran, D. C., & Cunningham, L. (1987). Rates of on-task behavior throughout the year for kindergarten children in two alternative curricula. In D. C. Farran (Ed.), *Kindergarten project team research design, 1985–86* (pp. 121–134) (Technical Report No. 143). Honolulu: Kamehameha Schools/Bishop Estate, Center for Development of Early Education.

Feitelson, D., & Goldstein, Z. (1986). Patterns of book ownership and reading to young children in Israeli school-oriented and non-school-oriented families. *Reading Teacher, 39,* 924–930.

Feldman, D. H. (1980). *Beyond universals in cognitive development.* New York: Ablex Publishing.

Ferguson, C. A. (1977). Baby talk as simplified register. In C. Snow and C. A. Ferguson

(Eds.), *Talking to children: Language input and acquisition* (pp. 219–235). Cambridge University Press.

Fischer, K. W., & Bullock, D. (1984). Cognitive development in school-aged children: Conclusions and new directions. In W. A. Collins (Ed.), *Development during middle childhood: The years from six to twelve* (pp. 70–146). Washington, DC: National Academy Press.

Fisher, C. W., Filby, N. N., Marliave, R., Cahen, L. S., Dishaw, M. M., Moore, J. E., & Berliner, D. C. (1978, June). *Teaching behavior, academic learning time and student achievement: Final report of phase 111-B, beginning teacher evaluation study* (Technical Report No. V-1). San Francisco: Far West Laboratory for Educational Research and Development.

Flavell, J. H., & Wellman, H. M. (1977). Metamemory. In R. V. Kail & J. W. Hagen (Eds.), *Perspectives on the development of memory and cognition* (pp. 3–34). Hillsdale, NJ: Lawrence Erlbaum Associates.

Forman, E. A., & Cazden, C. B. (1985). Exploring Vygotskian perspectives in education: The cognitive value of peer interaction. In J. V. Wertsch (Ed.), *Culture, communication, and cognition: Vygotskian perspectives* (pp. 323–347). Cambridge University Press.

Fortes, M. (1938). Education in Taleland. *Africa, 11*(Suppl. 4), 14–74.

Foster, S. (1981). The emergence of topic type in children under 2, 6: A chicken and egg problem. *Papers and Reports in Child Language Development* (No. 20). Stanford, CA: Stanford University Press.

Frank, J. D. (1961). *Persuasion and healing.* Baltimore, MD: Johns Hopkins University Press.

Fullan, M. (1985). Change processes and strategies at the local level. *Elementary School Journal, 85*(3), 391–421.

Fullan, M., & Pomfret, A. (1977). Research on curriculum and instructional implementation. *Review of Educational Leadership, 47,* 335–397.

Gage, N. L. (1978). *The scientific basis of the art of teaching.* New York: Teachers College Press.

Gall, M. D., Ward, B. A., Berliner, D. C., Cahen, L. S., Winne, D. H., Elashoff, J. D., & Stanton, G. C. (1978). Effects of questioning techniques and recitation on student learning. *American Educational Research Journal, 15,* 157–199.

Gallimore, R., Boggs, J. W., & Jordan, C. (1974). *Culture, behavior and education: A study of Hawaiian-Americans.* Beverly Hills, CA: Sage Publications.

Gallimore, R., Dalton, S., & Tharp, R. G. (1986). Self-regulation and interactive teaching: The impact of teaching conditions on teachers' cognitive activity. *Elementary School Journal, 86*(5), 613–631.

Gallimore, R., & Tharp, R. G. (1976). *Studies of standard English and Hawaiian Islands Creole English* (Technical Report No. 59). Honolulu: Kamehameha Schools/Bishop Estate, Kamehameha Early Education Project.

Gallimore, R., & Tharp, R. G. (1981). The interpretation of elicited limitation in a standardized setting. *Language Learning, 31*(2), 369–392.

Gallimore, R., Tharp, R. G., Sloat, K. C. M., Klein, T. W., & Troy, M. E. (1982). *Analysis of reading achievement test results for the Kamehameha Early Education Project: 1972–1979* (Technical Report No. 102). Honolulu: Kamehameha Schools/Bishop Estate, Center for Development of Early Education.

Gal'perin, P. (1969). Stages in the development of mental acts. In M. Cole & I. Maltzman (Eds.), *A handbook of contemporary Soviet psychology* (pp. 249–273). New York: Basic Books.

Garnica, O. (1977). Some prosodic and para-linguistic features of speech to young children. In C. Snow & C. Ferguson (Eds.), *Talking to children: Language input and acquisition* (pp. 63–88). Cambridge University Press.

Gearhart, M., & Newman, D. (1980). Learning to draw a picture: The social context of an individual activity. *Discourse Processes, 3,* 169–184.

Gleason, J. B., & Weintraub, S. (1978). Input language and the acquisition of communicative competence. In K. Nelson (Ed.), *Children's Language, Vol. 1* (pp. 163–210). New York: Gardner Press.

Glidewell, J. C., Tucker, S., Todt, M., & Cox, S. (1983). Professional support systems: The teaching profession. In A. Madler, J. D. Fisher, & B. M. DePaulo (Eds.), *Applied research in help-seeking and reactions to aid* (pp. 189–212). New York: Academic Press.

Goldenberg, C. (1987). Low-income Hispanic parents' contributions to their first-grade children's word-recognition skills. *Anthropology and Educational Quarterly, 18,* 149–179.

Goldenberg, C. (in press-a). The home literacy environment of low-income Hispanic kindergarteners whose parents are recent arrivals from Latin America.

Goldenberg, C. (in press-b). The school's effects on parent–child literacy interactions in the homes of low-income Hispanic kindergarteners.

Goldsberry, L. (1986, April). *Colleague consultation: Another case of fools rush in.* Paper presented at the annual meeting of the American Educational Research Association, San Francisco.

Golinkoff, R. (Ed.), (1983). *The transition from prelinguistic to linguistic communication.* Hillsdale, NJ: Lawrence Erlbaum Associates.

Good, T., & Grouws, D. (1979). *Experimental study of mathematics in instruction in elementary schools* (NIE Grant 677-003). Columbia: University of Missouri.

Good, T. L., & Weinstein, R. S. (1986). Schools make a difference: Evidence, criticism, and new directions. *American Psychologist, 41*(10), 1090–1097.

Goodlad, J. (1984). *A place called school.* New York: McGraw-Hill.

Greenfield, P. M. (1984). A theory of the teacher in the learning activities of everyday life. In B. Rogoff & J. Lave (Eds.), *Everyday cognition: Its development in social contexts* (pp. 117–138). Cambridge, MA: Harvard University Press.

Griesemer, J. L., & Butler, C. (1983). *Education under study: An analysis of recent major reports on education.* Chelmford, MA: Northeast Regional Exchange.

Griffin, G. A. (1985). The school as workplace and the master teacher concept. *Elementary School Journal, 86*(1), 1–16.

Griffin, P., & Cole, M. (1984). Current activity for the future: The Zo-ped. In B. Rogoff & J. V. Wertsch (Eds.), *Children's learning in the "zone of proximal development" (New Directions for Child Development, No. 23)* (pp. 45–64). San Francisco: Jossey-Bass.

Grimmett, P. P., Housego, I., & Suddaby, M. (1986, April). *Implementing district-wide peer coaching: The role of central office supervisors.* Paper presented at the annual meeting of the American Educational Research Association, San Francisco.

Grimmett, P. P., Moody, P. R., & Balasubramaniam, M. (1986, April). *District-wide implementation of peer coaching: A case study of one step toward successful change.* Paper presented at the annual meeting of the American Educational Research Association, San Francisco.

Gross, B., & Gross, R. (Eds.). (1985). *The great school debate: Which way for American education?* New York: Simon & Schuster.

Guskey, T. R. (1986). Staff development and the process of teacher change. *Educational Researcher, 15*(5), 5–12.

Guthrie, J. T. (1973). Reading comprehension and syntactic responses in good and poor readers. *Journal of Educational Psychology, 65,* 294–299.

Haertel, G. D., Walberg, H. J., & Weinstein, T. (1983). Psychological models of educational performance: A theoretical synthesis of constructs. *Review of Educational Research, 53*(1), 75–91.

Hakes, D. T. (1982). The development of metalinguistic abilities: What develops? In S. Kuczaj, II (Ed.), *Language development. Vol. 2: Language, thought & culture* (pp. 163–210). Hillsdale, NJ: Lawrence Erlbaum Associates.

Hall, M. A. (1976). *Teaching reading as a language experience.* Columbus, OH: Charles E. Merrill.

Halliday, M. A. K. (1975). *Learning how to mean: Explorations in the development of language.* London: Edward Arnold.

Hao, R. K. (1980). *Comparative data on reading programs: KEEP and Kalihi public schools* (working paper). Honolulu: Kamehameha Schools/Bishop Estate, Center for Development of Early Education.

Hao, R. K. (1983). *Using a comprehension strategies continuum to train teachers to make instructional decisions* (working paper). Honolulu: Kamehameha Schools/Bishop Estate, Kamehameha Educational Research Institute.

Hawkins, B. (1988). *Scaffolded classroom interaction and its relation to second language acquisition.* Unpublished doctoral dissertation, Department of Applied Linguistics, University of California, Los Angeles.

Heath, S. B. (1982). What no bedtime story means: Narrative skills at home and school. *Language and Society, 11*(2), 49–76.

Heath, S. B. (1983). *Ways with words: Language, life, and work in communities and classrooms.* Cambridge University Press.

Herreshoff, M. J., & Speidel, G. E. (1987). Child talk in large group storybook discussions in kindergarten. In D. C. Farran (Ed.), *Kindergarten project team research design 1985–86* (pp. 121–134) (Technical Report No. 143). Honolulu: Kamehameha Schools/Bishop Estate, Center for Development of Early Education.

Hess, R., & Shipman, V. (1965). Early experience and the socialization of cognitive modes in children. *Child Development, 36,* 377–388.

Hiebert, E. H. (1983). An examination of ability grouping for reading instruction. *Reading Research Quarterly, 18*(9), 231–255.

Hilgers, T., & Molloy, M. (1981). "Your Holiness, What's your favorite color?" Talking with the Dalai Lama. *American Benedictine Review, 32,* 189–199.

Hirsch, E. D. (1987). *Cultural literacy: What every American needs to know.* Boston: Houghton Mifflin.

Hoetker, J., & Ahlbrand, W. (1969). The persistence of recitation. *American Educational Research Journal, 6,* 145–167.

Hoffman, S. J. (1982). *Preschool reading related behaviors: A parent diary.* Unpublished doctoral dissertation, University of Pennsylvania, Philadelphia.

Homme, L. (1966, November). Contingency management. *Clinical Child Psychology Newsletter, 4.*

Huberman, M. A. (1981). *ECRI, Masepa, North Plains: Case study.* Andover, MA: Network.

Hyland, J. T. (1984). *Teaching about the constitution: Relationships between teachers' subject matter knowledge, pedagogic beliefs, and instructional decision-making.* Unpublished doctoral dissertation, University of California, Los Angeles.

Hyland, J. T., Gallimore, R., & Schneider, P. (in press). Knowing what they teach and teaching what they know: Improving teaching in eighth grade U.S. history classes. In L. C. Solomon (Ed.), *From the campus to the classroom: The practical application of educational research.*

Inagaki, K. (1981). Facilitation of knowledge integration through classroom discussion. *Quarterly Newsletter of the Laboratory of Comparative Human Cognition, 3*(3), 26–28.

Inagaki, K., & Hatano, G. (1968). Motivational influences on epistemic observation. *Japanese Journal of Educational Psychology, 6,* 191–202.

Inagaki, K., & Hatano, G. (1977). Amplification of cognitive motivation and its effects on epistemic observation. *American Educational Research Journal, 14,* 485–491.

Jackson, P. (1968). *Life in classrooms.* New York: Holt, Rinehart & Winston.

Johnson, D. W., Maruyama, G., Johnson, R., Nelson, D., & Skon, L. (1981). Effects of cooperative, competitive, and individualistic goal structures on achievement: A meta-analysis. *Psychological Bulletin, 89,* 47–62.

Johnson, J. L., & Sloat, K. C. M. (1980). Teacher training effects: Real or illusory? *Psychology in the Schools, 17,* 109–115.

John-Steiner, V. P. (1985). *Notebooks of the mind.* Albuquerque: University of New Mexico Press.

John-Steiner, V. P., & Oesterreich, H. (1975). *Learning styles among Pueblo children: Final report to National Institute of Education.* Albuquerque: University of New Mexico, College of Education.

John-Steiner, V. P., & Tatter, P. (1983). An interactionist model of language development. In B. Bain (Ed.), *The sociogenesis of language and human conduct* (pp. 79–97). New York: Plenum Press.

Jordan, C. (1977). *Maternal teaching modes and school adaptations in an urban Hawaiian population* (Technical Report No. 67). Honolulu: Kamehameha Schools/Bishop Estate, Kamehameha Educational Research Institute.

Jordan, C. (1978a). *Peer relationships among Hawaiian children and their educational implications.* Paper presented at the annual meeting of the American Anthropological Association, Los Angeles.

Jordan, C. (1978b). Teaching/learning interactions and school adaptations: The Hawaiian case. In *A multidisciplinary approach to research in education: The Kamehameha Early Education Program* (pp. 31–38) (Technical Report No. 81). Honolulu: Kamehameha Schools/Bishop Estate, Center for Development of Early Education (revised version of a paper presented at the annual meeting of the American Anthropological Association, Houston, December 1977).

Jordan, C. (1981a). *Educationally effective ethnology: A study of the contributions of cultural knowledge to effective education for minority children.* Doctoral dissertation, University of California, Los Angeles (available on microfilm from University Microfilms Library Services, Ann Arbor, MI).

Jordan, C. (1981b). The selection of culturally compatible teaching practices. *Educational Perspectives, 20*(1), 16–19.

Jordan, C. (1983). Cultural differences in communication patterns: Classroom adaptations and translated strategies. In M. Clark & J. J. Handscombe (Eds.), *TESOL '82: Pacific perspectives on language, learning and teaching* (pp. 285–294). Washington, DC: Teachers of English to Speakers of Other Languages.

Jordan, C. (1984). Cultural compatibility and the education of ethnic minority children. *Educational Research Quarterly, 8*(4), 59–71.

Jordan, C. (1985). Translating culture: From ethnographic information to educational program. *Anthropology and Education Quarterly, 16,* 106–123.

Jordan, C., D'Amato, J., & Joesting, A. (1981). At home, at school and at the interface. *Educational Perspectives, 20*(1), 31–37.

Jordan, C., & Tharp, R. G. (1979). Culture and education. In A. J. Marsella, R. G. Tharp,

& T. Ciborowski (Eds.), *Perspectives in cross-cultural psychology* (pp. 265–285). New York: Academic Press.

Jordan, C., Tharp, R. G., & Vogt, L. (1985). *Compatibility of classroom and culture: General principles, with Navajo and Hawaiian instances* (working paper). Honolulu: Kamehameha Schools/Bishop Estate, Center for Development of Early Education.

Joyce, B. R., Bush, R. N., & McKibbin, M. D. (1981). *Information and opinion from the California staff development study: The compact report.* Sacramento: California State Department of Education.

Joyce, B. R., & Clift, R. (1984). The Phoenix agenda: Essential reform in teacher education. *Educational Researcher, 13*(4), 5–18.

Joyce, B. R., Howey, K., & Yarger, S. (1977a). *Preservice teacher education.* Palo Alto, CA: Booksend Laboratories.

Joyce, B. R., Howey, K., & Yarger, S. (1977b). Reflections of preservice preparation: Impressions from the National Survey, Part I. *Journal of Teacher Education, 28*(5), 14.

Joyce, B., & Showers, B. (1980). Improving in-service training: The messages from research. *Educational Leadership, 37,* 379–385.

Joyce, B., & Showers, B. (1987). Low-cost arrangements for peer coaching. *Journal of Staff Development, 8,* 22–24.

Joyce, B., Showers, B., & Rolheiser-Bennett, C. (1987, October). Staff development and student learning: A synthesis of research on models of teaching. *Educational Leadership, 45,* 11–23.

Keenan, E. O., & Schieffelin, B. B. (1976). Topic as a discourse notion: A study of topic in the conversations of children and adults. In C. Li (Ed.), *Subject and topic* (pp. 335–384). New York: Academic Press.

Keogh, B. K., & Hall, R. J. (1984). Cognitive training with learning-disabled pupils. In A. W. Meyers & W. E. Craighead (Eds.), *Cognitive behavior therapy with children* (pp. 163–192). New York: Plenum Press.

Kerr, D. H. (1983). Teaching competence and teacher education in the United States. *Teachers College Record, 84*(3), 525–552.

Klein, T. W. (1988). *Program evaluation of the Kamehameha Elementary Education Program's reading curriculum in Hawaii public schools: The cohort analysis 1978–1986* (working paper). Honolulu: Kamehameha Schools/Bishop Estate, Center for Development of Early Education.

Knoblock, P., & Goldstein, A. P. (1971). *The lonely teacher.* Boston: Allyn & Bacon.

Kohlberg, L., & Wertsch, J. V. (in press). Language and the development of thought. In L. Kohlberg (Ed.), *Developmental psychology and early education.* New York: Longman.

Kohlberg, L., Yaeger, J., & Hjertholm, E. (1968). Private speech: Four studies and a review of theories. *Child Development, 39,* 691–736.

Kol'tsova, V. A. (1978). Experimental study of cognitive activity in communication (with specific reference to concept formation). *Soviet Psychology, 17,* 23–38.

Korth, W., & Cornbleth, G. (1980). In search of academic instruction. *Educational Researcher, 9,* 9.

Krashen, S. D. (1981). *Second language acquisition and second language learning.* New York: Ablex Publishing.

Lareau, A. P. (1986, April). *Perspectives on parents: A view from the classroom.* Paper presented at the annual meeting of the American Educational Research Association, San Francisco.

Leggett, D., & Hoyle, S. (1987). Preparing teachers for collaboration. *Educational Leadership, 45,*(3), 58–63.

Leinhardt, G., & Greeno, J. G. (1986). The cognitive skill of teaching. *Journal of Educational Psychology, 78*, 75–95.

Leming, J., & Hollifield, J. (1985). Cooperative learning. A research success story. *Educational Researcher, 14*, 1.

Lemke, J. L. (1982). *Classroom communication of science: Final report* (SEDR-79-18961). Washington, DC: National Science Foundation. (ERIC Document Reproduction Service No. ED 222 346)

Lenz, A. J., & Gallimore, R. (1973). A behavioral comparison of two "good" teachers. In S. MacDonald & G. Tanabe (Eds.), *Focus on classroom behavior: Readings and research* (pp. 36–44). Springfield, IL: Charles C Thomas.

Leont'ev, A. N. (1981). The problem of activity in psychology. In J. V. Wertsch (Ed.), *The concept of activity in Soviet psychology* (pp. 37–71). Armonk, NY: M. E. Sharpe.

Leont'ev, A. N. (1983). The mastery of scientific concepts by students as a problem of educational psychology. In A. N. Leont'ev (Ed.), *Selected psychological works* (Vol. 2). Moscow: Pedagogika. (Original work published 1935)

Levin, J., Hoffman, N., & Badiali, B. (1986). *Rural teachers' perceptions of the effectiveness of various supervisory practices.* Paper presented at the annual meeting of the American Educational Research Association, San Francisco.

Little, J. (1981). *The power of organizational setting: School norms and staff development.* Paper presented at the annual meeting of the American Educational Research Association, Los Angeles.

Little, J. W. (1982). Norms of collegiality and experimentation: Workplace conditions of school success. *American Educational Research Journal, 19*(3), 325–340.

Lomov, B. F. (1978). Psychological processes and communication. *Soviet Psychology, 17,* 3–22.

Lortie, D. C. (1975). *Schoolteacher.* University of Chicago Press.

MacDonald, S., & Gallimore, R. (1971). *Battle in the classroom.* Scranton, PA: Intext.

MacDonald, S., & Gallimore, R. (1972). Introducing experienced teachers to classroom management techniques. *Journal of Educational Research, 65,* 420–424.

McLaughlin, M. W., & Marsh, D. D. (1978). Staff development and school change. *Teachers College Record, 80*(1), 69–94.

McNamee, G. D. (1979). The social interaction origins of narrative skills. *Quarterly Newsletter of the Laboratory of Comparative Human Cognition, 1*(4), 63–68.

Mason, J. M. (1977). *Reading readiness: A definition and skills hierarchy from preschoolers' developing conceptions of print* (Technical Report No. 59). University of Illinois at Urbana–Champaign, Center of the Study of Reading.

Mason, J. M., & Allen, J. (1986). A review of emergent literacy with implications for research and practice in reading. *Review of Research in Education, 13,* 3–48.

Mason, J. M., & Au, K. H. (1986). *Reading instruction for today.* Glenview, IL: Scott, Foresman.

Mason, W. S. (1961). *The beginning teacher* (Circular No. 644). Washington, DC: U.S. Department of Health, Education, and Welfare, Office of Education [cited in Pickle, J. (1984). Relationships between knowledge and learning environments in teacher education. *Journal of Teacher Education, 25*(5), 13–17].

Medley, D. (1977). *Teacher competence and teacher effectiveness.* Washington, DC: American Association of Colleges for Teacher Education.

Mehan, H. (1979). "What time is it, Denise?" Asking known information questions in classroom discourse. *Theory into Practice, 28*(4), 285–294.

Meichenbaum, D. (1977). *Cognitive behavior modification: An integrative approach.* New York: Plenum Press.

Meichenbaum, D., & Asarnow, J. (1979). Cognitive-behavioral modification and metacognitive development: Implications for the classroom. In P. C. Kendall & S. D. Hollon (Eds.), *Cognitive-behavioral interventions: Theory, research, and procedures* (pp. 11–35). New York: Academic Press.

Miller, P. (1982). *Amy, Wendy, and Beth: Learning language in South Baltimore:* Austin: University of Texas Press.

Minick, N. (1987). Implications of Vygotsky's theories for dynamic assessment. In C. S. Lidz (Ed.), *Dynamic assessment: An interactional approach to evaluating learning potential* (pp. 116–140). New York: Gilford Press.

Minick, N. J. (1985). *L. S. Vygotsky and Soviet activity theory: New perspectives on the relationship between mind and society.* Unpublished doctoral dissertation, Northwestern University.

Moerk, E. L. (1983). *The mother of Eve – as a first language teacher.* New York: Ablex Publishing.

Moll, L. C., & Diaz, S. (1985). Ethnographic pedagogy: Promoting effective bilingual instruction. In E. Garcia & R. Padilla (Eds.), *Advances in bilingual education research* (pp. 127–149). Tucson: University of Arizona Press.

Morrison, T. (1860). Methods of instruction. *Barnard's American Journal of Education, 9,* 294–320.

National Commission on Excellence in Education. (1983, April). *A nation at risk.* Washington, DC: United States Government Printing Office.

Nerlove, S. B., & Snipper, A. S. (1981). Cognitive consequences of cultural opportunity. In R. H. Munroe, R. L. Munroe, & B. B. Whiting (Eds.), *Handbook of crosscultural human development* (pp. 423–474). New York: Garland Press.

Newport, E. L. (1976). Motherese: The speech of mothers to young children. In N. J. Castellan, D. B. Pisoni, & G. R. Potts (Eds.), *Cognitive theory* (Vol. 2). Hillsdale, NJ: Lawrence Erlbaum Associates.

Newson, J. (1977). An intersubjective approach to systematic description of mother–infant interaction. In H. R. Schaffer (Ed.), *Studies in mother–infant interaction* (pp. 47–61). New York: Academic Press.

Ochs, E. (1982). Talking to children in western Samoa. *Language in Society, 11,* 77–104.

Ochs, E., & Schieffelin, B. B. (1984). Language acquisition and socialization: Three developmental stories and their implications. In R. Shweder & R. LeVine (Eds.), *Culture theory: Essays on mind, self, and emotion* (pp. 276–320). Cambridge University Press.

Ogbu, J. U. (1982). Cultural discontinuities and schooling. *Anthropology and Educational Quarterly, 13*(4), 290–307.

Ogbu, J. U., & Matute-Bianchi, M. E. (1986). Understanding sociocultural factors: Knowledge, identity, and school adjustment. In Bilingual Education Office, California State Department of Education (Ed.), *Beyond language: Social and cultural factors in schooling language minority students* (pp. 73–142). Los Angeles: California State University, Evaluation, Dissemination and Assessment Center.

Oldenquist, A. (1983). "Social triage" against black children. *American Education, 19*(4), 12–18.

Ong, W. (1982). *Orality and literacy: The technologizing of the world.* London: Methuen.

Palinscar, A. S. (1986). The role of dialogue in providing scaffolding instruction. *Educational Psychologist, 21,* 73–98.

Palinscar, A. M., & Brown, A. L. (1984). Reciprocal teaching of comprehension-fostering and comprehension monitoring activities. *Cognition and Instruction, 1,* 117–175.

Paris, S., Lipson, M., & Wixson, K. (1983). Becoming a strategic reader. *Contemporary Educational Psychology, 8,* 293–316.

Perret-Clermont, A. N. (1980). *Social interaction and cognitive development in children.* New York: Academic Press.

Peters. A. (1987). *The development of collaborative story telling.* Paper presented at the Third International Conference on Thinking, Honolulu.

Peterson, R. O., Chuck, H. D., & Coladarci, A. P. (1969). *Teaching standard English as a second dialect to primary school children in Hilo, Hawaii. Final report, Vol. 1* (Project No. 5-0692, Contract No. OE6-10-176). Washington, DC: U.S. Department of Health, Education, and Welfare, Office of Education, Bureau of Research.

Pettit, G. A. (1946). *Primitive education in North America.* University of California Publications in American Archaeology and Ethnology, No. 43 (Whole No. 1).

Phillips, S. U. (1972). Participant structures and communicative competence: Warm Springs children in community and classroom. In C. B. Cazden, V. John, & D. Hymes (Eds.), *Functions of language in the classroom* (pp. 370–394). New York: Teachers College Press.

Phillips. S. U. (1983). *The invisible culture: Communication in classroom and community on the Warm Springs Indian Reservation.* New York: Longman.

Price-Williams, D. R., Gordon, W., & Ramirez, M., III. (1969). Skill and conservation: A study of pottery-making children. *Developmental Psychology, 1,* 769.

Reid, W. A. (1987). Institutions and practices: Professional education reports and the language of reform. *Educational Researcher, 16*(8), 10–15.

Rice, J. M. (1893). *The public school system of the United States.* New York: Century.

Roberts, R. N. (1979). Private speech in academic problem-solving. A naturalistic perspective. In G. Zevin (Ed.), *The development of self-regulation through private speech* (pp. 295–323). New York: Wiley.

Roberts, R. N., & Mullis, M. (1980). *A component analysis of self-instructional training.* Paper presented at the annual convention of the Western Psychological Association, Honolulu.

Roberts, R. N., & Tharp, R. G. (1980). A naturalistic study of children's self-directed speech in academic problem-solving. *Cognitive Research and Therapy, 4,* 341–353.

Rogoff, B. (1982). Integrating context and cognitive development. In M. E. & A. L. Brown (Eds.), *Advances in developmental psychology* (Vol. 2) (pp. 125–170). Hillsdale, NJ: Lawrence Erlbaum Associates.

Rogoff, B. (1986). Adult assistance of children's learning. In T. E. Raphael (Ed.), *The contexts of school-based literacy* (pp. 27–40). New York: Random House.

Rogoff, B. (in press). The joint socialization of development by young children and adults. In L. M. & S. Feinman (Eds.), *Social influences and behavior.* New York: Plenum Press.

Rogoff, B., & Gardener, W. (1984). Adult guidance of cognitive development. In B. Rogoff & J. Lave (Eds.), *Everyday cognition: Its development in social contexts* (pp. 95–116). Cambridge, MA: Harvard University Press.

Rogoff, B., & Lave, J. (Eds.). (1984). *Everyday cognition: Its development in social contexts.* Cambridge, MA: Harvard University Press.

Rogoff, B., Malkin, C., & Gilbride, K. (1984). Interaction with babies as guidance in development. In B. Rogoff & J. V. Wertsch (Eds.), *Children's learning in the "zone of proximal development" (New Directions for Child Development, No. 23)* (pp. 30–44). San Francisco: Jossey-Bass.

Rogoff, B., Mistry, J., Radziszewska, B., & Germond, J. (in press). Infants' instrumental social interaction with adults. In S. Feinman (Ed.), *Social referencing, infancy, and social psychological theory.* New York: Plenum Press.

Rogoff, B., & Wertsch, J. V. (Eds.). (1984). *Children's learning in the "zone of proximal development."* San Francisco: Jossey-Bass.

Rosenholtz, S. J. (1985). *Teacher's experience and learning: Do all the good die young?* (interim report to the National Institute of Education). Champaign: University of Illinois.

Rosenholtz, S. J. (1986). Career ladders and merit pay: Capricious fads or fundamental reforms? *Elementary School Journal, 86*(4), 513–529.

Rosenholtz, S. J., Bassler, O., & Hoover-Dempsey, K. (1985a). Organizational conditions of teacher learning. *Teaching & Teacher Education, 2,* 91–104.

Rosenholtz, S. J., Bassler, D., & Hoover-Dempsey, K. (1985b). *Organizational inducements for teaching* (interim report to the National Institute of Education). Champaign: University of Illinois.

Rosenshine, B. (1976). Classroom instruction. In N. L. Gage (Ed.), *The psychology of teaching methods: The 75th yearbook of the National Society for the Study of Education.* Chicago: National Society for the Study of Education.

Rosenshine, B. (1979). Content, time and direct instruction. In H. Walbert & P. Peterson (Eds.), *Research on teaching: Concepts, findings and implications.* Berkeley, CA: McCutchan Publishing.

Rosenshine, B., & Berliner, D. C. (1978). Academic engaged time. *British Journal of Teacher Education, 4,* 3–16.

Rosenshine, B., & Stevens, R. (1986). Teaching functions. In M. C. Wittrock (Ed.), *Handbook of research on teaching* (3rd ed.) (pp. 392–431). New York: Macmillan.

Rutter, M., Maughan, B., Mortimore, P., & Ouston, J. (1979). *Fifteen thousand hours: Secondary schools and their effects on children.* Cambridge, MA: Harvard University Press.

Sachs, J. (1977). Adaptive significance of input to infants. In C. Snow & C. Ferguson (Eds.), *Talking to children: Language input and acquisition* (pp. 51–61). Cambridge University Press.

Sarason, S. B. (1971). *The culture of the school and the problem of change.* Boston: Allyn & Bacon.

Sarason, S. B. (1972). *The creation of settings and the future societies.* San Francisco: Jossey-Bass.

Sarason, S. B. (1983). *Schooling in America: Scapegoat and salvation.* New York: Free Press.

Sarason, S. B., Davidson, K. S., & Blatt, B. (1986). *The preparation of teachers: An unstudied problem in education* (2nd ed.). Cambridge, MA: Brookline Books.

Saxe, G. B., Gearhart, M., & Guberman, S. R. (1984). The social organization of early number development. In B. Rogoff & J. V. Wertsch (Eds.), *Children's learning in the "zone of proximal development" (New Directions for Child Development, No. 23)* (pp. 19–30). San Francisco: Jossey-Bass.

Schacter, F. F. (1979). *Everyday mother talk to toddlers.* New York: Academic Press.

Schaffer, H. R. (Ed.). (1977). *Studies in mother–infant interaction.* New York: Academic Press.

Schieffelin, B. B. (1985). Acquisition of Kaluli. In D. I. Slobin (Ed.), *The crosslinguistic study of language acquisition. Vol. 1: The data* (pp. 525–593). Hillsdale, NJ: Lawrence Erlbaum Associates.

Schlechty, P. C., & Vance, V. S. (1983). Recruitment, selection, and retention: The shape of the teaching force. *Elementary School Journal, 83,* 469–487.

Schneider, P. J, Hyland, J. T., & Gallimore, R. (1985). The zone of proximal development in eighth grade social studies. *Quarterly Newsletter of the Laboratory of Comparative Human Cognition, 7*(4), 113–119.

Schultz, J., Erickson, F., & Florio, S. (1982). Where's the floor? Aspects of the cultural organization of social relationships in communication at home and at school. In P. Gilmore

& A. Glatthorn (Eds.), *Children in and out of school: Ethnography and education* (pp. 88–123). New York: Harcourt, Brace; Washington, DC: Center for Applied Linguistics.

Scribner, S. (1984). Studying working intelligence. In B. Rogoff & J. Lave (Eds.), *Everyday cognition: Its development in social contexts* (pp. 9–40). Cambridge, MA: Harvard University Press.

Scribner, S., & Cole, M. (1973). Cognitive consequences of formal and informal education. *Science, 182,* 553–559.

Scribner, S., & Cole, M. (1981). *The psychology of literacy.* Cambridge, MA: Harvard University Press.

Sergiovanni, T. J. (1975). *Professional supervision for professional teachers.* Alexandria, VA: Association for Supervision and Curriculum Development.

Sharan, Y., & Sharan, S. (1987). Training teachers for cooperative learning. *Educational Leadership, 45*(3), 20–25.

Shavelson, R. J., & Stern, P. (1981). Research on teachers' pedagogical thoughts, judgments, decisions, and behavior. *Review of Educational Research, 51,* 455–498.

Shiel, G. (1987, April). *The influence of teachers' literary interpretations of basal reader selections on their instructional decisions in directed reading lessons.* Paper presented at the annual meeting of the American Educational Research Association, Washington, DC.

Shotter, J. (1978). The cultural context of communication studies. Theoretical and methodological issues. In A. Lock (Ed.), *Action, gesture, and symbol* (pp. 43–78). New York: Academic Press.

Showers, B. (1984a, April). *Peer coaching and its effects on transfer of training.* Paper presented at the annual meeting of the American Educational Research Association, New Orleans.

Showers, B. (1984b). *Peer coaching: A strategy for facilitation transfer of training.* Eugene: University of Oregon, Center for Educational Policy and Management.

Shulman, L. S. (1986). Those who understand: Knowledge growth in teaching. *Educational Researcher, 15*(2), 4–14.

Shuy, R. W. (1986, April). Secretary Bennett's teaching: An argument for responsive teaching. *Teaching and Teacher Education, 2,* 315–323.

Sizer, T. R. (1984). *Horace's compromise: The dilemma of the American high school.* Boston: Houghton Mifflin.

Slavin, R. E. (1983). When does cooperative learning increase student achievement? *Psychological Bulletin, 94,* 429–445.

Sloat, K. C. M. (1981). Characteristics of effective instruction. *Educational Perspectives, 20*(1), 10–12.

Sloat, K. C. M., & Hao, R. (1980). *A pilot study of field-based guided practice in positive reinforcement* (working paper). Honolulu: Kamehameha Schools/Bishop Estate, Kamehameha Early Education Program.

Sloat, K. C. M., Tanaka-Matsumi, J., Ah Ho, M., & Sueoka, S. (1977). *Training teachers to use positive reinforcement through guided practice in the classroom* (Technical Report No. 68). Honolulu: Kamehameha Schools/Bishop Estate, Kamehameha Early Education Program.

Sloat, K. C. M., Tharp, R. G., & Gallimore, R. (1977). The incremental effectiveness of classroom based teacher training techniques. *Behavior Therapy, 8,* 810–818.

Snow, C. (1972). Mothers' speech to children learning language. *Child Development, 43,* 549–565.

Snow, C. (1977a). The development of conversation between mothers and babies. *Journal of Child Language, 4,* 1–22.

Snow, C. (1977b). Mothers' speech research. From input to interaction. In C. E. Snow & C. E. Ferguson (Eds.), *Talking to children: Language input and acquisition* (pp. 31–49). Cambridge University Press.

Snow, C. E. (1983). Literacy and language: Relationships during the preschool years. *Harvard Educational Review, 53,* 165–189.

Snow, C. E., & Ferguson, C. A. (Eds.). (1977). *Talking to children: Language input and acquisition.* Cambridge University Press.

Speidel, G. E. (1981a). *Psycholinguistic abilities and reading achievement in children speaking nonstandard English* (Technical Report No. 91). Honolulu: Kamehameha Schools/ Bishop Estate, Kamehameha Early Education Program.

Speidel, G. E. (1981b). Language and reading. Bridging the language difference for children who speak Hawaiian English. *Educational Perspectives, 20*(1), 23–30.

Speidel, G. E. (1982). Responding to language differences. In G. E. Speidel (Ed.), *Oral language in a successful reading program for Hawaiian children* (Technical Report No. 105). Honolulu: Kamehameha Schools/Bishop Estate, Kamehameha Early Education Program.

Speidel, G. E. (1983a). *Can findings from first language acquisition be useful for second dialect learning.* Paper presented at the seventh biennial meeting of the International Society for the Study of Behavioural Development, Munich.

Speidel, G. E. (1983b). *Language and reading: The role of dialogue.* Paper read at the 17th annual meeting of TESOL, Toronto.

Speidel, G. E. (1984). *Conversation and language learning in the classroom.* Paper presented at the Third International Congress for the Study of Child Language, Austin, Texas.

Speidel, G. E. (1987a). Language differences in the classroom. Two approaches for developing language skills in dialect-speaking children. In E. Oksaar (Ed.), *Sociocultural perspectives of language acquisition and multilingualism.* Tubingen: Gunter Narr Verlag.

Speidel, G. E. (1987b). Conversation and language learning in the classroom. In K. E. Nelson & A. van Kleeck (Eds.), *Child language* (Vol. 6). Hillsdale, NJ: Lawrence Erlbaum Associates.

Speidel, G. E., & Dowhower-Vuyk, S. (1981). *Developing children's discourse skills.* Paper presented at the Hawaii Educational Research Association, Honolulu.

Speidel, G. E., & Pickens, A. L. (1979). Art, mental imagery and cognition. In A. Sheik & J. T. Shaffer (Eds.), *The potential of fantasy and imagination* (pp. 199–213). New York: Brandon House.

Speidel, G. E., & Tharp, R. G. (1978). Teacher-training workshop strategy: Instructions, discrimination training, modeling, guided practice, and video feedback. *Behavior Therapy, 9,* 735–739.

Speidel, G. E., & Tharp, R. G. (1980). *The effectiveness of art and language instruction on the intelligence and achievement scores of disadvantaged dialect-speaking kindergarten children* (Technical Report No. 84). Honolulu: Kamehameha Schools/Bishop Estate, Kamehameha Early Education Program.

Speidel, G. E., Tharp, R. G., & Gallimore, R. (1974). *Explorations in teacher training* (Technical Report No. 7). Honolulu: Kamehameha Schools/Bishop Estate, Kamehameha Early Education Program.

Staats, A. W. (1968). *Learning, language, and cognition.* New York: Holt, Rinehart & Winston.

Stallings, J. (1980). *The process of teaching basic reading skills in secondary schools.* Menlo Park, CA: SRI International.

Stallings, J. (1981). *Testing teachers' in-class instruction and measuring change resulting from staff development.* Mountain View, CA: Teaching and Learning Institute.

Starr, I. (1978). *The idea of liberty.* St. Paul, MN: West.

Stauffer, R. G. (1969). *Teaching reading as a thinking process.* New York: Harper & Row.

Stauffer, R. G. (1970). *The language-experience approach to the teaching of reading.* New York: Harper & Row.

Stedman, L. C., & Smith, M. S. (1983). Recent reform proposals for American education. *Contemporary Education Review, 2*(2), 85–104.

Stevens, R. (1912). *The question as a measure of efficiency in instruction: A critical study of classroom practice* (Contributions to Education No. 48). New York: Teachers College, Columbia University.

Summers, A., & Wolfe, B. (1977). Do schools make a difference? *American Economic Review, 67,* 639–652.

Super, C., & Harkness, S. (Eds.). (1980). *Anthropological perspectives on child development (New Directions for Child Development, No. 8).* San Francisco: Jossey-Bass.

Tafoya, M. (1983). *The red & the black: Santa Clara pottery.* Posterboard, Wheelwright Museum of the American Indian, Santa Fe, NM.

Tanaka-Matsumi, J. (1977). *KEEP consultation research strategies, 1971–76* (Technical Report No. 58). Honolulu: Kamehameha Schools/Bishop Estate, Kamehameha Early Education Program.

Tanaka-Matsumi, J., & Tharp, R. G. (1977). Teaching the teachers of Hawaiian children: Training and consultation strategies. *Topics in Culture Learning, 5,* 92–106.

Teale, W. H. (1978). Positive environments for learning to read: What studies of early readers tell us. *Language Arts, 55,* 922–923.

Teale, W. H. (1986). Home background and young children's literacy development. In W. H. Teale & E. Sulzby (Eds.), *Emergent literacy: Writing and reading* (pp. 173–206). New York: Ablex Publishing.

Teale, W. H., & Sulzby, E. (Eds.). (1986). *Emergent literacy: Writing and reading.* New York: Ablex Publishing.

Terrell, T. (1982). The natural approach to language teaching: An update. *Modern Language Journal, 66,* 121–131.

Tharp, R. G. (1975). The triadic model of consultation: Current considerations. In C. A. Parker (Ed.), *Psychological consultation: Helping teachers meet special needs* (pp. 135–151). Reston, VA: University of Minnesota and the Council for Exceptional Children.

Tharp, R. G. (1979, October). *Culture, behavior modification, and education.* Paper presented at the annual meeting of the Southern California Conference on Behavior Modification, Los Angeles.

Tharp, R. G. (1982). The effective instruction of comprehension: Results and description of the Kamehameha Early Education Program. *Reading Research Quarterly, 17*(4), 503–527.

Tharp, R. G. (1984). The triadic model. In J. A. Tucker (Ed.), *School psychology in the classroom: A case study tutorial.* University of Minnesota: National School Psychology In-Service Training Network.

Tharp, R. G. (1985, October). *Wholism and the "observational-learning complex": A comparative study of comprehension instruction among Navajo and Hawaiians.* Paper read at a meeting of the National Indian Education Association, Spokane, WA.

Tharp, R. G. (1987, January). *Culture, cognition, and education.* Symposium conducted at the Third International Conference on Thinking, Honolulu.

Tharp, R. G. (in press). Psychocultural variables and constants: Effects on teaching and learning in schools. *American Psychologist.*

Tharp, R. G., & Gallimore, R. (1975). *The mutual problems of Hawaiian-American students*

298

References

and public schools (Technical Report No. 1). Honolulu: Kamehameha Schools/Bishop Estate, Kamehameha Early Education Program.

Tharp, R. G., & Gallimore, R. (1976a). Basketball's John Wooden: What a coach can teach a teacher. *Psychology Today, 9*(8), 74–78.

Tharp, R. G., & Gallimore, R. (1976b). *The uses and limits of social reinforcement and industriousness for learning to read* (Technical Report No. 60). Honolulu: Kamehameha Schools/Bishop Estate, Kamehameha Early Education Program.

Tharp, R. G., & Gallimore, R. (1979). The ecology of program research and evaluation: A model of evaluation succession. In L. B. Sechrest (Ed.), *Evaluation studies annual review* (Vol. 4) (pp. 39–60). Beverly Hills, CA: Sage Publications.

Tharp, R. G., & Gallimore, R. (1982). Inquiry processes in program development. *Journal of Community Psychology, 10*, 103–118.

Tharp, R. G., & Gallimore, R. (1985). The logical status of metacognitive training. *Journal of Abnormal Child Psychology, 13*(3), 455–466.

Tharp, R. G., Gallimore, R., & Calkins, R. P. (1984). On the relationship between self-control and control by others. *Advances en Psicologia Clinical Latinoamericano, 3*, 45–58.

Tharp, R. G., Jordan, C., Speidel, G. E., Au, K. H., Klein, T. W., Calkins, R. P., Sloat, K. C. M., & Gallimore, R. (1984). Product and process in applied developmental research: Education and the children of a minority. In M. E. Lamb, A. L. Brown, & B. Rogoff (Eds.), *Advances in developmental psychology* (Vol. 3) (pp. 91–144). Hillsdale, NJ: Lawrence Erlbaum Associates.

Tharp, R. G., & Wetzel, R. (1969). *Behavior modification in the natural environment.* New York: Academic Press.

Thomas, B. (1985). *Remarks to Chicago United Education Committee.* Chicago: Comprehensive Health Council, 108 North State, #1201.

Tough, J. (1982). Language, poverty, and disadvantage in school. In L. Feagans & D. C. Farran (Eds.), *The language of children reared in poverty* (pp. 3–18). New York, Academic Press.

van Kleeck, A. (1982). The emergence of linguistic awareness. A cognitive framework. *Merrill-Palmer Quarterly, 29*, 237–265.

Veenman, S. (1984). Perceived problems of beginning teachers. *Review of Education Research, 54*(2), 143–178.

Venezky, R. L., & Winfield, L. F. (1979). *Schools that succeed beyond expectations for teaching* (Technical Report No. 1). Newark: University of Delaware, Studies on Education.

Vogel, S. A. (1975). *Syntactic abilities in normal and dyslexic children.* Baltimore: University Park Press.

Vogt, L. (1982). Comprehension teaching strategies to bridge home and school language. In G. Speidel (Ed.), *Oral language in a successful reading program for Hawaiian children* (pp. 74–94). (Technical Report No. 105). Honolulu: Kamehameha Schools/Bishop Estate, Center for Development of Early Education.

Vogt, L. (1985). *Training for responsive teaching* (working paper). Kamehameha Schools/Bishop Estate, Center for Development of Early Education.

Vogt, L. A., Jordan, C. J., & Tharp, R. G. (1987). Explaining school failure, producing school success: Two cases. *Anthropology & Education Quarterly, 18*, 276–286.

Vygotsky, L. S. (1956). *Izbrannie psibhologicheskie issledovania* (Selected psychological research). Moscow: Izdatel'stvo Akademii Pedagogicheskikh Nauk.

Vygotsky, L. S. (1960). *Razvitie vysshikh psikhicheskikh funktsii* (The development of higher mental functions). Moscow: Izdatel'stvo Akademii Pedagogicheskikh Nauk.

Vygotsky, L. S. (1962). *Thought and language.* Cambridge, MA: MIT Press.

Vygotsky. L. S. (1978). *Mind in society: The development of higher psychological processes* (M. Cole, V. John-Steiner, S. Scribner, & E. Souberman, Eds. & Trans.). Cambridge, MA: Harvard University Press.

Vygotsky, L. S. (1981). The genesis of higher mental functions. In J. V. Wertsch (Ed.), *The concept of activity in Soviet psychology*. Armonk, NY: M. E. Sharpe.

Vygotsky, L. S. (1987). *Collected works of L. S. Vygotsky: Vol. 1: Problems of general psychology* (translated by N. Minick; series editors Robert W. Rieber and Aaron S. Carton). New York: Plenum Press. (Original work published 1982 in Russian)

Walberg, H. J. (1986). Syntheses of research on teaching. In M. C. Wittrock (Ed.), *Handbook of research on teaching* (3rd ed.) (pp. 214–229). New York: Macmillan.

Wallace, A. F. C. (1961). *Culture and personality*. New York: Random House.

Ward, B. A., & Kelley, M. A. (1971). *Developing children's oral language: Minicourse 2* (Far West Laboratory for Educational Research and Development). Beverly Hills, CA: Macmillan Educational Services.

Warren, D. (1985). Learning from experience: History and teacher education. *Educational Researcher, 14*(10), 5–12.

Watson, D. R., & Tharp, R. G. (1988). *Self-directed behavior* (5th ed.). Monterey, CA: Brooks/Cole.

Watts, D. (1982). Can campus-based preservice teacher education survive? Part II. *Journal of Teacher Education, 33*(2), 37–41.

Weisner, T. S. (1976). Urban–rural differences in African children's performance on cognitive and memory tasks. *Ethos, 4*(2), 223–250.

Weisner, T. S. (1979). Urban–rural differences in sociable and disruptive behavior of Kenya children. *Ethnology, 18*(2), 153–172.

Weisner, T. S. (1984). Ecocultural niches of middle childhood: A cross-cultural perspective. In W. A. Collins (Ed.), *Development during middle childhood: The years from six to twelve* (pp. 335–369). Washington, DC: National Academy of Sciences Press.

Weisner, T. S., & Gallimore, R. (1977). My brother's keeper: Child and sibling caretaking. *Current Anthropology, 18*(2), 169–190.

Weisner, T. S., & Gallimore, R. (1985). *The convergence of ecocultural and activity theory.* Paper read at the annual meeting of the American Anthropological Association, Washington, DC.

Weisner, T. S., Gallimore, R., & Jordan, C. (1982). *Demographic description of KEEP families in cohorts I through V, by sample source and cohort* (Technical Report No. 99). Honolulu: Kamehameha Schools/Bishop Estate, Kamehameha Early Education Program.

Weisner, T. S., Gallimore, R., & Jordan, C. (1986). *Unpackaging cultural effects on classroom learning: Hawaiian peer assistance and child-generated activity.* Los Angeles: University of California, Department of Psychiatry & Biobehavioral Sciences.

Weisner, T., Gallimore, R., & Tharp, R. G. (1982). Concordance between ethnographer and folk perspectives: Observed performance and self-ascription of sibling caretaking roles. *Human Organization, 41*(3), 237–244.

Wells, G. (1985). Preschool literacy-related activities and success in school. In D. R. Olson, N. Torrance, & A. Hildyard (Eds.), *Literacy, language, and learning: The nature and consequences of reading and writing* (pp. 229–255). Cambridge University Press.

Wells, G. (1986). The language experience of five-year-old children at home and at school. In J. Cook-Gumperz (Ed.), *The social construction of literacy* (pp. 69–93). Cambridge University Press.

Wertsch, J. V. (1978). Adult–child interaction and the roots of metacognition. *Quarterly Newsletter of the Laboratory of Comparative Human Cognition, 2*(1), 15–18.

Wertsch, J. V. (1979). From social interaction to higher psychological process: A clarification and application of Vygotsky's theory. *Human Development, 22,* 1–22.

Wertsch, J. V. (1981). *The concept of activity in Soviet psychology.* Armonk, NY: M. E. Sharpe.

Wertsch, J. V. (1985a). *Culture, communication, and cognition: Vygotskian perspectives.* Cambridge University Press.

Wertsch, J. V. (Ed.). (1985b). *Vygotsky and the social formation of mind.* Cambridge, MA: Harvard University Press.

Wertsch, J. V., Minick, N., & Arns, F. A. (1984). The creation of context in joint problem-solving. In B. Rogoff & J. Lave (Eds.), *Everyday cognition: Its development in social contexts* (pp. 151–171). Cambridge, MA: Harvard University Press.

Wertsch, J. V., & Schneider, P. J. (1979). *Variations of adults' directives to children in a problem solving situation.* Unpublished manuscript, Northwestern University.

Wertsch, J. V., & Stone, C. A. (1979). *A social interactional analysis of learning disabilities remediation.* Paper presented at an international conference of the Association for Children with Learning Disabilities, San Francisco.

Wertsch, J. V., & Stone, C. A. (1985). The concept of internalization in Vygotsky's account of the genesis of higher mental functions. In J. V. Wertsch (Ed.), *Culture, communication, and cognition: Vygotskian perspectives* (pp. 162–179). Cambridge University Press.

White, K. R. (1982). The relation between socioeconomic status and academic achievement. *Psychological Bulletin, 91,* 461–481.

White, M. A. (1975). Natural rates of teacher approval and disapproval in the classroom. *Journal of Applied Behavior Analysis, 8,* 367–372.

White, S., & Tharp, R. G. (1987). *Training handbook for coding teacher questions* (Technical Report No. 141). Honolulu: Kamehameha Schools/Bishop Estate, Center for Development of Early Education.

White, S., Tharp, R. G., Jordan, C., & Vogt, L. (1987, January). *Cultural patterns of cognition reflected in the questioning styles of Anglo and Navajo teachers.* Paper presented at the Third International Conference on Thinking, Honolulu.

Whiting, B. (1980). Culture and social behavior: A model for the development of social behavior. *Ethos, 8*(2), 95–116.

Whiting, B., & Whiting, J. (1975). *Children of six cultures.* Cambridge, MA: Harvard University Press.

Wist, B. O. (1940). *A century of public education in Hawaii: 1840–1940.* Honolulu: Hawaii Educational Review.

Wittrock, M. C. (1974). Learning as a generative process. *Educational Psychologist, 11,* 87–95.

Wittrock, M. C. (1978). The cognitive movement in education. *Educational Psychologist, 13,* 15–29.

Wittrock, M. C. (Ed.). (1986). *Handbook of research on teaching* (3rd ed.). New York: Macmillan.

Wood, D. J. (1980). Teaching the young child: Some relationships between social interaction, language, and thought. In R. Olson (Ed.), *The social foundations of language and thought* (pp. 280–296). New York: Norton.

Wood, D. J., Bruner, J. S., & Ross, G. (1976). The role of tutoring in problem solving. *Journal of Child Psychology and Psychiatry, 17*(2), 89–100.

Wood, D., McMahon, L., & Cranstoun, Y. (1980). *Working with under fives.* London: Grant McIntyre.

Wong, J., & Au, K. H. (1985). The concept-text-application approach: Helping elementary students comprehend expository text. *Reading Teacher, 38*(7), 612–618.

Wyatt, J. D. (1978–1979). Native involvement in curriculum development: The native teacher as cultural broker. *Interchange, 9,* 17–28.

Yarger, S. J., Howey, K. R., & Joyce, B. R. (1976). *Improving teacher education.* Washington, DC: Association of Teacher Education.

Zetlin, A. G., & Gallimore, R. (1980). A cognitive skills training program for moderately retarded learners. *Education and Training of the Mentally Retarded, 15*(2), 121–131 [reprinted in J. Jacobs (Ed.). (1980). *Mental retardation: A phenomenological approach.* Springfield, IL: Charles C Thomas].

Zetlin, A. G., & Gallimore, R. (1983, October). The development of comprehension strategies through the regulatory function of teacher questions. *Education and Training of the Mentally Retarded, 18,* 176–184.

Author index

303

307

Subject index

A-B-C Triad: schematically defined, 23; *see also* triadic analysis
academic courses, 1, 2, 4, 16, 99; evaluation of, 205–6; in-service teacher training, 189, 205–6
academic engaged time, 16, 167, 172–4; congruent participation structures, 152; effects of teacher training on, 194–5, 196, 207–9; KEEP learning centers, 123–4; KEEP reading program, 120
accountability: of teachers, 2, 23–4, 188–9
achievement: of KEEP comparison groups, 116–18; KEEP reading program, 116–18
acquisition: of new behaviors, 53
activity settings: analysis of teacher training, 189–91; and assisted performance, 71–2; case study, 113; components of (who, why, what, how, and where), 74–9, 130, 132–5, 162–3; cultural issues, 170–1, 181–5; definition of, 72–4; design of, 80–2, 90–2, 111, 130, 161–2, 182–5; ecocultural niches, 74–6; effective schooling, 71–2, 91–2, 161–2, 191; emergent literacy, 101–2; goal, 77–8, 134, 146; impact of culture, 184; instructional conversation as, 108–11, 121, 130, 132–5, 159–62; in KEEP program, 123, 130; meaning, 78–9, 134; Native Hawaiians, 181–2; Navajos, 182–5; operations, 75–6, 79; orchestration of, 161–2, 217; schema, 78; scripts, 75; of society, 45, 130; stages of ZPD, 124; for teacher training, 125–9, 190–1, 196–216, 217, 271
Anglos, 79, 102, 263–5
Arizona, 115, 150
art instruction, 153
arts and sciences faculties, 4, 272–4
assisted performance: of adults, 31–2, 125–9, 190–1; of children, 40–1, 95–6, 120, 122–3, 124, 131–2, 135–6, 146, 148, 150, 153–8, 224; of consultants, 127–9, 213–14; culturally compatible, 171–2; definition, 20, 30–2, 36–7; example, 19–20; frequency of peer assistance, 179; in instructional conversation, 135–6, 138–46, 153–8, 160, 260, 263–5; in Native Hawaiian families, 181; by peers, 124, 135–6, 161–2, 170, 177, 178–81, 186–7; by project team, 215–16; reciprocities, 88–9, 150; restraint in, 88; by self, 38, 46, 54, 86–8, 110, 126, 159–60, 197, 224, 249, 250–2, 252–8, 258–63; social organization of, 71–2, 82–92, 124, 190–1, 217–19; in supervision, 83–4, 124, 217, 223; of teachers, 22, 24, 26, 31, 43, 124–9, 190–2, 192–6, 200, 212, 217–19, 223, 224, 234–7, 249, 250–2, 270–1; of teacher trainers, 127–9, 214–15; teaching, 21, 26, 31, 41–2, 146, 153–8, 168, 249, 258–65; triadic analysis of, 82–8; varieties of peer assistance, 179–81; in whole group, 166–9, 175; of word meaning, 143–4; in Zone of Proximal Development, 31, 71–2, 123–4, 150, 153, 161; *see also* cognitive structuring, contingency managing, feeding back, instructing, means of assistance, modeling, questioning, tailoring assistance
at-risk children: educationally, 148, 165–6
automatization, 29, 36–9, 88, 91; teaching skills, 249, 252–3, 256–7, 260–1, 265

"back-to-basics," 266
behavior management, 18, 161–2, 164–5, 170–3, 226, 254–7, 258–9; assisting performance, 164; cultural factors, 171–2; evaluation of, 172–4; time spent on, 167–8; training teachers, 192–6, 254–7; whole group, 166–7; *see also* classroom management

308

propositional knowledge, 217–19; "knowing how," 97; "knowing that," 217–19
psychotherapy, 39, 66
punishments, 51

questioning (as means of assistance), 33; acquisition of new behavior, 53; assessment vs. assistance, 59–60; definition, 57–62; examples, 60–2, 98–9, 138–41, 142–5, 145–6, 154–8, 180–1, 184–5, 220; in KEEP reading lessons, 122; language development, 97–8; nonformal sources, 84; reading lessons, 150; and requests, 58–9; responsive, 211, 219–22; social studies, 153–8; teacher self-assistance, 253; in teacher training, 233–4, 230, 240, 250, 253; varieties of, 150; vs. directives, 58–9; in whole group, 166
questioning techniques, 13–15, 18, 57–9, 223; assessment questions, 59–60, 110, 152; assisting questions, 59–60; "known information" questions, 140, 263; reading instruction, 110–11, 122; responsive questions, 211, 219–22; *see also* recitation

reading: instructional conversation, 109–11, 132; language experience approach, 146–7; program strands, 120; schooling, 106; social context, 111; teaching of, 108–11, 132, 147–50; *see also* literacy development, reading comprehension
reading comprehension: assisting development, 237; case example, 47, 120; frequency in schools, 110–11; instructional conversation, 109–11, 131–2; language development, 131–2, 134, 146; language experience approach, 146–7; teaching, 19–20, 132, 108–11, 132, 147–50, 259–65; time spent in KEEP, 120, 196
reading curriculum, *see* curriculum
reciprocal influence, 29, 36, 88–90; effects on teachers, 89–90, 231
reciprocal teaching, 17
recitation, 4, 18; beyond, 247; definition of, 14; examples of, 13–15; frequency of, 14–15, 99, 110, 153, 161, 260; persistence of, 161, 174, 188–90, 247, 260–1, 264–5, 267, 270–1, 274–5; and questioning, 59–60, 231–2; reading instruction, 110, 153; responsiveness, 231–2; and school organization, 23, 26,

81, 189–91, 274–9; and teacher cognition, 260–1; technical teaching, 16; whole group, 174, 185
recursion: through Zone of Proximal Development, 38–9, 249, 258–9
reform, 21; conceptualization of process, 189–90; curriculum, 188–90; of education, 1–2; history of school, 266–9, 275–6; obstacle to, 190–1, 266–9, 270–1, 272; process of, 189–90, 272–4, 276–9; public impatience, 111, 267–8; resources for, 200, 272–4; role of universities, 272–4; of schools, 1–4, 21, 189–91, 266–9; strategies, 2, 189–90; symbolic, 3; teacher training, 189–91; of teaching, 1–4, 21, 99, 188–91, 266–9
reinforcement: age of children, 168; cultural compatibility, 171–2; frequency of, 192–5, 196; in KEEP program, 123, 167–8, 172–4; material, 51; social, 51, 53, 168; symbolic, 51; teacher training, 193–6, 207–9
research and development, 115; resources for, 272–4; school reform, 272–4; as source of assistance, 127–9
researchers: program developers, 213–14; as source of assistance, 127–9, 211, 214
responsiveness: activity settings, 124; in Center One, 122–3, 141; to child's ZPD, 40–1, 95–6, 150, 231; definition of, 226; effects of task on, 41; example, 153–8, 219–22; frequency in Center One, 141; instructional conversation, 111, 260–1; in KEEP reading lessons, 122; ratio of teacher-student talk, 233–4, 234–5; recitation, 231–2; simplify speech, 95; systematic modification, 95, 97; tailoring, 135–6, 156–8; to teacher in training, 192, 197–200; in teaching, 122–3, 146, 150, 153, 156, 190, 219–22, 229–31, 231–34, 259–63; "tuned," 40–1, 95–6, 135–6; in whole group, 175
retreats, 81, 128, 212, 213
rewards, 51
rural areas, 74–5, 173

St. John, Gospel of, 94
Santa Monica, 277
scaffolding, 7, 33–4, 242–3, 251, 262
schema, 67, 78, 223, 272
schooled concepts, *see* concepts
schooling: activity analysis of, 71–2, 91–2, 161–2, 191; and assisting performance, 22, 31, 80–2, 265; cognitive